A Pub Crawl
Through History

A Pub Crawl Through History

The Ultimate Boozers' Who's Who

Mike Pentelow
and
Peter Arkell

JANUS PUBLISHING COMPANY
London, England

First published in Great Britain 2010
by Janus Publishing Company Ltd,
105–107 Gloucester Place,
London W1U 6BY

www.januspublishing.co.uk

British Library Cataloguing-in-Publication Data
A catalogue record for this book is available from the British Library

ISBN 978-1-85756-701-4

Cover Design: Janus Publishing
Cover Image supplied by: Peter Arkell

Printed and bound in India

Dedicated to Alan Dalton (1946–2003)

A passionate campaigner for health and safety in
the workplace who helped research many a hostelry

Contents

Introduction

Commoners who have pubs named after them are particularly uncommon people indeed, compared to members of the aristocracy, and what earned them this rare distinction is the purpose for this book.

There are thousands of pubs called the King's Head and the like, but only a handful called The Labouring Man; such as the one pictured in Pulborough, West Sussex. There are hundreds named after individual monarchs and barons, such as King George, Queen Victoria, the Marquis of Granby who set up his ex-soldiers as tavern keepers, the Duke of York and other aristocrats and autocrats, who often suppressed any revolts by the common people. Yet there are only two commemorating Robert Kett, who led the rebellion against the fencing off of common land in 1549; and only one Jack Straw's Castle in honour of the leader of the peasants' revolt of 1381, and even that has recently been turned into flats; and only one Joseph Arch, who formed the agricultural workers' union, which became the biggest trade union in the country.

History, it is now widely recognised, is just as much about these representatives of the common people – and not just kings and queens as was taught to generations of schoolchildren in years gone by. This book aims to redress that balance and celebrate the lives of untitled people – whether famous, infamous or unfamous – whose many and various contributions have been recognised by having pubs named in their honour.

These characters constitute a very mixed bunch. There are criminals (including highwaymen, smugglers, pirates, witches and murderers); pioneering discoverers (including inventors and explorers); rebels, revolutionaries and reformers; war heroes, writers, entertainers and sports stars. The pubs are situated throughout England, Scotland, Wales, Northern Ireland, the Republic of Ireland, the Isle of Man and even Germany. To give a sense of history, they are listed by characters in chronological order of birth, followed by the pubs' details.

What better way to get a taste of history than to embark on this national pub crawl and have a pint in each and every one of them? The authors certainly enjoyed the experience and, en route, found many characters as colourful as those listed in this *Boozers' Who's Who*. One occasion, in a remote valley, the authors were suspected of being private detectives spying on the landlord on behalf of a jealous husband. These suspicions were allayed by the production of a Transport and General Workers' Union membership card as proof of identity. Hostility rapidly turned to hospitality and after plentiful refreshments, we were even allowed to sleep overnight in an adjoining barn.

At another pub while taking photographs of the interior we were approached by a very burly bouncer, who demanded to know if we had got permission from the management. After we said that we hadn't realised it was necessary, he was about to boot us out, when he asked what the pictures were for. We explained it was for a book about pubs named after working people rather than lords and ladies and his attitude immediately changed as he said, 'Go ahead then, sod management.'

The pubs are equally as varied as the characters they are named after, from the seedy to the salubrious. We have decided not to rate them, or the beers they purvey, as they can change so rapidly. We have, however, shown at the end which ones are listed in the 2009 real ale guides.

Existing Pubs

These are pubs that had not been renamed or demolished at the time of going to press. Most of these pubs take on the exact title of the character they are named after. Where this is the case, the name of the character is followed by just the address of the pub or pubs. Where there is a variation, it is followed by the name of the pub as well as the address and details.

1. Thomas Becket (c. 1118–c. 1170)

(i)   The Thomas Becket, 21 Best Lane, Canterbury, Kent, CT1 2JB
      (Tel: 01227 464384). Punch Taverns.
(ii) Thomas-A-Becket, 146 Rectory Road, Worthing, West Sussex, BN14 7PJ
      (Tel: 01903 266643). Fullers.

The patron saint of brewers Thomas Becket was a merchant's son, whose first job was as a clerk to the sheriff of London. After an unsaintly life, Thomas became the Archbishop of Canterbury, a job where he acquired a penchant for wearing lice-ridden hair shirts and washing the feet of peasants.

In a power struggle for land between the crown and the church, which had very little to do with the peasants, he famously took the side of the church. This ended in his murder in Canterbury Cathedral after King Henry II, as reported 400 years later by Shakespeare, declared to his knights, 'Who will rid me of this troublesome priest?'

Romantic legend has it that Becket's mother was a Saracen princess, who followed his crusader father back from the Holy Land. In fact, his mother Rohesia, known as Matilda, was a burgher woman from Caen and his father Gilbert was a merchant from Normandy.

Thomas was born at 90 Cheapside, London, on the corner of Ironmonger Lane, which is marked by a plaque, and he completed his education in France at the University of Paris. When he returned to London, both of his parents had died, which is when he became a clerk. His main hobby was hawking and hunting and it is said that one day his hawk plunged into a river while trying to kill a duck. Thomas dived in to save it and was swept towards a mill, which would have killed him, but at the last moment the mill's wheel stopped, by chance, and saved his life.

He then got a civilian job with the Archbishop of Canterbury and decided to make a career in the church. In 1154, he was ordained an archdeacon and he befriended Henry II. The following year, the king made him chancellor of England. In 1159, Henry raised an army of mercenaries to reconquer some land in France. In the resulting war, Thomas fought enthusiastically on his behalf, leading assaults and engaging in single combat. Indeed, a fellow clergyman remarked, 'You look more like a falconer than a cleric'. The rebuke was received with good humour by Thomas. In 1161, the existing Archbishop of Canterbury died and Henry offered Thomas the job.

Hops in the Church of St Thomas a Becket in Lewes for the annual Thanksgiving service.

His reply, in the slight stutter which afflicted him, was, 'Should God permit me to be the Archbishop of Canterbury, I would soon lose your majesty's favour, and the affection with which you honour me would be changed into hatred. For there are several things you do now in prejudice of the rights of the church which make me fear you would require of me what I could not agree to; and envious persons would not fail to make it the occasion of endless strife between us.'

But he took the job anyway and sure enough, before long, they were squabbling over who should have the land and the revenue from it: the crown or the church? The new archbishop excommunicated anyone who disagreed with him and the king confiscated castles and property from anyone who disagreed with him. Finally, the struggle developed into who had the higher authority to punish their opponents – the church through ecclesiastical courts or the crown through civil courts?

It had to end in tears. After being accused of contempt of court by the king, Thomas fled to France. Henry confiscated all of his property and banished all of his friends and relatives. Thomas then threatened to excommunicate the king and so it went on.

Shortly after Thomas returned, four knights forced their way into Canterbury Cathedral and accused him of being a traitor. They tried to drag him out, but he successfully resisted, so they set about him with their swords. After the third blow, he fell to his knees and said, 'For the name of Jesus and for the defence of the church I am ready to embrace death'. The next stroke severed the crown of his head from his skull.

His corpse was buried the next day in the crypt without any religious service. His grave became a place of pilgrimage and four years later, the king was forced to make public penance there. But in 1536 the body of Thomas was disinterred and burned for high treason by order of Henry VIII, who said he was 'a rebel and traitor to his prince'. This only seemed to increase Thomas' posthumous popularity and thus he was made a saint and had a hospital in Southwark, London, named after him, along with a pub with a boxing ring at 320 Old Kent Road in London and a school near the Worthing pub which bears his name.

Close to the Worthing pub is the tiny remnant of an ancient fig garden in South Street, West Tarring, which was reputed to have been planted by Beckett in 1162. In the Church of St Thomas-A-Becket in Cliffe High Street, Lewes, East Sussex, the local brewer Harvey has an annual thanksgiving service for the new season's hops every October.

At the hop....dancing at the Thanksgiving Festival in Harvey's Brewery, Lewes.

2. William Wallace (c. 1272–c. 1305)

(i)   2 Airthrey Road (corner of Gogie Road), Stirling, FK9 5JR
      (Tel: 01786 472740). Belhaven.
(ii) (Recently renamed The Gunmakers), 33 Aybrook Street, Marylebone,
      London, W1U 4AP (Tel: 020 7487 4937). Punch Taverns.

Wallace became famous as Braveheart in leading Scottish resistance to the English occupation by King Edward I at the end of the thirteenth century. The Stirling pub named after him was erected in 1877, within 'a spear's throw' of his great triumph over the English invaders at Stirling Bridge in 1297 and within

the shadow of the Wallace Monument. He was also taught at an early age a few miles south of Stirling at Dunipace by an uncle who was a priest.

He was 6 foot 7 inches tall – at a time when average height was around 5 foot – and his favourite weapon was a claymore sword with a 5 foot double edged blade and a handle almost a foot long carried on his back, with which he could slash through armour in a whirling movement.

William's father Malcolm refused to swear allegiance to Edward, who declared himself the superior lord of Scotland, and was killed by an

English knight called Fenwick in 1291. In the same year, young William was accosted by five Englishmen, who said he was too well dressed for a Scot and demanded his knife. He used it to kill or wound them all and made his escape. A little later he was fishing by a river, when five English soldiers demanded his whole catch. He offered half, but they took the lot and one attacked him with a sword. Although he was unarmed, Wallace used his fishing rod to hit his assailant, then he grabbed his sword and killed him and two others before the remaining pair fled.

The modern statue at the foot of the monument.

In 1296, Edward's troops butchered around 20,000 men, women and children at Berwick over a period of three days – and then only stopped when the king saw a woman giving birth to a baby as she was being hacked to pieces by a frenzied soldier. Shortly afterwards Edward became King of Scotland.

Wallace continued to resist and he killed several English soldiers in various skirmishes. He was later captured and thrown into a dungeon to be fed on rotten herrings, after which he became feverish and went into a deep coma. Assuming he was dead, the English threw him into a dungheap and left him to rot. He was taken away for burial by a nurse, who noticed a faint flickering of his eyelids and spoon-fed him back to life. When fit again he formed a band of about fifty relatives. They heard that Fenwick, the knight who had killed William's father, was in the area with a hundred and eighty soldiers. The fifty Scots ambushed them, killing about a hundred, including Fenwick, for the loss of just three of their own. The Scots seized the hundred and eighty horses, which were heavily laden with provisions and wine, which 'right happily they consumed on the spot'.

In 1297 Wallace was in Lanark, where his lover 19-year-old Marion Braidfute lived with their young daughter, when he was taunted by an English soldier, who claimed the local priest was the real father of Marion's child. In the ensuing struggle, Wallace and his supporters killed fifty English soldiers, but Marion was killed in retribution. Wallace returned at night and killed the sheriff and captain of the garrison, who had been responsible for her murder. This triggered off the first war of independence.

Wallace soon had 3,000 armed men and after a significant victory over the English at Stirling Bridge, the invaders were cleared out of Scotland. In this battle, Wallace waited until most of the English cavalry had crossed the bridge and then sounded a horn to signal to his colleague under the bridge to pull its pins and destabilise it. The trapped cavalry subsequently either sank in the marshland or drowned in the river.

Wallace, a commoner, was effectively leader of Scotland, an unprecedented position. He was given the title of Guardian of the Kingdom of Scotland and he later set up a structure that cut through feudalistic ties. But Edward returned with superior weapons in the form of new longbows and won a battle at Falkirk in 1298, after which Wallace's career declined.

The Wallace Monument.

By 1304, only Wallace and his few remaining supporters fought on after the surrender of the Scottish nobles. He was finally captured and taken to London, where a show trial was staged on 23 August 1305. He was charged with sedition, homicide, robbery, arson and other felonies, but was not allowed to plead. Even so, he said he had never taken an oath of allegiance to the King of England and thus was not a traitor, but conceded the rest in the cause of the war of independence.

Without bothering with a formal verdict, the judges read out the punishment. He was hung, drawn and quartered at Smithfield that same day; a death crueller in reality than depicted in the 1995 film *Braveheart* of his life, starring Mel Gibson.

As a warning and as an example to others, his head was placed on London Bridge, his right arm on a bridge at Newcastle-upon-Tyne, his left arm at Stirling, his right leg at Berwick and his left leg at Perth. But his example, in fact, proved to be an inspiration to others further afield for many centuries; Garibaldi being known as the Wallace of Italy.

A statue of Wallace, chiselled from two huge blocks of sandstone weighing 6 tons each by sculptor Tom Church, was erected in 1996 at the foot of the Wallace Monument. A stone mason recovering from heart surgery, Church, was inspired by watching the film *Braveheart*.

3. Robin Hood (c.1290–c. 1346)

The Robin Hood Inn, Clipstone Road, Edwinstowe, Sherwood Forest, Notts, NG21 9JA.

The legendary outlaw Robin Hood, who 'robbed from the rich and gave to the poor', had his marriage to Maid Marian blessed in St Mary's Church, Edwinstowe, in the heart of Sherwood Forest; the original ceremony having taken place under a nearby greenwood tree.

Also near this pub is the Major Oak, where Robin and his merrie men hid inside its hollow trunk from the Sheriff of Nottingham and his men. The tree's trunk is now 33 feet in circumference, its branches spread out over 92 feet, it weighs 23 tons and its age is estimated at between 800 and 1,500 years old. Another hollow oak tree nearby in Birklands woodland was known as Robin Hood's Larder, where he stored his stolen venison, but it was blown down by a storm in 1961. Robin, according to local folklore, made his bows from the wood of yew trees at St Swithin's Church in nearby Wellow.

The Major Oak in Sherwood Forest, where Robin Hood hid.

Records show the existence of a Robert Hood (c. 1290–1346) of Wakefield at a time when Robin was a common nickname for Robert. In 1316, he was fined for taking dry wood and in 1322, he was ordered by his landlord the Earl of Lancaster to join the rebellion against King Edward II. When the rebellion failed, the earl was beheaded and his followers, including Hood, who was an archer, were outlawed. They fled at first to Barnsdale Forest in Yorkshire, which was linked to Sherwood Forest. In 1324, they became reconciled with Edward II, but in 1327, it was the King's turn to be executed by having a red hot poker thrust up his anus.

Robin's time was fixed as being during the reign of Edward II by Joseph Hunter, the assistant keeper to the Public Records Office, who spent a lot of his time during the nineteenth century documenting ballads about him. One in particular related to incidents in 1323, while others refer to Robin being in Sherwood Forest when Edward II came to Nottingham and pardoned many outlaws, which occurred at about the same time.

Writing in 1952, the historian James Walker also concluded that Robert Hood of Wakefield was the real man behind the legend. Earlier,

Scottish historians John Fordun (who died in 1386) and Andrew of Wyntoun (c. 1350–c1425) placed Robin as existing around 1260–1280 onwards. Another, John Major or Mair (c. 1467–1550), estimated in 1521 that he lived in the reign of Richard the Lionheart (1189–1199), which has been the version taken up by most makers of films and television series about Robin. Richard, incidentally, was French born, he spoke no English and he only reigned for six months in England. In fact, the original Robin Hood stories and ballads span many centuries and it is possible there were many generations of outlaws who took up the name.

A new statue to Robin and Marian was unveiled in Edwinstowe High Street opposite the library in 1998 and each year in August there is a Robin Hood festival around the Major Oak and Sherwood Forest Visitor Centre. The centre is at Sherwood Forest Country Park, Edwinstowe, Notts NG21 9HN (Tel: 01623 823202). The pub can be found on the intersection of the B6034 and B6030.

4. William Tell (fourteenth century)

Hero of Switzerland, 142 Loughborough Road, Camberwell, London, SW9 7LL (Tel: 020 7274 2763). Punch Taverns.

This pub is named after William Tell, the legendary hero who liberated Switzerland from Austrian oppression in the revolt of 1308 against the bailiffs. When passing through a square in Altdorf with his young son, Tell refused to salute a hat in Austrian colours hanging on a pole. He was immediately seized by Austrian soldiers for showing a lack of respect and he was brought before the Austrian governor named Gessler.

Gessler decided that Tell's punishment would be to shoot an apple on his son's head with his crossbow from fifty paces. They were marched back into the square, where an indignant crowd gathered to witness the event. But Tell shot the apple without harming his son and the crowd duly applauded. Gessler noticed that Tell had brought out a second arrow and asked why. Tell was hesitant at first, until Gessler threatened to have him executed if he did not answer, but would spare his life if he did.

'It was to pierce your heart if my first arrow had killed my son,' replied Tell.

Outraged at this reply, Gessler decided to punish him, while sticking to the letter if not the spirit of his promise, by ordering Tell be jailed for life in the dungeons of Kusnacht Castle.

Tell was chained in a boat to make the journey there, but not far from port a huge storm raged that looked like it might blow the boat onto rocks. The crew told Gessler that only Tell could save them, so he was released and he subsequently managed to steer the boat to safety. As it reached land, Tell jumped to freedom and then he made his way to Kusnacht Castle to hide behind some bushes and await Gessler. When

Gessler arrived that same night, Tell killed him with an arrow from his crossbow and rid the country of tyranny.

Another pub called the William Tell Tavern in Stephens Street, Dublin, has since been renamed the Hairy Lemon.

5. Wat Tyler (executed 1381)

80 High Street (corner of Bullace Lane), Dartford, Kent, DA1 1DE
(Tel: 01322 272546). Free house.

The Peasants' Revolt of 1381 was sparked off by the third poll tax imposed by the young King Richard II in just four years. Dartford was one of the early towns to rebel on 5 June under the incitement of Abel Ker from nearby Erith. Wat Tyler rose to lead the rebels, who took over his hometown Maidstone on 7 June and Canterbury on 10 June (seizing the sheriff and making a bonfire of all his records), and then he marched to London on 11 June.

According to a plaque outside the pub, Wat Tyler and his followers 'called at this ancient tavern (so it is said) to quench their thirst with flagons of ale' before proceeding to London to demand from the king 'that you make us free for ever, ourselves, our heirs and our lands and that we be called no more bond or so reputed.'

When they met the king at Mile End, they accused the lords of being traitors to the king, and demanded they should no longer be serfs to the lords. The king promised he would grant them freedom and permission to catch traitorous lords and bring them to him. Tyler and others went to the Tower of London, where they captured the Archbishop of Canterbury, the Chancellor Simon Sudbury and the Treasurer of England Sir Robert Hales, whom they deemed responsible for the poll tax. They then took them to Tower Hill and beheaded them.

On 15 June the king and Tyler met at Smithfield, where Tyler shook the king's hand roughly and said, 'Brother be of good cheer for in the next fortnight you will have 40,000 more of the common people with you and we shall be good companions'. When the king asked him to disperse his followers, Tyler replied 'with a great oath' that he would not leave until he had a charter signed and sealed. He demanded there should be no more serfdom, but that all men should be free, with one condition attached: that there should be no more lords except the king, that the possessions of the church be taken from the clergy and that all lands should be divided among the commoners. The king agreed to this, reserving only for himself the regality of the crown, and ordered Tyler and his followers to return home without delay.

Tyler responded by ordering a jug of water to rinse out his mouth 'in a very rude manner' followed by a jug of ale, which he drank in one great draught, before remounting his horse. The Mayor of London William of Walworth then arrested Tyler for showing contempt for the king. In the struggle, Walworth stabbed Tyler in the neck and others plunged their swords into his body.

Tyler's supporters carried him to the hospital for the poor at St Bartholomews, but he was dragged from there by Walworth, who beheaded him in the middle of Smithfield and later took his head on a pole to the king in a field by St John in Clerkenwell. The king thanked the mayor greatly for what he had done and knighted him.

After the king had left many of the peasants were killed. But some escaped and, according to one report, they returned in disarray to the pub in Dartford, which was their meeting place, then called the Rose and Crown, but unofficially known as the Wat Tyler for the last 600 years.

The king naturally broke all his promises and the revolt was crushed. Indeed, four hundred years later, Thomas Paine praised Tyler for his valour in standing up against the odious and detested poll tax. He repeated what was probably a popular myth that Tyler had killed a tax collector with a hammer when he visited his Deptford home and indecently examined one of his daughters to ascertain whether or not she was over the age of 15 and so liable to pay poll tax.

Paine said of Tyler, 'All his proposals made to Richard were on a more just and public ground than those which had been made to John by the Barons ... If the Barons merited a monument to be erected in Runnymede, Tyler merits one in Smithfield.'

Sadly, the only commemoration of him at Smithfield is the dagger which killed him, which is held in Fishmongers Hall. But a road has been named after him at Blackheath in south-east London (Wat Tyler Road), where the peasants had gathered for a mass meeting.

In the 1840s, the Chartists formed a Wat Tyler brigade and he appeared on the banners of the Sheffield Chartists. One of their songs concluded,

'For Tyler of old, a heart-chorus bold
Let Labour's children sing!'

On the six hundredth anniversary of the revolt, the TUC paid tribute to him when its general secretary Len Murray opened the Wat Tyler Country Park at Pitsea in Essex.

6. Owain Glyndwr (c. 1359–c. 1416)

(i) St John's Square, Cardiff, Glamorgan, South Wales, CF10 1GL
     (Tel: 029 2022 1980). Laurel Pub Company.
(ii) Llanddona, Beaumaris, Isle of Anglesey, North Wales, LL58 8UF
     (Tel: 01248 810710). Free house.

The leader of the Welsh national revolt against the English, which lasted from 1400 to 1409, Owain Glyndwr was known for perfecting the art of guerrilla warfare; the lessons of which were learned nearly 600 years later in Latin America by his admirer Che Guevara. While the English armies trundled slowly along the well-trodden valley routes, Owain's men moved swiftly along the highland ridgeways. When the armies had passed by, the Welsh guerrillas launched lightning raids from their mountain hideouts on the English settlements and castles.

During the height of the revolt in 1404, Cardiff was captured by the rebels. It was only after a long siege when surrounded by hundreds of troops from Somerset and Devon that they lost control of it. A statue of Owain now stands in Cardiff city hall.

Owain had been described as 'an exemplary warrior' during his previous military career in the English army, for which he fought from 1384 to 1387 in Scotland and France; later to be his allies. He lived at Glyndyfrdwy, south of Denbigh in north Wales, and claimed that some of the land occupied by his neighbour Reginald Grey, Lord of Ruthin, was really his. When Owain went to Westminster to stake his claim, he was disdainfully dismissed by the lords, who said they did not care for him 'and his barefooted rogues'.

Enraged by this he returned home and took the law into his own hands by plundering and burning Grey's estates in Ruthin on the 16 September 1400 with two hundred and fifty men. The situation rapidly escalated into a national rising against English tyranny, whereby Welsh labourers from England seized weapons and joined him and in April 1401, they captured Conway Castle with less than fifty men. By the summer of 1403, the whole of Wales was ablaze with revolt and the English had lost control of the countryside, unable to collect any revenue for the following three years. The Welsh rebels even crossed the River Severn into England and returned with booty.

In order to forge the sense of national unity to attain independence from the yolk of England, Owain proclaimed himself Prince of Wales; a title which the English had usurped. The last Welsh Prince of Wales

Llewelyn ap Gruffudd had died in 1282 and was from a Gwynedd dynasty, whereas Owain was from a Powys dynasty. There was no legitimacy to Owain's claim to the title, but he saw it as an important symbolic gesture to cement unity for national independence and his leadership of the revolt was never challenged. His standard was a golden dragon on a white field.

He delegated authority to local commanders and gave them the same loyalty that they showed him. This allowed him to go abroad on missions to forge alliances with England's enemies, such as France and Scotland. This was rewarded in 1405, when 1,100 French soldiers arrived with heavy stocks of wine in February and a further 2,500 men in July. They helped capture Carmarthen, where the English had their headquarters for south-west Wales. But in 1407, the French signed a truce with England and returned home.

In 1409 Owain's wife Margaret Hanmer of Flintshire and two of their daughters and three grandsons were captured when Harlech Castle finally fell. Their son-in-law Edmund Mortimer had been killed earlier in this siege. The English Prince of Wales burned Owain's house at Glyndyfrdwy.

However, Owain was never captured or betrayed and he continued living in mountain thickets and caves as far afield as Beddgelert in Caernarfonshire, Llangelynnin in Merionethshire, and Craig Gwrtheyrn Hill Fort in Carmarthenshire. He was last seen in 1416 and it was not until 1421 that his son Maredudd ab Owain gave himself up in return for a pardon from the king. Owain may have starved to death in the mountains, but legend has it that he was buried in the churchyard at Monington, a small village near Cardigan, where he haunted the home of his son-in-law; and the home of another son-in-law at Scudmore.

Penal statutes were brought in to punish the Welsh, barring them from all important positions and from marrying the English. In Chester, the Welsh were barred from keeping taverns, from selling ale or wine, or from even being within the city walls after dark on pain of death. The revolt did, however, hasten the end of serfdom in Wales, as so many serfs had fled from their masters and refused to return or submit to their obligations unless granted tenurial rights to the land and a measure of freedom.

Shakespeare portrayed Owain with some degree of sympathy in his play *Henry IV*, Part One and in more recent times he was described as the father of modern Welsh nationalism.

Owain Glyndwr`s story is told on this pillar in the Cardiff pub.

7. Mother Shipton, real name Ursula Sontheil (1488–1561)

Mother Shipton Inn, Low Bridge, Knaresborough, North Yorkshire, HG5 8HZ (Tel: 01423 862157). Scottish & Newcastle.

The cave where Mother Shipton was born, near the inn.

Born illegitimately in a cave, Ursula Sontheil acquired an early reputation as a witch and a child of the devil. After marrying a carpenter Toby Shipton, she achieved long-lasting fame as a prophetess. Her mother Agatha was a 15-year-old orphan when she gave birth to Ursula in the cave next to this pub by the River Nidd. A great crack of thunder and the smell of sulphur heralded the birth of the 'huge and mis-shapen' baby (she had a crooked spine and hunched back), who 'jeered and laughed' until the storm was silenced. Shortly afterwards, Agatha was prosecuted in court for prostitution, but she caused uproar by revealing that the judge had made two of his servants pregnant and the case was dismissed.

When Ursula was two years old, her mother joined a convent and fostered her out. One day, her foster mother came home and found the front door open and the sound of dreadful wailing noises. She went to fetch a clergyman and they found that Ursula, still only two, had left her cradle and was sitting on the iron bar in the kitchen chimney, smiling mischievously.

Her physical deformities attracted unkind remarks as she grew older and she was said to use her witchcraft powers to get revenge against those who made them. Indeed, two so-called 'worthy gentlemen' called her 'the devil's bastard' and 'hag face'. She turned the ruff around the neck of one into a toilet seat and the hat on the head of the other into a chamber pot.

She became Mrs Shipton by marrying Toby in 1512 at the age of 24. The following month, a neighbour told her someone had stolen her new smock and petticoat. Ursula said she knew who had done this and that the items would be returned on the following market day. This duly happened and she became respected as a prophetess. She also correctly forecast the death of a young nobleman, the stabbing to death of a Lord Mayor in York and the falling of the steeple at York's Trinity Church.

Her life became endangered, however, when she described Cardinal Thomas Wolsey, who was both Lord Chancellor and Archbishop of York, as 'the mitred peacock', whose great honour would come to nothing. In particular, she was widely reported as having prophesied he would not see York, despite being its archbishop. Wolsey sent Lord Percy, Lord D'Arcy and the Earl of Northumberland, to silence her. She told them, 'I said he might see York, but never reach it'. They told her that Wolsey had said when he reached York he would have her burned at the stake.

'We shall see,' she replied. Then she threw her headscarf in the fire, but it did not burn, and neither did her walking stick when she held it in the flames. Taking it out again, she declared, 'If this had burned I might have too.' She then told the three lords that they would all be killed on the pavements of York.

Wolsey then travelled from London towards York, stopping at Cawood, 10 miles south of the city, to climb a tower to see it. He satisfyingly remarked that he had confounded Mother Shipton's claim that he would never see York. He was then corrected, that she had said he would not reach it.

'I vow that I will have her burned when I get there, and I soon will be,' he reacted angrily.

Almost immediately he was arrested for high treason and was escorted back towards London, but died at Leicester on the way. Later, the three lords were all killed on the pavements of York as Henry VIII crushed their rebellion ... and Mother Shipton's reputation became unchallenged.

She even correctly predicted the year of her own death, after which she was buried on unconsecrated ground on the outskirts of York. On her tombstone, which has now disappeared, read the inscription:

> Here lies she who never lied,
> Whose skill so often has been tried.
> Her prophecies shall still survive
> And ever keep her name alive.

Many of her prophesies did, indeed, become true long after her death. These included the beheading of Charles I, the Great Plague, the Great Fire of London and the advent of motor vehicles, iron ships, aeroplanes and submarines. In the inn named after her is the table that belonged to Guy Fawkes when he lived in nearby Scotton in 1592.

A table in the Mother Shipton Inn.

8. Robert Kett (1492–1549)

(i) Lime Tree Avenue, Wymondham, Norfolk, NR18 0HH (Tel: 01953 602957). Greene King.

(ii) Kett's Tavern, 29 Kett's Hill, Norwich, NR1 4EX (Tel: 01603 628520). Free house.

A rebel army of 20,000 Norfolk farm labourers was led against the landowners by Kett, who lived in Wymondham in the summer of 1549. The immediate issue which sparked off the rebellion was the fencing off of the common land, which many smallholders depended on to graze their animals, by the unpopular large landowners.

On 7 July of that year, after drinking plentifully at the annual fair in Wymondham, many of the locals pulled down the fences which had been put up to enclose the common land at nearby Morley. The following day, they set off to do the same at another local village called Hethersett, their target being the fences that had been put up by landowner John Flowerdew. Flowerdew pointed out that Kett had also fenced off land in Wymondham and offered cash to the crowd to pull down Kett's fences instead. Kett, a tanner by trade, surprised everybody by offering to help them to pull down his own fences and lead their protest.

In a speech at his house, below the church in a meadow near the tan pits, he promised to subdue the power of great men and right the hurts done by 'the importunate lords' to the common pastures. 'Whatever lands I have enclosed shall again be made common unto ye and all men, and my own hand shall first perform it,' he declared. 'Never shall I be wanting where your good is concerned. You shall have me if you will, not only as a companion, but as a captain, and in the doing of so great a work before us, not only as a fellow, but for a general standard bearer and chief.'

A server in the local Abbey church, he had bought some land in 1540, which had belonged to the Abbey after it had been dissolved in the previous year. His religious convictions meant he was outraged by the callous disregard of many large landowners for the plight of the poor commoners. After pulling down his own fences, he and the crowd returned to uproot Flowerdew's fences in Hethersett, where Kett urged his followers 'to be of good comfort' and to follow him 'in defence of their common liberty'.

On 9 July the crowd assembled again under an oak on the common outside Wymondham, where Kett roused them with the words, 'I refuse not to sacrifice my substance, yea my very life itself, so highly do I esteem the cause in which we are engaged'. A tree marked 'Kett's Oak', which still stands in a lay-by just south of Hethersett on the B1172, is said to be where this meeting took place. Their numbers swelled when the cry for freedom went up with the demand 'thatt all bonde men may be

Kett's Oak, near Hethersett, Norfolk.

ffre for god made all ffre with his precious blode sheddying'; echoing the sentiments of John Ball's sermon back in the1381 Peasants' Revolt.

They then marched towards Norwich and set up camp on the outskirts of the city at Mousehold Heath. The artist Samuel Wale depicted Kett at this camp under the 'Oak of the Reformation' in a picture, on which the pub sign is based.

Kett declared, 'What we want is liberty, and the power, in common with our so called superiors, of enjoying the gifts of nature'. The Oak of Reformation is where Kett held councils, administered justice, issued edicts, and appointed twenty-five governors for the surrounding areas. They drew up a list of twenty-nine complaints, mainly against economic exploitation, and concluded, 'We pray that all bond men may be made free.'

They commandeered 3,000 bullocks, 20,000 sheep and immense quantities of corn from the gentry, which they shared out publicly under the Oak of Reformation. The landowners who had enclosed the land were tried, convicted and imprisoned by the rebels. An army of 1,400 soldiers was then routed by the rebels. But then a much larger one of 12,000 plus 1,200 foreign mercenaries finally conquered them after seven weeks. A total of 3,000 rebels were slaughtered and a further 300 captured and executed.

After losing the battle, Kett was imprisoned in Guildhall in Norwich, before being executed at Norwich Castle on 7 December 1549. On the same day his brother William, a butcher, was hanged in chains from the west tower of Wymondham Church – a slow, painful death, which was often cut short by friends of the condemned shooting them with arrows – for his part in the uprising. The heads of the defeated rebels were then displayed on the walls of Warwick Castle as a warning to others.

A plaque placed at the entrance to Norwich Castle in 1949 honours Kett as 'a noble and courageous leader' and the town sign in Wymondham, outside Becket's Chapel at the end of Damgate, shows him rallying the peasantry under an oak tree. His name also lives on through Robert Kett Junior School in Hewitts Lane, Wymondham and through a play written in 1909 by G. Colman Green called *Kett the Tanner.*

Kett was described as bold, hardy, of unbridled spirit, resolute, confident, wise ... and a natural successor to Geoffrey Litster, a dyer from Felmingham,

who was the chief leader in Norfolk of the 1381 Peasants' Revolt. They temporarily entered Norwich and occupied the castle in June of that year. Bishop Despenser crushed that revolt and sentenced Litster to drawing and hanging and held up his head to prevent it knocking on the ground while he was being dragged to the place of his hanging at North Walsham.

Another farm workers' leader addressed a meeting from Kett's Oak, when Jack Boddie, General Secretary of the National Union of Agricultural and Allied Workers, spoke to unemployed workers taking part in the People's March for Jobs in the 1970s. Jack also fought for the preservation of the tree, when it looked as if its survival was threatened from lack of support.

9. Hugh Sexey (1556–1619)

Sexey's Arms, Sexeys Road, Blackford, Near Cheddar, North Somerset, BS28 4NT (Tel: 01934 712487). Free house.

Hugh Sexey was a self-taught plough boy and stable boy, who became a pirate and, eventually, a wealthy lawyer and royal auditor. The various phases of his life are depicted on the pub sign, which shows him as a young boy. A lamb represents his time as an agricultural worker, a ship his time at sea and a castle and coat of arms for his later eminence.

After being orphaned he was raised by nuns, who put him to work on farms at an early age. But the call of the sea appealed to his sense of adventure and before long, he became a pirate – or privateer as pirates who gave part of their plunder to the crown were known. Untypical of this profession, however, he used his ill-gotten gains to finance a less risky way of fleecing the rich, by studying and qualifying as a lawyer in London.

His social standing advanced from yeoman to esquire during the 1580s and he became deputy auditor to the crown. He was appointed as royal auditor to Elizabeth I in 1599 and retained the position under James I after her death. This made him a rich man and he was able to purchase much land around Bruton in Somerset, where he was born, and elsewhere in the county, including both Blackfords; the one where the pub is located, near Cheddar, and the other near Bruton and Wincanton.

Mindful of his poor beginnings, he left money in his will for a trust to help the less well off, which has been used to build hospitals and schools. The first hospital was built at Bruton in 1632 for twelve 'aged and impotent persons'. Its first master was sacked for drunkenness and neglect. The first school, also in Bruton, was for twelve boys. Money was also provided for poor boys from the village to have seven-year apprenticeships in mechanical trades. The school has since grown to cater for 400 pupils, including girls. In addition, there is a Hugh Sexey Middle School at Wedmore, which is situated near this pub. Sexey's Trust also owns many dairy, sheep and cattle farms in the area; probably the ones on which he used to work.

10. William Shakespeare (1564–1616)

The Shakespeare Inn, Chapel Street, Welford-on-Avon, Warwickshire, CV37 8PX (Tel: 01789 750443). Enterprise Inns.

Shakespeare was also known as Shagspere and Shakeshaft during his acting career, but sadly no pubs are called either of these. This particular inn that has been named after him is the nearest to his birthplace of Stratford-upon-Avon; where only a hotel bears his name in the town itself.

His father John was one of Stratford's two ale tasters, whose job it was to check on the quality of the local brewing and to bring to court anyone who fell below standard. He was also a part-time constable and a bailiff with the responsibility of a Justice of the Peace; although he could not read or write. Despite John's trade as a wood dealer, his son could hardly be described as a 'chip off the old block'. Young William shared neither his father's respect for law nor his illiteracy and he became both a deer poacher and a playwright.

In 1582 he married Anne Hathaway in a shotgun wedding and before long he had three children, including twins. In 1592 he travelled to London to become an actor, often performing on barrels at inns. The Vagabonds Act of the time stipulated that any 'common players' not part of a troupe belonging to a baron were to be stripped, whipped and thrown out of the parish. Luckily, Shakespeare was patronised by Lord Strange and so avoided this fate.

Another member of the aristocracy to befriend him was the 4th Earl of Southampton, a young, feminine-looking man, whose beauty Shakespeare praised in his Sonnets. This, and letters between them, led to speculation that they had a gay relationship, at a time when sodomy carried the death sentence. Other sonnets contained confessions by

Shakespeare of adultery with a married woman; possibly Jane D'Avenant, wife of the inn keeper of the Crown Tavern in Oxford,

where Shakespeare stayed on journeys between London and Stratford. A further intimate friend of both Jane and the Earl was Shakespeare's rival dramatist Christopher Marlowe (1564–1593) who was killed in a brawl at a tavern in Deptford. There is an anecdote of another adulterous act by Shakespeare, where his fellow actor Richard Burbage was playing Richard III and made an assignation to sleep with a woman, who lived near the playhouse, after the performance. She told him to announce himself as Richard III to keep his identity secret. Shakespeare overheard this, left before the end of the play, went to the woman's house, announced himself as Richard III and went to bed with her. When Burbage turned up and also announced himself as Richard III, he was given a message from Shakespeare, 'William the Conqueror came before Richard III'.

Shakespeare died of a fever following a drinking bout, according to the Vicar of Stratford John Ward. In Shakespeare's will the only reference to his wife Anne Hathaway was, 'I give unto my wife my second best bed with the furniture'. He was buried at Holy Trinity Church in Stratford, where the inscription on his tombstone, written by him, read:

> Good frend for Jesus sake forebeare
> To digg the dust enclosed heare
> Bleste be ye man ty spares thes stones,
> And curst be he ty moves my bones.

This was to discourage the practice at the time of digging up the bones of the dead in order to make room for more burials.

His bones may well have turned in his grave in 1818 though, when Thomas Bowdler edited an edition of his works, which cut out all the 'profane and obscene' parts.

11. William Butler (early sixteenth century)

Old Dr Butler's Head, 12 Masons Avenue, Moorgate, London, EC2V 5BB
(Tel: 020 7606 3504). Shepherd Neame.

Self-professed quack William Butler bought this pub in 1616 in order to sell ales, which he claimed cured various ailments. He got a boost when King James I (1566–1625) had an excruciatingly painful bad back and went to Butler as a last resort. After prodding the king's back, Butler said he should try his medicinal ale, brewed from his own secret formula, which was 'flamed with a variety of spices and tinctures'. The king quaffed large quantities of the draught ale and got so intoxicated that the pain went away. So grateful was he that he gave Butler an honorary degree in medicine and made him his court physician.

His remedies were hardly founded on medical science, however. For epilepsy, for example, he fired pistols without warning inches from the sufferer's ear. Those suffering from malarial fever he threw head first into the River Thames through a trapdoor on London Bridge. Amazingly, people queued up in large numbers to receive this treatment and eventually, a whole chain of taverns, displaying signs of Butler's head, stocked his so-called medicinal liquors.

12. Guy Fawkes (1570–1606)

Guy Fawkes Arms, Main Street (corner of Harikil Lane), Scotton, North Yorkshire, HG5 9HU (Tel: 01423 862598).

It was while living as a child in Scotton, a quarter of a mile from this pub, that Guy Fawkes became a devout Catholic ... paving the way for his later attempt to blow up the government that persecuted his faith. He was born on the site of the present Young's Hotel in High Petersgate, Stonegate, York and was baptised at St Michael-le-Belfry Church opposite on 16 April 1570, in the Protestant faith of his father Edward.

But he came under the influence of the forbidden Catholic faith of his mother Edith Jackson, when attending St Peter's school in York, where three of his fellow pupils later became Catholic priests, who were executed by being disembowelled alive at Lancaster in 1601. A couple of others, Jack and Kit Wright, joined him in the Gunpowder Plot to blow up Parliament and were shot when captured.

When Guy was aged 8 his father died and two or three years later, his mother remarried a Catholic called Dionysius Baynbridge, also known as Denis Bainbridge, and joined him at Scotton, just west of Knaresborough and north of Harrogate. In 1591 he is believed to have married Maria Pulleine, who bore him a son, Thomas, but both mother and son died shortly afterwards.

He then became a footman for the 1st Viscount Montague in Cowdray, Sussex, who disliked and sacked him. But he was taken on again by the 2nd Viscount, waiting at table. In 1593 he enlisted as a soldier in the Spanish army in Holland, where his religion was not a bar to advancement, and he fought in it for ten years, rising to the rank of captain and achieving a reputation as a courageous man of action, who was also able to argue intelligently. For a soldier, he led an unusually clean life. He was tall and powerfully built, with thick, reddish-brown hair, a flowing moustache and a bushy beard.

In 1603 he went on a mission to Spain, still technically at war with England, to try and persuade King Philip III to invade England and restore the Catholic faith. He told him that the recently crowned King James I was a heretic, who intended to drive all papists out of England and who was not to be trusted in any peace talks. Although Philip was friendly towards Guy, who changed his name to Guido during this trip, he had, in fact, decided not to invade England or support the Catholics there.

The Gunpowder Plot was sparked off by a bill that James introduced in April 1604 to class all Catholics as outlaws ... thus breaking a promise he had made as James VI of Scotland to introduce religious toleration. Guy and four others, including his school friend Jack Wright, attended the first meeting on 20 May at the Duck and Drake Inn at The Strand in London. They realised that Spain was not committing itself to any military support and they would have to take action themselves, as Parliament was continuing to pass anti-Catholic laws and was executing priests. James ordered the extermination of the Jesuits and a peace treaty was signed with Spain, without any clause about religious toleration.

The blowing up of Parliament was seen by the conspirators as a last resort – describing it as tyrannicide – to alert the world to the outrageous suffering they were being subjected to. Kit Wright and others joined the plot bringing their number to thirteen. Thomas Percy, who was Jack Wright's brother-in-law, rented a storeroom under the House of Lords on 25 March 1605 along with a room on the first floor, where he installed Guy as his servant, using the alias John Johnson. By 20 July they placed thirty-six barrels of gunpowder in the storeroom. Guy then went to Flanders to try and enlist foreign support and was observed there by English government spy Captain William Turner, who reported him to Robert Cecil, Earl of Salisbury, the king's chief minister.

Back in London it was decided that Guy was to light the fuse and then escape by boat across the Thames. He would then go over to the Continent to explain to the Catholic powers the reasons for such action. Final plans were made in taverns such as The Mitre in Bread Street, Mansion House, London EC4, and the Irish Boy in The Strand.

Lord Monteagle, who was the brother-in-law of one of the plotters, got to hear of the plan and was anxious to dissociate himself from it. So it seems likely he contrived to have a letter giving details about the plot written and delivered to him. It arrived on 26 October and he took it to the government.

At 10 p.m. on 4 November Guy picked up the watch to time the fuse and went to the storeroom. But just after midnight on the morning of 5 November he was caught – dressed in a cloak and dark hat and booted and spurred 'as though for flight' – and arrested. He freely admitted he had intended to blow up the king and the lords and had no regrets for his actions, other than the fact he had not succeeded. When the king himself came to question him and asked how he could 'conspire so hideous a treason', he replied that a dangerous disease required a desperate remedy.

Guy's iron resolve of self-control impressed even the king. However, it did not prevent him ordering that he be tortured. 'The gentler tortures are to be first used unto him,' he commanded, only to be made gradually worse. 'God speed your good work.'

So he was taken to the Tower of London, where the 'gentle' manacles were used. He was hung by the wrists against the wall and left dangling for hours as the manacles were gradually tightened, permanently maiming him. He was then put on the rack, with his wrists and ankles tied to rollers, which stretched him slowly and, on 7 November, dislocated his body. It was only then that he began talking, although he still did not reveal any names until the next day.

He and the other seven surviving conspirators were displayed on a scaffold in Westminster Hall for a show trial on 27 January 1606. To the disgust of the king, who was present, they smoked tobacco 'as if hanging were no trouble to them'.

Guy surprisingly pleaded not guilty – over some technical inaccuracy in the indictment – but was not allowed to make a defence. Found guilty of high treason, he and the others were

A painting in the pub of the arrest of Guy Fawkes.

told of their punishment: to be drawn head down behind a horse, to have their genitals cut off and burned in front of their face, to be hanged and, before death, to have their bowels and heart hacked out, and afterwards to have their heads cut off. Then, their dismembered bodies were to be publicly exposed and left 'prey for the fowls of the air'.

Guy was the last to be executed on 31 January 1606, at Old Palace Yard, Westminster. He was reported to be 'weak with torture and sickness' and had to be helped up the ladder by the hangman. Mercifully, he got high enough to have his neck broken by the drop, so was not conscious during the remaining barbarities of his execution.

13. Moll Cutpurse, real name Mary Frith (1584–1659)

Moll Cutpurse, 58 High Road, Tottenham, London, N15 6JU.

The female highway robber Mary Frith, also known as Moll Cutpurse, was born with clenched fists – the sign of a wild and adventurous spirit – and she became known as 'the Roaring Girl'. Her father, a shoemaker in Barbican, tried to get her apprenticed as a saddler, but she refused, in keeping with her determination not to submit to discipline, so he put her on a ship destined for Virginia to be sold on the plantations there, but she escaped before it even left London.

An anonymous biography of her published in 1662 said that in her childhood she was 'a very tomrigg or rumpscuttle', who 'delighted and sported only in boys' plays and pastime, not minding or companying with the girls'. She grew to be a 'lusty and sturdy wench', who fought well with a distaff. She disliked housework and 'had a natural abhorrence to the tending of children', so, after being forced into domestic service, she rapidly rebelled and turned to crime instead.

She gained notoriety as a pickpocket, a fortune teller (illegal in those days), a receiver, a forger, and a highway robber. So well known did she become as a receiver that people who had been robbed went to her Fleet Street house to retrieve their property for an agreed percentage of its value. The only penance she showed was once at Paul's Cross after drinking six pints of ale and being 'maudlin-drunk'.

On one occasion she robbed General Fairfax on Hounslow Heath, shot him through the arm, and killed two horses

on which his servants were riding. For this, she was sent to Newgate prison and was sentenced to death, but was released after paying Fairfax £2,000, a considerable fortune at the time, proving how successful she had been in crime. Indeed, a large gang of thieves were under her control and she was friendly with highwaymen, such as Captain Hind and Richard Hannam. She also trained a vicious dog to accompany her on these missions. Although she suffered from dropsy, it was believed that this was kept at bay by her constant smoking.

Moll Cutpurse robbing a general on the highway (depicted in a Dunlop advert in the 1950s).

A popular comedy called *The Roaring Girle*, written by Thomas Middleton and Thomas Dekker and performed in 1611, depicted her as the heroine. Her portrait was on the front of the published version, depicting her in men's clothing with a pipe and a sword.

Her own view of herself was, 'When viewing the manners and customs of the age, I see myself so wholly distempered, and so estranged from them, as if I had been born and bred in the Antipodes'. She died in her house in Fleet Street and was buried in the church of St Bridgets (or Brides).

14. Oliver Cromwell (1599–1658)

(i) 13 Wellington Street, St Ives, Huntingdon, Cambridgeshire, PE27 5AZ (Tel: 01480 465601). Free house.

(ii) 71 St Edith's Marsh, Bromham, near Devizes, Wiltshire, SN15 2DF (Tel: 01380 850293). Enterprise Inns.

Britain's only republican head of state so far, Oliver Cromwell (apart from his son) famously told portrait artist Peter Lely to paint him 'warts and all'. The metaphorical warts in his life include his massacres of the Irish people, the execution of the radical 'levellers' in his own army and, arguably, regicide. On the other hand, he had the enormous sense of purpose and strength of character to win two civil wars for Parliament over the royalists. He saw himself as a local policeman, who was good at settling neighbourly squabbles but not good at making the rules. His pronounced belief in tolerance was way ahead of public opinion, but he was forced, or otherwise, into some very intolerant actions.

Born in Huntingdon, he was the descendant of an ale brewer and innkeeper from Putney; where the famous radical debates in Cromwell's new model army took place from 1647 to 1648. At the age of 17 he went to Cambridge University, where he excelled at 'football, cudgels, or any other boisterous sport or game'. A year later, when his father died, he went to London for three years to study law.

His first radical act took place in 1630, when he successfully objected to a new charter, which would have taken common land away to the detriment of the poorer people in Huntingdon. From 1631 to 1636 he was a townsman of nearby St Ives, where a statue of him stands in Market Hill, near the pub named after him and opposite The Golden Lion Pub. Later, in the 1630s, he had a form of nervous breakdown and a period of depression, followed by conversion to the puritan cause. He was elected MP for Cambridge in 1640 and zealously defended the rights of commoners against proposed enclosures at Somersham in Huntingdonshire.

With the outbreak of the first civil war in 1642, he rose through the ranks of the parliamentary army to become lieutenant general, always leading from the front, once getting wounded in the neck. He said he preferred his troops to be plain men rather than gentlemen and his remarks about wanting to see an end to all noblemen in England led to him being branded an 'incendiary' in Parliament.

After beating Prince Rupert in a battle near York in 1644 he became nicknamed 'Ironside'. Cromwell beat the prince even more decisively the following year at Naseby, where Charles I managed to escape, but he

nevertheless left behind papers proving he was trying to get armed support from foreign countries. Charles I surrendered in 1646 and Cromwell was one of those who supported a negotiated settlement with the king and 'fair and moderate treatment' of the royalists in the cause of national unity.

But the king stubbornly refused to make any concessions to Parliament and fled to the Isle of Wight in November 1647. Cromwell, his patience with the king exhausted, told Parliament in January 1648 that it would have to govern without Charles I, whom he described as 'an obstinate man whose heart God has hardened'.

Later in the same year, another royalist uprising led to the second civil war. This ended with the capture and execution, on 30 January 1649, of the king at Cromwell's instigation. Many in the victorious parliamentarian army were dissatisfied with Parliament for the lack of democracy in its constitutional reforms and at how gradual they were. These included the 'levellers' or 'diggers', who believed in, and practised, communal farming and the sharing out of land. When they published their own programme and planned to impose it with arms, Cromwell had the levellers arrested and some of the mutineers executed. Cromwell criticised the levelling principle for 'reducing' all to equality and for making tenants as rich as landlords. He was then made commander in chief, before being sent to Ireland with an army of 12,000. His first act was to attack the garrison at Drogheda, to kill 2,500 men and to deport the rest as slave labour to sugar plantations in Barbados. The next massacre took place in Wexford, where 2,000 people were slaughtered. Describing this as 'a righteous judgement of God upon these barbarous wretches', Cromwell said Wexford would now be a good place to establish a new colony and invited people from New England to settle there. He saw the Catholic clergy as the 'chief promoters of rebellion' and ruthlessly suppressed Catholic worship in Ireland.

In January 1650, he was sent to wage war on Scotland with 16,000 troops, because it was supporting the king's son (later Charles II). After suffering from a fever, which brought him close to death on three occasions, Cromwell finally defeated the future Charles II and his Scottish army in September 1651, forcing him to flee abroad.

When the new Parliament failed to legislate for some of the freedoms that had been fought for, the army stepped in to take over in 1652. Cromwell, accompanied by musketeers, marched into the chamber and took away the speaker and the mace, referring to it contemptuously as a bauble, leaving Cromwell in sole power. After refusing the offer to be made king, he was installed as 'Protector' in December 1653. Eventually, an accommodation was made whereby he would have executive power, while Parliament had legislative power. Laws were passed against duelling, cock fighting, horse racing and swearing.

Further conflicts between Cromwell and Parliament resulted in him establishing military rule, with soldiers empowered to enforce laws on vice and morals. As he dissolved Parliament prior to this, Cromwell opined, 'The people will prefer their safety to their passions.' Anabaptist preachers were imprisoned for attacking the government in their sermons, but Jews, who had been expelled in 1290, were allowed back into the country in 1655; one motive being that the conversion of the Jews was said to be a sign of the coming of Christ. Catholics in England were less persecuted during this period without any laws being passed against them.

Cromwell's powers as Protector were increased in 1657; including his right to appoint his successor, who, briefly, was his son Richard. As

The Cromwell statue in St. Ives.

symbols of his authority he replaced black clothes and a sword with ermine and a sceptre. Charles II, in exile, offered a knighthood and £500 a year to anyone who would slay 'a certain base mechanic fellow called Oliver Cromwell'.

In 1658, Cromwell suffered from 'a bastard tertian ague' (a form of malaria fever, which he originally contracted in the bogs of Ireland) and died in Whitehall on 3 September, the day after a great storm. His body was embalmed and, after a lavish funeral costing £60,000, he was buried at Westminster Abbey in Henry VII's chapel at the east end of the middle aisle.

After the restoration of Charles II (in 1659), Cromwell's body was exhumed on 26 January 1661 and was taken to be hanged on gallows at Tyburn on 30 January; the twelfth anniversary of the execution of Charles I. While waiting for this indignity the body was kept upstairs in the Old Red Lion, now called Cromwell's Bar, at 72 High Holborn, WC1. His trunk was then buried under the gallows and his head was put on a pole on top of Westminster Hall, before being buried in Sidney Sussex College, where he had studied, in Cambridge University.

15. Mother Red Cap, real name Jinney Bingham (1600–1680)

(i) Mother Red Cap bar, World's End, 174 Camden High Street, London, NW1 0NE (Tel: 020 7482 1932).

(ii) Mother Red Cap, Prospect Road, Bradway, Sheffield, South Yorkshire, S17 4JA (Tel: 0114 236 0179). Samuel Smith.

(iii) Mother Red Cap, 80 Latimer Road, Luton, Bedfordshire, LU1 3XD (Tel: 01582 730913). Greene King.

(iv) Mother Red Cap, 665 Holloway Road (corner of Witley Road), Archway, London N19 5SE (Tel: 020 7263 7082). Punch Taverns.

Also known as Mother Damnable, The Witch Queen of Kentish Town, Jinney Bingham disposed of several husbands before being celebrated as the legendary Mother Red Cap. Her cottage stood where the World's End Pub, which was called the Mother Red Cap until 1986 and still has a bar named after her, is now located at 174 Camden High Street, on the corner of Kentish Town Road, London, NW1.

In those days, this was wasteland and the cottage was built by her father Jacob, a local brick maker, for her and her boyfriend 'Gypsy' George Coulter, when she had a baby at the age of 16. Soon afterwards, George was found guilty of stealing sheep in nearby Holloway and was hanged at Tyburn. Jinney's next partner was a hard drinking man called Darby, who brutally beat her when frequently intoxicated. She enlisted the help of her parents and Darby mysteriously disappeared. Later, Jinney's parents were convicted of using witchcraft to kill a woman and were hanged at Tyburn. Her third husband named Pitcher ended up burned to death in the cottage oven.

Jinney Bingham (Mother Red Cap), who lived in Camden, North London, where she was known as a witch.

She was tried for his murder but was acquitted after a neighbour said Pitcher 'often got into the oven to hide himself from her tongue'. The next mysterious death in her cottage was that of her lodger, who was a wealthy royalist on the run from the Roundheads (Cromwellians). It was rumoured that she had used witchcraft and poison to kill him, but the inquest failed to establish this.

Sheffield.

The local people, however, became convinced that this red-hatted woman was a witch, especially as she always had a large black cat by her side and wore a cape with bats on it. They often baited and taunted her and she responded by screaming profanities at them from her gate. Another fugitive from the authorities to be sheltered in the cottage by Jinney was highway robber Moll Cutpurse. A coach carrying Lord Rochester and various others was passing her cottage, when they saw a crowd baiting her yet again. Rochester joined in before continuing to Belsize Park, where he got drunk. He decided to return to her cottage dressed up as the devil with horns and a forked tail to frighten her. Jinney was not in the slightest bit intimidated, however, and he skulked off suitably chastened.

Her legendary figure was described in 1870 by Samuel Palmer's History of St Pancras as having 'a large broad nose, heavy shaggy eyebrows, sunken eyes, and lank and leathern cheeks; her forehead wrinkled, her mouth wide and her looks sullen and unmoved. On her shoulders was thrown a dark grey frieze, with black patches, which looked at a distance like flying bats'. This is confirmed by an engraving of her as Mother Damnable published in 1793. A popular rhyme of the time ended:

> 'Her features were shrivelled and brown as a mummy's hide,
> And she passed for a witch, whose amusement was homicide.'

On the eve of her death, neighbours were said to have seen Satan entering her cottage. The next morning, her dead body was found by the fireplace holding a crutch with a teapot hanging from it full of a noxious brew of herbs, drugs and liquid. This was fed to her cat, which promptly died. The undertaker had to break her rigoured limbs to get her into the coffin, which he buried at midnight under a local tree.

A pub called Mother Red Cap has been in Archway since the seventeenth century, the first one being at the top of Highgate Road. At one time it had a picture of a woman with a pot of ale in one hand and cakes in the other, with the inscription:

> 'Old Mother Red Cap, according to her tale,
> lived twenty and a hundred years by drinking this good ale;
> It was her meat, it was her drink and medicine beside,
> And if she still had drunk this ale she never would have died.'

Samuel Pepys dropped in with his wife to escape the rain on 24 September 1661 and laughed at the barmaid, because she looked so much like the picture on the sign.

In the eighteenth century, bowling, quoits and skittles were played in the pub. Now it is pool and darts; sadly, the pub has not seen fit to replace the sign, which blew off in a storm many years ago. Mother Red Cap also became a general term for 'ale wives', hence pubs of this name in Sheffield, Luton and other parts of the country.

16. Alice Lisle (c. 1614–1685)

Rockford Green, Ringwood, Hampshire, BH24 3NA (Tel: 01425 474700). Fullers.

Decapitated at the age of 70 for harbouring a rebel against James II, Alice Lisle was the widow of one of the judges who had sentenced Charles I to death. The notorious Judge Jefferies ordered her to be burned to death on the day of the verdict, but she was eventually beheaded a few days later after refusing to confess in order to save her life. She was a great supporter of religious dissent and had sheltered both royalist and Roundhead refugees in the past.

In 1630 she had married John Lisle, a Cromwellian who became a regicide in 1649 as a judge in the trial of Charles I. When the monarchy was restored in 1660 he fled to Switzerland, but was assassinated by royalists in 1664. Alice chose to stay in England and live in the New Forest at Ellingham in Moyles Court, Ringwood, near this pub, where she became known for her sympathy for nonconformist ministers.

A couple of weeks after the battle of Sedgemoor, in which the Duke of Monmouth's rebellion against the king was defeated in July 1685, one of the rebels, a fiery nonconformist minister called John Hicks or Hickes, sought shelter at her home. She agreed to let him stay in her malthouse, thinking his offence was nothing more serious than illegal preaching. One of the soldiers hunting Hicks was Colonel Thomas Penruddocke, whose father had been condemned to death by John Lisle. He was thus able to get his revenge on Lisle's widow when he tracked Hicks to her property. The arrests were made the next day and Alice was tried on 27 August at the 'Bloody Assizes' in Winchester, accused of 'traitorously entertaining, concealing, and comforting' Hicks and causing meat and drink to be delivered to him. So old, infirm and hard of hearing was she that she was allowed an assistant to 'stand by her'. Jefferies was openly hostile to her and her witnesses, one of whom he denounced in court as 'a strange prevaricating, shuffling, snivelling, lying rascal' when he refused to say Alice had supplied Hicks with beer. When the same witness said that all Alice was interested in was whether or not Hicks was a nonconformist, this equally angered the judge, who blasted him again. Finally, the witness said, 'Tell me what you would have me say.'

Entry to the pub is through a swinging turnstile.

Another witness gave evidence against Alice, but she pointed out that his evidence was biased, because he had robbed her and was avoiding prosecution himself by getting her convicted. In her own defence, Alice said she had heard warrants were out for the arrest of Hicks for preaching in private meetings and that she did not know he had been fighting. 'I was, indeed, willing to shelter Hicks, knowing him to be a dissenting preacher, and that there were warrants out against him upon that account,' she said. This was not treason, she added. She also pointed out that she should not be tried for harbouring a traitor until Hicks had been convicted of being one. The king's soldiers who had conducted the search, she said, had put her in 'great consternation and dread', as they were 'very rude and could not be restrained by their officers from plundering my house.'

In a hostile summing up, Jefferies referred to the 'share her husband had in the death of King Charles I' and 'reports of her rejoicing at the death of King Charles'. He told the jury that the charges were 'as plain as the sun at noon day' and that the 'preservation of the government, the life of the king, the safety and honour of their religion' were all at stake.

The jury asked whether or not it could equally be seen as treason to receive a rebel before he was convicted of treason as after. The judge told them, 'It is all the same.'

After half an hour the jury returned and said they had doubts over whether or not the accused knew Hicks had been in Monmouth's army. Again, the judge brushed aside their doubts and said, 'Come, come, gentlemen, 'tis a plain proof. But if there were no such proof, the circumstances and management of the thing is as full proof as can be; I wonder what it is you doubt of.'

Finally, the jury reluctantly found her guilty. The next day the judge ordered her to be burned on that very afternoon ... unless she confessed,

in which case her execution may be respited. There was a delay, however, during which Alice refused to confess, but successfully asked the king to change her method of execution to beheading.

This took place in Winchester market place on 2 September 1685. In her dying speech, she declared the jury had found her guilty without sufficient evidence. Indeed, many considered her execution to be a judicial murder and when William and Mary squeezed on to the throne, the prosecution was ruled to be irregular and the verdict 'injuriously extorted' by 'menaces and violences and other illegal practices.' She was buried at Ellingham near her Moyles Court home.

17. John Evelyn (1620–1706)

299 Evelyn Street (corner of Grove Street), Deptford, London, SE8 5RA
(Tel: 020 8692 6588). Fullers.

Diarist and author John Evelyn was a recognised authority on landscape gardening, who took forty-two years stocking his garden in Sayes Court near this pub. Then, Peter the Great, the Russian tsar, rented the house and ruined the garden in a drunken act of vandalism. He insisted his servant push him in a wheelbarrow all over the cherished flower beds and Evelyn's favourite holly hedge. This happened in 1698 and, despite the £162 7s damages he received from the Tsar, who was studying the local shipbuilding industry, it would have tested Evelyn's support for royalty.

Born in Wotton, just south of Dorking, his family was from Normandy and he spent his infancy in Lewes, Sussex. He refused to go to Eton and instead went to a free school. Later, he went to Middle Temple and Balliol, where he left without a degree after spending most of his time dancing, playing music and arguing. After living in Holland he returned to London and did a little studying, but mainly concentrated on 'dancing and fooling'.

In 1642 during the civil war he fought for the royalists at Brentford and was pressed into joining the king's army, but stayed for just three days. He was described as a 'hearty royalist whose zeal was tempered by caution'. In 1652 he thought the royalist cause was hopeless and settled at Sayes Court with his wife Mary Browne (1635–1709), whom he had married when she was just 12 years old and living in Paris with her father, the British ambassador.

With the restoration of the monarchy he was back in favour and held minor offices in the government, being responsible for improving the streets and regulating the mint. But he never rose to high office, because of his dislike of intrigue and because of his disgust at the behaviour of courtiers – views that he confided to his friend and fellow diarist Samuel Pepys.

Evelyn's own diaries were not published until long after his death, when they were found in an old clothes basket at Wotton in 1817. They covered the years 1641 to 1706, containing vivid portrayals of his contemporaries, and were bought for £8 million by the British Museum around the year 2000.

During his lifetime he had thirty-six books published, including *Fumifigium, on the Inconvenience of the Air and Smoke of London Dissipated* in 1661, *Sculptura, on the Art of Engraving on Copper* (the title of which varies in different editions) in 1662 and *Sylva, on the Discourse of Forest Trees* in 1664.

Throughout the plague he stayed in Deptford and helped care for the sick and wounded, including Dutch prisoners of war. In 1694 he rented out Sayes Court and lived with his brother in Wotton. He was appointed treasurer of Greenwich Hospital from 1695 to 1703, and finally moved his remaining property from Sayes Court in 1700. It became a workhouse from 1759 to 1848 and then in 1881 it was turned into almshouses to accommodate old residents on parish relief, and finally into what Evelyn would presumably have approved of: public gardens.

18. Giles Cannard (executed 1625)

Cannards Grave, Castle Cary Road (A37), Shepton Mallet, Somerset, BA4 4LY
(Tel: 01749 347708). Free house.

Giles Cannard was believed to be the last man hanged for sheep stealing in England and this pub was built at the site of his execution in around 1625. He ran a hostelry near this site on the Fosse Way crossroads, a mile south of the village, which was often used by stagecoach passengers. Cannard would get them intoxicated in order to rob them, sometimes murdering them to cover up the crime. Many smugglers, highwaymen and bandits used the pub as a hideout and Cannard would often tip them off as to which travellers had valuables and when they would be leaving. Then, of course, they would be robbed on the road. Cannard was accused by merchants from nearby Frome of being complicit in these robberies, but no action was taken against him.

Cannard also indulged in highway robbery and rustling as far afield as Glastonbury, Frome and Warminster, which was to be his downfall. Some ten stolen sheep were found in his yard, for which he claimed he had been framed by his enemies in Frome, but he was later found guilty and hanged from the gibbet.

Cannards Grave Inn was built on this spot and there have been numerous reports of ghostly hauntings inside it. Rev H. Allen, rector of Shepton Mallet, wrote in 1662 that Cannard's 'soul could not rest and frequently visits the scenes of his former abode while in the flesh'. He also noted that rumours abounded about Cannard's smuggling, gambling, illegal drinking and profanities.

19. Thomas Tripp (seventeenth century)

10 Wick Lane, Christchurch, Dorset, BH23 1HX
(Tel: 01202 490498). Free house.

Smuggler, brigand and local hero, Thomas Tripp was arrested in this pub in the early seventeenth century and he was taken to the Tower of London to be hanged. The source for this information comes from the current landlord John Lovell, who has a roguish sense of humour and claims to be Tripp's descendant.

Whatever the truth about this, the pub certainly plays up to the smuggling theme with pictures and other decor, and it has a genuinely seedy atmosphere.

20. Samuel Pepys (1633–1703)

146 High Street, Huntingdon, PE29 3TF (Tel: 01480 437877). Admiral Taverns.

The great naval reformer and diarist Samuel Pepys was brought up as a Roundhead from 1644 to 1645 during the civil war at Huntingdon Grammar School, where Oliver Cromwell had also been educated. Pepys, the son of a poor tailor, was living at Brampton, a mile south west of Huntingdon, at the time and later owned a house there, which he inherited from his uncle Robert in 1661.

At the age of 15 he returned to London in time to witness the decapitation of Kings Charles I, which caused him to remark, 'The memory of the wicked shall rot.'

In 1650 he won a scholarship to Cambridge University and three years later, he was 'solemnly admonished' for being 'scandalously overserved with drink' after enjoying the 'coarse bluntness' of the local taverns and their barmaids. He was highly amused on revisiting the university some years later to be treated to 'some alcoholic excess' by the same governors who had reprimanded him as a student.

On getting a job as a government clerk for £50 a year in London he liked to stroll around mixing with all classes. He would normally rise at dawn and play his flageolet (a small flute), lute or viol (the predecessor of the violin). For breakfast he would have a draught of ale and pickled onions at the Harp and Ball – sometimes his heavy drinking the night before would cause him to vomit the onions – and then spend a short time in the office. At lunch he would be back in a tavern, where he liked to sing and hear bawdy songs, before an afternoon trip to the theatre, a visit to prostitutes in St James's Park and finally a few more hours in the office.

The diary that he kept from 1660 to 1669 reveals many of his sexual encounters, often in pubs. These include Betty Martin in the Trumpet Tavern, Mary from the Harp and Ball, Mrs Martin in the Swan Tavern, Betty Lane ('I had my full liberty of towzing her'), and Deborah Willet, whose breasts he fondled in an alehouse. Pepys, a bottom fetishist, had been forced to sack Deborah after his wife caught him fingering her. He also gave detailed descriptions of his bouts of constipation in the diary.

But many passages dealing explicitly with sex and defecation were not included in published editions until the 1970s.

In 1665 he became responsible for ordering supplies of victuals to the navy and he received a customary backhander of £500 for giving out one contract alone to supply victuals to the garrison in Tangier. He was not above condemning the corrupt practices of the day, while also benefiting from them. Another example of this was when he used money, which should have been used to pay seamen in the navy, to pay instead the crew of his own private vessel the *Flying Greyhound* and keeping the £500 worth of booty that it plundered from the Dutch for himself, instead of handing it over to the crown. As a result his personal wealth increased from £25 in 1660 to £6,200, plus the house in Brampton, just six years later.

A parliamentary enquiry into charges of embezzlement implicating the king was held in 1668, to which Pepys gave evidence for three hours, bolstered by a pint of mulled wine and a dram of brandy. Many of the committee members went to dinner during this and after coming back half drunk, they dropped the charges.

Pepys made enemies among the aristocracy who held high positions in the navy when he proposed in 1677 that officers should first serve as midshipmen in order to pick up basic navigational and sailing skills. Against their will, and that of Prince Rupert, these regulations were introduced.

Shortly after this Pepys was accused in Parliament of promoting Popery in the navy – perhaps because of his close association with the Catholic Duke of York, later King James II, who was the Lord High Admiral – and piracy ... resulting in him being committed to the Tower in May 1679 for treason and piracy. His good friend and fellow diarist John Evelyn visited him there and they dined on roasted fowl.

One of the chief accusers was Colonel John Scott, whom Pepys was investigating for fraud, who claimed Pepys had spied for the French. Scott later fled the country after killing a coachman. The trial was postponed several times and the charges were eventually dropped in February 1680.

By the time James II came to the throne in 1685, Pepys had risen to be Secretary of the Navy, Master of Trinity House and President of the Royal Society, where he took part in an experiment, killing a dog with opium.

But after William of Orange outwitted the British navy, controlled by Pepys, and invaded the country from Holland to take the crown in 1688, Pepys' political future was in danger once again.

In May 1689 he was arrested and charged with treason. Although released in July, he was rearrested again the following June, accused of giving information to the French. The charges were finally dropped in October 1690, when he was released. While in prison he had three painful operations on the ulcer in his kidneys. When his kidney was opened up after death, a 'great quantity of a most foetid purulent matter gushed out' and large, sharp, pointed stones were found, which had pierced his parenchyma.

21. William Nevison (1639–1684)

Nevison Inn, 96 Plank Lane, Leigh, Lancashire, WN7 4QE (Tel: 01942 671394). Punch Taverns.

The highwayman William Nevison once feigned death from the plague while in Leicester jail to avoid the gallows. He painted blue spots on his breast, hands, face and body to simulate the symptoms of the plague. His accomplices, one masquerading as a doctor, pronounced him dead and took him away in a coffin. When he resumed his old trade, extorting money on the highway from carriers and drovers, who had heard of his reported death, they became convinced they were seeing his ghost.

He was born in Pontefract, Yorkshire, and at the age of 13 he became the ringleader of a young gang renowned for its rudeness and debauchery. At school he stole various items including a silver spoon, apples and poultry, for which he was severely punished by his teacher, whom Nevison was determined to wreak revenge upon, later stealing £10 of his money and his horse, which he rode to London over a period of four days. There, he cut the horse's throat to avoid being identified through it and worked for a brewer. He then stole another £200 and fled to Holland, where he was clapped in jail but escaped and joined an English regiment serving the Spanish army.

Returning to England he became a highwayman again and achieved a reputation for being both obliging to women whom he robbed and charitable to the poor. In Robin Hood-style on one particular occasion he stopped a sequestrator and relieved him of the money he had confiscated from widows and orphans and then returned it to them. He did, however, take an extra £500 from the sequestrator as a service charge.

In 1676 he was tried and convicted in York, under his alias John Bracy, of robbery and horse stealing. He was granted a reprieve on the promise that he would shop his accomplices, but he thought better of it and so remained in jail for some years after.

On his release he was drafted into the army, but soon deserted and took up his old trade again. Charles II issued a warrant for his arrest, under the name John Nevison, and offered a reward of £20 for his capture. The notice stated that Nevison had murdered someone who had tried to enforce a magistrate's warrant for his arrest and that he had threatened to kill any Justices of the Peace who issued further ones. Nevison's headquarters were at the Talbot Inn in Newark.

For a while, however, he went to London and drank cups of 'rum booze' with a 'ragged regiment of beggars', who initiated him into their ranks. This involved having a quart of ale poured over his head, reading a lesson from the 'devil's horn book' and forsaking God in favour of the devil. He was also given a 14-year-old beggar girl, whom he married in a ceremony involving a decapitated hen and a 'dry cow turd' broken over her head. They then got as 'drunk as beggars' and sang bawdy songs.

The William Nevison pub.

According to the historian Thomas Macaulay, it was really Nevison who made the legendary ride from near London to York, which is normally attributed to Dick Turpin. It took place in May 1676, when he committed a robbery in Gadshill, near Gravesend, Kent at 4 o'clock in the morning and then rode the 200 miles to York by 7 o'clock in the evening. He spoke to the mayor at a nearby bowling green and when Nevison was tried for the crime, he was acquitted after the mayor gave evidence of having seen him that same day and the jury thought it was impossible to have made the journey so fast. He later confessed and was given the nickname of Swift Nick.

It was in Yorkshire that he met his end, where he was shot and then arrested in a public house at Thorp, a village near Wakefield, by Captain Hardcastle on 1 March 1684, and taken the 13 miles to York to be hanged. A popular ballad about him contained the lines:

'He maintained himself like a gentleman,

Besides he was good to the poor;

He rode about like a bold hero,

And gained himself favour therefore.'

22 William Penn (1644–1718)

The Pennsylvanian, 115–117 High Street, Rickmansworth, Herts, WD3 1AN (Tel: 01923 720348). Wetherspoon.

William Penn was the Quaker who founded Pennsylvania in America after being jailed four times in England for his beliefs. He lived at Basing House, 20 High Street, Rickmansworth, which is near the local history museum, for five years, after getting married there to Gulielma Springett in 1672, and is buried 5 miles west in the village of Jordans.

Penn was born near the Tower of London, where he would be locked up for heresy twenty-four years later. At the age of 18 he was expelled from Oxford University for dissent and for protesting against compulsory attendance at the Anglican chapel. Some four years later he was sent to Cork in Ireland to manage the estate of his father, also called William, who was an admiral in the British navy. It was here that he attended meetings addressed by Thomas Loe and became a Quaker. This resulted in Penn being jailed and disowned by his family.

His first major writing work, entitled *Sandy Foundation Shaken*, attacking the doctrine of the Holy Trinity, caused a furore when it was published in 1688. As already mentioned, he was imprisoned for heresy as a result. It was while he was incarcerated in the Tower that he wrote his next book called *No Cross, No Crown* against both organised religion and royalty.

After being released it was not long before he was arrested again in 1670, for addressing a Quaker meeting in London. He and a fellow preacher William Meads were charged with conspiring to cause a riot. The jury was directed by the judge to find the pair guilty and when they refused and delivered a non-guilty verdict the judge ordered that they be locked up in Newgate Prison, until they changed their minds. This became a cause *celebre* and a higher court ordered their release and established the precedent that juries could deliver their own verdicts without being coerced by judges. In the meantime, the judge fined Penn for wearing a hat in court and jailed him for refusing to pay the fine.

The following year he was imprisoned at Newgate for preaching again. He later wrote a book entitled *Primitive Christianity Revived* and expressed the view, 'True godliness doesn't turn men out of the world but enables them to live better in it, and excites their endeavours to mend it.' In practice, he was able to improve the world with Quaker settlements in what were then the American colonies. In 1675 he went to West Jersey on the eastern bank of the Delaware River and promoted liberty and democracy.

Then, in 1681, he was given a large tract of land on the western bank by Charles II in payment of a debt to Penn's father, who had died in 1670. He wanted to call it just Sylvania, meaning 'wooded place', but the king insisted it be called Pennsylvania in honour of Penn's father. The land really belonged to the Native Americans, of course, so Penn insisted on paying them money for it and agreeing a treaty with them. Voltaire later remarked this was the only treaty that was never sworn to and never broken.

Penn thought he had got possession of the colony through divine providence and that he was called upon to set up a model community as an example to other nations. He passed laws guaranteeing freedom of conscience and religious toleration. He also framed the constitution that contained his famous phrase that 'governments, like clocks, go from the motion men give them, and as governments are made and moved by men, so by them they are ruined too.'

From 1682 to 1684 he supervised the building of the colony's capital Philadelphia, which became known as 'the city of brotherly love'. After that he returned to England, where James II had become king, and Penn helped to persuade him to release 1,200 Quaker prisoners. Because of this, Penn had supported James, so when he was ousted by William and Mary in 1688, he was suspected by them of treason, but not prosecuted.

In 1699 he returned to Pennsylvania, but financial mismanagement forced him to sell his ownership of it. In 1707 he spent six months in a debtors' prison, until a group of supporters paid his debts. He suffered a stroke in 1712, which left him disabled for the rest of his life.

23. William Kidd (c. 1645–1701)

Captain Kidd, 108 Wapping High Street, London, E1W 2NE (Tel: 020 7481 5759). Samuel Smith.

William Kidd was hanged for murder and piracy – both of which he committed – but his trial was clearly unfair and he was used as a political scapegoat by the Tories to discredit the aristocratic Whig financial backers, who were his lords and masters.

Captain Kidd sign.

Born in Greenock he went to sea as a boy, emigrated to America in his 20s, became a 'privateer' in the West Indies in 1689 – plundering French ships and sharing the loot with King William III – and was an established merchant shipowner by the 1690s.

The eastern coast of America was swarming with pirates, so in 1695 the king decided to crack down on them by dismissing the New York Governor Colonel Fletcher, who was soft on them in return for a share of their take, and replacing him with Lord Bellamont, an Irish peer, with orders to crack down on the pirates. Bellamont decided to finance Kidd to capture the pirates – and any ships sailing for France with whom England was at war – in exchange for the lion's share of any booty. Bellamont was joined in this venture by Sir John Somers (Lord Keeper of the Great Seal and subsequently Lord Chancellor), the Duke of Shrewsbury (Secretary of State), Sir Edward Russell (First Lord of the Admiralty and later Lord Orford) and the Earl of Romney (Master General of Ordnance). Even the king promised to invest £3,000, but had second thoughts.

These gentlemen paid eighty per cent of the cost of the project and Kidd and his partner, the other twenty per cent. The first ten per cent of any booty was to go to the king. Of the rest, sixty per cent was to go to Bellamont and his backers, fifteen per cent to Kidd and only twenty-five per cent to the crew. Normally, in privateering agreements, the crew got sixty per cent. Kidd realised this might cause problems and tried to wriggle out of the deal, but was told this could be seen as being disloyal to the king. Romney and Russell both 'promised to stand by me' if there was any trouble, Kidd later stated, so he reluctantly agreed and was supplied with a commission from the king – with the crown's seal on it, dated 11 December 1695 – empowering him to seize pirates and capture ships or goods belonging to France.

Their ship the *Adventure Galley* left Deptford in the Thames in December 1695 with a crew of seventy well-chosen men. However, they failed to salute a navy yacht at Greenwich, which fired a shot at them to make them show respect. Impudently, the crew turned their backs on the yacht and slapped their bottoms in derision. The navy responded by sending a press gang on board and carrying off the crew and replacing them with their own rejects.

Kidd needed another eighty crew members when arriving in New York and found the only way to hire them was to increase their share of the profits to the traditional sixty per cent, plus compensation for loss of a limb, amounting to six hundred pieces of eight or four able slaves. But when, after a year at sea, they had seized nothing, the crew grew restless; they had no sleeping quarters anyway. They suggested capturing any ships, whether or not they were pirates or French, and when an English ship appeared, Kidd's gunner William Moore proposed they plunder it. Kidd rejected this and managed to stave off a near mutiny. He later got into a violent argument with Moore and hit him over the head with an iron bucket worth eight pence (it was meticulously noted at Kidd's trial), fracturing his skull, after which he died the next day.

Skulduggery of a different nature was then resorted to be Kidd. He was aware that ships of many nations carried 'passes' from England, France and other major powers for production when challenged on the high seas. So when approaching a vessel he would fly the French flag to trick the other ship into producing a French pass. Even though this did not prove it was French owned, he used it as an excuse to seize the vessel. Later at his trial he intended to use these French passes as evidence, but they were suppressed by the prosecution; and it must be pointed out that little evidence that ships attacked were really French had been demanded when the king was taking his share.

Using this ploy, Kidd relieved a Portuguese ship of opium and other goods belonging to the East India Company, an Armenian one under the command of an English captain of guns and gold coins, and at least three other non-French ships.

In Madagascar, Kidd came across a pirate ship, the *Mocha Frigate*, commanded by Robert Culliford and ordered his men to attack it. Instead, they deserted and joined Culliford, threatening to kill Kidd if he did not also join Culliford, so he did.

The East India Company, annoyed at having their opium and other goods stolen, sent a letter to the Lords Justices in London, accusing Kidd of piracy. When it emerged that Whig Lords had financed Kidd, the Tories made maximum political capital.

Kidd, armed with the French passes that he had taken from the ships he had plundered and armed with the king's commission, assumed he would be protected by Lord Bellamont in New York. So he sailed there, arriving in June 1699. Bellamont had orders to arrest him and lured him into port by sending him a message that His Majesty's Council had said 'you may safely come hither, and I make no manner of doubt but to obtain the King's pardon for you'. Thus it was that Kidd came in and met his English wife Sarah Oort and two daughters – who had been aged 3 and 4 respectively when he had left them three years earlier – in a moving but short-lived reunion. When he met Bellamont he was asked to produce his log and he replied his crew had destroyed it when they had mutinied. Bellamont arrested him and clapped him in prison in solitary confinement in irons weighing 16 pounds. His booty was then seized and sent to the Treasury in England.

In February 1700 he was shipped back to London, arriving in April. By then his mind was temporarily unhinged and he asked for a knife to kill himself. Instead, he was taken to Newgate Prison, which was so overcrowded that prisoners slept three to a bed covered in lice. There, he was kept in close confinement for over a year, being allowed no exercise or visitors. He was not even allowed to meet anybody to prepare a defence.

In March 1701 he was suddenly called without warning before the House of Commons. If he had given more evidence about the Whig sponsors of his crimes, then it is possible the Tories would have pardoned him. Instead, he pleaded his innocence and they ordered his prosecution. By the time he appeared at the Old Bailey in May he had been imprisoned for nearly two years.

His main evidence – the French passes which he had given to Bellamont – was withheld from him; and did not appear again

A noose in the pub marks where Captain Kidd was hanged.

until 219 years later in the Public Record Office. In addition to this, he was not given a defence counsel until an hour before the trial; after two years of waiting in jail. He was not allowed to testify in his own defence and neither could his counsel cross-examine the two deserters who gave evidence against him in return for a pardon.

On the charge of murdering gunner William Moore, he pleaded provocation, as Moore had been mutinous and insolent. On the piracy charges, he stated some of the ships he captured were French and that the others he was forced to capture by a mutinous crew. Found guilty and sentenced to hang, he was asked if he had anything to say and replied, 'I have nothing to say but that I have been sworn against by perjured and wicked people.'

On 23 May he was taken, reeling drunk, from his cell and carried through the street mobs to Execution Dock at Wapping, near this pub. At the gallows he refused to confess his guilt. The rope broke at the first attempt to hang him and he had to be retrieved from the mud by the river. After he was hanged at the second attempt his body was chained to a post by the river and left there until the tide had ebbed and flowed over it three times. The body was then tarred and bound in chains – with the head set in a metal harness – and was hung from a gibbet at Tilbury Point as a warning to other pirates. Robert Culliford, responsible for much of Kidd's enforced piracy, was given a royal pardon.

Kidd's effects worth £6,472 were seized by the crown and used to build Greenwich Hospital. A special ballad of the time, called *Captain Kidd's Farewell to the Seas*, went as follows:

> My name was Captain Kidd, when I sail'd, when I sail'd,
> And so wickedly I did, God's laws I did forbid,
> When I sail'd, when I sail'd.
> I roam'd from sound to sound, And many a ship I found,
> And them I sunk or burn'd, When I sail'd.
> I murder'd William Moore, And laid him in his gore,
> Not many leagues from shore, When I sail'd.
> Farewell to young and old, All jolly seamen bold,
> You're welcome to my gold, For I must die, I must die.
> Farewell to Lunnon town, the pretty girls all round,
> No pardon can be found, and I must die, I must die,
> Farewell, for I must die. Then to eternity, in hideous misery,
> I must lie, I must lie.

24 Nell Gwynne (1650–1687)

(i) Nell of Old Drury, 29 Catherine Street (opposite Theatre Royal, Drury Lane), London, WC2B 5JS (Tel: 020 7836 5328). Free house.

(ii) Nell Gwynne Tavern, 2 Bull Inn Court (off Strand between Adelphi and Vaudeveville theatres), London, WC2R 0NP (Tel: 020 7240 5579). Free house.

Nell Gwynne, the most famous mistress of Charles II, started selling oranges at the age of 13 in the Theatre Royal (opposite Nell of Old Drury) and two years later she made her stage debut there in a play by John Dryden, who recognised her natural wit and wrote future plays to accommodate it.

Her mother Eleanor worked as a barmaid in the Rose Tavern, next door to the theatre, on the corner of Catherine Street and Russell Street. She got Nell a job as a barmaid in a bawdy house further up Drury Lane in Macklin Street, where she lost her virginity and became a child prostitute as well. This was owned by Madam Ross, where Jack Shepherd was taken after his second escape from Newgate.

Bull Inn Court, where the Nell Gwynne Inn now stands, is where Samuel Pepys describes seeing 'the mighty pretty Nell' on his way to the Strand in 1667. This was when she was aged 17 and involved in a troilistic relationship with the dissolute poet Charles Sedley and the foul-mouthed Charles Buckhurst, also a poet. This pub was where a well-known actor William Terris was stabbed to death in 1897 by an Adelphi stagehand called Richard Prince, who was subsequently sent to Broadmoor.

Nell had no qualms about her position as a 'kept woman'. When her coachman got into a fight she asked him why and he replied that the other man had described her as a whore. She laughed and said, 'But I am a whore.' The coachman solemnly proclaimed, 'You may be called a whore, but I will not be called a whore's coachman.'

On another occasion in her coach she was booed by the crowd, who mistook her for another of the royal mistresses, Louise de Keroualle, who was a French Catholic. Nell poked her head out of the window and cried out, 'Pray, good people, be civil! I am the Protestant whore!' This delighted the crowd, who turned to cheering. This same Louise de Keroualle (the Duchess of Portsmouth) once bumped into Nell in Whitehall and, complimenting her fine clothes, said that she looked fine enough to be a queen. Nell retorted, 'You are right, madam, and I am whore enough to be a duchess.'

Nell was popular for not using her position with the king to try and curry political favour, unlike his other women. It was expressed in a poem of the time:

> Hard by Pall Mall lives a wench call'd Nell.
>
> King Charles the Second he kept her.
>
> She hath got a trick to handle his prick
>
> But never lays hands on his sceptre.
>
> All matters of state from her soul she does hate,
>
> And leaves to the politic bitches.
>
> The whore's in the right, for 'tis her delight
>
> To be scratching just where it itches.

Nell's father Thomas died in a debtor's prison when she was just a child and her mother Eleanor, an alcoholic, supported Nell and her sister Rose as best she could.

Nell's first serious affair was with the actor Charles Hart. When she moved on to Charles Buckhurst, who gave her £100 a year to live with him, she referred to him as her Charles II. Then, before she was aged 18, she bedded the real Charles II (king) by disposing of her rival Moll Davis by

spiking her drink with an emetic 'with immediate and tumultuous results' (vomiting). She thereafter nicknamed Charles II as her Charles III.

Spurning the use of crocodile dung, which was used as a contraceptive barrier at the time, she gave birth to his son Charles, in 1670, while living in the Cock and Pie, where she often served the king with pigeon pie in bed, which is where Bush House now stands. The following year the king moved her into Pall Mall, where she gave birth to his second son James. Despite his generosity the king rarely carried money and when drinking incognito in taverns, Nell invariably had to pay, once observing that she had got 'into the poorest company that ever she was in at a tavern'.

In 1679, her mother, who consumed 40 pints of brandy a day, drowned after falling into a ditch while drunk between Chelsea and Fulham. In 1680, Nell's 8-year-old son James died in Paris 'of a sore leg'. In 1681 Nell was riding across Bagshot Heath, when she was stopped by a highwayman known as Old Mob (Thomas Simpson, who was hanged in 1691). She handed over her valuables and when he asked for 'something personal', she kissed him and he gave her back her rings as a result.

On her death she was buried in the chancel at St Martins and in her will, she gave money to take poor debtors out of prison and to get paupers released from prison at Christmas time.

25. William Dampier (1651–1715)

97 Middle Street, Yeovil, Somerset, BA20 1LW (Tel: 01935 412533). Wetherspoon.

The pirate and scientific explorer William Dampier was born at East Coker, just 2 miles south of Yeovil. The son of a tenant farmer, his father died when William was 10 and his mother when he was 16. At this young age, he went to sea on a Weymouth trading ship.

In his early twenties he fought against the Dutch as an able seaman in the royal navy and was wounded and discharged, after which his father's ex-landlord gave him a job as assistant manager on his plantation in Jamaica, but he soon got bored with that. So he got a job on a coastal trader taking rum and sugar to a logging area and exchanging it for logs with the lumberjacks. Eventually, he joined them, describing them as 'a wild set' who drank a lot of punch. Work was hard, earnings high and debauchery excessive. They also combined this with piracy and buccaneering. Dampier worked with them from 1676 to 1678, during which time he amassed a small fortune.

After that he returned to England and married a woman called Judith. But within a year he was globetrotting again via Jamaica to the South American coast, where he joined a party of buccaneers – or privateers as he called them. They seized and plundered a number of Spanish ships, and then joined some pirates for a year, during which time there were frequent mutinies and desertions. From Virginia he joined another vessel, which sailed to the African coast, and seized a Danish ship at Sierra Leone. He described this as a voyage of discovery rather than piracy.

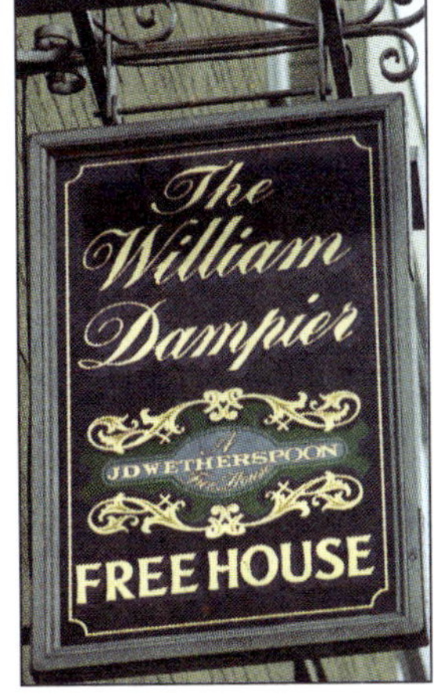

Eventually, he joined a band of nearly 1,000 buccaneers sailing in as many as ten ships at a time raiding the coast of South America. They came across some shipwrecked Spaniards on an island in the Gulf of San Miguel in 1680 and fraternised with them. They then met some Moskito Indians, whose language Dampier knew. 'We told them they were Wankers, which is the name they commonly give to Spaniards, in their own language,' he reported. The Indians wanted to put the Spaniards to death, but the English intervened to save them, which they benefited from when later captured by another large contingent of Spaniards. Dampier became the first Englishman to step ashore on Australian soil when he landed on the north-west shore in 1688.

In the same year, he visited what was then called Cachao (now Hanoi in Vietnam), where chief officials had to be eunuchs. Dampier saw one castrate himself in order to further his career. He observed marijuana being used in the following year at Achin (now Banda Aceh). 'They have here a sort of plant called ganga, or bang,' he wrote. 'It appeared to me like hemp. It is reported of this plant that if it is infused in any liquor it will stupefy the brains of any person that drinks thereof. Some it keeps sleepy, some merry, putting them into a laughing fit, and others it makes bad; but after two or three hours they come to themselves again.'

Another trip from Mexico to the Dutch Indies involved great hardship for the crew and they reached Guam with just three days' provisions left. Captain Swan, who was in command, heard that if they had run out of food, the crew had planned to kill and eat him and then all other officers. Swan remarked to Dampier, 'You would have made them but a poor meal.' Dampier agreed, 'for I was as lean as the captain was lusty and fleshy.'

After excessive drunkenness and debauchery, the crew left Swan behind and cruised around China for 18 months, after which Dampier decided he wanted to desert. Instead, he was dumped by the crew with three others and some Malay prisoners on a remote island called Nicobar, from which it was thought they would never escape. But they befriended the natives, bought a canoe from them and put to sea, trusting to Dampier's navigational skills. Surviving a terrible storm, they reached Sumatra exhausted and suffering from fever, which killed two of them.

Dampier was detained against his will as a master gunner at Bencoolen Fort, but managed to escape on a ship called the *Defence* in January 1691. He made it back to England with his only possession being a 'curiously tattooed Menangis islander', whom he passed off as an Indian prince and intended to make money by exhibiting him. But he was forced to sell this 'amiable savage', who soon afterwards caught smallpox and died.

In 1697 Dampier published his memoirs *Voyage Round the World*, which was a best seller, going through four editions in less than two years. He followed this up with *A Discourse of Winds* in 1699 on meteorological geography based on his observations, which was later used by Captain Cook and Admiral Nelson. It greatly interested the naval secretary Samuel Pepys and the Royal Society, which nevertheless never invited him to join, because of his rural working-class origins. The government then commissioned him to explore and chart the Australian coast, which he did on the *Roebuck* from 1698 to 1699.

His name lives on through Dampier Archipelago and Dampier Port (both on the west coast of Australia), Dampier Strait off New Guinea, which he found in 1700, and a plant named after him brought back from East Lewis Islands.

On the voyage back the ship sank off Ascension Island, which was then an utterly desolate island, but he and the crew found a spring of fresh water near the top of the mountain, now known as Dampier's Spring, and lived for six weeks on goats and turtles. They were rescued by a squadron of British warships.

Although he was a skilled, scientific observer, he was no good as a leader. After hitting his lieutenant and putting him in irons, Dampier was court-martialled for cruelty and oppression. So he went back to privateering, leaving Ireland with a hundred and twenty-six men and twenty-six guns in 1703, first anchoring by two rocks, then called the Sovereigns Bollocks (but now simply the Sovereigns), off Kinsale.

A portrait of William Dampier inside the Wetherspoon's pub.

He was reported to be frequently drunk (he liked rum punch, brandy and South African white wine), foul-mouthed and oppressive. One of his officers was marooned and another deserted. Finally, he was left with just thirty men. They left the ship on the coast of Peru after seizing a Spanish one and crossing the Pacific to a Dutch settlement, where they were imprisoned. Dampier finally returned to England in 1707 with no wealth and his reputation tarnished by accounts of his misdemeanours published by his opponents.

As a result he got no more work from British shipowners, so worked as a pilot for a Dutch privateer from 1708 to 1711, operating around Cape Horn and the Cape of Good Hope. The vessel returned to London with £200,000 worth of booty, but it took eight years to distribute it ... four years after Dampier's death. He had, however, received enough from the capture of a rich Spanish treasure ship in 1712 to live out the last few years of his life in comfort. Indeed, his name was given to a Royal Navy survey in 1848. One of his crew members Alexander Selkirk was cast away on an island 400 miles from Chile and was picked up by him four years later. This inspired the novel *Robinson Crusoe* by Daniel Defoe.

It is not known where Dampier was buried, but there is a memorial to him at St Michael's church in East Coker, where he was born, with the inscription, 'Buccaneer, explorer, hydrographer, and captain'.

26. Daniel Defoe (1660–1731)

102 Stoke Newington Church Street (junction with Defoe Road), London, N16 0LA (Tel: 020 7254 2906). Charles Wells.

Bankruptcy drove Defoe to become a novelist and his experiences in a debtor's prison provided some of his plot lines. His unsuccessful business ventures included trading in beer, wine and spirits ... and making scent from the musk of cats' anal glands. The son of a butcher, he was educated at a dissenting academy in Newington Green and he took part in the rebellion of 1685 against James II and fought in the battle of Sedgemoor. He was able to slip away in dense fog and so avoid being sentenced to death by the infamous Judge Jeffreys as most of his fellow conspirators were. His fear of capture was described in his novel *Colonel Jack*.

He was made bankrupt in 1692 and was committed to Fleet Prison; ironically, he was later consulted by the government on the problem of the National Debt. In May 1703, he was back in prison at Newgate for writing *The Shortest Way with Dissenters*, which was a satire on Tory intolerance. This led to a charge of seditious libel and, in addition to time in prison, he was fined £130, bound over for seven years' good behaviour and was put in the pillory for three days. A month before, another pamphleteer had been savagely stoned almost to death in the pillory. But Defoe was surrounded by cheering supporters, who pelted him with flowers. When he was released he made money from working for the Secret Service under the Tory Speaker of the House of Commons, Robert Harley. He also made money from writing first pamphlets and articles, and then books. In 1794 he wrote his first novel *Advice from the Scandalous Club* about magistrates getting drunk, singing bawdy songs and 'pissing over the balcony on the people's heads', among other things.

Although he preached religious tolerance, he supported the Scots for still (in 1708) executing atheists, sodomites and adulterers as a 'necessary severity', which should be restored in England; perhaps he was being satirical again.

In 1709 he moved to what is now Stoke Newington Church Street and four years later, with his £400 a year from the Secret Service, he was able to move over the road to a three-storey building on what is now Defoe Street (there is a blue plaque in honour of him at 95 Stoke Newington Church Street) which had four acres of land on which he grew lime trees.

He praised the Derbyshire beer, which he sampled at Buxton on his *Tour of Great Britain* (published in three volumes from 1724 to 1726), adding, 'The nearer we approached to Yorkshire ... so the ale advanced nearer to its perfection.'

In 1724 he wrote the life story of hanged highwayman Jack Sheppard. The following year, Defoe's gall stones caused such pain that he had them operated on before the introduction of anaesthetics. Some three attendants held him down, while a surgeon passed a tube through his penis to the urethra and then cut him between the anus and the scrotum to insert a catheter while the stones were removed. He described this as suffering as much as being broken alive on the Wheel.

He died in 1731 and was buried at Bunhill Fields in Finsbury, the cemetery for Dissenters, where his wife Mary joined him a year later. No tombstone was erected to him there, however, until 1870, when money raised by readers of

Bust of Daniel Defoe with his original tombstone in Stoke Newington Library.

Christian World led to one inscribed: 'Daniel Defoe (author of *Robinson Crusoe*) who died April 24, 1731 in his 70th year'. A few days later it was stolen and not found again until 1940, when it emerged on a bombed-out building in Southampton. It was presented to Stoke Newington Borough Council in 1958 and is now on view in the library on the corner of Stoke Newington Church Street and Edward Street.

His great novel *Robinson Crusoe* was recommended for natural education by Rousseau of the French Revolution and was used by Karl Marx to explain the theories of labour value. A pub named Robinson Crusoe is situated at the opposite end of Stoke Newington Church Street, on the corner of Green Lanes. The Defoe Pub, which changed its name from Steptoes in 2000, sells a Defoe Ale, brewed by Charles Wells in Stratford upon Avon.

27 Jonathan Swift (1667–1745)

Dean Swift, 40 Francis Street, Dublin 8 (Tel: 00353 1 453 3519). Free house.

The satirist Jonathan Swift was Dean of nearby St Patrick's Cathedral from 1713 for the rest of his life. His early scruples, against entering the church merely for financial support, were overcome in 1694, when he was ordained as a deacon in order to accept a sinecure as master of the rolls for £120 a year. Lord Berkeley later offered him a rich deanery in Derry, if he greased his palm with £1,000, which Swift rejected out of hand and called the lord a scoundrel. In 1700, however, he was given the job as Vicar of Laracor, near Trim in County Meath, for which he got £250 a year and became known as the 'mad parson'. His income was further boosted by an extra £400 a year, when he was made Dean of St Patrick's. One of his first tasks was to boost the wine and beer cellar of the deanery in Kelvin Street, with forty-six bottles of Alicante wine.

His favourite meal there was mutton pie and half a pint of wine, served by his cook, whom he described as an 'old and ugly woman'. He employed her, he explained, because 'the ladies of my acquaintance would not allow me one with a tolerable face'. One visitor, indeed, confirmed that the cook's face was 'much roughed by smallpox, and furrowed by age'. Other visitors noticed the food she cooked was either raw or burned.

The 'ladies of my acquaintance' whom Swift referred to were Hester 'Stella' Johnson, whose tutor he had been in England, and Esther

'Vanessa' Vanhomrigh, whom he had also met in England. Both women frequently stayed at the deanery and it was rumoured that in 1716 he had actually married Stella, who organised his parties in the deanery with a plentiful supply of punch and claret. A portrait of her with a feather in her hair still hangs in the deanery.

Swift had hoped for a bishopric, but this was denied him by Queen Anne, who was displeased by his outspoken attacks on religious cant in a satire *A Tale of a Tub* published in 1704. Swift got on better with King William III, who taught him how to cut asparagus.

Swift was born at 7 Hoey's Court in Dublin, which is no longer there, but its site is marked by a plaque in Little Ship Street, near St Patrick's Cathedral. It was seven months before Jonathan's birth that his father of the same name had died, so the lad was taken by his mother to her family in Leicester for some years, but he eventually returned to Dublin to be brought up by his uncle Godwin Swift.

At Trinity College in Dublin from 1682 to 1689 he was described as an unsatisfactory student, who only obtained his degree by 'special grace'. He was constantly fined for non-attendance and was publicly censured for this and his insolence. He liked walking expeditions and staying in wayside inns, where 'lodgings for a penny' were advertised and where he could enjoy the rough talk of wagoners and hostlers.

Initially, his politics led him to support the 'revolution principles' of the Whigs, but their support of religious dissenters led him to switch his allegiance to the Tories. His views on Irish nationalism also changed over the years. Originally, he proclaimed his pride to be an Englishman, even though he 'happened to be dropped' (as he put it) in Ireland. But he grew to hate the oppression that Ireland was put under by the English and said that government, without the consent of the governed, was the 'very definition of slavery' and if Irishmen were not to be slaves, the remedy was in their own hands.

In 1724 he became a national hero, when one of his pamphlets led to the withdrawal of a coin, which would have meant an excessive patent being paid to the English. It was two years before this that he had published another pamphlet entitled *The Benefit of Farting Explained*. It

Gullivers Travels ... is Dean Swift a tiny Lilliputian or is the Guinness from the land of the giants?

warned that suppression of farts caused other ailments, such as colic, rumbling and belching. Praising farting as a great promoter of mirth, he suggested that if a group of people of different sizes farted together, it would be musical in the same way as a ring of bells or a set of organ pipes.

His great classic *Gulliver's Travels* was published in 1726 and became an instant success, expressing his rage at human misery and depravity, much of which he saw in the streets around his deanery. His fee of £200 was all he ever received for any of his writings, many of which were published anonymously.

His satire took on an extra edge when he published in 1729 *A Modest Proposal for preventing the Children of the Poor from being a Burden to their Parents or Country, and for making them beneficial to the public.* It suggested the children of the poor be sold to the rich to eat. At the same time he wrote about his 'rage and resentment' at the 'mortifying sight of slavery, folly, and baseness' all around him, especially in the 1720s, when the famine led to an increase in beggars and when the depression made many local weavers unemployed.

Swift reacted by giving badges to the 'local' beggars to distinguish them from the 'foreign' ones, which he told to go back to where they had came from. When the starving families of weavers came to him for help he refused donations, but lent them money, to be repaid weekly with interest, to set up other trades. This could have been when he was dispirited by an attack of the piles.

In later years he suffered from a form of vertigo in the region of his ear, which made him giddy, as well as becoming deaf and paralysed. An abscess in his eye broke in 1742, after which he did not recognise his friends and sank into lethargy ... the symptoms of which have been diagnosed in more recent times as being Meniere's Disease. A commission of lunacy pronounced him incapable of conducting his affairs and committed him to the care of guardians.

On his death he was buried next to his long time love Stella Johnson in the west end of the nave of St Patrick's Cathedral. His epitaph, written by himself in Latin, translates as, 'He has gone where savage indignation can lacerate his heart no more'.

The majority of his estate, around £8,000 to £10,000, he bequeathed for the building of St Patrick's Hospital for Imbeciles, which opened in 1757 for the treatment of fifty mentally ill patients. Swift explained this gift in a poem:

> He gave the little wealth he had,
>
> To build a house for fools and mad,
>
> And showed by one satirical touch,
>
> No nation wanted it so much.

28 Rob Roy (1671–1734)

(i)   Rob Roy Inn, 45 Main Street, Buchlyvie, FK8 3LR (Tel: 01360 850219). Scottish & Newcastle.

(ii) Rob Roy, 101–103 Beaumont Street, Toxteth, Liverpool, L8 0XA. Currently up for sale.

The Rob Roy, Toxtteth, Liverpool.

Rob Roy MacGregor caught the public imagination by stealing two herds of cattle from Buchlyvie at the age of 20. The main target was a valuable herd belonging to Sir Alexander Livingston, which was being driven to Stirling through the village. Rob ran a 'watch', which was a 'protection' scheme for cattle owners, but Sir Alexander foolishly refused to pay for it. Apart from teaching him a lesson, Rob had other motives: the need for food and redressing injustice. His father Donald had been imprisoned in Stirling Castle (where a statue to Rob now stands nearby) and also in Edinburgh for two years for not taking an oath of allegiance to the new King William. When he finally yielded, he was told he would not be released until he had paid the prison expenses of sixpence a night for the time of his incarceration. In order to obtain this money, government troops seized his property the day after the funeral of his wife Margaret. The family had already suffered from hunger owing to a series of bad harvests.

Rob and his men went into Buchlyvie waiting for Livingston's herd. When the local men working in the fields saw them, they suspected that their cattle were the target, so they went to nearby villages to get assistance and returned armed with cudgels. Not wishing to have an unnecessary fight with them, Rob took his men to the surrounding heathland of Kippen Muir to await the herd there.

When it came into sight as the sun was setting he gave the order to descend, but their way was blocked by the villagers. At first he ordered his men to beat them aside with the flat of their broadswords, but when this failed they had to use the blades, forcing the villagers to flee. Wishing to make his peace with them, after taking Livingston's herd, he found all the villagers had deserted. Disgusted at their lack of courage he took their cattle as well.

His next skirmish in the area was against a more spirited opposition and saw him suffer his only defeat in a duel – and he fought at least twenty-two opponents. He met a Lowland fop called Henry Cunninghame at a party in Arnprior, 2 miles east of Buchlyvie. After imbibing much whisky, Rob insulted Henry for his mannerisms. Everyone was amazed when Henry immediately challenged Rob, a feared swordsman with long arms for his average height, to a duel. Henry's friends hid his sword but, undeterred, he found another rusty old one and rushed at Rob with such fury and unexpected skill that he drove him off the field.

Rob's birth was registered at Buchanan, 8 miles west of Buchlyvie, and he was born in Glengyle at the head of Loch Katrine, about 10 miles north-west of Bucklyvie, where he later lived in caves when on the run. At the age of 18 he had fought with his father for the Jacobites in a battle they won at Killiecrankie. Although Protestants they supported James, because they thought he would support the Highland way of life more than King William. Through fighting with Jacobites, Rob admired his Catholic colleagues and never supported religious discrimination.

In 1693 he married Mary MacGregor in the parish of Buchanan, but then had to take the surname of his mother's clan, Campbell, because of a penal code passed against his clan, forbidding the use of its name. This increased his contempt for the law and his determination to defy it.

He was captured in 1695 in Glasgow and was found guilty of stealing Livingston's cattle at Buchlyvie four years earlier, for which he faced transportation, but he escaped after his friends bribed the guards. From 1702 to 1712 he earned a legal living as head drover for herds of up to 1,000 strong, taking them from the Outer Hebrides as far as Norwich in England. But in 1712 one of his chief drovers ran off with some cash, which was to be paid to the Duke of Montrose for his cattle. Rob started paying back the Duke but needed more time to collect debts owed to him. The Duke refused to allow this and sued him, but offered to drop the case if Rob would agree to give false evidence that one of his aristocratic rivals, the Duke of Argyle, was a Jacobite.

This greatly offended Rob's sense of honour and he flatly refused. So in February 1713, his land and goods were all confiscated and he was proclaimed an outlaw. In the following month, his family was evicted and their home was destroyed by troops, who physically assaulted Mary. From then on Rob targeted the Duke of Montrose for his criminal enterprises, stealing his cattle, grain and rent from his larger tenants, always giving them receipts signed Rob Roy. He never took money from Montrose's smaller tenants; in fact, he often gave grain to the poorer ones which he had stolen from their landlord. When one of them was threatened with eviction by Montrose, Rob gave her the money to pay the bailiffs and then robbed it back from them as they returned to Stirling.

Montrose retaliated by burning Rob's house down in 1716 and then again when he rebuilt it a few months later, also putting a price on his head. Rob hit back with a vengeance by kidnapping Montrose's rent collector,

The Rob Roy, Buchlyvie

relieving him of £3,227 and sending a ransom note to Montrose demanding damages for destroying his house. Montrose managed to capture Rob and took him to Stirling on horseback. But one of the guards escorting him owed Rob a favour and he cut the thong binding him as they crossed a river and he dived underwater and escaped. This added to his legendary reputation as one who could not be contained by the authorities.

In 1717 he was arrested again by the Duke of Atholl, who tricked him with a false guarantee of safety to meet him. He also wished him to give perjured evidence against the Duke of Argyle. Once more he escaped, with the help of friends after getting the guards drunk. He was captured a fourth time and again escaped when one of the troopers' horses refused a craggy passage, leaving a gap for him to escape into the hillside.

In 1722 he prevented some evictions of tenant farmers for rent arrears following several bad harvests by ambushing the law officers and by making them swear not to return. Rob's reputation became even more widespread in 1723, when Daniel Defoe wrote a fictional account of his life entitled *Highland Rogue* and in 1726 he was pardoned.

Towards the end of his life a minister spotted him in his congregation and – looking him in the eye – condemned robbery as a sin. Rob saw him afterwards and was told a widow had complained of the price he had given her for a cow, which she was forced to sell to stave off starvation. The next day Rob returned the cow and refused to take any money back for it. The following Sunday the minister told this to the congregation and said it was 'worthy of imitation by the hard-hearted gentry of my parish.'

Rob died on 28 December 1734 and was buried on New Year's Day 1735 at Balquhidder Church. But there was no ringing of the church's bronze bells, for he had stolen them some years earlier.

29. G. F. HANDEL (1685–1759)

28 Thomas Street (corner of Thomas Court), Dublin 8.

The composer, organist and conductor George Frederick Handel first performed his greatest work, the Messiah, at the Great Music Hall, Fishamble Street, Dublin in April 1742. Handel, born Georg Friedrich in Lower Saxony, arrived in England in November 1710. He became the conductor in residence for the Duke of Chandos at Stanmore near Edgware in Middlesex in 1717.

By 1723 he was able to afford a house in London's Mayfair, at 25 Brook Street, where he lived for the rest of his life and wrote most of his masterpieces. In 1727 he became a British citizen and ten years later he had a stroke, which left his right hand partly paralysed.

In 1741 he composed the Messiah at Brook Street, where his servant found him weeping over its score, and took it to be premiered in Dublin, staying there with it until the following year. One of these performances was in aid of 'the relief of the prisoners in the several jails and for the support of Mercer's Hospital in Stephen's Street, and the Charitable Infirmary in Inn's Quay'. He was particularly pleased with the choirs from Christchurch and St Patrick's cathedrals.

He was a great supporter of the Foundling Hospital for Abandoned Children (now the Thomas Coram Foundation) in London's Bloomsbury and he donated the original manuscript of the Messiah to it and also performed it in charity concerts, raising £7,000 for the hospital in 1750. Handel Street in London WC1 was built and named in his honour near the Foundling Hospital in 1803 – the year in which Robert Emmet was publicly executed, for leading a failed uprising, outside the Dublin pub now named after Handel.

Handel also played the organ unpaid on Sundays at his parish church St George's in Hanover Square. Before coming to England he had worked in Hanover for the future King George I, but was never intimidated by royalty. One member of the royal family was said to have warned another, 'Hush! Handel's in a passion!' His rages, however, were short-lived and he never bore a grudge. He drank a lot and when depressed, he was nicknamed Great Bear.

In 1751 he lost the sight of one eye and two years later he became completely blind, when he composed *An Anthem* for the foundling hospital, after which he gave regular public organ recitals.

30. Alexander Pope (1688–1744)

Pope's Grotto, 72 Cross Deep (corner of Pope's Grove), Twickenham, Middlesex, TW1 4RB (Tel: 020 8892 3050). Youngs.

The poet and satirist Alexander Pope lived in a Palladium-style villa opposite this pub (on the opposite corner of Pope's Grove), where St Catherine's School for girls now stands. It was in the cellars of this villa that his famous grotto was built and later extended into the tunnel under Cross Deep, which linked up to his 5 acres of garden on the banks of the Thames, now called Pope's Villa at 19 Cross Deep, which houses St James Independent School for boys, where he moved in the spring of 1719 and spent the rest of his life there.

Writing in 1725, he stated, 'When you shut the doors of this grotto, it becomes on the instant, from a luminous room, a camera-obscura, on the walls of which all objects of the river, hills, woods and boats are forming a moving picture in their visible radiations; and when you have a mind to light it up it affords a very different scene.

'It is furnished with shells, interspersed with pieces of looking glass in angular forms; and in the ceiling is a star of the same material, at which, when a lamp (of an orbicular figure of thin alabaster) is hung in the middle, a thousand pointed rays glitter, and are reflected over the place.'

It became a museum to mineralogy and mining, with stalagmites and materials from Peru, Egypt, Italy, Germany, Norway and the West Indies. The lining consisted of marbles from Devon and Cornwall, seashells and feldspar. The grotto remains in the grounds of St James' School. The garden, which he constantly mentioned in his poetry, contained the earliest and finest cedar trees from the Lebanon and a famous Spanish weeping willow (only the second ever planted in England), cuttings of which were sent to the Empress of Russia.

The son of a Catholic linen merchant Pope was born in Lombard Street in the city area of London and became known as 'little nightingale' for the beauty of his voice in infancy. A severe illness, possibly tuberculosis of the spine, at the age of 12 deformed his figure and stunted his growth; he never grew taller than 4 foot 6 inches. A cow nearly killed him as a child, but he managed to escape. In middle age he became weaker and had to wear a bodice of stiff canvas. He could not dress without help and wore three pairs of stockings to cover his thin legs.

After going to school at Marylebone, he moved to Twyford near Winchester, where he was whipped and expelled for satirising one of the masters. The invective of his satire later made him famous and he befriended the other master of the medium Jonathan Swift. By the age of 16, Pope's first essays and poems were being published, one of which was put to music by George Frederick Handel. Pope's greatest commercial success though was his translation of Homer's *Iliad,* issued between 1715 and 1720, which earned him an estimated £10,000 and financial security for life. One of his more radical poems *Essay on Man* was published anonymously in 1733 and took on a deist theme, attacking orthodox, organised religion. This became his best-known work on the Continent and influenced Voltaire. His fingers were badly cut in a coach accident crossing a stream and he nearly lost the use of them. After this, he constantly called his servant to dictate ideas to, often in the middle of the night.

On his death he left much of his fortune to Martha Blount (1690–1762), whom he had first met in 1705 and was said to have been his mistress. In 1718 he had paid her an annuity of £40 for six years on condition that she did not get married to anyone else. He was still intimate with her in his dying days and his spirits rose whenever she visited him. He was buried by the side of his parents at the Church of St Mary the Virgin in Twickenham by the east wall. A monument to him was erected by the north wall in 1761.

The pub was built by Young's brewery in 1852 on part of Pope's old garden, but was destroyed by V2 bombs in the World War II, to be replaced by a wooden building, until the present structure was opened in 1959. It is recommended in Camra's Beer, Bed & Breakfast guide, edited by Jill Adam and Susan Nowak.

Stained glass portrait of Pope in the pub.

31 William Hogarth (1697–1764)

The Hogarth, 58 Broad Street, Teddington, Middlesex, TW11 8QY
(Tel: 020 8977 3846).

Taverns were very much the haunts of the great engraver and painter William Hogarth. One of his very first caricatures was drawn when, as an apprentice engraver, he saw a man badly injured in a tavern brawl. Rather than going to his aid, the 5 foot tall Hogarth calmly drew the agonised face of the victim instead. One of his earliest jobs was to paint the sign for The Man with a Load of Mischief pub at 53 Oxford Street in London, depicting a man with a gin-swilling woman and a monkey on his back.

The Kings Head at the northern end of Tottenham Court Road was another of his favourite haunts. It appears in his famous painting the *March to Finchley* in 1750, which depicted soldiers outside it who were incapable of moving because of their 'entanglements with women, drink and crime'. Hogarth offered it to King George II, but he was so disgusted by its scenes of debauchery that he rejected it. So Hogarth raffled it off, giving the last 157 unsold tickets to the Foundling Hospital for children in Coram Fields, one of which was the winning ticket. A fine engraving of this picture can also be seen in The Hogarth pub, along with the *Rake's Progress* and *Harlot's Progress* series of prints. Indeed, two of his most famous pictures are *Gin Lane* and *Beer Street*, depicting the widespread intoxication of the era.

Born in the poor Smithfield neighbourhood of London, Hogarth was only 10 years old when he saw his father, who ran a coffee house, jailed for debt for five years; he died prematurely six years after his release. At the age of 15 Hogarth became an apprentice engraver and started by decorating beer tankards. He taught himself to paint in his spare time and soon his pictures became very popular. He was irked somewhat when pirate copies were made of them and sold without any payment to him. So he campaigned for a copyright act (known as Hogarth's Act), which was passed in 1735.

In 1748 he was arrested on suspicion of being a spy in France when drawing fortifications in Calais. A nobleman once commissioned Hogarth to paint a biblical scene of the Israelites and the Egyptians in the Red Sea. He demanded such a low price, however, that Hogarth got his own back by covering the entire canvas in red. When asked where the Israelites and Egyptians were, he said, 'They are all drowned.'

A young woman asked him to teach her to draw caricatures and he replied wistfully, 'Alas! young lady, it is not a faculty to be envied. Take my advice, and never draw caricature – by the long practice of it I have lost the enjoyment of beauty. I never see a face but distorted. I have never the satisfaction to behold the human face divine.'

His latter years were spent in poverty at what is now called Hogarth House, in Hogarth Lane, Great West Road, London, W4, a few miles north of this pub at Chiswick. Hogarth frequently visited the pub to see his favourite dog. A few days before his death, bailiffs came to seize the bed in which he was sleeping for a small debt he was unable to pay. 'Spare me my bed for a little while,' he pleaded, 'until I can find another in the grave.'

His friend, the actor David Garrick, wrote the following epitaph, which is engraved on his headstone in Chiswick:

> Farewell, great painter of mankind!
> Who reached the noblest point of art,
> Whose pictured morals charm the mind
> And through the eye correct the heart.

32. Tom Cobley (1698–1794)

The Tom Cobley Tavern, Dragdown Hill, Spreyton, Devon, EX17 5AL
(Tel: 01647 231314). St Austell.

Farmer Tom Cobley was made famous by the folk song *Widdecombe Fair*. According to local legend, he left this pub, which was licensed in 1589, on his infamous journey to the fair. Indeed, he and seven others borrowed a grey mare to pull them in a gig to the fair. After a busy time at the fair, they got drunk on cider and overturned the gig on the way back, killing the mare in the process. The ghost of the mare could be heard groaning on Dartmoor on the eve of the fair ever since, according to the song. Each verse lists the

men involved ending with 'old uncle Tom Cobley and all'.

Uncle Tom Cobley bequeathed two shillings a week to his nephew of the same name in his will. But the nephew did not benefit from this act very much, as he died in the same year as his uncle. Uncle Tom was 96 when he died in the village and he was buried in the local graveyard.

33. Molly Mogg (1699–1766)

Molly Mogg's, 2 Old Compton Street, Soho, London, W1D 4TA (Tel: 020 7437 1786).

Molly Mogg was a celebrated beauty and the daughter of the keeper of the Rose Inn, now demolished, in Wokingham, Berkshire. Despite her beauty she remained unmarried after the death of her lover Mr Standen of Arborfield in 1730. She was, however, constantly 'the toast of the gay sparks of her day'.

One of these was John Gay (1685–1732) the satirist and writer, who in 1726 published a song about her entitled *Molly Mogg, Fair Maid of the Inn*. This was after Gay had stayed at the inn with fellow writers Alexander Pope and Jonathan Swift, where all three had been struck by her beauty. She must have felt something in return for Gay, because his portrait remained in the Rose until its demolition.

The London pub named after her is in the centre of Soho's gay community, so it is strangely appropriate that it was Gay who wrote about a molly (gay slang for a male prostitute).

He wrote about half a crown (12.5p) being able to get you a Molly. But describing the real Molly, he wrote:

> When she smiles on each guest, like her liquor
>
> Then jealousy sets me agog

To be sure there's a bit for the Vicar,

And so I shall love Molly Mogg.

According to the pub's folklore, Molly later became a lover of Nelson's friend, became involved in a scandal and died destitute in Newgate. John Gay's most famous work *The Beggar's Opera* was published two years after *Molly Mogg*. He was buried at Westminster Abbey with his own epitaph:

Life is a jest, and all things show it;

I thought so once, and now I know it.

34. Jack Sheppard (1702–1724)

The Shepherd, Blackmore Road, Kelvedon Hatch (Doddinghurst), Essex, CM15 0AT (Tel: 01277 372389). Gray & Sons.

Robber and highwayman Jack Sheppard, whose name was sometimes spelled Shepherd, achieved immense fame, or infamy, for his many spectacular escapes from prison. When he was finally hanged for housebreaking, a huge crowd of 200,000 gathered to witness it; he was

even found with a knife concealed about him then, ready to cut the rope. He was frequently on the run and often hid in a secret space behind the fireplace of this fifteenth-century inn. 'He played the lute – and it was here when I took over the place,' said landlord Steve Richbell.

Born in London's Spitalfields, young Sheppard became a carpenter like his father. Then, in the Black Lion in Drury Lane, he met a burglar called Blueskin Blake (later executed) and some women 'of abandoned character', including Elizabeth Lion (known as Edgeworth Bess), who led him astray. He later started robbing the houses where he was employed as a journeyman carpenter.

Edgeworth Bess was caught and locked up in St Giles Roundhouse, where Sheppard knocked down the beadle guarding her, broke down the door and carried her off in triumph. Not long afterwards, Jack himself was caught and shut up in the same roundhouse, but he broke through the roof and escaped into the night.

After being caught pickpocketing, Jack and Bess were banged up in Newgate Prison in a cell 75 feet from the ground, surrounded by a 25 feet high wall. With the aid of a file he removed his fetters and then overcame several obstacles with Bess and got out of the prison in an escape that

Detail from the reverse side of The Shepherd sign.

attracted enormous publicity. In a foolhardy show of bravado, he failed to put distance between himself and the prison, but instead stayed to drink in the local taverns. Before long he was captured again, when he was sentenced to death and put back in Newgate. The jailers put him in an especially secure cell called 'The Castle' and then handcuffed him to a large staple fixed to the floor. He managed to wriggle free of the handcuffs and with a bent nail he picked the lock on the leg irons, which were also attached to the staple. Using his broken chains, he smashed the iron bars in the chimney stack and managed to break a hole big enough to gain entry into an unlocked cell above. He then made his way through the prison chapel and broke through several more locked doors in his bid for freedom once more, where he then sheltered in a cow house in a field by Tottenham Court Road.

Once more, however, he returned to the alehouses near Newgate and, when senseless from brandy, was recaptured once more. This time he was weighed down with 300 pounds of chain, fastened to the floor and guarded day and night. The jailers earned several hundreds of pounds by charging the public 3s 6d (17.5p) a time to look at him. Sheppard dictated his life story to Daniel Defoe, who was then a reporter on *Applebee's Journal*, and had his portrait painted by fashionable artist Sir James Thornhill.

On the day of the execution he was offered, as was traditional for those being taken from Newgate to Tyburn, a bowl of ale at St Giles. He swigged some of it and exclaimed, 'Give the remainder to Jonathan Wild,' (who had betrayed him). The following year, Wild was executed and he delighted the crowd by picking the pocket of the priest, who was performing the last rites.

When Sheppard reached Tyburn he cursed the sheriff for not removing his irons. The sheriff became suspicious and searched him once more, finding the concealed knife in his possession. Being light in weight he suffered longer than normal at the end of the rope, but his friends' plan to resuscitate him, with hot blankets and a nearby surgeon, came to nowt. When he was cut down his body was taken to a public house in Long Acre and he was later buried in the churchyard at St Martins-in-the-Fields, where the funeral was arranged by Defoe.

Several histories of his life appeared, a pantomime called *Harlequin Sheppard* played in a Drury Lane theatre, a farce entitled *The Prison-breaker, the Adventures of Jack Sheppard* was also popular at Bartholomew Fair and several songs and poems were written about him.

When Newgate was dismantled in 1902, Tussaud's waxworks exhibition bought one of the doors and a wrought iron grill, which he had broken through between the chapel staircase and the roof.

35. Dick Turpin (1705–1739)

Arterial Road (north side of A127, London to Southend Road, between the A130 and A132), Wickford, Essex, SS12 9HZ (Tel: 01268 726205).
Spirit/Millers Kitchens.

The most famous highwayman of all time Dick Turpin broke into organised crime at Hadleigh, just south-east of this pub, where he joined a gang of smugglers and deer thieves. This was when he was on the run from the constabulary for stealing cattle from the butcher, who had sacked him for selling stolen meat, in East London.

Dick was born in the Essex pub kept by his father John – the Bell in Hempstead, which was later known as the Royal Oak, and the Crown, but is now called the Blue Bell. After being an apprentice butcher in Whitechapel he married Hester (or Esther) Palmer of East Ham, daughter of the landlord of the Rose & Crown Inn at Clay Hill, Enfield, at which point he started a butchery business at nearby Waltham Abbey.

When his practice of stealing cattle to provide stock for his shop was discovered, he fled to join the gang which operated between Hadleigh and Plaistow. After that he stole deer from Epping Forest, where he lived in a cave between High Beach and Loughton Camp (a pub later being named Dick Turpin's Cave at High Beach Hill) and he also partook of some housebreaking in Essex and East London with Gregory's Gang.

In 1735, they spread their net wider and raided the house of a rich farmer in Charlton, Kent. While looting the place they found some mince pies in the larder and impudently ate them in front of their captives. Then they found some brandy and started drinking that, too – while also hospitably offering it to the farmer and his wife, saying mockingly that they were 'as welcome as could be to it'. The humour was lost on the wife, who fainted and had to be revived with the brandy. On another occasion they held the landlady of an inn over the fire, until she revealed the location of her valuables. A large reward was offered for the capture of the gang, resulting in three of them being seized in a Westminster alehouse and their subsequent hanging. Turpin was in the same alehouse at the time, but he escaped through a window.

He decided it was safer to operate alone for a while and turned to highway robbery. One of those he held up at Stamford Hill on the Cambridge road outside London was Tom King, who turned out to be another notorious highwayman, and they became partners, operating from Dick's cave in Epping Forest.

The partnership came to an end in 1737, when the horse they had stolen from a man at the Green Man in Leytonstone was traced to the Red Lion on the corner of Whitechapel Road and Leman Street, where they were staying. As a constable was arresting King in the pub yard, Turpin arrived and aimed his pistol at the constable, but shot his companion by mistake. Before King died, he told the authorities that Turpin could be found at the White House Inn on Hackney Marshes, where he often hid.

Turpin's execution announcement in the Wickford pub.

Perhaps knowing this, and that the price on his head had doubled to £200, he fled instead to Yorkshire. Popular legend, as told in the novel Rookwood by Harrison Ainsworth in 1834, has it that he rode the whole way in a single day on his horse Black Bess, who sank exhausted to the ground at York race course. This story is more likely to be true of another highwayman William Nevison, before Turpin was born. Either way, Turpin settled at Welton, 10 miles from Beverley, and set up as a horse dealer, once more stealing his stock.

He attracted the attention of the authorities by shooting a cock belonging to his landlord when returning half drunk from a hunt. This led to a brawl in an inn at which he was arrested. He gave his name as Palmer (his wife's maiden name), but the prison authorities required independent corroboration of his identity. So he wrote under that name, from York prison, to his brother-in-law in Hempstead, who refused to pay the postage to accept the letter. It was returned to the local post office, where the handwriting was recognised by Dick's former schoolmaster, who reported this to the local magistrate for a £200 reward. His true identity established, he was charged with horse stealing, was found guilty and was sentenced to death.

During the twenty-six days before this was carried out, he joked and drank with his many visitors and ignored appeals to repent. He expressed regret at killing his partner in crime Tom King and confessed to one other murder and several robberies. But he seemed less interested in how this would be treated in the next world than how he looked whilst leaving this one. So he bought new clothes for the event and gave the hangman £3 10s (£3.50) to pay for five mourners.

The execution took place at Knavesmire in York, where he chatted to the hangman for half an hour until the crowd grew impatient, at which point he mounted the scaffold and threw himself off 'in resolute fashion'. His body lay in state at the Blue Boar, Castlegate, York and was buried at St George's Churchyard, Fishergate Postern, York. When surgeons disinterred it for dissection this aroused the fury of the mob, who retrieved it and reburied it in lime to prevent similar attempts. The iron fetters he was bound in, weighing 28 pounds, are on show in York Museum.

36. William Cookworthy (1705–1780)

Tregonissey Road (corner of Lewis Way), St Austell, Cornwall, PL25 4DL (Tel: 01726 72020). St Austell.

The 'father of the English porcelain industry' William Cookworthy was the self-educated son of a weaver, who never made a penny out of his great discovery. He was a Quaker pacifist, who disapproved of making money from any trade connected with war and who dismissed those of his faith who did as being 'artful' and 'managing'. Cookworthy was not a good businessman and the china clay factory, which he opened in Plymouth in 1768, lasted for only two years. It was four years later that he sold the patent

to the production method he had invented without ever making any profit.

Born in Kingsbridge, Devon (17 miles east of Plymouth), his father died when William was 14 years old and the family – he had six brothers and sisters – was impoverished within a year or so. To save the coach fare he walked the 200 miles to London to become an apprentice at a wholesale chemist. After six years he had become a skilled pharmaceutical and mineralogical chemist and returned to Devon in 1726 to set up as a chemist in Plymouth.

He married another Quaker Sarah Berry in 1735 and they had five daughters, but Sarah died young in 1745. In the same year, Cookworthy was shown some china clay from an American ship at Plymouth. He had read about its production in China and decided to look for its raw materials in Cornwall. The following year he saw miners repairing furnaces with clay at Godolphin, near Penzance, which was extracted from local pits. He took these samples back to his laboratory and found it could be used in making porcelain.

But the real breakthrough came soon after when, using his divining rod, he discovered a purer clay at St Austell in the parish of St Stephen-in-Brannel. There then followed 20 years of experiments, mainly by trial and error, mixing it with Cornish rocks to perfect the production method of Britain's first real 'hard paste' porcelain, which eventually became a flourishing industry. The china clay pits around St Austell are of enormous size, being nearly 300 feet deep and a mile in circumference.

Cookworthy's expertise was sought in many other fields, such as which rocks to use in the construction of the famous Eddystone Lighthouse, 14 miles west of Plymouth, in 1759, which lasted 123 years before being replaced. And he was consulted by doctors in trying to find the cause of Devonshire Colic, a disease affecting cider drinkers. One theory was that it was a form of poisoning from the lead contained in cider presses. Cookworthy was unable to detect any metal traces in cider made from leaden presses, but this could have been owing to the unadvanced methods of the day. He also helped to promote the health of sailors by selling medicines and a 'portable soup' made from oxen offal, which looked like glue but protected them from scurvy and 'other putrid disorders'. In fact, Captain Cook was one of his customers, whom he entertained at home.

Uncharacteristically, William and his brother Jacob had a three-year feud with a fellow Quaker Joseph Veal of St Austell. Jacob had got engaged to Elizabeth Hingston in 1741, but then refused to pay the £200 bond demanded by Elizabeth's father James Hingston (which William had been involved in negotiating), because he could not afford it. Hingston accused Jacob of acting 'basely and knavishly' towards his daughter and approved of her getting engaged to Veal instead. There then followed a prolonged wrangle in Quaker circles over whether or nor the original engagement still stood. Jacob finally conceded in 1744.

In the same year, William set off another controversy at Quaker meetings in Plymouth: his disapproval of buying war-captured goods during the War of the Austrian Succession. Cargoes from

A green lake in Cornwall...one of Cookworthy's china clay pits near St Austell.

captured ships were auctioned in a profitable trade for, among others, local wealthy and influential Quakers. Cookworthy objected that this compromised their anti-war principles, but he failed to get support.

An even more squalid form of profiteering involved the supplying of coffins to French prisoners of war, who died from the pestilential conditions in which they were incarcerated. The Plymouth mayor's cousin got the contract for this ... and decapitated the corpses to get them in shorter coffins to save on costs. Cookworthy told this tale to his friend Dr John Wolcot – the writer of anti-establishment satire under the pseudonym of Peter Pindar – who used it in his poem *The Plymouth Carpenter & The Coffins*. A couple of local labourers' sons Henry Bone and John Opie were helped by Cookworthy's generosity to become established artists.

Examples of Cookworthy's absent-mindedness abound. He once mistook a pickling tub, half-filled with food, for 'a cloacinian receptacle' (a quaint term for a chamber pot) and used it as such. A couple of times he put on other people's clothes without noticing. On another occasion he befriended a fellow traveller at an inn and then picked up the latter's saddle bag, and its valuable contents, by mistake. Cookworthy had gone several miles before the hue and cry caught up with him and found him 'trotting soberly along and looking as little like a rogue as possible'. He taught himself Greek, Latin and French, which he used to translate theological works, notably the works of Emanuel Swedenborg, the Swedish mystic.

A stained-glass window depicting Cookworthy in his pottery is situated in the Guildhall at Plymouth, the town where he lived in Nut Street. Portraits were disapproved of in Quaker circles at his time, but a silhouette (considered acceptable) survives. Kingsbridge, where he was born, has a William Cookworthy Museum at 108 Fore Street. The William Cookworthy pub is used as a training centre for St Austell Brewery and is located behind John Keay House, which is the head office of the English China Clay company.

37. Benjamin Franklin (1706–1790)

Franklin Tavern, 157–158 Lewes Road, Brighton, East Sussex, BN2 3LF (Tel: 01273 602995). Spirit.

So much was achieved by the great American statesman and inventor Benjamin Franklin, despite him only receiving two years' formal education. By the age of 10, he was working at making candles for his father Josiah and two years later, he was an apprentice printer to his brother James on a newspaper in Boston. James was imprisoned for mocking the clergy and in his absence, the teenage Benjamin kept the paper going.

The two fell out, however, and Benjamin, at the age of 17, ran away, illegally breaking the terms of his apprenticeship, and settled down in Philadelphia, where he published the *Philadelphia Gazette*. He became a commercial success and within a few years he gained some lucrative contracts to print the currencies for Philadelphia, New Jersey, Delaware and Maryland.

In 1731 he helped form the world's first public library and in 1737 he became deputy postmaster of Philadelphia. He invented the Franklin stove in 1744, which heated homes more safely and economically, but he refused to patent the invention in the interest of the public good. At the age of 42 he retired from business and concentrated on experimenting with electricity, bringing out fully the distinction between positive and negative electricity. Famously, he flew a kite in a thunderstorm in 1752 to prove that lightning was electricity and from this act, he invented the lightning rod to protect buildings from being struck.

In 1764 he went to London to challenge the English policy of taxing the American colonies without allowing them representation. While he did not succeed in this, he did have some success with his landlady Margaret Stevenson and her daughter Polly, having affairs with them both; Polly was later at his side when he died. He also joined the notorious Hell Fire Club with John Wilkes.

After returning to America, Franklin helped to draft its declaration of independence in 1776 with Thomas Jefferson and Thomas Paine. Jefferson stated that the only reason Franklin was not allowed to write the entire declaration was because he would have included too many jokes in it. On signing the declaration on 4 July, Franklin commented, 'We must indeed all hang together or, most assuredly, we shall all hang separately.'

He was sent to France to get assistance in the resulting war against Britain, and managed to persuade the French to supply war munitions and money, which helped win the war. Franklin remained in Paris as ambassador and helped negotiate the Treaty of Paris in 1783, which ended the war between Britain and America. A couple of years later he returned to Philadelphia and continued inventing.

At the age of 83 he invented bifocal spectacles after getting fed up with having to change glasses when reading. Other inventions included swim fins, the glass armonica (a musical instrument) and a flexible urinary catheter – after his older brother John suffered from kidney stones. Finally, as he found it difficult to reach books on high shelves in his old age, he invented a tool called a long arm, which was a long wooden pole with a grasping claw at the end.

His sexual appetite was undiminished in old age, as was his penchant for strolling about naked in the open air. He was completely unselfconscious about his own nudity. On one occasion he saw a friend's maid approaching with a letter to deliver to him. Forgetting he was naked, he went towards her to collect it, upon which she fled screaming and later told her master she had been chased by an Indian chief, who must have killed Franklin.

A couple of months before his death he signed a petition to congress urging the abolition of slavery. His ready wit lives on in many quotations, but perhaps the most pertinent to this publication is, 'There are more old drunkards than old doctors'.

38. Samuel Johnson (1709–1784)

118 Mitcham Lane, Streatham, London, SW16 6NR (Tel: 020 8696 9362). Youngs.

One of the most quoted writers in the English language, Samuel Johnson was physically deformed and suffered from flatulence. The deformities were caused at birth, when his mother did not have sufficient milk to suckle him and so put him in the care of a nurse. The baby contracted a tubercular infection (scrofula) from the nurse, which disfigured his face, left him deaf in the left ear, almost blind in the left eye and visually impaired in the right eye. A bout of smallpox as a child further disfigured his face. The flatulence was possibly connected to his eating habits, as he gobbled his food 'so fast that the veins stood out on his forehead'. An irked clergyman described, in pained terms, Johnson's feeding manners in Fleet Prison, where he was detained for debt, as worse than those of Eskimos and Hottentots.

Born in Lichfield, Staffordshire, the son of a bookseller, he had an uncle who was a local boxing champion and he taught him how to defend himself as a child. This proved useful in his later years, when he was attacked by four robbers in London and was able to keep them at bay until help arrived. At the age of 19 he went to Oxford University with the help of money his mother had inherited, but it soon ran out and he had to drop out after a year. This made him depressed and he developed convulsive tics, jerks and twitches, which remained with him for life. His recovery was helped by Henry and Elizabeth Porter, who befriended him. When Henry died, Johnson married Elizabeth, who was 20 years older than him but who had a dowry of £600 in 1735. He used the money to invest in a school, but it failed, and he lost nearly all of his money.

In search of work, he decided to go to London in 1737, with his pupil David Garrick, who became a famous actor. They were so poor that they had to share a horse for the journey, taking it in turns to ride or walk. Johnson had just four pence (under 2p) and Garrick threepence (just over 1p) when they arrived. Johnson took lodgings in what is now Eastcastle Street, near Oxford Circus, when it was on the edge of Marylebone Fields, where highwaymen operated. He lived on bread and water and became very shabby.

In 1738 he published a poem called *London,* which expressed his disgust at how the poor were oppressed there. In his early days he was a victim of this, so when he did have money in his later years he was always generous in giving to the poor and homeless. When his wife followed him down to London he found better rooms to live in Streatham, but these were more expensive. Often when working late in Central London he would walk the streets at night to save travel or extra lodging costs.

In 1747 he was commissioned to compile the first ever Dictionary of the English Language, for which he became famous. He was paid £1,575, but it took nearly nine years and he had to pay six assistants out of this. It was published in 1755, with 41,000 words having been defined and their meanings illustrated with 114,000 quotations. Among them was his self-deprecating definition of 'lexicographer' as 'a writer of dictionaries, a harmless drudge'. He also described 'pension' as an allowance to 'state hirelings', and the Board of Excise as 'wretches' who levied 'hateful' taxes. This led to some embarrassment when he accepted a £300 a year pension from the board in 1762.

He was far from a compliant state hireling, however, strongly voicing his opposition to the government's wars with France for possessions in North America. These, he likened to the quarrels of two

Statue of Johnson in the Strand.

robbers over booty taken from a victim; but the English were worse, in his view, for their treatment of the natives. He also supported the Americans in their War of Independence from the English and he detested slavery.

When his wife died in 1752, after becoming addicted to alcohol and opium, Johnson was distraught with grief. 'Marriage has many pains, but celibacy has no pleasures,' he ruefully ruminated. He decided not to remarry, having famously observed that this would show 'the triumph of hope over experience'. Neither did he seek solace in prostitutes, disapproving of a trade that dealt 'with women like a dealer in any other commodity ... as an ironmonger sells ironmongery'. Lines in his diary of 1771, however, allude to him dabbling in bondage, using 'shackles and handcuffs' with Hester Thrale, the wife of an MP.

Johnson hated public hangings at Tyburn, including that of his preacher friend Rev. William Dodd, who was hanged for forgery in 1777. While in jail, Dodd hurriedly penned his autobiography, which prompted Johnson's famous remark, 'When a man knows he is to be hanged in a fortnight it concentrates his mind wonderfully'. Johnson was less kind about other preachers, 'A woman's preaching is like a dog's walking on his hind legs. It is not done well, but you are surprised to find it done at all'. But perhaps his most famous saying of all is, 'Patriotism is the last refuge of a scoundrel'.

39. David Garrick (1717–1779)

(i)   The Garrick, 25 High Street, Stratford-upon-Avon, Warwickshire, CV37 6AU (Tel: 01789 292186). Greene King.

(ii) Garrick Arms, 8 Charing Cross Road, London, WC2 0HG (Tel: 020 7240 5556). Greene King.

(iii) Garrick's Head (recently closed), Winton, Greater Manchester.

Garricks Head, Winton, Greater Manchester.

Undoubtedly one of the most successful and popular actors ever, David Garrick arrived penniless in London in 1737. He and his friend Samuel Johnson had shared a horse between them, taking it in turns to ride and walk all the way from their native Litchfield.

At first Garrick became a wine merchant with his brother. But he knew treading the boards suited him better than treading grapes and he took the theatrical world by storm in 1741. By 1747 he had earned enough money to become part-owner of the Drury Lane Theatre and never looked back from then on, leaving a fortune of £100,000 at the end of his life.

A skilful fencer and a graceful dancer, he was only 5 foot 4 inches tall, but was very popular with women. His first love was the actress Peg Woffington, with whom he lived without getting married. They separated after six months but continued to be friends, until Garrick rejected her proposal of marriage. Garrick then met Viennese dancer Eva Maria Veigel, whom he married in 1749 and he stayed with her for the rest of his life, living in a house five minutes' walk from Drury Lane.

He had a good cure for piles ... six grains of opium, forty grains of white lead powder and a large piece of fresh butter. This was spread on linen and applied as

The Garrick Inn, Stratford upon Avon

cold as possible to the posterior. His death was caused by a combination of gout, herpes and kidney trouble.

40. Martha Gunn (1726–1815)

Martha Gunn Inn, 100 Upper Lewes Road, Brighton, East Sussex, BN2 3FE (Tel: 01273 681671). Courage.

Fisherwoman Martha Gunn became known as Queen of the Dippers when catering for Brighton's growing attraction as a sea-bathing resort. She and the other dippers would plunge the visitors vigorously in and out of the water, as it was believed to be good for their health in the 1750s. The female dippers had a reputation for roughness, being described by the artist John Constable as 'hideous amphibious animals ... whose language, both in oaths and voice, resembles men, all mixed together in endless indecent confusion'.

During the French invasion scare of 1794 the large and rotund Martha and her dippers, armed with mops and buckets, were depicted in a cartoon as 'icons of working people repelling the invaders while Mr Pitt, the prime minister, peeps timidly out of a bathing machine'. Bathing machines were little huts on wheels, which were pushed into the sea to allow bathers to undress without being seen by others. This *Morning Herald* cartoon by J. Nixon, entitled 'Failed French Invasion or Brighton in a Bustle', is on display in the Fishermen's Museum at 200 Kings Road Arches in Brighton (on the shore opposite the Old Ship Hotel). Outside the museum is a boat named the *Martha Gunn*. There are also other pictures of her in the museum, where she is described as 'the working person who gave birth to new Brighton' when it developed from a small fishing village called Brighelmstone to the resort of Brighton.

One of Martha's customers was King George IV, whom she had bathed since he was a young prince. According to her descendent Brighton taxi driver John Maguire, Martha was also a tobacco smuggler and prostitute, who became the lover of the prince.

More official sources allude to this discreetly with phrases such as she 'received in after years very marked attention from the prince' and that 'she was a great favourite of the prince who granted her free access to his kitchen'. And it was here that she used to steal butter to rub into her rheumatic knees to ease the pain. She hid the butter, which was expensive in those days, in her undergarments before leaving. On one occasion the prince observed her secreting a pound of butter in this way and, without letting on, he mischievously started chatting to her, steered her towards the hot stove and then prolonged the conversation ... so that the butter would

Bartender shows picture of Martha Gunn with a young Prince of Wales (later George IV).

melt in her drawers. When it duly did and formed a puddle on the floor, he told the cook that Martha must have wet herself – but what a fine lady she must have been to produce such a golden pool!

One of Martha's dipping customers, a young woman, attempted to drown herself, but Martha rescued her and drew out of her the reason for her unhappiness. It emerged the young woman had been made pregnant by a duke, who had abandoned her. Martha put her in touch with the local abortionist, a woman whose other customers included discarded lovers of the prince.

The seawater certainly seemed to benefit Martha's health, as she lived to the age of 88 and was working until the year before her death. She outlived her husband Stephen – a fisherman, who also manned the local lifeboat and helped to smuggle tobacco and spirits into nearby Shoreham from Holland – and all her children; including Elizabeth, who died at the age of 13 from a lung infection.

Martha Gunn's grave in Brighton.

In her final year she was spotted by a visitor who knew her well and he asked how she was. She replied, 'Well and hearty, thank God, sir, but rather hobbling. I don't bathe, because I ain't so strong as I used to be, so I superintend on the beach, for I'm up before any of 'em; you may always find me and my pitcher at one exact spot, every morning by six o'clock.' Even though she had lost her teeth, she added that she was looking forward to devouring some Christmas pudding.

She lived at 36 East Street in Brighton, where an Italian restaurant called Al Forno now stands, inside which is a plaque to her. She was buried in the south-east corner of the churchyard of St Nicholas, on Dyke Road, which is the oldest church in Brighton. A portrait of her by John Russell now hangs in the tea room of the Royal Pavilion, Brighton.

41. John Wilkes (1727–1797)

Wilkes' Head, 16 Edward Street, Leek, Staffordshire, ST13 5DS.

John Wilkes, the son of a distiller, became a champion of the common man, parliamentary reform, religious toleration and American independence. 'Wilkes and Liberty' became a popular slogan on the streets of London, when crowds demanded his release from the Tower of London, where he was locked up from 1768 to 1770: twelve months for sedition and ten for obscenity and blasphemy. The sedition was for criticising the king's speech (by George III) about the terms of ending the war with France. Wilkes' anti-royalty feelings were also demonstrated by his statement that he was a bad card player, because 'I cannot tell a king from a knave'. Even when he proposed a toast of long life to George III, he told his son the Prince of Wales that it was only to delay his accession to the throne as George IV. The obscenity and blasphemy charges arose from a pornographic publication called *Essay on Women*, which he had published privately for friends. It was while he was in prison that his followers formed The Society for Supporting the Bill of Rights, which raised funds for him and the developing of a radical movement.

Back in 1757 he had been elected as MP for Aylesbury and in 1768 as MP for Middlesex. His devil-may-care attitude was exemplified in one of these elections when he bribed the captain of a ship carrying the voters of his opponent to go to Norway. He was said to be extremely ugly with a hideous squint, but a charm that carried all.

In 1764 he fled to Paris, where he was asked by Madame Pompadour how far press liberty extended in England, to which he famously replied, 'I am trying to find out.' While in France he was banned from Parliament in England, where he had been elected for Middlesex. On his return to England he was re-elected three times, but was expelled each time on the grounds that he had libelled the troops who had shot and killed protesters demonstrating outside his jail (the St George's Field massacre).

Wilkes` Head landlord keeps his award-winning real ales in good condition.

One of his greatest opponents in Parliament was the Earl of Sandwich, who had never forgiven Wilkes for a prank he had played on him at the Hell Fire Club, where Wilkes drank claret and port. It involved a baboon, dressed as the devil, jumping on Sandwich's back. Sandwich expressed the view that Wilkes would die of the pox or on the gallows. Wilkes rejoindered, 'That depends my lord on whether I embrace your principles or your mistress.'

In 1774 he was elected Lord Mayor of London and he was finally allowed to take up his seat in Parliament, where he moved several reform bills covering issues such as liberty of the press. Many public houses honoured Wilkes by naming themselves after him and hanging his portrait on the signs outside. Wilkes liked to tell the story of an old woman who pointed at one of the signs and said to him, 'Aye, Wilkes swings everywhere but where he ought'. This particular pub was built around the time of Wilkes' death.

42. James Cook (1728–1770)

Captain Cook Inn, 60 Staithes Lane, Staithes, North Yorkshire, TS13 5AD (Tel: 01947 840200). Free house.

It was while aged 12 working in a shop at Staithes that the great explorer James Cook, the son of an agricultural labourer, first came into contact with the sea. The shop, which has since eroded into the sea, was on the seafront next to the Cod and Lobster pub. It was owned by William Sandison, who sold fishermen's equipment, chandlery goods and ale. It was a noisy, busy village that was cramped at the end of a narrow valley between the sea and the cliffs, where young Cook could 'feel the spray on his cheeks, hear the crashing of the surf and the cry of the gulls as they wheeled above the fishing boats'. In an area where smuggling was rife, he also learned to bring small boats inshore in the dark, which served him well later against the French on the St Lawrence River in North America.

At the age of 18 he had a disagreement with Sandison in the shop and went to work instead for John Walker, a Quaker shipowner, at Whitby, 10 miles away. Cook lived in the attic of the house belonging to Walker in Grape Lane, Whitby, where the Captain Cook Memorial Museum is now located. He was apprenticed to Walker from 1746 to 1749 and continued

Seafaring landlord of the Capt. Cook Inn.

working for him until 1755. The first ship he sailed on for Walker was the *Freelove Collier* in 1747.

At the start of the war against France in 1755, while a mate on a vessel in the Thames, he volunteered to join the navy, to avoid being press-ganged, and by 1759 he was serving in North America. After the war he was the first to sail all around New Zealand and to chart it accurately, and the whole east coast of Australia. Indeed, New South Wales was so-called, because he thought it resembled the Welsh shores of the Bristol Channel.

After thirty of his crew of eighty-five died from scurvy and fever he determined to cut this by introducing a new diet. This included celery boiled with peas and wheat, with spruce beer (made from the juice of wort) to drink. Only one crew member died when this diet was tried on a voyage from 1772 to 1775 taking in the Antarctic Circle, when he also discovered New Caledonia and Southern Georgia. His paper on this method of preserving seamen's lives earned him a medal from the Royal Society in 1776.

On reaching the Hawaiian Islands in 1779, he discovered that the local sugar cane made a very palatable beer. He also liked a glass of punch. While anchoring there in Krakatoa Bay, he was at first treated with respect by the natives. But after having one of them flogged for stealing on board, another stole one of the ship's boats. When Cook went ashore to retrieve it he was surrounded and then clubbed and stabbed to death. His body was then dismembered and partly burned. His crew burned and destroyed an entire village in revenge.

Before going to Staithes (where there is a Captain Cook Heritage Centre in the High Street), he was born in a small farm worker's cottage, which had previously been an alehouse known as the Bear in Marton in Cleveland.

The death of Cook, a painting in the Capt. Cook Heritage Centre, Staithes.

43. Oliver Goldsmith (1728–1774)

(i) 46 Dame Street, Dublin 2.

(ii) 89 St Mary's Road (corner of Onslow Road), Southampton, Hants,
     SO14 0AH (Tel: 02380 390911).

The novelist, poet and dramatist Oliver Goldsmith spent most of his life in poverty, even when his works were successful, and died in debt to the tune of £2,000. Born in Pallas, near Ballymahon, Co Longford, he listened as a child to the ballads of local peasants and he scribbled his own rhymes even before he could write legibly. His formal education was interrupted by smallpox which permanently disfigured him.

At the age of 17 he went to Trinity College in Dublin as a 'sizar', which meant that he had to do menial work in exchange for reduced fees. This included sweeping the floor and being a waiter at meals. He

Sign in Southampton.

resented this and described it as 'a contradiction for men to be at once learning the liberal arts and at the same time treated as slaves; at once studying freedom and practising servitude'. Even with the reduced fees he had to pawn his books and write street ballads, which he sold for five shillings each, to make ends meet.

He avoided lectures as much as possible and in 1747 was admonished for abetting a riot in which bailiffs were ducked in the college cistern. In the same year he tried, and failed, to get a scholarship, but was consoled with a grant of thirty shillings a year. While celebrating this he got into an argument with his tutor, after which he ran away to Cork for a while and then returned. He suffered real poverty when his father died in 1747, yet gave the blankets from his bed to a poor woman and her five children.

Eventually he got his BA in 1749 and applied for Holy Orders. The bishop rejected the application though, because Goldsmith had neglected his preliminary studies and had turned up wearing scarlet breeches.

For a while he spent most of his time in the Ballymahon Inn, telling stories and playing his flute. When given £50 by relatives to start as a lawyer in London he lost it gambling in Dublin. In 1752 he went to Edinburgh to study medicine, but left the following year to travel on the Continent mainly by foot. While sailing to France his ship was forced by the inclement weather conditions to shelter at Newcastle, where he was arrested as a suspected French spy. As he spent two weeks in prison, the ship put to sea and sank with the loss of all those on board.

On finally reaching France he travelled widely on foot, repaying peasants for their hospitality by playing his flute for their entertainment. He ended up in London penniless and virtually destitute, trying to earn a living as an actor, a school usher, a chemist's assistant and as a physician - despite the dubious nature of his medical degree from his unfinished course.

But it was as a writer for the *Monthly Review* that gave him his first adequate salary in 1757. Even so, he had just one chair in his lodgings when he was visited by a bishop, who was amused to see him lend his neighbour some coal in a chamber pot. His first poem published in 1764, called *The Traveller*, described his excursions abroad and it proved to be very successful. This was followed by an even greater success, his novel *The Vicar of Wakefield*, in 1766. His £60 payment for this was used to release him from custody after his landlady had him arrested for non-payment of rent.

In between drinking at the Crown Tavern in Islington, attending masquerades and gambling, he wrote a biography of Charles Parnell, which was published in 1770. When a magazine 'alluded insultingly' in 1773 to Goldsmith's passion for Mrs Mary Horneck, he went round to their office to fight the publisher. During the fisticuffs a lamp got broken and covered

Statue of Oliver Goldsmith in Dublin.

them both in oil. His most popular play *She Stoops to Conquer* earned him a lot of money in the same year, but this was mostly squandered on his 'feckless habits'.

He died the following year in London from a fever, which was probably aggravated by the pressure of debt, and he was buried in the Temple. A monument was later erected in Westminster Abbey.

44. William Cowper (1731–1800)

Cowper's Oak, High Street, Weston Underwood, Bucks, MK46 5JB
(Tel: 01234 711382). Enterprise Inns.

The suicidal and sometimes insane poet William Cowper spent 27 years in this village and the neighbouring one of Olney. Much of his best work, such as *The Task*, which influenced Wordsworth, was written in what is now known as Cowper's Alcove near this pub.

Born with weak eyesight this was cleared at the age of 14 by a severe attack of smallpox. When working as a young man in London, he had a forbidden affair with his cousin Theodora Cowper and he also went to watch lunatics for amusement in Bedlam Asylum in Bishopsgate - although angry with himself for this. Soon, however, he was in a lunatic asylum himself in St Albans, after trying to strangle himself with a garter in 1763. Indeed, during his lifetime he made three suicide attempts. The first had been when he bought a bottle of laudanum to drink, but failed to swallow it, threw it out of the window and went to drown himself in the river instead. But the sight of a porter by the bank inhibited him. The final attempt was through hanging, but he was cut down by his long-term companion Mrs Unwin, who had originally been his landlady in Cambridge.

Throughout his life he was subject to delusions, hearing voices and strange fancies. He said he felt a violent blow had struck his brain 'without touching the skull'. He also felt a need to sacrifice himself or be doomed to eternal perdition - an illusion that he never completely eradicated. Being bullied at school might have caused his morbidity and depression. Another theory proffered by the politician Charles Greville, who knew him, was that he had gone mad because he was a hermaphrodite, whereas essayist William Hazlitt opined that Cowper was effeminate. Cowper's mother died when he was 6 years old, while giving birth to his brother John, and his father died when William was 25.

Cowper's Alcove where the poet wrote much of his best work.

He had his first poem published at school, but after leaving, he trained to be a solicitor. Despite a lack of diligence in his studies, he was called to the bar and became a commissioner of bankruptcy. But he resigned from this job and became deeply in debt himself after his spell in the St Albans private madhouse. He then settled in Cambridge, where he met Mrs Mary Unwin (née Cawthorne), the daughter of a draper, who was seven years older than Cowper. In 1768 he moved with her to Olney, a mile north of Weston Underwood, where his friend John Newton the curate employed him as a lay curate on parish work, such as visiting the sick

and the dying. This earned him nicknames such as 'the Squire' and 'Sir Cowper'. He became engaged to Mrs Unwin, but it was broken off when he had a fresh attack of mania.

In Olney, Cowper lived in the house called Orchard Side in Market Place, where the Cowper and Newton museum now stands. It was here that he started composing hymns, of which the most famous was *God Moves in a Mysterious Way*, as well as poems.

In 1871 he met and befriended Lady Austen (née Ann Richardson) at Clifton, near Olney, and she encouraged him to write poetry and ballads again, some of which, such as *John Gilpin*, became very popular. They ranged from humorous observations to stinging attacks on slavery and public schools. Perhaps his most famous line was *Variety's the very spice of life, That gives it all its flavour.* He also wrote love poems to Lady Austen, who wore a lock of his hair.

His move to Weston Underwood took place at the end of 1786 and soon afterwards he had a fresh attack of insanity, which lasted six months. It was around this time that Mrs Unwin prevented him from hanging himself. His recovery was rapid but never complete. In 1795, he and Mrs Unwin moved to North Tuddenham, near East Dereham, Norfolk, where she died in 1796 and he four years later. He is buried in the St Edmund's chapel of East Dereham Church, where a tablet has been erected in his memory.

45. James Watt (1736–1819)

80–92 Cathcart Rd (opposite Watt Place), Greenock, Renfrewshire, Scotland, PA15 1DD (Tel: 01475 722640). Wetherspoon.

The inventor James Watt, who improved the efficiency of the steam engine, was born in Greenock and his surname lives on as the unit of electric power. There is a statue of him outside his birthplace, at the bottom of William Street, about two minutes' walk from the pub.

During his school years in Greenock he was jeered at by his fellow pupils for being dull and spiritless because of his feeble health. When he left school he went to work in his father's workshop – who was at various times a shipwright, a carpenter and a joiner – making models. This skill was to serve him well in his later years, when testing his theories about steam power on models he made himself.

He later moved to Glasgow and London to learn the skills of mathematical instrument making. But because he had not served a proper apprenticeship, he was prevented from opening his own workshop to the public in Glasgow, but instead was allowed to make instruments for the university. In 1763, the university asked him to improve the poor performance of a steam engine invented by Thomas Newcomen in 1710. After experiments with a kettle, discovering the latent heat of steam, he came up with the idea of separate condensers: one hot and one cold. This proved a huge leap forwards, but he was unable to afford to patent it until 1769.

He then got industrialists to develop it in Birmingham and he was working on how to improve its rotary motion with the use of a crank, when one of his workmen called Pickard stole his plans and patented them before him. But Watt

Statue of James Watt outside his birthplace in Greenock.

put this setback behind him and in 1782, he patented a new system, which prevented steam from escaping and from being wasted, and so continued driving pistons.

It is debatable as to whether or not Watt discovered the chemical composition of water (until then considered one of the elements) before or after Henry Cavendish. Watt's paper on this was submitted to the Royal Society in November 1783, but was not publicly read to members until April 1784, after Cavendish's had been read in January of that year.

Watt's other inventions included a machine for copying letters and another for reproducing sculptures. A further machine was to help the generation and inhalation of gases in order to cure patients, including his son Gregory, who suffered from consumption. His other son, also named James, went to study in Paris in 1789 and took part in the revolution there. He never forgot his roots in Greenock and he provided the town with an improved harbour, a new waterworks and its first library.

46. Thomas Paine (1737–1809)

White Hart Street (corner of Norwich Road), Thetford, Norfolk, IP24 1AA (Tel: 01842 755631). Free house.

World fame can truly be claimed for Thomas Paine, who was born in a cottage on the site of this pub and hotel. Yet he also had his fair share of infamy, which endangered his life on many occasions in England, France and America. A plaque on the building, financed by American airmen in 1943, praises him for expressing 'the democratic aspirations of the American Republic through such splendid writing as Common Sense, Crisis, and The Age of Reason'. However, despite this contribution and risking his life fighting for American independence, as well as drafting its declaration of independence, he was barred from voting there.

A nearby statue of him, sculpted by Charles Wheeler and erected in 1964, has an inscription recording the fact that Paine was made an honorary French citizen for his part in that country's revolution. Yet he was sentenced to be guillotined there and only escaped execution by exceptional circumstances. A pub called Rights of Man existed for many years in Brandon Road, Thetford, but was closed in the 1990s, because of trouble caused by its customers, who were mainly poachers.

At the age of 19 Paine signed articles at Wapping in London to go to sea as a privateer – a form of piracy, which was legalised if part of the booty was given to the government. He just missed the ship, however, and it was later captured by the French, who killed over 150 of the crew, with just 17 surviving. After working as a stay maker (his father's profession) for a couple of months, he signed on for another privateer and spent seven months at sea.

Paine's father was a Quaker, yet Thomas had an early attraction to Methodism after hearing John Wesley preach in Thetford. When living at 20 New Street in Sandwich, Kent in 1759, Paine became a Methodist lay preacher. In the same year, he married local woman Mary Lambert, but she died in childbirth less than a year later.

Paine moved to Lincolnshire to become an excise man, lodging in such pubs as The George in Grantham and The Windmill at Alford, but was sacked, seemingly unjustly, after claims of corruption by an unnamed informant in 1765. For a while he worked as a stay maker again, next to the Old Beehive Inn at Diss, Norfolk, and then he did some teaching in London.

In 1768 he got another excise job in Lewes, Sussex, staying there until 1774, where he lived at Bull House, which had been the Bull Inn on the corner of Bull Lane and Westgate Street. Harveys, the local brewery in Lewes, produces a premium bitter named Tom Paine (5.5 per cent alcohol by

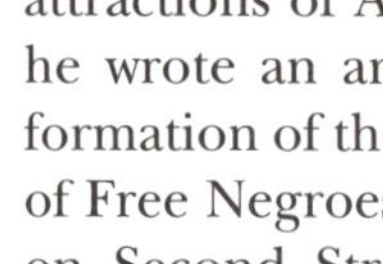

Plenty of bottle ... Thomas Paine strong pale ale, brewed in Lewes, Sussex.

volume), which it brands as 'a taste of independence'. His portrait graces some of their beer mats as well. While at Lewes he joined the Headstrong Club, which had debates in the White Hart Inn as members consumed ale and oysters. He was sacked again by the excise in 1773, this time for seeking a rise and for being absent without leave.

In London he met Benjamin Franklin, who persuaded him of the attractions of America, to where he sailed in 1774. Shortly after arriving he wrote an article against the African slave trade, which inspired the formation of the world's first anti-slavery society, The Society for the Relief of Free Negroes Unlawfully Held in Bondage. This was at the Sun Tavern on Second Street in Philadelphia on 14 April 1775. Paine published *Common Sense* in 1776 and gave all the considerable royalties to the cause of American independence.

In 1777, when the British were winning the war against independence, it was Paine who raised the morale of the Americans with a pamphlet that proclaimed, 'We fight not to enslave, but to set a country free, and to make room upon the earth for honest men to live in.' But when he made accusations about public money for purchasing arms from France being embezzled in 1779 he became unpopular, resigned from Congress and was beaten up in the street more than once.

Back in favour in 1781, he was sent on a mission to France to enlist support for the American cause and, when attacked by British ships off Greenland, he took up arms with the rest of the crew to beat it off. They were welcomed on the southern shores of Brittany with oysters and cider.

After American independence was won, Paine concentrated his thoughts on designing an iron single span bridge to cross 400 to 500 feet over the river at Philadelphia. His plans were rejected, so he returned to England to try and get them accepted there in 1787.

He took up residence in the Yorkshire Stingo Pub on the south side of Marylebone Road in London (opposite where Lisson Grove now is). While a prototype of the bridge was erected next to it he sampled the pub's strong ale and played on its bowling green. The bridge, spanning 110 feet, was completed in September 1790, but it failed to attract any investors.

He then started writing *The Rights of Man* in support of the French Revolution, after having been in Paris from November 1789 to March 1790. This was written while he lodged at the Angel Inn in Islington, North London. After completing part one on his fifty-fourth birthday on 29 January 1791, he celebrated in the inn with several bottles of wine and brandy and then slept until noon the next day.

He then returned to Paris to promote the cause of republicanism and was there when King Louis XVI fled from the capital. Paine, however, was nearly hanged from a lamp post, being mistaken for an aristocrat because he was not wearing a tricolour hat.

Back in London he was arrested at the London Tavern for debt on 21 May 1792 and was summoned to appear on charges of seditious libel in *The Rights of Man*; the book denounced class-divided society and the use of taxes to finance wars of conquest to make the rich richer and the poor poorer, and was suppressed until 1817. Following a warning that he might face the death penalty he fled to France. He was found guilty in his absence at a trial before a hand-picked jury, being described as a traitor and 'a drunken roisterer'.

On landing in Calais he was made an honorary citizen and he was elected to represent the port at the national convention. He was also made a member of the committee to draft a new republican constitution. He argued against the summary execution of the king, but for a fair trial and his exile to America. 'Avidity to punish is always dangerous to liberty,' he declared. 'He that would make his own liberty secure must guard even his enemy from oppression; for if he violates this duty he establishes a precedent that will reach to himself.' This plea for clemency was narrowly defeated and Robelpierre's Reign of Terror followed, which Paine opposed as a violation of the revolution's standards of the rights of man and which he blamed for preventing the revolution from spreading through Europe. Many of his friends were executed in 1793 and seeing his own life in continual danger he feverishly wrote the *Age of Reason*, which was an attack on organised religion.

Despite popular misconceptions, he was not an atheist but believed in deism, which recognised God as a benevolent creator of the universe, but did not believe the Bible was anything more than a collection of stories based on hearsay. All churches, he stated, were 'human inventions to terrify and enslave mankind and monopolise power and profit'. But he also opposed the forcible extermination of religious belief by the Jacobins, which he saw as making atheism a new dogma.

He put the finishing touches to *Age of Reason* on Christmas Eve 1793,and was then arrested at 4 a.m. on Christmas Day. He managed to pass the manuscript to a friend and it was published in February 1794.

By June he was semi-conscious from jail fever (typhus) and on 24 July the public prosecutor put Paine's name on the list to be executed the next day. Accordingly, the jailer chalked a mark on his door. But the door was open to allow some breeze in,

Statue of Thomas Paine in Thetford.

because Paine was sweating so badly from the fever. Consequently, when the door was shut at night, the chalk mark was on the inside and was not seen by the executioner ... 'the destroying angel passed by it,' as Paine described it.

A few days later, Robespierre was ousted and executed, so ending the Reign of Terror. It was nearly another four months, however, before Paine was finally released on 6 November, haggard and stooped, with chest pains and paralysed hands.

He wanted to return to America, but feared being captured at sea by the British and taken back to London to be executed on the sedition charge. Finally, he returned to America in 1802, to find himself condemned in the press as 'a depraved atheist' and 'a drunken infidel'. Taking it in his stride, he refused to sue, because of his belief in press freedom. He said he would have if there had been a law punishing liars and the money given to the poor, but he would not sue for personal damages. One result of the campaign of vilification, however, was that stagecoach companies barred him for fear that God would strike him and their property with lightning. And in 1806 he was barred from voting when turning up at the polling station.

After contracting gout and having a stroke he drank a quart of brandy a day to relieve the pain; he was also fond of rum and wine. Living in penury at the age of 75, he lodged in stench and squalor over a cheap tavern at 63 Partition Street, New York. One of his friends Thomas Emmet (brother of Robert Emmet, who was executed in Ireland) was so shocked at the conditions that he paid for better lodgings for him at Herring Street in Greenwich Village. He moved 80 yards to his final resting place at 59 Grove Street in May 1809, where he died on 8 June.

The night before, his doctor had asked him, 'Do you wish to believe that Jesus Christ is the son of God?' He replied, 'I have no wish to believe on that subject.' He asked to be buried on Quaker ground with a headstone engraved 'Author of Common Sense'. This was rejected.

47. James Boswell (1740–1795)

(i) Boswell's Pub, 14 Mandeville Place (corner of Hinde Street), Marylebone, London, W1M 6BE. (Tel: 020 7936 5599)
(ii) Boswell's, 24 Hys, Tombland, Norwich, Norfolk, NR3 1RF.

James Boswell mixed writing and drinking with alacrity when living a few yards from this London pub. His home was in Queen Anne Street from 1788 to 1790; he then lived for the rest of his life within half a mile at what is now 122 Great Portland Street. His life's work constituted the biography of his friend Samuel Johnson, whom he had first met in London in 1763. Published in 1791, this was one of the first 'warts and all' biographies.

Earlier on, he had been persuaded by a friend not to give up drinking while writing it, for fear it would be too dull an account.

Boswell's Pub in London.

Later, he advised him not to drink more than four glasses of wine and a pint of beer a day until he had finished the book. The early stages of his work routine included several brandies at breakfast until he was 'quite intoxicated', two visits to his favourite prostitute Betsy Smith, a visit to Bedlam Lunatic Asylum, where he sang *Maid of Bedlam* with a pretty inmate, followed by two bottles of claret at supper time.

He liked having sex with prostitutes in public places while standing up. Worried about picking up venereal diseases, he wore an early condom sheath made out of a sheep's intestine. Sadly, this did not prevent him from catching gonorrhoea seventeen times in his life. His early attempts at sexual gratification involved rubbing himself up against trees.

He also got excitement from attending public executions. This was heightened when he befriended the keeper of Newgate Prison, who gave him access to the prisoners just before execution and then to the scaffold as they slowly died. After they were cut down he would examine their faces closely. When twin brothers Daniel and Robert Perreau were executed in 1776 for forgery, Boswell began an affair with Daniel's mistress and fellow forger Margaret Rudd, who escaped the noose herself by giving evidence against the twins. The affair lasted on and off until 1787, when she was imprisoned for debt.

In 1790 Boswell was locked up overnight in the Watch House in Oxford Street (close to Boswell's Pub) and the following day he was reprimanded by a magistrate for causing a disturbance on the previous night; he had noisily cried out the hours in the street, claiming the duty watchman was not doing his job properly. Then, in June 1793, he was mugged while drunk in Great Titchfield Street (the street next to his Great Portland Street home). He was knocked down, robbed and left stunned in the gutter until a passer-by summoned assistance and took him home. His head and arms were so badly cut and bruised that he was confined to bed for several days and he was still not fully recovered eight weeks later. Yet he was at pains to make it clear that 'I was robbed and left lying in the gutter – not found lying (drunk) in the gutter and then robbed' (which, given his habits, was just as likely). He went on to say, 'This, however, shall be a crisis in my life. I trust I shall henceforth be a sober, regular man.' Within two years he died from kidney failure, complicated by gonorrhoea and a tumour on his bladder.

Boswell's in Norwich

Earlier in his life he had written a book about Corsica, a country which he visited after being inspired by the case for its liberty when meeting Voltaire and Rousseau in Italy. His biography of Johnson was enriched by many anecdotes and witticisms, involving banter between the subject and his acquaintances, which Boswell played his part in provoking. Original editions of this book are framed on the wall of the London pub, as is an original letter signed by Boswell on 11 April 1774, about his tour of Scotland, including the Hebrides, with Johnson. Barred from the pub are musical instruments, dogs and soiled clothes.

48. Isaac Gulliver (1745–1822)

Gulliver's Tavern, Wimborne Road (corner of School Lane), Kinson, Bournemouth, Dorset, BH11 9AD
(Tel: 01202 768019).

Smuggler Isaac Gulliver used a tunnel that emerged in this tavern for his clandestine activities. At other times he was more brazen … such as when he led a 2-mile convoy of horses taking three shiploads of contraband from Bournemouth (where the pier now is) to the Bourne Valley. Large and fearless (his nerve was legendary), he led his gang of fifty men mounted on a white charger, carrying brandy, silk and tobacco. His men were dressed in shepherd smocks and powdered wigs, earning them the nickname of Whitewigs. The wig powder itself evaded a high duty, so this was an extra expression of defiance to the customs officials.

Although known as 'Old Gulliver, the Gentle Smuggler', Isaac did, on occasion, resort to violence, which led to the deaths of law enforcement officers. One such incident occurred in the Cranbourne Chase area (about 15 miles north-west of Kinson), where the customs officers had shown the temerity to seize smuggled tea and spirits. In retaliation, Gulliver masterminded an attack on them with clubs in order to reclaim the booty, which he sold in Bath, Bristol and even further afield. He also used a pistol, which is now displayed in the Russell-Cotes Museum in Bournemouth.

A favourite picking-up point of his was Branksome Chine (3 miles south-west of Kinson). Others in the area were Pug's Hole and Talbot Woods. The booty was often hidden in Kinson Church's tower and in a tomb near its entrance. Another of his haunts was Howe Lodge in Brook Road, Kinson, which, when it was demolished in 1958, was found to be riddled with secret doors, passages and recesses, as well as a tunnel to his other home in Poole

(6 miles south-west of Kinson). He also lived for a time in Longham (2 miles north-west of Kinson). Once, when tracked down by revenue officers to Kinson, he escaped by feigning his death and staging his own funeral, to the extent of having his coffin buried containing stones.

He had less to fear from the authorities, however, when George III granted him informal immunity after Gulliver unmasked a plot by the French on the king's life. George III was reported to have said, 'Let Gulliver smuggle as much as he likes.'

By 1776 he was able to afford to buy North Eggardon Farm near Dorchester (20 miles west of Kinson) and he later became a respectable wine merchant, who commissioned both Henry Perlee Parker and Thomas Gosse to paint his portrait. Gulliver even became the warden of Wimbourne Minster Church (5 miles north-west of Kinson), where he was buried under its tower. A play about him was written by Joan Pitts in 1975 entitled *The Gentle Smuggler*.

49. Spence Broughton (1746–1792)

Noose and Gibbet, 97 Broughton Lane, Attercliffe, Sheffield, S9 2BE
(Tel: 0114 261 7182). Free house.

The body of executed highwayman Spence Broughton was left to rot in a cage near this pub for thirty-six years as a deterrent to others. 'Gambling was my ruin,' he wrote from his death cell to his widow Eliza. It was this that led to him squandering the wealth from a farm his wealthy parents had bought him in Sleaford and a considerable dowry from his marriage to Eliza.

He left her and his children to mix with 'lewd' women and criminals in London. There, he met a young man from Sheffield, who had carried mail to and from the city. As a result, Broughton and two accomplices Shaw and Oxley decided to rob the mail from the Sheffield to Rotherham coach. On 29 January 1791 they successfully stopped the coach at Ickles on Attercliffe Common, midway between Sheffield and Rotherham. They tied the driver to a hedge and ran off on foot, unable to afford a horse, with bills of exchange worth £123, which they cashed in on their return to London.

One of the shopkeepers that accepted the stolen bills, which the bank refused to honour, recognised Oxley later and reported him to the Bow Street Runners, who arrested him in October. Oxley informed on Broughton and Shaw, who had since taken part in another robbery, to

The pub mural depicting Broughton's execution.

save his own neck; he later escaped in suspicious circumstances. Shaw was also let off in return for giving 'king's evidence' against Broughton. His trial took place in York on 24 March 1792 and lasted just one day.

After the guilty verdict, the judge gave the sentence of death and ordered that his body be gibbeted (put in a metal cage and hung from gallows) to deter others. The body, he said, would be 'suspended betwixt heaven and earth (as unworthy of either) to be buffeted by the winds and storms'. From his cell, Broughton wrote to his wife that 'my awful sentence ... chills me with horror.' The thought of his remains being 'buffeted about by the storms of heaven, or poached by the summer's sun,' he added, 'freezes my blood.' He was hanged on 14 April, reportedly saying it was the happiest day of his life and he died a murdered man. The following day his body was gibbeted in front of a crowd of 40,000

people. The landlord of the nearest pub, the Arrow Inn (later renamed the Pheasant Inn), made a fortune from crowds viewing the body.

A few days later, Broughton's widow visited the Arrow and wept at the sight of her husband outside. When one of the fingers fell off the corpse it was used to make a bone china mug. The corpse became a local landmark and was not removed until 1827, when a local landowner complained it encouraged trespassers on his adjoining property. A replica now stands outside this pub in a street which has now been named after him.

Gibbeted body of Spencer Broughton outside the pub.

50. Jeremy Bentham (1748–1832)

31 University Street (corner of Huntley Street), Fitzrovia, London, WC1E 6JL (Tel: 020 7387 3033). Punch Taverns/T&J Bernard.

An eccentric inventor, moral philosopher and law reformer, Jeremy Bentham always said he was born old and grew young. He had taught himself to read by the age of 3, had learned Latin and Greek at 4 and French at 6, had won a place at Oxford University at 12 and had gained his bachelor's degree at 15 and his master's degree at 18, which is when he also qualified as a barrister at Lincoln's Inn Fields. In his later years he took up badminton at 75 and he loved playing billiards, chess, the violin, and drinking home-brewed ale.

Among his inventions was an early fridge for storing bullocks' hearts, sprats and smelts. He also invented a new language and coined words such as international, codify, minimise and maximise.

As a moral philosopher he is best known for creating the concept of utilitarianism, which is devoted to achieving the greatest happiness for the greatest number of people; one of his most enthusiastic disciples being Daniel O'Connell. Bentham became convinced that this was most likely to be achieved by democratic government and universal suffrage – quite radical views in those days. He was also an early proponent of the welfare state, sexual freedom for all and women's rights.

Pub sign. (New)

After qualifying as a barrister he quickly became disillusioned with the legal profession and advocated radical law reforms, many of which (originally advanced in his book *Introduction to the Principles of Morals and Legislation*) have since been enacted. Recognising the class nature of the British judicial system, he stated that the Magna Carta says 'justice shall be denied to no man; justice shall be sold to no man', yet in practice it was 'denied to nine-tenths of the population [the poor] and to the remaining one-tenth [the rich] it is sold at an unconscionable price.'

All punishment he considered to be in itself evil and he believed that it should only be used if it excluded a greater evil. His views on prison reform earned him the wrath of King George III and the British establishment, but great respect in revolutionary France. In 1792, he was made an honorary French citizen and he addressed the country's national assembly on the need to emancipate its colonies. He was feted again in 1825 at the Courts of Justice in Paris, when he

Pub sign. (Old)

was given a standing ovation and sat next to the president. The following year he became a founder of University College at 43 Gower Street in London, close to the pub now bearing his name. This was the first non-sectarian college, where religious instruction was omitted from its curriculum – hence, its nickname of Godless Gower Street.

Of dwarfish stature, he had long white hair, which flowed down his back, and he always wore a yellow straw hat and embroidered carpet slippers. Every day he beavered away in a damp, gloomy room writing fifteen pages of his thoughts and refusing to see anyone until dinner at 7 p.m.; his published writings amounted to eleven volumes and his unpublished ones are stored away in many dusty old trunks. He nicknamed himself the Hermit, his house in London's Queen Square as the Hermitage, his cat The Reverend Doctor Sir John Langborn, his teapot Dick and his walking stick Dapple.

On his death he requested that the organs of his body be used for medical research – and that his head be embalmed and placed on his skeleton dressed in his Quaker clothes (an auto-icon as he called it). While his body was being dissected, a violent thunderstorm raged and his body was lit up by flashes of lightning. His auto-icon is preserved in a glass case at the end of the South Cloisters of the main building of University College London in Gower Street. His skeleton is placed in the boardroom for meetings of the college governors and he is recorded in the minutes as being present but not voting. The embalmed head became distorted both with time and from being used as a football by students, so it has now been replaced with a wax effigy. His ghost was said to chase staff around University College Hospital in Gower Street (before it recently moved to Euston Road), while waving his walking stick Dapple at them.

51. John Rann (1750–1774)

Sixteen String Jack, Coppice Row, Theydon Bois, Essex, CM16 7DS
(Tel: 01992 813182). McMullens.

John Rann was a highwayman and dandy, who was tried for his life and acquitted numerous times, before finally going to the gallows. His nickname 'Sixteen String Jack' came from the eight silk ribbons he wore on each of the knees of his breeches, said to be one for each of his acquittals. It was his love of finery that led him into crime to pay for it.

Born in Bath, he earned a living as a lad peddling goods from the back of a donkey. Later, he moved to London where, in 1770, he became a coachman in Portman Square. His wages for this, however, were not sufficient enough to pay for his taste in flowered satin waistcoats, in gambling at cards, and in women who were attracted to him despite the marks left on him from smallpox. When he was sacked he turned to pickpocketing and highway robbery.

In April 1774, he was in the dock for the first time at the Old Bailey accused of highway robbery, but was acquitted. He then befriended a prostitute and receiver of stolen goods, Ellen Roche, with whom he lodged in Covent Garden. At the end of May the same year, they both found themselves in the dock at Bow Street for stealing a watch and some money. Jack wore in his buttonhole a bunch of flowers and a nosegay as big as a birch broom. Again, they were acquitted.

He was arrested for burglary in July and, although once more acquitted, he was warned by the court that he was lucky to escape and should mend his ways. He immediately got drunk and – dressed in a scarlet coat and waistcoat, white silk stockings and a laced hat – he solemnly declared himself on oath as a highwayman. Shortly afterwards, he was arrested for debt and was thrown into Marshalsea Prison. His criminal friends clubbed together to pay the £50 owed and he was free again. But he was arrested for debt once more while drinking in an alehouse in Tottenham Court Road. The impudent Jack managed to persuade the bailiffs to lend him five shillings to buy them a bowl of punch, after which he escaped. By then he was becoming something of a celebrity and huge crowds followed him round when he visited Barnet races dressed in a blue satin waistcoat trimmed with silver.

On 26 September 1774 he stole a watch and some money from a Dr William Bell on the Uxbridge Road near Ealing. Ellen pawned the watch with

Mr Cordy in Oxford Street, who became suspicious and reported the matter. The next day Jack, Ellen and two others were arrested and ended up at the Old Bailey once more. Jack again dressed for the occasion, this time in a pea-green coat and waistcoat, ruffled shirt, white buckskin breeches and a silver laced hat. Rather cocksurely he ordered, in advance, a splendid supper to celebrate yet another expected acquittal with his friends. But they were found guilty: he being sentenced to be hanged and Ellen to 14 years' transportation. The pre-ordered supper thus went cold and uneaten as he went to his cell. But he was later allowed to be visited by seven girls to dine with him in jail. He was the gayest of the party, proposing the toast, 'Let us eat, drink, and be merry, for tomorrow we die.'

He finally made the journey from Newgate to Tyburn on 30 November 1774, where he was strung up, still wearing his sixteen strings. As a poem, framed on the pub wall, concludes:

> The cart drove off from the gallows,
>
> He had now paid for his crime,
>
> As the famous sixteen silk strings fluttered
>
> For the very last time.

52. Sarah Siddons (1755–1831)

47 High Street, Brecon, Wales, LD3 7AP (Tel: 01874 610666).

The great Shakespearean actress Sarah Siddons was born at this pub, then called the Shoulder of Mutton Inn, on 5 July 1755, when her parents were on tour with a troupe of strolling players. She was baptised on 14 July at the nearby Church of St Mary and a few days later was on the road in the company cart heading for her parents' next performance at Llandrindod. Her father Roger Kemble was a Catholic and her mother Sarah was a Protestant. Between them they brought up the boys as Catholics and the girls as Protestants.

Young Sarah's first public performance was at the age of 11, when she and other family members at the Kings Head, High Street, Worcester entertained all those who had purchased packets of a certain brand of tooth powder in a local promotion. Sarah played Rosetta in *Love in a Village* opposite her future husband William Siddons and she sang between the acts.

Siddons was a lowly member of the cast from Birmingham and when Sarah 'bestowed her affections' on him, her father forbade the match and sacked him. At his benefit, coincidentally held in Brecon, he recited a doggerel lamenting the plight of a discarded lover, for which he got his ears boxed by Sarah's mother. Earlier, her father had forbidden her to marry any actor at all. But Sarah doggedly stuck by her choice of man in Siddons. Exasperated, her father exclaimed he was not only a member of a dubious profession but also the worst one in the troupe. 'Exactly,' replied Sarah. 'No one can call him an actor.' Eventually, her father reluctantly gave his consent and the couple married at Trinity Church in Coventry on 26 November 1773.

David Garrick heard of her reputation and hired her for £5 a week at Drury Lane in London in 1775. She was out of work the following year, however, after appearing as Julia in a play called *Blackamoor*, which was damned and caused a riot at one performance. So it was back to touring the provinces and after appearing at Manchester, she became very popular again and finally returned to Drury Lane in 1782.

It was said that her face was so expressive that the passion was communicated to the audience before she spoke. William Hazlitt wrote of her, 'Power was seated on her brow, passion emanated from her breast as from a shrine'. Her salary was increased from £5 to £20 a week and people would queue before breakfast to get tickets to see her. Society portrait artist Sir Joshua Reynolds painted her as the *Tragic Muse* and wrote his signature on the hem of her garment in the picture, explaining, 'I would not lose the honour this opportunity afforded to me for my name going down to posterity on the hem of your garment.' Amid all this adoration and adulation she refused countless requests to attend expensive dinners in order to be with her five children.

In 1783 she played her first Shakespearean role in London as Isabella in *Measure for Measure*. That same year she visited Dr Samuel Johnson and noticed there was no chair for her to sit on. He told her, 'Madam, you who so often occasion a want of seats to other people, will the more easily excuse the want of one yourself.'

When she went to Edinburgh the following year there were 2,575 applications, from as far as Newcastle, in one day for the 630 seats available. On tour in northern England she played the role of a tragic queen, who commits suicide by taking poison. As she raised the cup to her lips the spellbound silence was shattered by a shout of encouragement from the gallery, 'That's reet, Molly. Soop it oop, ma lass, soop it oop.' For just nine performances in Edinburgh she was paid a total of £967, a huge amount of money in those days. Yet she was accused of stinginess for demanding payment for a benefit performance for an actor down on his luck, which led to her being booed off stage at Drury Lane. She returned to deny the charge and was vindicated in the press.

In 1785 she played Lady Macbeth in London for the first time and her performance in the sleepwalking scene has become the standard interpretation ever since. This was the part she played in her last professional performance in 1812; and also the few benefits she did until 1819. In conversation with the poet Samuel Rogers she once mused, 'Perhaps in the next world women will be more valued than they are in this.'

Her ghost is said to haunt the electricity sub-station at 228 Baker Street, overlooking Regents Park in London, where she lived and gave frequent large parties, and died from erysipelas.

53. Jack Fuller (1757–1834)

Jack Fullers, Oxley Green, Brightling, East Sussex, TN32 5HD (Tel: 01424 838212).

'Mad Jack' Fuller was an eccentric builder of follies, providing work for local, unemployed villagers. He was orphaned when very young and the resulting lack of parental control might explain some of his eccentricities.

The family iron foundry at Heathfield meant he was rich and able to live in Brightling Park (called Rose Hill at the time). A bulky man weighing 22 stone, one of his nicknames was 'Hippopotamus'; the others being 'Mad Jack' and 'Honest Jack'. A jolly and rough-spoken man, who wore his hair in a pigtail, he consumed large amounts of beer and port.

His outspoken and boisterous outbursts got him into trouble in Parliament after he was elected MP for East Sussex in 1801. He insulted the speaker as the 'insignificant little man in the wig' and was taken into custody by the Sergeant at Arms in 1810. He then lost interest in politics and did not stand again for re-election. He declined a peerage from William Pitt the Younger, stating, 'I was born Jack Fuller, and Jack Fuller I'll die.' Instead, he threw himself into promoting science and the arts, becoming a founder member of the Royal Institution and becoming a patron of the painter J. M. W. Turner, who painted *Hastings Fishermen on the Sands* and other pictures for him.

When unemployment became high after the Napoleonic wars, Fuller embarked on his massive building programme, with the help of the architect Sir Robert Smirke:

- The Rotunda Temple in Brightling Park is 25 feet high and was said to be used by the unmarried Fuller to entertain ladies of ill repute and to store his wine in the summer. It was also used by smugglers as a hideout and a storing place.

- The Sugar Loaf, also in Brightling Park, was built 35 feet high in one night, so that he could win a bet he had made that the spire of St Giles Church at Dallington could be seen from his grounds.

- The Tower, also 35 feet high, south-east of Brightling was another of his follies.

- The Pillars in Brightling Park were built to mark the grave of his favourite horse.

The biggest provider of employment, however, was the 4 mile long and 6 feet high wall around his estate, for which he paid out a total of £10,000 in wages to numerous labourers over many years. Other projects which were not follies but which provided much needed employment were also financed by him:

- The Observatory, between Brightling and Burwash, was built to serve his interest in astronomy, which was stimulated after Sir William Herschel (1738–1822) discovered Uranus.

- The Obelisk (Brightling Needle), built on the second highest point in Sussex, 646 feet above sea level, north-west of Brightling Park, had a beacon to warn of invasion.

- The Belle Tout Lighthouse on the cliffs of Beachy Head was built in 1831 to prevent ships from running aground; Fuller also provided Eastbourne with its first ever lifeboat.

He was also very generous to the Church of St Thomas-a-Beckett in Brightling, providing it with the largest barrel organ in Britain, nine

bassoons and twelve trombones to accompany the choir, and five new bells. There is a bust of him in this church and in its yard he is buried under a 25 foot high pyramid. It was built from November 1810 to June 1811 and was designed by Sir Robert Smirke, based on the Tomb of Cestius in Rome. Apparently, Fuller twice advertised for hermits to live in it for a year. Local legend has it that Fuller was buried in it, sitting at an iron table, with a bottle of claret and a full meal before him, dressed for dinner and wearing a top hat. Broken glass was strewn on the floor to keep the Devil out.

Jack Fuller's tomb..

54. Robert Burns (1759–1796)

11–13 Townhead Street, Steveston, Ayrshire, KA20 3AQ (Tel: 01294 465102).

Known as the 'Ploughman Poet', Burns started work at the age of 13 thrashing corn on his father's small, infertile farm and at the age of 15 he was its principal labourer. 'I was born a very poor man's son,' he stated, and life was as 'the cheerless gloom of a hermit with the unceasing moil of a galley slave.'

In 1778 he went to a summer school at Kirkoswald, where he learned 'to look unconcernedly on a large tavern bill and mix without fear in a drunken squabble.' Here, he was able to hold his own in logical debate with his supposed social superiors.

In 1781 he went to Irvine (3 miles south of the Steveston pub) to learn flax dressing. 'This turned out a sadly unlucky affair,' he recalled. 'My partner was a scoundrel of the first water, and, to finish the whole business, while we were giving a welcome carousal to the New Year, our shop, by the drunken carelessness of my partner's wife, took fire and burned to ashes, and I was left, like a true poet, not worth a sixpence.' Also while at Irvine the bisexual Burns befriended a sailor named Richard Brown, who 'encouraged him to looser ways' and, according to Burns, 'did me mischief.' He also made 'acquaintances of a freer manner of thinking and living' than he had been used to and afterwards, he stated, 'for three months I was in a diseased state of body and mind, scarcely to be envied by the hopeless wretches who have just got their sentence.' It was Brown who suggested Burns should send his poems (*Corn Rigs* was probably one of them) to magazines, which led to them being published. Burns had been reading the poetry of Robert Fergusson, who became the 'chief formative influence in making him a great poet' while at Irvine. At this time he was also afflicted with 'alarming symptoms of pleurisy' and the first signs of a recurring rheumatic fever.

One of the great loves of his life Mary Campbell, known as 'Highland Mary', lived in the parish. Another woman, Maria Riddel, was greatly offended by his behaviour, probably at a Hogmanay in Irvine, for which he apologised. The gentlemen, over wine, discussed the Rape of the Sabines and decided to enact it when they rejoined the ladies. 'When Robert had carried out his part with hearty despatch and all the latitude that the occasion called for,' according to one report, 'he was stupefied to find himself alone.'

In 1784 he met Jean Armour, who was to become his wife and the mother of many of his children. After she became pregnant with twins in 1786, he signed a legal document agreeing to marry her, which he planned to do after seeking his fortune in Jamaica. But her father destroyed the document and forbade the match, bringing Burns to the verge of insanity. With the money from the publication of his first poems in 1786 he booked his passage to Jamaica, but when the twins (a boy and girl) were born, he decided to stay in Scotland.

He was unaffected by the fame that his poems and songs brought him, suspecting it would be only temporary. He wrote to a friend, 'You will bear me witness that when my bubble of fame was at the highest, I stood unintoxicated with the inebriating cup in my hand, looking forward with rueful resolve to the hastening time when the blow of calamity should dash it to the ground with all the eagerness of vengeful triumph.'

A significant year for Burns was 1788, when he finally married Jean, when they had twin girls who died within a month, and when he started working for the Board of Excise. His views in support of the French Revolution and the American Revolution often threatened his job with the Excise and in 1793, he was suspended for being a 'Friend of the People'. He also got in trouble for responding to a toast to the health of Pitt with a counter one to 'a greater man than Pitt: George Washingon'. He was also accused of sedition for proposing another toast, in the presence of an army captain, that 'may our success in the present war be equal to the justice of our cause' (which he doubted).

Robert Burn's statue over-looking the Thames, on the London Embankment.

In 1791 he had an affair with Anna Park, a barmaid at the Globe Tavern in Dumfries, who gave birth to his daughter Elizabeth, whom Jean took in with her own children. The following year Jean had a daughter, which she also called Elizabeth; Burns, in fact, fathered three daughters of this name, with three different mothers. He certainly liked wassailing and womanising. Of the former, he confessed, 'Occasional hard drinking is the devil to me.' His love of the latter was expressed in his poetry, such as *Nine Inch Will Please a Lady* and his bawdy songs, such as the collection entitled *The Merry Muses of Caledonia*, which were not published uncensored until 170 years after his death. That death came in 1796 from rheumatic heart disease. Jean gave birth to his final son Maxwell on the day of his funeral.

55. William Wilberforce (1759–1833)

(i) Trinity House Lane (corner of Silver Street), Kingston-upon-Hull, East Yorkshire, HU1 2JD (Tel: 01482 586099). Wetherspoon.

(ii) Previously the junction of Dean Street and Forge Lane, East Farleigh, near Maidstone, Kent (now a private house).

The sign of the pub that used to be in East Farleigh, Kent.

The great campaigner for the abolition of slavery William Wilberforce was also a heavy gambler at cards and a taker of opium. He was born at 25 High Street, Hull, which is now the Wilberforce House Slavery Museum (a few minutes walk from the existing pub). There is a statue of him outside the museum and another on a column in Wilberforce Drive. His final days were spent in East Farleigh, Kent, where the previous pub named after him was located.

A few days after his twenty-first birthday he was elected MP for Hull on 11 September 1780. It cost him many hogsheads of ale for the electors, who were confined to the 1,500 freemen of Hull. About 300 of them lived in London, so he had to buy them suppers in 'the different public houses of Wapping'. He held the seat until becoming MP for York in 1784; and he later represented the rotten borough of Bramber in Sussex, without elections, from 1812.

Although a landowner and believer in free markets, he supported government measures to relieve the agricultural poor in times of famine from poor harvests and he also gave £3,000 of his own money to them in 1800 (which would be worth about £160,000 now).

It was at Teston, near East Farleigh, that Wilberforce had the horrors of slavery graphically described to him in 1783 by the rector Rev James Ramsay. He had been a naval chaplain in the West Indies and had seen the slaves brutally beaten, being kept in overcrowded conditions and being fed on near-starvation rations. Wilberforce took up their case with zeal and in 1787, also in Kent, persuaded Prime Minister William Pitt to support the legislation for its abolition. This was when they were walking in the grounds of Pitt's estate at Holwood Park in Keston, near Orpington. Their conversation took place at the root of an old tree, now called Wilberforce Oak, which still stands, with a Wilberforce seat beside it. He spearheaded the campaign and moved the first of his annual motions to Parliament in 1790, where he succeeded in getting the capture and transportation of new slaves abolished in 1807. But it was not until 1833 that the abolition of slavery itself was achieved, just a week before Wilberforce's death. Even then, it was only gradually phased out in the British colonies.

The Wetherspoon's pub in Hull.

Although a Methodist, he became a heavy gambler at cards in London clubs and gave it up for the unusual reason that he was winning too much and felt sorry for the losers. He was a good singer and mimic, who sometimes got into dangerous situations for his cruel impersonations of members of the gentry. An illness that he contracted in 1788 had to be treated with opium and he continued to take it for the next 20 years after the ailment had been cured.

Active in the Society for Bettering the Conditions of the Poor, he also opposed laws which oppressed Catholics and he supported factory reform to limit the working day. He was financially ruined in 1830, after investing in his son William's dairy farm in St John's Wood, London, which failed. Another son, Robert, let him live with him at the Old Vicarage in Lower Road, East Farleigh and was the vicar at the local church from 1832 to 1840. Robert and his brother Henry, who was vicar there from 1843 to 1850, and William's wife are all buried in the church by the south wall.

The pub in the village was previously called the New Inn, being renamed the William Wilberforce in around 1949 or 1950, when William Foster was the landlord and it was owned by Whitbread. The sign showed Wilberforce holding a broken chain of fetters. It was delicensed in about 1980 and is now a private residence called Rivendell. Another Whitbread pub had the same name and sign at the aforementioned Holwood Park.

56. Margaret Catchpole (1762–1819)

Cliff Lane, Ipswich, Suffolk, IP3 0PQ (Tel: 01473 252450). Pubmaster.

Margaret Catchpole was twice sentenced to death: once for horse stealing and once for jail breaking. But she was reprieved on both occasions and was transported for life to Australia.

Born in Ipswich, she became a maid and nurse for Rev Richard Cobbold. Her horsemanship became famous locally when she rode bareback from Nacton to Ipswich to fetch a doctor for her seriously ill mistress.

Margaret then fell in love with a local smuggler called William Laud. In order to meet him in London, she stole one of Rev Cobbold's horses, a strawberry coloured one, in 1797 and rode the 70 miles in ten hours dressed as a young man. But the unusual colour of the horse made it easy for her to be identified and she was arrested. She was sentenced at Bury St Edmunds assizes to be hanged. But Rev Cobbold, whose horse she had stolen, made a powerful appeal on her behalf and she was reprieved and sentenced to transportation for seven years instead. She was locked up in Ipswich Prison awaiting the sentence and incredibly managed to escape. Using just a gardening frame, a linen line and prop, the 5 foot 2 inch woman managed to scale a 22 foot wall topped with spikes.

Mural inside the pub showing Margaret being transported.

Although disguised as a sailor, she was recognised and arrested again in 1799. The following year, she was sentenced to death and reprieved, but this time was transported for life. In 1801, she made the six-month voyage to Botany Bay in New South Wales. There, she made a new start and became a well respected midwife in Hawkesbury, where the local hospital's maternity ward is named after her. She also became a farmer and owned a general store in Hawkesbury.

In 1814 she was granted a pardon, but stayed on in Australia, where she died from influenza, caught from one of her patients, in Newtown, Sidney. Her name lived on through a novel published in 1847 called *The History of Margaret Catchpole, A Suffolk Girl*, by her former employer Rev Richard Cobbold. Telling the story of a criminal being redeemed after transportation, it was based on his first-hand knowledge of her and letters she wrote to him from Australia.

57. William Cobbett (1763–1835)

4 Bridge Square, Farnham, Surrey, GU9 7QR (Tel: 01252 726281). Free house.

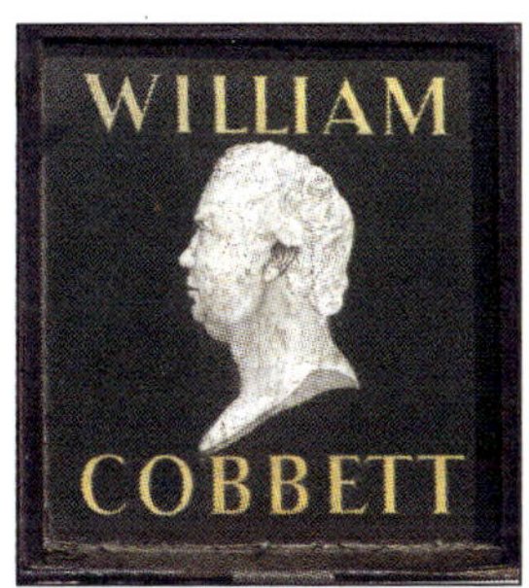

A self-educated farm labourer, who became the leading radical journalist in the movement for parliamentary reform, William Cobbett was born and raised on a small farm, where this pub now stands. His radical campaigns against corruption in high places led to him being imprisoned and exiled for so-called sedition and libel.

His eyewitness accounts of the miserable living conditions of farm workers as he rode on horseback around the country were read by thousands in his own journal *The Political Register*. These accounts were published in book form as *Rural Rides* in 1830, the year of the great labourers' revolt. The revolt spread like wildfire through Surrey and the southern counties and resulted in 19 farm workers being hanged, 481 being transported to Australia and 400 being imprisoned.

When hardly tall enough to climb gates and stiles, Cobbett's first job in the fields was as a bird scarer, protecting turnip seeds and peas. He was then employed weeding wheat, leading a horse at harrowing barley, hoeing peas and finally, ploughing and reaping in the harvest. He also worked in a hop garden a mile away from Farnham at Bourne, which he showed his young son on one of his rural rides on 27 September 1822. He told him how he and the other young workers used to skive off to roll down a nearby sandhill. As they proceeded from there to nearby Wrecklesham, they came across an old childhood friend of his among labourers on 'parish work' (a form of work for dole). This consisted of breaking stones into very small pieces for the roads. Because of the depression, there were hops to be

Cartoon in the pub.

picked, but the farmers could not afford to employ labourers to do the work. Cobbett gave the men some money to buy bread, cheese and beer.

Three years later, on 27 October 1825, he was in the area again with his son and he pointed out his birthplace. He also showed him Waverley Abbey, where he had worked at the age of 8 collecting strawberries ... but ate a good few of them instead of passing them on to his employer Sir Robert Rich. It was near here as a lad that Cobbett had fallen from a tree into the river while trying to get a crow's nest. Another tree he showed his son was a hollow elm with a circumference of 17 feet, which he had seen a huge cat enter; he had then been beaten by his parents for exaggerating its size. But he had later seen a similar one in America - a great wild grey cat species called Lucifee.

At the age of 20 he caught a coach to London and joined the army, where he served for eight years as a sergeant major in Canada. Here, he disapproved of a form of corruption, whereby captains would keep some of the money they had been paid for their soldiers' food rations, meaning that the officers' personal purses fattened as their men starved. His attempts to get this practice stopped made him enemies, who falsely accused him of corruption. When he followed this up by agitating for an increase in soldiers' pay, he had to flee the country to France to avoid imprisonment.

After a spell in America, where he was fined 5,000 dollars for libel in one of his pamphlets, he returned to England in 1800. A couple of years later, he started his famous weekly *Political Register*, which he continued publishing for the rest of his life. He was convicted for libel for one of his outspoken articles in the cause of the Irish and was later imprisoned for two years and fined a massive £1,000 in 1810 for his attacks on flogging in the army. After serving the full two years he came out of prison financially ruined, but threw himself into agitation for reform and saw his Political Register reach an enormous circulation when he reduced its price to tuppence (just under 1p).

His frequent calls in its columns for the abolition of rotten boroughs – parliamentary seats that were bought without election – and the extension of the vote to all male adults led to the government prosecuting him for incitement to sedition in 1831. He defended himself and was discharged by a hung jury. The following year, he was elected as a radical MP for Oldham, where he continued, like the Chartists, demanding universal suffrage, annual parliaments and secret ballots. He also spoke in favour of factory legislation, the cause of the Irish and the relieving of agricultural distress.

On his rural rides he had estimated that the farm labourers produced about fifteen times as much food as they were able to buy on their near-starvation wages of nine shillings a week or less. Seeing a huge abundance of food being produced, he had declared, 'What injustice, what a hellish system it must be, to make those who raise it skin and bone and nakedness, while the food and drink and wool are almost all carried away to be heaped on the fundholders, pensioners, soldiers, dead-weights, and the other swarms of tax-eaters! If such an operation do not need putting an end to, then the devil himself is a saint.'

For the last four years of his life, he leased Normandy Farm near Farnham and on the day before he died, he insisted on being carried around its fields to look at the crops. He died on the farm and was buried in Farnham churchyard.

58. Theobald Wolfe Tone (1763–1798)

(i) Wolfe Tone Tavern, 17 Wolfe Tone Road, Cork, Republic of Ireland.
(ii) Wolfe Tone Square, Bantry, West Cork, Republic of Ireland. Free house.

Theobald Wolfe Tone readily gave his life for the cause of Irish independence. The son of a coach maker, he was born in Dublin as a Protestant, but was one of the founders in 1791 of the Society of United Irishmen, which dedicated itself to uniting Protestants and Catholics in the cause of independence. Originally, it tried to achieve this through constitutional methods, but when it became clear this was impossible, it resorted to armed rebellion.

As a youth he had a weakness for 'good liquor and bad language', as well as a reputation for being 'incorrigibly idle' at Trinity College, from which he was nearly expelled for acting as a second in a duel in which the opponent was killed. After marrying at the age of 22 and having a young daughter, he went to London in 1787 to earn money as a lawyer at No 4 Hare Court,

Wolfe Tone tavern in Cork

Middle Temple. He never opened a law book, however, and after returning to Dublin he gave up the profession.

The anniversary of the capture of the Bastille was celebrated in Belfast in 1791, which was witnessed with interest by Tone, who was becoming an ardent republican. 'To subvert the tyranny of our execrable government, to break the connection with England, the never failing source of all our political evils, and to assert the independence of my country – these were my objects,' he stated. 'To unite the whole people of Ireland, to abolish the memory of all past dissensions, and to substitute the common name of Irishmen in place of the denominations of protestants, catholics, and dissenters – these were my means.'

In 1792 he became assistant secretary of 'a club of United Irishmen' in Dublin, which was declared illegal by the government, but this was overruled in the courts. He discussed the possibility of gaining the assistance of revolutionary France in Ireland with his comrades, but when arrests were made in 1795, he fled to America, where he ran a small farm. While in America, he approached the French and in 1796, he sailed from New York to France, where he stayed at the Hotel des Etrangers, Rue Vivienne, Paris.

On 15 December a fleet of seventeen French ships carrying 15,000 soldiers, including Tone, who was an adjutant general in the French army, set off from Brest for the coast of Kerry. But a storm sprang up just as they were about to land and they were forced to retreat. Another attempt was made in September 1798, when just 1,000 soldiers sailed, and it landed at Lough Swilly on 10 October. They were heavily outnumbered and routed by the English. Indeed, Tone's brother Matthew was captured and executed and Tone himself was captured in French uniform.

At his trial he proclaimed, 'From my earliest youth I have regarded the connection between Ireland and Great Britain as the curse of the Irish nation, and felt convinced, that while it lasted, this country would never be free or happy.

'In consequence, I determined to apply all the powers which my individual efforts could move, in order to separate the two countries.

'That Ireland was not able, of herself, to throw off the yoke, I knew. I therefore sought for aid wherever it was to be found ... Under the flag of the French republic I originally engaged with a view to save and liberate my own country.

'For that purpose I have encountered the chances of war amongst strangers: for that purpose I have repeatedly braved the terrors of the ocean, covered as I knew it to be with the triumphant fleets of that Power which it was my glory and my duty to oppose.

'I have sacrificed all my views in life; I have courted poverty; I have left a beloved wife unprotected, and children which I adored, fatherless.

'After such sacrifices, in a cause which I have always considered as the cause of justice and freedom – it is no great effort at this day to add the sacrifice of my life.'

He asked to be shot as a soldier rather than hanged. When this was rejected, he cut his own throat with a penknife. He was buried at Bodestown Churchyard in Kildare, where his father Peter had become a farmer after becoming bankrupt.

59. Fletcher Christian (1764–c. 1793)

Fletcher Christian Tavern, 55 Main Street, Cockermouth, Cumbria, CA13 9JS (Tel: 01900 825856).

Probably the world's most famous mutineer, Fletcher Christian was born at Moorland Close, near Cockermouth, and was educated at Cockermouth Free Grammar School. He continued his studies at St Bees School near

Whitehaven (12 miles south-west of Cockermouth) and was probably there when the coastal town was raided by the celebrated pirate John Paul Jones.

At the age of 13, the Christian family went bankrupt and Fletcher and his younger brother were taken by their mother to the Isle of Man, where they had many relations, having descended from the Manx family of Milntown. This was in 1780, when another seafarer was on the island meeting his wife for the first time. His name was William Bligh ... whom Fletcher led the mutiny against on HMS *Bounty* in 1789. Bligh and Christian met on the Isle of Man, becoming firm friends, and Fletcher decided to follow a career at sea.

In April 1783, he signed up as a midshipman on the *Eurydice* at Spithead and was rapidly made up to acting lieutenant. He came under the command of his friend Lieutenant Bligh in 1786 on the *Britannia*. The pair's fateful voyage to the South Pacific on the *Bounty* started from Spithead in September 1787, with Christian as the master's mate. He was promoted to acting lieutenant and second in command in March 1788. The main purpose of the voyage was to collect fruit and plants, especially bread fruit trees from the South Sea Islands, to be planted in the West Indies.

They sailed via the Cape of Good Hope and Van Diemen's Land and reached Tahiti in October 1788. The islanders showed them great hospitality and many of the crew took advantage of this to form sexual liaisons with the women. In April 1789, however, Bligh ordered them to set sail again. Bligh became increasingly irritable, especially after an incident at Nomuka, when he took some islanders hostage to demand the return of some stolen articles, but had to release them without the goods being returned. This incident had echoes of the one which led to the death of Captain Cook, detailed elsewhere, with whom Bligh had sailed.

Fletcher had been the butt of Bligh's temper for some time, but the spark which finally ignited his fuse was to be accused by the captain, in front of the entire crew, of stealing some coconuts in the night. He decided to leave the Bounty on a hastily built raft. But when it became clear others were equally resentful of Bligh's despotic behaviour, the plan was adapted ... so Bligh ended up on the raft instead on 28 April. When Bligh resisted, according to his own account, Christian 'changed the cutlass he had in his hand for a bayonet, that was brought to him, and, holding me with a strong grip by the cord that tied my hands, he with many oaths threatened to kill me immediately if I would not be quiet.'

Bligh and eighteen other crew members were given 28 gallons of water, 150 lbs of pork, 6 quarts of rum, 6 bottles of wine, bread, a quadrant and compass. Amazingly, they managed to navigate the small craft 4,000 miles to the Dutch colony of Coupang. From there, Bligh reached Portsmouth in March 1790, less than a year after being set adrift, where a court martial cleared him of any misconduct and promoted him to vice-admiral.

Christian, along with eight mutineers, had sailed the Bounty back to Tahiti, where they picked up their lovers and six Polynesian men and their wives. They then cruised around the islands to the west, before heading south in search of obscurity, trying, unsuccessfully, to colonise the island of Tubuai. Eventually, they settled on Pitcairn Island, which in those days was either uncharted on British maps or was inaccurately located on them, and tales spread that they lived a life of paradise on the island under Christian's leadership.

In 1810, however, John Adams the last survivor of the mutineers on the island was found and he claimed Christian, whom he said was leader and sole cause of the mutiny, had been killed by Tahitans four years after they landed. Another mutineer, however, Peter Heywood (one of those to be captured and found guilty but not executed) was convinced he saw Christian in Devonport in 1808. This supported a story that Christian had escaped from Pitcairn Island in 1808 and had visited his relatives in Cockermouth later that year and in 1809. Fletcher's elder brother Edward, who was an attorney, defended the reputation of his brother and the other mutineers, three of whom were hanged, by unearthing records to show that Bligh was a

Picture in the Fletcher Christian Tavern of Capt. Bligh being cast adrift after the mutiny on the Bounty.

tyrant, who drove his men to insubordination. A debate between Edward and Bligh took place through a series of pamphlets, until Bligh died in 1817 at the age of 63.

60. Daniel Lambert (1770–1809)

20 St Leonards Street, Stamford, Lincolnshire, PE9 2HN.

The most corpulent man to have his bulk authentically corroborated at the time, Daniel Lambert died in a Stamford pub weighing 52 stone 11 pounds. He was 5 feet 11 inches tall, 3 feet 1 inch round each leg and 9 feet 4 inches round the waist. It took 112 feet of elm to make his coffin, which was put on wheels to roll him down the hill from the Waggon and Horses Inn, where he died, to St Martin's church, to be buried.

Another local link is that his father, who later becoming a jail keeper in Leicester where Daniel was born, had been a huntsman for the Earl of Stamford. After being apprenticed in the engraved button trade in Birmingham, Daniel took over from his father at Bridewell Prison, Leicester in 1791, when he was a normal weight, being a keen walker, swimmer and sportsman. But his body ballooned to 32 stone by 1793 and by 1805, he was too big to do his job properly and resigned on an annuity of £50 a year, which was granted in recognition of his 'wise and humanitarian nature'.

At first he found his weight a matter of annoyance, but in 1806 he decided to make some capital out of it and went to London in a specially constructed carriage to put himself on show in Piccadilly, and the following year in Leicester Square. He became a very popular attraction. One journal noted, 'When sitting he appears to be a stupendous mass of flesh, for his thighs are so covered by his belly that nothing but his knees are to be seen, while the flesh of his legs, which resemble pillows, projects in such a manner as to nearly bury his feet.'

Quick-witted he was skilled at repartee. After his success in London he went on tour and had been to Cambridge and Huntingdon in June 1809, before reaching Stamford where, according to the local paper, he 'attained the acme of mortal hugeness' and died from fatty degeneration of the heart. His walking stick and a portrait of him are held in the nearby George Hotel,

A giant appetite...the menu in the Daniel Lambert.

a suit of his clothes are on display in Stamford Town Hall and a waistcoat of his lies in Kings Lynn Museum. His portrait also adorned many tavern signs in London and the East Midlands for a time. This pub (previously known as The Reindeer) took the title in the 1980s.

61. William Wordsworth (1770–1850)

The Wordsworth, Main Street, Cockermouth, Cumbria, CA13 9JS
(Tel: 01900 822757). Punch Taverns.

The poet laureate William Wordsworth was born a few hundred yards from this bar at what is now Wordsworth House on the corner of Main Street and Low Sand Lane. He went to school in the town, where he learned very little, his mother remarking on his 'stiff, moody, and violent temper', which she prophesied would be harnessed for great good or evil. Full of audacity, he greatly resented being punished for it, so he fully appreciated the liberty he was allowed at nearby Hawkshead Grammar School, where he went at the age of 8 years old. It was here that he went on lonely strolls in awe of the mountains, which were to inspire his poetry. He also went rambling, fishing, boating, bird-nesting, riding and skating. Even more freedom was allowed him at St John's College in Cambridge from 1787 to 1790, after which he and a companion set off on foot, with just a few belongings tied in a handkerchief, to tour Europe.

In France he was very much fired with enthusiasm for the ideals of the revolution and he also had a daughter by a French woman called Annette Vallon. He befriended an ardent republican Michel de Beaupuy, who showed him starving peasants, whose poverty they were fighting against, a cause he became converted to. Wordsworth's eyes glowed with 'remarkable fire' according to his radical friends, including James Leigh Hunt, William Hazlitt and Thomas de Quincey. In fact, it was the poverty of the French peasants that Wordsworth condemned in his first published poems in 1793, followed by a letter in support of the revolution and the principles of *Rights of Man* by Thomas Paine. Coleridge described Wordsworth at this time as 'a republican, and at least a semi-atheist'. The government thought both Wordsworth and Coleridge sufficiently revolutionary to be spied upon.

In 1802, Wordsworth married Mary Hutchinson and they had five children, including John, who became Vicar of Brigham, near

Cockermouth. Wordsworth gradually became respectable and conservative, supporting the Tory party and repressive measures introduced to suppress popular discontent and opposing Catholic emancipation and the Reform Bill. He also became a little pompous, once boasting to Charles Lamb, 'I could write like Shakespeare if I had a mind to.' Lamb quickly rejoindered, 'So it is only the mind that is lacking.'

Asked at a party the funniest thing he had ever said, Wordsworth recalled it was when a Dalesman he met walking near Grasmere asked if he had seen his wife anywhere along the road and he had answered, 'My good man, I did not even know that you had a wife.'

His poems never really sold in great numbers until 1837, when an American edition came out with a print run of 20,000. In 1843 the

government decided he had become safe enough to be the new poet laureate, but he only agreed to it on being assured no official verses would be required from him. For the inauguration ceremony before Queen Victoria, he had to borrow some breeches from fellow poet Samuel Rogers, somewhat smaller than him, and he only just managed to squeeze into them. But they were so tight that when he knelt down before the queen, he had to be helped up again.

He is buried in Grasmere, where he lived at Dove Cottage, Town End, from 1799 for the rest of his life.

62. Elizabeth Wallbridge (1770–1801)

The Dairyman's Daughter, Craft Village, Sandown Road, Arreton, Isle of Wight, PO30 3AA (Tel: 01983 539361). Free house.

The conversion of Elizabeth Wallbridge from an 'evil, carnal, selfish, and ungodly' young woman to a most devout Methodist was told in a nineteenth century best seller. Originally issued as a tract in 1841, *The Dairyman's Daughter* by Rev Leigh Richmond, vicar of the neighbouring parish of Brading, finally sold over ten million copies and was translated into dozens of languages. Following her early death from consumption, she was buried at St George's Church in Arreton, where her grave was visited by thousands after the publication of the book.

As a child, she lived with her family in a little cottage on the south side of Sandown Road, where her father was a dairyman, and she left home to work 'in service'. Until the age of 26 she was, in her own words, 'wilful, proud, selfish and irreligious' and 'a fallen, depraved, careless soul'. Betsy, as she was known, was also 'fond of dress and finery' and one particular Sunday, she went to a local church to show off her new dress,

which lacked 'a modest sense of propriety and decency'. The visiting preacher, a ship's chaplain, gave as his text, 'Be ye clothed with humility', whereupon she looked at her gay dress and 'blushed for shame on account of my pride'. After that she became 'quite an altered creature', reading the Bible and becoming 'quite sober'.

When her younger sister died, Betsy returned to the family home to help her 70-year-old father to run his dairy; he relied on day labour and the keeping of a few cows on a few acres of rented ground to make a living. Her father was described in Rev Richmond's booklet as 'a venerable old man, whose long hoary hair and deeply wrinkled countenance commanded more than common respect'. He needed a walking stick and had bent shoulders and a feeble gait. Rev Richmond buried Betsy's younger sister and at the funeral he prayed 'that the poor may become rich in faith, and the rich be made poor in spirit'.

Soon afterwards, Betsy developed consumption (tuberculosis) and Rev Richmond observed, 'The pale, wasting consumption, which is the Lord's instrument for removing so many thousands every year from the land of the living, made hasty strides on her constitution.' In dying she 'departed with a smile' and was decorated with leaves and flowers in the coffin. The inscription on her gravestone reads:

> Stranger, if e'er by chance or feeling led
>
> Upon this hallowed turf thy footsteps tread,
>
> Turn from the contemplation of this sod,
>
> And think of those whose spirit rests with God.

This pub has its own Scarecrow Brewery on the premises.

63. Daniel O'Connell (1775–1847)

22 Aston Quay (southern end of O'Connell Bridge), Dublin 2. Free house.

Known as 'the Liberator', Daniel O'Connell was responsible for the Catholic Emancipation Act being passed in 1829 and as an agitator, he drew crowds of up to a million for further reform. He became a radical when he was a law student attending the trial of Thomas Hardy on trumped-up charges of treason in London in 1794. As a qualified lawyer, O'Connell later proved remarkably successful at defending those accused of terrorist offences. This rankled with the establishment and they may have encouraged John Norcot D'Esterre (an officer of the Marines and 'one of the surest shots that ever fired a pistol') to challenge O'Connell to a duel over a mild criticism of Dublin corporation in 1815.

O'Connell accepted and hundreds turned up to watch the event on the snow-covered ground at Bishop's Court, just outside Dublin. D'Esterre took the first shot, but it hit the ground by his opponent's feet. O'Connell then shot him in the thigh, with the intention of wounding him. D'Esterre died the next day and O'Connell vowed never to take part in a duel again and he granted a pension to the widow. He kept his word and refused all challenges, including one from Disraeli, after they had traded insults.

In 1823, O'Connell founded the Catholic Association and later the Campaign for Catholic Emancipation. A by-election in County Clare was called in 1828 and O'Connell stood against the government because it was not pledged to emancipation. O'Connell won, but was not allowed to take his seat in Parliament, because he was a Catholic. The resulting furore led to emancipation being enacted the following year.

He and his followers were crucial in voting through the Reform Bill in 1832, but afterwards he became opposed to social reforms, such as limiting the use of child labour and establishing minimum rates of pay. While he opposed the transportation of the Tolpuddle Martyrs in England, he denounced trade unions in Ireland. And while he condemned slavery as 'abominable', he abstained in a debate when the choice was put between expensive sugar grown by free men and cheap sugar grown by slaves.

In 1843 his campaign in Ireland for repeal of the union with England drew huge crowds: half a million came to hear him at Mallow, three-quarters of a million at Mullaghmast and a whole million at Tara. The stage was set for an even larger final rally in Dublin on Sunday 8 October and people set off from all over Ireland for it. The government banned it at the last minute, but in practice it would have been impossible to contain so many people. Instead of challenging the ban, O'Connor called off the demonstration. Not only did he lose public credibility for this, but he was also arrested for making seditious speeches and 'attempting to alter the constitution by force'. A hand-picked jury, which excluded any Catholics or supporters of repeal, found him guilty and he was sentenced to a year in prison, of which he served six months.

O'Connor's climbdown meant that the British government did not have to quell disorder in Ireland and was therefore able to concentrate all its forces on repressing the Chartist campaign for universal suffrage in England. O'Connor himself seemed proud of this, stating that the government was only able to contain Chartism, 'because the troops which were necessary to struggle against rebellion, sedition and treason in England were not required to maintain the good order which prevailed in Ireland.' His reputation was further diminished by his inactivity during the so-called famine of 1845. Throughout this four-year potato famine the Irish were producing enough other food to feed themselves more than twice over, but they had to export most of it to pay rent to absentee landlords in England. A movement to withhold the rent instead of starving was opposed by O'Connell; his son John, also an MP, said, 'I thank God I live among a people who would rather die of hunger than defraud their landlords of rent!'.

Daniel O'Connell's statue in Dublin's O'Connell Street.

O'Connell put his faith in the English government, appealing to it to stop the export of corn out of Ireland and to impose a tax on landlords. It refused the export ban and imposed a tax on landlords based on the number of tenants they had, which resulted in them evicting their tenants and burning their houses. Subsequently, a million and a half Irish people starved to death.

A dispirited man, O'Connell left Ireland for the last time in January 1847 and set off for Rome, where he wished to die and be buried. He reached as far as Genoa before dying, but his heart was taken to the vaults of Glasnevin Cemetery in Rome. A statue of him stands in O'Connell Street, Dublin.

64. Humphry Davy (1778–1829)

Sir Humphry Davy, 32 Alverton Street, Penzance, Cornwall, TR18 2QN
(Tel: 01736 362013). St Austell.

Born and educated in Penzance, Sir Humphry Davy is today best known for the miners' safety lamp he invented, which saved thousands of lives by preventing pit explosions from firedamp. This he did in 1815, by which time he was already famous for founding the science of electrochemistry and for discovering six new elements (including potassium, sodium and chlorine).

The son of a wood carver, he went to Penzance Grammar School, where he acquired a reputation for being precocious and lazy. He possessed a remarkable memory, however, which he used to address crowds from a cart in the market place on the subjects of his latest reading ... aged just 8.

The folklore of Penzance was a particular interest of his and he became a storyteller of it. 'The applause of my companions was my recompense for punishments incurred for being idle,' he commented. He also stated, 'I consider it fortunate I was left much to myself as a child, and put upon no particular plan of study ... What I am I made myself.'

He composed poems and ballads from the age of 17 about local landmarks, such as Mount's Bay and St Michael's Mount. About the same time, he acquired a taste for experimental science, being encouraged by a local Quaker saddler Robert Dunkin, who demonstrated the rudiments of science with an electrical machine that he had constructed.

In 1795, the year after his father's death, Humphry became an apprentice to Penzance surgeon John Bingham Borlase, acting as a chemist. John Tonkin, who had adopted Humphry's mother when she was a child, allowed the youngster to experiment in his garret, much to the alarm of the neighbours, who feared he would blow them all up. His eldest sister complained her dresses were ruined by corrosive substances as part of his experiments.

Humphry moved to Bristol to work for the Pneumatic Institution experimenting on the pain-relieving qualities of various gases. Indeed, he discovered that laughing gas (oxide of azote or nitrous oxide) could be used as an anaesthetic when made pure, using a specific method he discovered. To test it, he breathed it for nearly seven minutes and it 'absolutely intoxicated me'. Other experiments of breathing in gases nearly killed him, when one mixed with air formed nitrous acid and severely injured his mucous membrane. When breathing carburetted hydrogen gas, he 'seemed sinking into annihilation' and took several hours to recover.

When Gregory Watt (son of James Watt, the inventor who developed the steam engine) lodged at the house of Humphry's mother, he taught him more about chemistry and in return, he examined Humphry's researches into heat and light and helped to get them published in 1799.

In 1801 he went to London as director of the chemical laboratory, assistant lecturer in chemistry and assistant editor of journals for the Royal Institution. A year later, he became its professor of chemistry and a year after that, he was elected a fellow of it. His versatility was shown in 1805 though, when he wrote a prologue to a comedy performed at Drury Lane, and he was promoted to director of his laboratory at a salary four times what he had been earning four years earlier.

A couple of years later in 1807, he was elected as secretary of the Royal Institution and worked on developing the chemical action of the voltaic battery. Later that same year, he was able to report, 'I have decomposed and recomposed the fixed alkalis (potash and soda), and discovered their bases to be two new inflammable substances (potassium and sodium) very like metals, but one of them lighter than the other, and infinitely more combustible; so that there are two bodies decomposed, and two new elementary bodies found.'

Soon after this, John Children constructed a great battery and the Royal Institution followed suit with an even more powerful one, which Davy used to demonstrate the existence of chlorine as a new element, which could be used as a bleaching agent.

He gave a lecture to the Royal Society about his discoveries in electricity, which made him famous throughout Europe and led to the Institute of France awarding him the Napoleonic Prize. At the end of this momentous year he became severely ill for several months while disinfecting Newgate Prison.

His international reputation grew and he was given an honorary degree from Trinity College in Dublin after a lecture on the application of chemistry to agriculture. He then went to Italy to experiment in producing a torpedo and shocked the dignitaries there by how meanly he was dressed.

Back in London, he was approached by Rev Gray to do something about the destruction of human life from explosions in coal mines. Davy immediately experimented on specimens of firedamp from Newcastle and two months later, in October 1815, he had produced a safety lamp that surrounded the flame with wire gauze. This contained the gas explosion within the lamp. At about the same time, George Stephenson invented a

Humphry Davy's statue in Penzance.

different type of safety lamp, but it was Davy's that was adopted in the mines.

When the Geological Society of Cornwall was formed in Penzance, he backed it financially and contributed a paper on the geology of the county. He was well liked locally as a benevolent and amiable man. He encouraged a young blacksmith's son Michael Faraday (1791–1867), for example, as his assistant, who went on to invent the first electric motor and became hailed as the 'father of the electrical industry'.

In 1820, Davy was elected as president of the Royal Society and three years later was asked to invent a way of preventing the copper bottoms of ships from decaying. He came up with zinc protectors, which were installed on royal navy ships. Unfortunately, they later proved to attract large numbers of shellfish, which caused another problem.

An apoplectic attack paralysed him in 1826, forcing him to resign as the Royal Society President and he then went to Italy to recover, where he discovered a new species of eel, which linked the ancient muraena and the conger.

A skilful angler, he wrote a book about fly fishing before dying in Geneva, where he is buried in Plain-Palais Cemetery. There is a tablet to his memory by a window dedicated to him in Westminster Abbey and there is also a white marble statue of him, which was erected in 1872 at Penzance.

The pub named after him has the Latin motto *Igne constricto vita* (constricting fire saves life) on its sign and it also has a poem written by E. C. Bentley in 1905 displayed in the doorway, which reads:

Sir Humphry Davy

abominated gravy,

he lived in the odium

of having discovered sodium.

65. Tom Cribb (1781–1848)

36 Panton Street (corner of Oxendon Street, between Leicester Square and Haymarket), London, SW1Y 4EA (Tel: 0207 839 3801). Shepherd Neame.

Old sign

Tom Cribb, born in Hanham near Bristol, became the British boxing champion in the bare-knuckle days of 1809, when he beat Jem Belcher in the thirty-first round on a wintry day on Epsom Downs. In the crowd was the Duke of Clarence, whom Tom later acted for as a bodyguard at his coronation as King William IV. Cribb had been near defeat several times during this fight, but was saved by his renowned resilience.

And he certainly needed to draw on this ability to recover when beating the black American boxer Tom Molineaux in 1810 on Copthall Common near East Grinstead; Molineaux and his cornerman Bill Richmond were the first black boxers to challenge for the world championship and both were beaten by Cribb. In the twenty-eighth round, Cribb appeared to be beaten three times, before being knocked heavily to the ground. After the thirty seconds that was allowed to contestants in those days to regain their feet, Cribb failed to respond to the referee's call. Cribb's second Jem Ward rushed across the ring and accused Bill Richmond of putting two bullets in Molineaux's fists to increase his punching power. It took four minutes for this to be proved untrue, but they were vital for Cribb to recover, while the American shivered in the cold wet weather. This is one of the earliest recorded acts of gamesmanship – similar to the ripped glove of Cassius Clay, later Muahammad Ali, in 1963, which gave him time to recover after he had been floored by Henry Cooper.

Nearly an hour later in the thirty-third round, Molineaux sank slowly to the ground and told Richmond through swollen, blood-splattered lips that he could fight no more. Cribb was rewarded with the first ever boxing title belt, made from lion skin, which was presented to him by King George III.

A rematch with Molineaux was arranged for the following year, but Cribb realised he would have to be a lot fitter and lighter (he weighed 16 stone) if he was not to risk defeat. Captain Barclay Allardyce became his trainer and took him to Scotland. On the second day, Allardyce made him walk 60 miles to get something to eat. After nine weeks, he lost 3 stone and was ready for the fight. He was so transformed that when Molineaux saw him in the ring, he did not recognise him and declared, 'This is not

New sign

Master Cribb. This is a strange man whom I do not know.' He later admitted it had completely undermined his confidence.

This time, Cribb won more comfortably, breaking his opponent's jaw in the nineteenth round, and with his prize money bought the Union Arms (the pub now named after him), which had been there since 1785. He retired as champion in 1820.

Earlier he had left home for London at the age of 13 and got a job unloading barges at the wharves. This was dangerous work and twice he was nearly killed in accidents. Once, he fell between two coal barges and became trapped and another time he slipped while carrying a heavy package of oranges, which crushed his chest, after which he was spitting blood for several days. After a spell in the navy he returned to London in 1804 and started fighting publicly in January 1805. For only his second purse he received 40 guineas, which was a small fortune in those days.

George Nichols was one of the few to beat him, but Cribb dispatched the likes of Ikey Pig, George Maddox, Tom Blake and Jem Belcher on his way to the top. After retiring from the ring he became a coal merchant and ran the Union Arms, before having to hand it over to his creditors when made bankrupt in 1839. He died in 1848 and was buried at St Mary's Church in Woolwich. A monument to him in this churchyard overlooks the Woolwich Ferry.

66. George Stephenson (1781–1848)

Great Lime Road (by railway bridge), West Moor, Newcastle-upon-Tyne, Tyne & Wear, NE12 7NJ (Tel: 0191 2681073). Scottish & Newcastle.

The 'father of the railways', George Stephenson built his early steam engines when living and working about 500 yards from this pub. This was from 1804 to 1822, when he was working as a mechanical engineer at West Moor Pit in Killingworth's Highpoint Colliery and living alongside it at Dial Cottage, Great Lime Road. This cottage was filled with material for his experiments in order to develop new engines and his obvious talents led to him being promoted to engine wright in 1812. It was behind this cottage, on the wagon way, which crossed the road to its east, that he constructed his first locomotive called Blucher in 1814, which could pull 30 tons uphill at 4 miles an hour.

The following year, he invented a safety lamp that did not explode when used near highly flammable gases in the mines, at about the same time as a separate safety lamp was invented by Humphry Davy. But Stephenson devoted his main energy into making more powerful and more comfortable locomotives, constructing a further sixteen while at Killingworth.

At the end of his time in the area he was rewarded with the job of overseeing the construction of the Stockton to Darlington railway line and designing its first locomotive called Locomotion. This was built by Robert Stephenson and Co., the world's first locomotive building company in the world, set up by him and his son in Forth Street, Newcastle. The line was opened in front of huge crowds on 27 September 1825 and the 9 mile journey took just under two hours. And so Stephenson became known as 'father of the railways'.

His fame spread even further when his steam engine The Rocket won a race at Rainhill, just east of Liverpool, in 1829, which was held to decide which one would be used on the new Liverpool–Manchester railway line. The Rocket won hands down, with a world record speed of 35 miles per hour, and he gained a prize of £500. The line opened in 1830 and was the first to carry passengers rather than cargo.

After that, Stephenson went from strength to strength, being chief engineer on most of the lines laid in the 1830s, and he was also adviser on the Belgian state railway, the first continental railway operated solely by steam. He also won the battle with his rival Brunel over whether or not the gauge of the new lines should be narrow or broad. Stephenson's view that they should be narrow prevailed.

He was born in the Northumberland colliery village of Wylam (about 7 miles west of Newcastle) and as a child he was employed as a cowherd. At the age of 17 he followed in his father's footsteps and became a fireman on the colliery's pumping engine. He taught himself to read and write and progressed to

The cottage where Stephenson lived and constructed his first locomotive.

working on steam-driven winding engines that hauled the coal wagons, which had fascinated him since childhood. This helped him secure the job in Killingworth, where he moved with his first wife Frances Henderson and their baby son Robert. Sadly, Frances (known as Fanny) died two years later in 1806 from tuberculosis. Stephenson married again twice. His later success enabled him to buy Tapton House, near Chesterfield, in 1838, where he retired. In the last year of his life, he founded the Institution of Mechanical Engineers.

The pub which has taken his name is right next to the bridge which supports the main east coast railway line from London to Aberdeen. In 2004, it won the Best Beer Pub of the Year award, thanks to its Rivet Catcher beer from the local Jarrow Brewery.

67. Dolly Peel (1782–1857)

137 Commercial Road (corner of Portberry Way), South Shields, Tyne & Wear, NE33 1SQ (Tel: 0191 427 1441).

Known as 'Queen of the Smugglers', Dolly Peel not only smuggled brandy and cigars, but she also smuggled fugitive sailors out of the hands of the

press gangs, by hiding them under her voluminous petticoats. From a seafaring family, she became a fishwife hawking fish in the town.

One day, her husband Ralph, also described as Cuthbert, was being chased by a press gang, when he reached home – the top floor of a house in Shadwell Street (since renamed Wapping Street), where Dolly was born – just ahead of his pursuers. When the gang broke in, Dolly, who was a large woman, barred their way upstairs. They tried to force their way past her 'but their efforts were unavailing for she possessed phenomenal strength and the muscles of a man'. She kept them at bay long enough for her husband to make his escape through a window on to the roof. He was captured later, however, and forced on to a man-o'-war ship destined to fight in the Napoleonic wars.

Dolly, alarmed at losing her breadwinner, decided to join him and so stowed away on the same ship. She had a nerve of iron and on being discovered was put into service in the cockpit, where crude surgery was performed on wounded sailors, in the height of battle, and her fighting spirit became admired. There, she cooked for and tended the wounded.

On her return to South Shields she became known as a 'Robin Hood figure', selling fish by day and smuggling by night. She became notorious for being able to obtain anything that was ordered – mostly brandy, tobacco, cigars, lace and scent – from 'sundry shady looking luggers' that landed the contraband at Marsden Beach. From there, it was transferred to a large cave just south of where Marsden Grotto now stands. It was then delivered to customers under the very noses of the excise men as Dolly once more showed her steely nerve.

Her infamy spread and a play was written about her activities, which was performed for many years. Indeed, she herself wrote poems and songs, even though she had received no formal education, including one about the loss of a Sunderland ship called the Dove. She was also a good storyteller. Another facet of her ability to entertain was to pretend to sell boxes of pills in the market place and to imitate the sales patter of quack doctors. She also had a talent for repartee. When one man told her 'you're a bonny canary', she riposted, 'I'm not a canary, you impudent fellow, I'm a water wagtail, ye may see by my feather.' Apart from her huge size, she also had 'an awkward gait and stentorian voice'.

In later years she became a well-known figure in the market place, standing aside noted characters of the day. She died aged 75 after a bad attack of bronchitis. On 29 April 1987, a statue of her was unveiled near her birthplace overlooking the Tyne, about a mile from the pub. It was sculpted in solid concrete by local shipyard worker Bill Gofton, then aged 36, in his home at Coston Drive. There is also a portrait of her in South Shields Central Library.

Statue of Dolly Peel overlooking the Tyne.

68. Peter de Wint (1784–1849)

De Wint, Moorland Avenue (corner of Tritton Road), Lincoln, LN6 7JJ (Tel: 01522 681521).

The water colourist Peter de Wint was imprisoned for a short while in 1803 for refusing to reveal that his fellow apprentice engraver William Hilton had run away to Lincoln. It was an offence to break apprenticeships in those days and the engraver who was their employer,

John Raphael Smith in London's Covent Garden, had no compunction about prosecuting de Wint for aiding and abetting this escape. In 1806, de Wint legally broke off his own apprenticeship, which had started in 1802, by paying Smith compensation of £300 and by agreeing to produce nine pictures for him each year for the next two years.

De Wint, born of Dutch parents in Stone, Staffordshire, married Hilton's sister Harriet from Lincoln in 1810 and the three of them shared several addresses in London. De Wint took on several pupils and became one of the most influential water colourists in the country. His subjects were mainly scenic views in the north and east, especially around Lincoln, where his wife's parents lived. One critic said, 'De Wint's brush strokes are like dragon flies skimming the solemn well of truth.' And leading critic John Ruskin said, 'De Wint despises all rules of composition, hates old masters and humbug, synonymous terms with him.' The artist Henry Fuseli said the best way to look at de Wint's rural scenes was with a pot of porter, while the novelist D. H. Lawrence said, 'To copy a nice de Wint is the most soothing thing I can do.'

He befriended the poets John Keats and John Clare, whose works he illustrated. When the latter was committed to a mental asylum, de Wint contributed to his expenses and visited him regularly. Clare expressed his gratitude by writing a sonnet to de Wint in his book, The Rural Muse. Although generous in many ways, de Wint resented dealers and middlemen taking a cut, so instead he tried to sell direct to patrons by putting on exhibitions himself.

One client was continually bemoaning the fact that the pictures he wished to buy always seemed to have 'sold' tags on them. De Wint suspected this was just an excuse not to buy anything and so played a trick on him at the next private showing. The client predictably pointed at a selection of pictures and said, 'Those are exactly the things I would like to possess, what a pity they are sold.' De Wint caught him out by replying, 'My dear fellow, I knew you would like them, so I put a ticket on them to keep them for you.' Many of his original works are held in the Usher Art Gallery in Lindum Road, Lincoln.

69. Sarah Moore (1787–1867)

57–59 Elm Road, Leigh-on-Sea, Essex, SS9 1SP (Tel: 01702 478164). Marstons.

Legendary 'sea witch' Sarah Moore was said to be able to curse pregnant women so that their babies were born with harelips and to burn people by flashing sparks from her eyes. She had a hare lip herself, as well as being dirty and toothless, with a hard, weather-beaten face and a hooked nose.

In August 1849, when already a widow, her only two sons George and John both died in a cholera epidemic. Miserable and lonely, she drowned her sorrows in gin and became increasingly bitter. A year later, she grew resentful of five local young mothers having newborn babies, so she cooked up a satanic brew in her copper pot and poured it on the doorsteps of all five of them. The register of St Clement's Church shows that all five babies died from 4 to 24 September 1850: Michael Going (five months old), Mark Osborne (six months old), Gertrude Le Grys (two months old), Elizabeth Lucking (infant) and John Thomas Axcel (six weeks old).

In the same year, she met a pregnant woman called Eliza Meddle and offered to tell her the sex of the baby in return for a few coins. Eliza rejected the offer, adding, 'I have got better things to do with my money than give it to you for gin.' Angrily, Sarah told Eliza she would have twins and that both would have harelips like her. When Eliza slapped Sarah's face, she added another curse that she and all her female descendants would have to bring up their children alone. Sure enough, three months later, Eliza gave birth to twins Elizabeth and William, both with harelips. William died of smallpox when his son was only 2 years old, leaving his wife to rear the child alone. Other mothers were left to bring up their children alone – the husband of one being electrocuted in a bath – right down to the 1960s.

Sarah's reputation for burning people by flashing sparks from her eyes was based on an incident that occurred on 28 February 1852. Again, the local register confirms the death by burning of 17-year-old Lizzie Hays and 4-year-old Emily Lungly on that day. Lizzie, who could not work because she was slightly retarded and suffered from warts and chilblains, was looking after Emily and two other children as they played in the alley on Victoria Wharf where Sarah lived. Sarah came out and told them to clear off and play in their own yard and then stormed off. The children noticed her door was not shut properly and so they went in and saw a squalid room with a copper pot bubbling away, an unfinished meal on a table with a candle and lots of dusty bottles on a shelf. Lizzie's 10-year-old sister Janie suggested they look at the bottles to see if any of them could cure Lizzie's warts and chilblains. Lizzie had just lit the candle and was looking at the bottles, when they heard Sarah returning. As the children fled from the door, they knocked the bottles over and their greasy contents spilled all over Lizzie and Emily. As Lizzie clasped Emily to protect her, the candle was tipped over their wet dresses.

Then the door opened and the angry sea witch cursed them for invading her cottage, after which Lizzie and Emily burst into flames. Sarah grabbed an old sack and ran towards them, but they were more scared of her than the flames and dashed into the street towards the creek. A doctor arrived too late and as a crowd gathered, young Janie pointed at Sarah and declared, 'She did it, the sea witch. She came in the door and sparks flashed from her eyes and they burst into flames.'

Emily's 10-year-old brother Tommy, who was the other child present, had a more rational explanation ... the liquid in the bottle that had spilled on their dresses was paraffin, which was set alight by the candle 'and when the witch came in the wind made it blaze'. The doctor suggested the 'sparks' might have been the reflection of the flames in her eyes. But Janie was adamant and added that Sarah had tried to catch them in a sack, which Tommy corroborated. It is entirely possible, of course, that she was trying to smother the flames with the sack. Anyway, Sarah went unpunished, but the story of her sparking eyes persisted for generations to come.

Many newborn babies were said to be born with harelips after their mothers offended Sarah. And her ability to correctly predict their sex was said never to have failed. Other predictions were based on visions which she experienced when pouring a mixture of seawater and Thames sand through her horny fingers from a fishermen's pan.

One story was told of her death after she put a curse on a new skipper of a smack who, unaware of her reputation, refused to give her a coin for wishing him a safe trip. A violent storm followed with thunder and lightning and, as the craft keeled over, the crew told him it was the curse of the witch. He grabbed an axe and hacked away at the tangled rigging which threatened to drag them under, and shouted, 'I'll kill that perishing witch.' With the third stroke of the axe the storm suddenly ceased and when they returned to the quay they found Sarah dead with three bloody blows on her head. The story was said to have happened during the great storm of 1870, but this was three years after she had died.

Sarah escaped any prosecution for witchcraft, but earlier women in Leigh were not so lucky. They included Joan Allen in 1574 and Alice Soles in 1622, both of whom were burned to death. The pub, which became named after Sarah in 2001, now has a cocktail bar (but no witch's brews available) and an area where children can dine – if only they knew what Sarah did to babies ...

70. Robert Peel (1788–1850)

7 King Street, Watford, Hertfordshire, WD18 0BW (Tel: 01923 227528)

Robert Peel, who was twice prime minister, is probably best known for forming the modern police force when home secretary in 1829. Police were originally nicknamed 'peelers' and even now are known as 'bobbies', after their founder. He also reformed the judicial system and removed over 110 death-penalty offences. He himself was nicknamed 'Orange Peel', because of his strong opposition to Catholic emancipation when he was Chief Secretary of Ireland from 1812 to 1818. By 1829, however, he had a change of heart and supported the Catholic Emancipation Act at Westminster.

As the modern Conservative Party became established and distanced itself from the old Tories in the 1830s, Peel became their first prime minister from 1834 to 1835. Many considered him more of a liberal, however, as he worked closely with the Whigs, and his chief disciple Gladstone went on to found the Liberal Party. Peel supported agitation, for example, as 'the marshalling of the conscience of the nation to mould its laws'.

Peel's second term as prime minister was from 1841 to 1846, when he helped relieve the distress of the poor by reducing food prices and when he supported the repeal of the Corn Laws import duties during the Irish famine. He died after his horse fell on top of him when he was riding up Constitution Hill in London.

71. Richard Oastler (1789–1861)

Park Street Market, Brighouse, West Yorkshire, HD6 1JL (Tel: 01484 401756). Wetherspoon.

A strong campaigner against the evils of child labour in factories, Richard Oastler ended up in prison for over three years. Born in Leeds, he was the son of linen merchant Robert, who was disinherited for becoming a Methodist. John Wesley frequently stayed at their house and on his last

A portrait of Oastler in the pub.

visit he lifted young Richard in his arms and blessed him.

Richard became an architect, but poor eyesight forced him to give this profession up and he became a steward for an absentee landowner instead. On 29 September 1830 he was shown around a Bradford factory and saw, for the first time, the exploitation of child labour. 'I had lived for many years in the very heart of the factory districts,' he recalled. 'I had been on terms of intimacy and friendship with many factory masters, and I had all the while fancied that factories were blessings to the poor.' On the very same day, he wrote a letter entitled 'Yorkshire Slavery' to the Leeds Mercury about it. His observations were denied and criticised by the factory owners, but he was able to prove them.

The following year he addressed a letter 'to the working classes of the West Riding', urging them to use their influence to prevent any MP being elected who did not 'unequivocally pledge himself' to support a limit of ten hours' work a day. He organised a mass meeting of thousands of working people from all parts of the clothing factory districts on a 'pilgrimage of mercy' to York in favour of such a bill. A bill making 12 years the age limit for those employed over eight hours a day was opposed by the owners, but Oastler went from town to town speaking in favour of it.

At a meeting in Blackburn on 15 September 1836, he criticised local magistrates for not even enforcing the limited factory acts which existed ... then hinted at using force in such circumstances, by teaching child workers to 'apply their grandmothers' old knitting needles to the spindles' in the factories. He was also forthright in his criticism of the use of poor law commissioners in supplying factories with agricultural labourers as cheap labour. This led to him being sacked by his employer, who also sued him for debt.

The magnificent organ overlooks the drinkers in the Richard Oastler pub which is a converted church.

Unable to pay it, he was sent to Fleet Prison in London on 9 December 1840 and he stayed there for more than three years.

While in prison, he wrote and published the agitational Fleet Papers and his supporters all over the country set up an Oastler Liberation Fund. This raised enough money to pay his debts and gain his release in February 1844. He continued agitating for a maximum ten-hour day, until this was finally enacted in 1847. The final loopholes to it, however, were not blocked until 1874.

Robert's own two children Sarah and Robert both died in infancy. Oastler, who campaigned against slavery from the age of 18, died at Harrogate and was buried in Kirkstall Churchyard, Leeds (10 miles north-east of this pub). There is a statue erected to him in Northgate, Bradford and a blue plaque lies at his birthplace in St Peter's Square, Leeds.

72. William Burke (1792–1829) and William Hare (died 1859)

Burke and Hare, 2 High Riggs (corner of Bread Street and East Fountainbridge), Edinburgh, EH3 9BX (Tel: 0131 622 7005). Free house.

William Burke and William Hare resorted to murder to provide bodies for dissection in Dr Robert Knox's anatomy school at 10 Surgeons Square, Edinburgh. They killed sixteen people in lodging houses which they ran (Log's in Tanners Close and later another in Gibbs Close, Cannongate), before being arrested. Both were Irishmen, who came over to Scotland to work on building the Union Canal at Mediston in 1818.

Burke, the son of a farmer, was born in the Parish of Urney near Strabane in County Tyrone. He worked as a baker, cobbler, weaver and an officer's servant in the Donegal Militia, before moving to Scotland, leaving his wife and two children behind. After finishing work on the canal, he became an itinerant farm labourer for a while. He befriended a prostitute and ex-canal worker Helen MacDougal and they tramped over southern Scotland together, finally settling at the Beggar's Hotel in Edinburgh. Burke scraped a living mending and selling shoes and as a dancing teacher.

Hare was born in Londonderry and later moved to Newry, where he worked as a farm labourer. After working on the Union Canal, he became a travelling huckster (aggressive salesman) for some time, until he settled in Edinburgh. Here, he met and stayed with a man called Logue, who died in 1826. Hare befriended Logue's widow Margaret Laird and they ran the inn and lodging house in Tanners Close as man and wife. Soon afterwards, Burke and Helen MacDougal became their tenants there.

In November 1827, an old pensioner named Donald who was also living there died, owing £3.50 rent. To recover this, Hare filled the coffin with tan bark and sold the body to Dr Knox for £7.50. This set Burke and Hare thinking that selling corpses was more profitable than cobbling shoes. When another of their tenants called Joseph (known as the Mumper or the Miller) was dying from fever, it discouraged others from lodging there, so Burke and Hare 'hastened' his death by plying him with whisky and suffocating him with a pillow, which left no signs of violence. They received £10 for his corpse from Knox.

The two Williams and their wives decided this was a profitable business worth pursuing, so on 11 February 1828, they lured an old woman hawker Abigail Simpson into the house and got her drunk, but then they lost their nerve. It was not until the next day that they suffocated her – Hare applying the pillow and Burke holding her kicking legs – and sold the body for another £10.

Mary Haldane, described as a 'worn out strumpet', was the next victim. Her half-witted daughter Peggy came looking for her missing mother; a trail that led her to Burke and Hare. Hare, with grim humour, offered to take her to join her mother and she, too, ended up under the surgeon's knife.

Mary Paterson, another one of their victims who was described as an 'attractive little harlot', had just been released by the police and was drinking with her friend Janey Brown on 9 April, when they were picked up by Burke, who took them to Gibbs Close. Janey ran out but Mary was suffocated and was sold to Dr Knox. Some of his students, who had used her services, recognised Mary and suspicions began to be aroused. A beggar woman called Effie, an unidentified female derelict, and an Englishman suffering from jaundice also ended up on the anatomist's slab.

An Irish beggar woman and her dumb grandson were the next victims. Burke strangled the old woman and broke the back of the lad over his knee. He then hired an old horse to pull the bodies in a large herring box to Surgeon's Square. But the nag stopped in the middle of Grassmarket and refused to budge. A porter had to be hired to carry the box on a barrow the rest of the way. In furious revenge, Burke slit the horse's throat. Several other victims, including Helen's own cousin Anne McDougal, were all sold for prices varying from £8 to £14.

The writing was on the wall for the murderers, however, when they chose a very well-known character to kill in October. This was a retarded youth called James Wilson, who was known throughout Edinburgh as 'Daft Jamie'. He put up a tremendous struggle, before he was overcome by their combined strength. As soon as his body was uncovered in the anatomy school he was recognised by the students. Knox quickly dismantled Jamie's face to prevent identification. But it heightened further the suspicions and only one more murder followed.

On the night of 31 October 1828, Burke lured another drunken beggar, a widow called Mary Docherty, back to Gibbs Close. A couple of other lodgers named James and Ann Gray were persuaded to stay at Tanners Close for the night, while the murder was committed. When they returned the next morning, they found Burke sprinkling whisky around the room and scattering straw to disguise the smell and sight of blood. They became suspicious when Burke refused to let Ann near her bed to collect her stockings. Later, they went to the bed, under which they found the body of the last victim. They were on their way to the police, when they bumped into the wives of the murderers, who took them to a pub to delay them, while the body was being collected in a tea chest.

When a policeman visited the lodgings and found no body he began to doubt the story. But when different times were supplied for the so-called departure of Docherty he became suspicious and a further search revealed blood. Reports of the arrests of the two men and women appeared in the Edinburgh press, which alerted Janey Brown to come forward and she was able to identify the clothes of Mary Paterson.

Hare escaped prosecution in return for giving king's evidence against Burke, who confessed to the murders. The trial of Burke and Helen started at 10 a.m. on Christmas Eve 1828 and continued right through until 10 a.m. on Christmas Day without any adjournment or break. Helen denied all knowledge of the crimes and was released after a verdict of 'not proven'. Nevertheless, she was nearly lynched by an angry mob and had to flee to Australia, where she died 40 years later. Margaret Hare, who was never tried, narrowly escaped a lynching also and returned to Ireland. Burke was found guilty and sentenced to death. He was found to have testicular cancer (possibly associated with syphilis), which probably would have killed him anyway. He claimed his testicle had been bitten by 'Daft Jamie' in his desperate struggle to defend himself.

The day before his execution, Burke complained he was still owed £5 for one of the bodies by Dr Knox and if he had it he could afford a decent coat and waistcoat for his final appearance on the scaffold. He was publicly hanged in front of a record crowd of up to 25,000 at Edinburgh's Lawnmarket on 28 January 1829 'amid the execrations of a vast assemblage, who cried out "Burke him! Burke him!"' He was immortalised in the English dictionary as 'burke', meaning to kill someone by smothering them. The similarly sounding berk is still rhyming slang based on Berkshire Hunt.

The next day, as part of the punishment, Burke's own body was dissected in the university medical school. His cranium was sawn off and an enormous amount of blood gushed out, making the classroom look like a butcher's slaughterhouse. The police had to be called when hordes of students clamoured to get in and witness the bloody scene. Several were injured on both sides and many windows were broken before it was agreed they could go in fifty at a time at the end of the dissection. The following day, the public were allowed to file past the carved-up corpse, of which up to 25,000 did. Then the flesh was stripped off and Burke's skeleton was placed in the university's Anatomical Museum, where it is on display to this day.

There was an attempt to indict Hare for the murder of James Wilson, but law officers decided he could not be legally put on trial after giving king's evidence. He was released from Tolbooth Prison in Edinburgh on 5 February 1829 and he fled to England, where he changed his name and is believed to have been blinded by fellow workers with quicklime, when they discovered his true identity. After that he had to resort to begging in London around the Rookery area, which is now New Oxford Street, before he died in 1859.

Dr Knox (1791–1862) also had to leave Edinburgh and ended up in London at a cancer hospital; most likely the Middlesex Hospital in Mortimer Street, a short distance from the New Oxford Street, where Hare roamed. A rhyme of the time went:

Burke's the murderer, Hare's the thief,

And Knox the boy who buys the beef.

Nowadays, students of anatomy examine living bodies... the striptease dancers who perform at the Burke and Hare pub.

Burke and Hare, nicknamed the 'Pubic Hair' by the locals because of its entertainment.

73. Ben Crouch (early nineteenth century)

Ben Crouch Tavern, 77a Wells Street, Fitzrovia, London, W1P 3RE
(Tel: 020 7636 0717). Spirit/Punch Taverns.

Bloodthirsty menu in the Ben Crouch Tavern.

Crouch was known as 'King of the Resurrectionists', when he led a gang of bodysnatchers supplying medical researchers in this part of London from 1809 to 1813. He did much to raise the price for bodies in this illegal trade by some pretty unsavoury methods, as will be seen. His gang, based in Southwark, was known as 'the Borough Boys' and their chief supplier was Joseph Naples, the head gravedigger of St James' Church in Clerkenwell.

Crouch was also an ex-prize fighter and so became friendly with one of his customers, fellow pugilist and great Scottish surgeon Robert Liston (1794–1847). They heard that the victim of a particularly rare disease had recently been buried and it would greatly advance research into this disease if they could acquire the body for examination. So one night Crouch and Liston went to the grave, dug up the body and put it in a sack. Having built up a thirst with this work, they decided to repair to the nearest tavern, taking care to hide the sack under a hedge outside, rather than lug it inside.

While Liston flirted with the barmaid, her brother spotted the sack outside and assumed it was loot hidden by thieves. Eagerly, he took it inside to show his sister, with a view to sharing the spoils. When they opened it and found the corpse his sister screamed and they both fled in revulsion. Crouch and Liston rapidly retrieved the body, gulped down their ale and made off in haste. Liston later achieved fame for conducting the first operation with a general anaesthetic in Europe, at University College Hospital in 1846 – as commemorated by a plaque at nearby 52 Gower Street.

Not all Crouch's customers were so salubrious, however. One of them was Joshua Brookes, who was dirty and smelly and he once refused to pay the price for two bodies. So the corpses were dumped unceremoniously in the road outside his abode at the bottom of the steps in Ramilles Street, a couple of hundred yards from this pub. This

The medical link with body-snatching is illustrated in the Ben Crouch Tavern.

A sculpture of Ben Crouch in the tavern.

exposed the nature of his experiments and an angry mob nearly destroyed his house. There was no more quibbling over prices after that. Another anatomist nearby supplied by Crouch was Joseph Carpue in Dean Street.

Public outcry grew when bodysnatchers such as William Burke and William Hare in Edinburgh, and John Bishop and John Head in London, resorted to murder to provide bodies. Bishop and Head, who drugged three victims with laudanum in rum and then drowned them in a well, were hanged in 1831.

It was partly to discourage such practices that in 1832, Jeremy Bentham became one of the first people to donate his body to medical research.

74. John Clare (1793–1864)

The Old John Clare, Hallfields Lane (corner of Pennine Way), Gunthorpe, near Peterborough, Cambs, PE4 7YH.

Even when his poems made him famous, John Clare continued to work as a farm labourer in the fields around Helpston, where he was born a few miles north-west of Peterborough. Crowds would come to his cottage, next to the Blue Bell (which is still at 10 Woodgate) in Helpston, and be amazed to find him dirty from his farm work.

'The first publication of my poems brought many visitors to my house out of mere curiosity,' he recalled, to see if, 'I really was the son of a thresher and a labouring rustic, as had been stated, and when they found it really was so they looked at each other as a matter of satisfied surprise, asked some gossiping questions, and on finding me a vulgar fellow that mimicked at no pretensions but spoke in the rough ways of a thorough bred clown, they soon turned to the door and departed.'

However successful a poet he was, he never wished to separate himself from ordinary men and women and he continued to be openly critical of the middle classes, 'pompous magistrates, pretentious miliary officers, and grasping farmers'. He despised hunting parsons but respected those clergymen who had sympathy for the poor. He was particularly enraged at the poor 'being a sort of foot cushion for the benefit of others'.

John's father Parker Clare was, indeed, a thresher and he was also a wrestler, who sang ballads 'over his horn of ale with his merry companions at the Blue Bell public house'. His mother Ann (née Stimson) was the daughter of a shepherd. John was their eldest child of four, two of whom, including his twin sister, died in infancy. John was twice saved from drowning and he also survived a dangerous fall when bird-nesting.

He started working at the age of 10 on a farm, where he learned to write in the dust on the barn walls. Then his next-door neighbour Francis Gregor, landlord of the Blue Bell, employed him for a year as a plough boy. On the way home, he made up rhymes and wrote them down on sugar bags. He kept these secret, however, fearing derision if it was found out he was a poet. It was only financial desperation which drove him to declare himself and to try and get his poems published. This was because his father was crippled with rheumatism and unable to work and John was also off work for a year as a result of fainting fits, which occurred after he saw a young farm worker killed from a fall off a hay load, which broke his neck. When 'released from my timid embarrassment of reserve from a free application of ale in the fair,' he recalled, he plucked up courage to sell his poems.

His published works included Poems Descriptive of Rural Life and Scenery (1820), The Village Minstrel and Other Poems (1821), The Shepherds Calendar with Village Stories and Other Poems (1827) and The Rural Muse (1835). He uncompromisingly demanded that his poems be published in his own dialect and idiosyncratic grammar. Despite their success, he was still in debt and sometimes had to work long hours burning lime in the kiln or digging ditches and planting hedges for the enclosures (privatising of common land), which he despised the social effects of.

After marrying Martha (Patty) Turner and having children to support, he joined the army at Peterborough for the two guineas enlistment fee. After being bullied by a corporal, John finally snapped and knocked him over and kicked him. The punishment was confinement to a black hole, but the corporal never troubled him again. Other ways of scratching a living included poaching – he often mixed with the gypsies, who taught him Romany slang and how to play the fiddle – and working in a pub (the New Inn, Peterborough), which he quit when the wages were cut.

When his poetry finally earned some revenue, he was able to visit London and mix with the likes of writers Hazlitt, Coleridge, de Quincey, Southey and Keats and the artist Peter de Wint, who illustrated his poems and kept in contact when Clare was later declared insane. Clare also liked London's seedy vaudeville theatres, such as the Royal West London Theatre in Tottenham Court Road, and it was near here, in Oxford Street, that he witnessed Byron's funeral procession in 1824 and was profoundly moved by it.

Later, Clare suffered delusions that he was Byron – and also Burns, Shakespeare, Nelson, the wrestler Jan Burns and the prize fighter Ben Caunt – and he was committed in 1837 to Dr Matthew Allen's Asylum in Epping. Another of his delusions was that he had married his childhood sweetheart Mary Joyce, who had died young, making his marriage to Patty bigamous, for which he thought his incarceration was a punishment.

In 1841, he met some gypsies, who offered to help him escape from the madhouse by hiding him in their camp. They left without fulfilling this promise, however, so he set off on his own, sleeping under hedges and eating grass from the roadside, 'which seemed to taste something like bread'. He got as far as Northamptonshire, before he was recaptured and confined for the rest of his life in Northampton General Asylum.

Towards the end he ruminated, 'If life had a second edition, how I would correct the proofs.'

75. Feargus O'Connor (1794–1855)

Land of Liberty, Peace and Plenty, Long Lane, Heronsgate, Rickmansworth, Herts, WD3 5BS (Tel: 01923 282226). Free house.

This pub takes its name from an adjoining Chartist settlement called O'Connorville after its founder Feargus O'Connor. This was a land experiment, organised by O'Connor, to provide smallholdings to working men as an alternative to factory employment. Shares were advertised in the Northern Star in 1845 and those who bought them for a few pennies a week qualified for a lottery for plots of land. Enough money flooded in to purchase five settlements around the country, the first of which was 103 acres at Heronsgate, which was to be divided into thirty-five plots, each with a cottage; previously the entire farm was cultivated by three men and a boy.

Because of legal difficulties setting up the Chartist National Land Company, the land was bought by O'Connor for £1,860 in March 1846. He also supervised the building of the cottages and captained the bricklayers in a cricket game on the village common in which they beat the carpenters. A school was also built and crops sown in time for the grand opening on May Day 1847, when the settlers took over their land.

They were welcomed by O'Connell, who warned them, 'There is a beer shop adjoining

Chartists, including Feargus O'Connor, started a settlement near the Land of Liberty pub.

your land; avoid it, I beseech you, as a pestilence, for if any enemy can be the means of ousting you from the lovely spot on which it was my pride to locate you, it will be man's greatest, most vicious and inviting enemy, drunkenness'; apparently, he liked a drop of brandy himself. That

particular beer shop became the Land of Liberty in honour of the Chartist settlement by the 1870s; although it did not get a full licence until after the Second World War, which meant it could not sell spirits up until then. In 1848, a parliamentary select committee ruled that the National Land Company scheme was

illegal and had to be closed down. In 1851, a Winding Up Act was passed and all the plots of land were sold in the years from 1853 to 1858. It had been a controversial experiment even in Chartist circles, many of whom saw it as a distraction from the main political thrust of the movement.

O'Connor was the most charismatic of the Chartist leaders and an impassioned orator, who always drew huge crowds. In 1837, he founded the Northern Star, a weekly Chartist journal published in Leeds, which had a national sale of over 40,000. In 1840, he was prominent in setting up the National Charter Association, which was the first national membership based organisation in Britain.

An article he wrote in the *Northern Star*, after the Newport uprising of November 1839, led to him being found guilty of seditious libel in 1840 and he was sentenced to 18 months' imprisonment in York Castle. When he was released in August 1841, after sixteen months, there were huge celebrations and poet Thomas Cooper wrote of him:

> The lion of freedom comes from his den,

> We'll rally around him again and again.

An O'Connor Liberation Medal was also struck with a portrait of him and the words 'Universal Suffrage and No Surrender'.

In March 1843 he was charged again, this time at Lancaster, for sedition, conspiracy, tumult and riot, after 'exciting disaffection by unlawfully encouraging a stoppage of labour'. But a procedural error meant he, and fifty-seven others were never sentenced. In the same year, he published a book called *A Practical Work on the Management of Small Farms.*

In November 1847, he was returned to Parliament for Nottingham as a Chartist MP; in 1835 he had been elected as MP for County Cork, but was not allowed to take his seat, because of lack of property qualifications.

Feargus O'Connor's statue in Nottingham.

In June 1852, he was pronounced insane (possibly in the final stages of syphilis) and he was confined to an asylum in Chiswick, where he remained until the month of his death, when his sister took him into her care at home. His funeral at Kensal Green on 10 September 1855 was attended by 50,000 people.

He lives on through a statue in the south-east corner of the Arboretum in Nottingham (known as the People's Park), near the corner of Peel Street and Addison Street, and a plaque at the Memorial Hall in Chorleywood, which marked the 150th anniversary of O'Connorville.

Charlie Chaplin (see separate entry) was a regular in the Land of Liberty when filming at the nearby Denham Studios. He particularly liked the cold ham on the bone served by landlady Vi Cornhill. One day, she ran out of ham and offered to provide any other order he wanted. So he suggested the order of the boot (the sack). So she found an old boot, cooked it and displayed it on the bar; reminiscent of Chaplin's film *The Gold Rush* in which he ate an old boot.

76. John Keats (1795–1821)

(i) John Keats at the Moorgate (and at the Globe), 83–85 Moorgate, London, EC2M 6SA.

(ii) Keats Green Hotel, 3 Queens Road, Shanklin, Isle of Wight, PO37 6AN (Tel: 01983 862742).

The poet John Keats was born near the Moorgate pub (just south of Keats Place) and he lived as a child in a tavern just north of it. He was baptised at St Botulph-without-Bishopsgate, which is a few streets to the east, near Liverpool Street Station. His father Thomas worked as an ostler at the Swan & Hoop Inn at 24 The Pavement (now Finsbury Pavement), which is the

northern extension of Moorgate. His father-in-law John Jennings had run the livery stables at the Swan & Hoop for twenty years before him.

In 1801, Thomas became manager of the inn and moved in with his wife Frances and son John. The inn was noted for its wine and heavy black porter. Then, in 1804, Thomas was killed in a horse-riding accident, when John was just nine. Riding along City Road (a further northern extension of Moorgate), his horse slipped on the cobbles and Thomas fell and cracked his skull. He died the next morning without regaining consciousness.

John's mother took out a short lease on the inn's livery stables, but within two months married another livery stables keeper called William Rawlings, at the same church, St George's in Hanover Square, where she had married Thomas.

John was apprenticed as an apothecary-surgeon, but cancelled the apprenticeship after five years in order to become a student at Guy's Hospital (just south of the river from Moorgate). In 1816, he qualified to practise as an apothecary (chemist), but abandoned the profession to become a poet.

In the same year, he met James Henry Leigh Hunt, who had just completed a two-year jail sentence for libelling the Prince Regent. He had called his royal highness 'a fat Adonis', who was a 'libertine in debt and disgrace' and a 'despiser of domestic ties' and a 'companion of gamblers and demireps [women whose chastity was suspect]'. Hunt had been fined £500 in addition to the sentence. His prison visitors included Byron, Lamb and others and he had continued to edit his journal the *Examiner* from behind bars. It was in this journal that he published Keats's sonnet *O Solitude* in 1816 and he continued supporting him throughout his life. He persevered with him even when Keats was savagely attacked in 1817 as a member of the 'low-born Cockney school of poetry' by the critic John Lockhart.

Depressed and embittered by these attacks, Keats went to the Isle of Wight in April 1817. He arrived at Cowes and stayed the night in Newport. The next day he explored Shanklin, where he was delighted by the landscape of woods and meadows sloping down to the Chine. There, he wrote a sonnet called *On The Sea* which started:

> Oh ye! who have your eye-balls vexed and tired,
>
> Feast them upon the wideness of the Sea –
>
> ... sit ye near some old cavern's mouth and brood ...

After writing this he said it 'did me some good' and 'I slept the better last night for it'.

He was upset by the large number of soldiers based in extensive barracks on the island and expressed extreme disgust with the government 'for placing such a Nest of Debauchery in so beautiful a place'. In his lodgings that night he found, written on the window by a previous lodger, 'O Isle spoilt by the Military!'

Keats returned to the island for a month in June 1819, where he caught a fever after being deluged by a heavy storm while riding outside the coach to save money on the journey down. It proved a fruitful month, as he was inspired to write *Endymion* – after seeing a vista of cottages 'covered with creepers and honeysuckles with roses and eglantines

peeping in at the windows' – and a play called *Otho the Great*, a new volume of poetry, including the sonnet *Bright star!*, as well as revise *The Eve of St Agnes*, recast *Hyperion* and start on *Lamia*. During this time, he stayed at Eglantine Cottage (now the Keats Cottage Hotel) at 76 High Street, Shanklin. In the winter of 1819, however, he became increasingly ill with tuberculosis, which reduced his output.

His friend and fellow anti-militarist Shelley invited him to join him in Italy, where the climate would benefit his health. So he left in September 1820, but settled in Rome before reaching Shelley. It was there that Keats died in the following February.

77. George Loveless (1797–1874) and the Tolpuddle Martyrs

The Martyrs Inn, The Main Road, Tolpuddle, West Dorset, DT2 7GS
(Tel: 01305 848249). Hall & Woodhouse.

The transportation to Australia for seven years of six Tolpuddle agricultural labourers, on highly questionable legal grounds, in 1834 rekindled the trade union movement. Trade unionism had been legalised in 1824 with the repeal of the Combination Acts. But the employers kept very much the upper hand and farmers cut wages from nine shillings to as little as six shillings, when the average family expenditure was nearly 14 shillings. This sparked the Captain Swing Riots of 1830 to 1831, which were savagely crushed, with 19 being hanged, 600 imprisoned and 500 transported, including 13 from Dorchester, near Tolpuddle.

In 1832 George Loveless, a Methodist lay preacher and agricultural labourer in Tolpuddle, sought a wage increase from the local farmers to ten shillings a week, which was agreed. But they soon reneged on this and reduced wages to seven shillings a week. 'The labouring men consulted together what had better be done, as they knew it was impossible to live honestly on such scanty means,' said Loveless. And so the Tolpuddle Friendly Society of Agricultural Labourers was formed in October 1833 by Loveless, who spelled out in its rules opposition to acts of violence and violation of the law. The initial meeting in October 1833 was attended by forty labourers, about half the adult population of the village.

On 24 February 1834, Loveless and five others were arrested, taken to Dorchester Jail and charged with taking a secret oath at a union meeting on 9 December 1833 under a 1799 Act for suppression of societies established for seditious and treasonable purposes, and under the 1797 Mutiny Act. The six were George Loveless, his brother James Loveless (1808–1873), James Brine (1813–1902), Thomas Standfield (1790–1864), his son John Standfield (1813–1898) and James Hammett (1811–1891). The trial took place in March 1834 before an openly prejudicial judge and a jury comprised entirely of farmers; and the men in the dock were not allowed to give evidence on their own behalf.

After the inevitable guilty verdict, Loveless said they had neither damaged property nor injured anybody. 'We were uniting together to preserve ourselves, our wives and our children from utter degradation and starvation,' he declared. As they were taken to prison ships for transportation, he scribbled the Song of Freedom, which went:

> God is our guide, from field, from wave,
>
> From plough, from anvil, and from loom;
>
> We come, our country's right to save.
>
> And speak a tyrant faction's doom;
>
> We raise the watchword, liberty,
>
> We will, we will, we will be free!

The injustice of their treatment led to 800,000 people signing a petition for their release. On Easter Monday on 21 April 1834, over

100,000 people marched with the petition from Copenhagen Fields in North London – as depicted on a mural painted by artist Dave Bangs in 1984 on the side of The Mitre pub in Copenhagen Street, London, N1 – to Parliament, where the home secretary Lord Melbourne refused to accept it. The authorities vindictively refused parish relief to the families of the convicted men, but trade unionists all over the country set up a fund to prevent their eviction from their cottages.

Radical MP Thomas Wakley campaigned vigorously for a pardon. He pointed out that the king's own brother the Duke of Cumberland had, as grand master of the Orange Lodges, sworn a secret oath. So it was a choice of transporting him as well, or pardoning the men. They were pardoned in March 1836, but the authorities in Australia, where they had all suffered terrible hardships, failed to inform them of this. It was not until 13 June 1837 that the first, George Loveless, arrived back in London, and August 1839 that the last, James Hammett, did.

Loveless wrote a pamphlet about their case called The Victims of Whiggery and, with three of the others, another on the horrors of transportation. Public collections raised enough money to buy them two farms in Essex, where five of them worked until emigrating to Canada in the mid 1840s. The exception was James Hammett, who stayed in Tolpuddle as a labourer for the rest of his life.

In 1875, he was awarded a gold watch by the newly formed agricultural labourers' union as a measure of 'the esteem and regard in which you are held by us as one of the early martyrs to the cause of unionism.' He said

A detail from the mural on the side of the Mitre pub in Copenhagen Street, North London, where 100,000 people marched demanding the release of the Tollpuddle Martyrs in 1834.

in response, 'We only tried to do good to one another, the same as you're doing now.' He also revealed it was his brother, not him, who was at the meeting where the oath had been taken. He took the blame though, because his brother's wife had just become pregnant.

Hammett's grave is in St John's Church, Tolpuddle, where a new gravestone designed by Eric Gill was installed in 1934 on the hundredth anniversary of his transportation, with the inscription, 'James Hammett, Tolpuddle Martyr, Pioneer of Trade Unionism.' In the same year, a thatched shelter was erected on the green near the bridge over the River Piddle, where they had met under a sycamore tree. Some fifty years later in 1984, a sycamore tree was planted beside it from a seedling of the original tree by the then TUC general secretary Len Murray. Every July, a rally to commemorate their struggle is held in front of the Tolpuddle Martyrs Museum and cottages, watched by Loveless as depicted in a sculpture by Thompson Dagnall called the Tolpuddle Six.

The pub sign contains the quote 'who was then the gentleman', taken from John Ball's cry during the 1381 peasants' revolt:

> When Adam delved and Eve span,
> Who was then the Gentleman?

> - cast off your yoke of bondage, and recover liberty!

78. Zachery Willsher (1799–1871)

Zach Willsher, 170 Church Road (corner of Manor Road), Thundersley, Essex, SS7 4PL (Tel: 01268 751781). Spirit.

This pub started as an alehouse run for the benefit of local farmworkers in the 1840s by Zachery Willsher, according to the plaque on the side of the building. The pub was built in 1979 on the site of an old off licence and coal yard. Zach was a woodman, who probably supplied timber to the local boat building trade, and he also owned a boathouse. According to the incomplete records of the time, he was born in either 1798 or 1799 in either Thundersley or Rayleigh; both part of the district of the Rochford Hundred. Three of his sisters were baptised under the surname of Wiltshire – in the days before the spelling of surnames was standardised – at St Peter's in Thundersley between 1798 and 1808, but no record exists of Zach being baptised in the same place, as was almost certainly the case.

He got married in the same church on 6 September 1819 to Elizabeth Haho or Hayhoe; both signed with an X in the days before most people were taught to read or write. They had at least six children (three of each), the oldest of which was Caroline, who was baptised at Holy Trinity Church in Rayleigh on 15 September 1822. This was followed by two boys: Robert in 1824 and Zach Junior in 1826, who had a son of the same name in 1853. A further three more followed in the 1830s: Eliza and Mary, and finally Aaron in 1839. His wife and children appear in the 1841 census (but not Zach himself) as living on 'the road leading to Daws Heath', which is probably close to the present junction of Daws Heath Road, Rayleigh Road and Hart Road.

He is listed as a 52-year-old 'retailer of beer' in the 1851 census, confirming the entry in White's Directory 1848. This was likely to have been at premises which later became The Woodman's, which exists today in a newer building. The 1861 census lists him as a beerhouse keeper and the 1866 Post Office Directory as a beer retailer. By 1871, he was listed as a widower living with his son-in-law in a cottage on Heath Road. He died in the same year on 24 May at the age of 72, when his occupation was described as woodman. One of his nephews William Wiltshire was transported to Australia for sheep rustling in 1846. Is it possible this was because he upset Sarah Moore, the sea witch (see elsewhere), who lived at nearby Leigh-on-Sea and was 59 years old at the time?

79. William Lovett (1800–1877)

The Chartist, 74 Commercial Road, Skelmanthorpe, West Yorkshire, HD8 9DS (Tel: 01484 863766). Admiral Taverns.

The Chartist pictured on this pub sign is William Lovett who, even though he was considered a moderate, was jailed for sedition and arrested many times. He was the chief drafter in 1838 of the famous People's Charter, which demanded annual parliaments, universal manhood suffrage, equal electoral districts, voting by secret ballot, abolition of property qualifications for MPs and payment of MPs.

Born in Penzance, Cornwall, his fisherman father was drowned at sea before William was born. At the age of 13 he became an apprentice rope maker but, as ropes were being replaced by chains, he then trained as a carpenter. He moved to London at the age of 21 and became a cabinet maker, joining the Cabinet Makers Society after a five year wait for eligibility. In the same year, he married a maid. Through attending evening classes at the London's Mechanics' Institute he met radicals, who introduced him to the cooperative ideas of Robert Owen. Lovett joined the London Co-operative Trading Association and in 1828, he became secretary of the British Association for the Promotion of Co-operative Knowledge.

William Lovett, leading Chartist, on the pub sign.

His first clash with authority came in 1831, when he was selected at random for compulsory service in the London Militia. When he refused, his property was seized as a punishment. He formed the Anti-Militia Association with the slogan 'No Vote, No Musket', which successfully campaigned to end compulsory service in the militia. This made him a national political figure.

The following year, he was arrested for attending a peaceful demonstration and was locked up in a dark cell, 9 feet square, with little air and 'a pailful of filth left by the last occupants, the smell of which was almost overpowering'. It was so damp that he had to keep walking round to keep alive. Eventually, he was released without charge.

He then joined the National Union of the Working Classes, campaigning for votes for all male adults, and Robert Owen's Grand National Consolidated Trade Union. In 1836 he founded the London Working Men's Association and at one of its meetings two years later, he drew up the famous People's Charter of political demands. He effectively became the leader of the Chartists.

He was arrested for sedition after making a speech in Birmingham in 1839. He had accused the Metropolitan Police of being 'a blood thirsty and unconstitutional force'. Found guilty, he was sentenced to twelve months in Warwick Prison. The food there was infested by beetles, so he tried to exist on bread and water alone, but this brought on horrible diarrhoea, which made him so weak he was taken to hospital. After nine months he was offered three months remission for good behaviour, but refused the offer, as it implied admission of guilt. On his release, his health had suffered so much in prison that he spent some time recuperating in Cornwall, before returning to London to open a book shop in Tottenham Court Road.

In obtaining the aims of the Charter, he was 'opposed to everything in the shape of a physical or violent revolution, believing that a victory would be a defeat to the just principles of democracy'. Many criticised him for this moderation, so he retired from politics in 1842 and concentrated on working-class education, forming the National Association for Promoting the Political and Social Improvement of the People. Financed by workers' subscriptions, it provided circulating libraries and lecturers.

His bookshop failed to make any money and he died in poverty. Pride of place in the pub goes to a replica of the Skelmanthorpe Flag of the Chartists; the original is in Huddersfield Museum. Written shortly after the 1819 Peterloo Massacre in Manchester – when the militia slaughtered 15 people and wounded 600 others who were asking for the vote – it pronounces:

> May Never A Cock in England Crow,
>
> Nor never a Pipe in Scotland Blow,
>
> Nor never a Harp in Ireland Play
>
> Till Liberty regains Her Sway.

As for Chartism, its success in immediate terms of results is unfairly judged as being limited. In 1842, it delivered a petition signed by 3,317,752 in favour of the six demands of the People's Charter. Indeed, it had more people on the streets protesting against wage cuts and demanding political reform than in any other year. In the same year there was a general strike in the Potteries, after which fifty-six people were transported and troops opened fire on Chartist crowds, including women and children, in Preston.

In 1848 six years later, the last great Chartist demonstration on the streets of London was confronted by thousands of middle-class men enrolled as special constables, along with troops armed with cannons commanded by the Duke of Wellington. The gloves were off and none of the six demands of the Chartists were granted immediately, but the government backed off on its proposed Poor Law Amendment Act to reduce food and other standards in the workhouses; and eventually, five of the Chartists' six demands were granted. That leaves annual elections for Parliament.

A replica of the Skelmanthorpe flag of the Chartists in the pub.

80. Lajos Kossuth (1802–1894)

The Independent, 65 Bingfield Street, Caledonian Road, London, N1 0AG.

Lajos (spelled as Louis or Lewis in England) Kossuth was the exiled fighter for Hungarian independence, who addressed popular demonstrations in Copenhagen Fields, which then adjoined the pub (Copenhagen Street remains just south of it). Kossuth (pronounced Kawsh-shoot) spent his life opposing the Austro-Habsburg empire's subjugation of his country and in 1859, the year he spoke in Copenhagen Fields, he received plenty of support in this country, as he recalled in his book *Memories of My Exile*, published in 1880.

Lajos Kossuth depicted addressing a meeting near this pub.

'The British nation has accustomed itself to identifying my name with the aspirations of the Hungarian nation for independence,' he wrote. 'The fact is proved beyond doubt ... by the reception I meet with whenever I appear at public meetings, and by the resolutions of sympathy and encouragement passed, and still passed, at a great many meetings.'

One of these meetings was chaired by the Lord Mayor of London, who introduced Kossuth as the 'last legitimate ruler of Hungary'; after the Hungarian revolution of 1848, Kossuth had been President briefly in 1849, until the republic was overthrown. These meetings helped to persuade the British government to remain neutral in the war between France and Austria, to prevent, in Kossuth's words, 'the fair name of Britannia (being) coupled with that of Austria, the despotic power and personified oppressor of national rights.' He had won a promise from France to support an independent Hungary, if England could be reconciled to the collapse of the Habsburg monarchy – a promise that failed to come to fruition.

Shortly after qualifying as a lawyer, Kossuth had been imprisoned in 1837 for publishing an illegal journal and he served three years behind bars. On his release, he edited another liberal publication. In 1847, he became the opposition leader in Hungary, calling for a modern government free of Austrian control and an end to the feudal system of serfs and nobles. In March 1848, the lower house approved his programme for constitutional reform and, because of popular unrest, the upper house dropped its opposition.

As peasants amassed in Budapest, the 'parliament' (diet) was persuaded by Kossuth to end some feudal ties, but his call for the emancipation of all was rejected and the majority of the population were excluded. He did, however, pass laws replacing the feudal diet at Bratislava with a Parliament at Budapest which was elected on universal suffrage. The country also acquired dominion status, with a separate Hungarian army, budget and foreign policy. In the revolutionary atmosphere of the time, this was all constitutionally conceded in Austria and so Hungary became a separate state, rather than a Habsburg province.

Statue of Lajos Kossuth in Budapest.

During this time of influence, Kossuth less creditably attacked the non-Magyar nationalities in Hungary and in April 1849, the Hungarian Parliament fully deposed the Habsburgs and elected Kossuth as Governor. But in the following month, the Russian army entered Hungary and restored the Habsburgs. Kossuth fled from the country, but was captured and imprisoned in Turkey. After pressure from Britain and America, he was released in 1851, whereupon he declared, 'Despotism and oppression never yet were beaten except by heroic resistance.'

After restraints were placed on him travelling, he eventually reached London, where he settled in 1852 for the rest of his life. In 1859, he had high hopes that, 'France will ally themselves with the Hungarian nation through me, its chosen representative, designated as such in the declaration of Independence.' But he would not allow Hungary to be used as a pawn in an international game. 'I will not allow one drop of blood to be sacrificed for the sole purpose of creating a diversion. I will call the nation to arms only if I can appear on the frontier with a force sufficient to allow the national forces to be organised, so that the liberation of the nation may only depend upon its own determination.'

He travelled to Italy, where the conflict between France and Austria was being fought, but the armistice between the two ended his hopes of Hungarian independence in his lifetime. While in Turin, he dissolved the Hungarian army there, signing the proclamation as President of the Hungarian National Committee, and returned to London.

81. Richard Cobden (1804–1865)

(i) Cobden Arms, 76 West Street, Bedhampton, Havant, Hants, PO9 1LN.
(ii) Cobden Arms, 28–30 Camden High Street, London, NW1 0JH
   (Tel: 020 7209 2472). Free house.
(iii) Richard Cobden, 2 Cobden Road, Worthing, West Sussex, BN11 4BD
   (Tel: 01903 236856). Punch Taverns.

By reducing the price of food to the poor through abolishing the Corn Laws, Richard Cobden became an extremely popular politician. When he was equally outspoken against war, however, his popularity temporarily waned and he lost his seat in Parliament.

Worthing pub sign.

Born the son of a poor farmer in a farmhouse called Durnford at Heyshott (15 miles north-east of Bedhampton) in West Sussex, his father, unable to make ends meet, was forced to sell the farm and 'farm out' his eleven children to be brought up by other people.

For a short while, the 10-year-old Richard lived in a shabby home at West Meon (10 miles north-west of Bedhampton). It was then his misfortune to be sent to a school in Yorkshire for five years of misery, under conditions of brutality, which were later exposed by Charles Dickens. After that, Cobden became a clerk in his uncle's warehouse in London and he then became a commercial traveller. In 1826, his employers closed down and Richard went to live at Fareham (8 miles west of Bedhampton).

A couple of years later, he and some friends borrowed enough money to set up a business selling Lancashire calicoes on commission in London. It thrived enough for them to be able to purchase a lease on a Lancashire factory three years later to print their own calicoes. This, in turn, prospered and Cobden purchased a house in Manchester.

From 1835 to 1837 he travelled the world and returned to write pamphlets warning that countries such as America, Ireland and Russia could soon become major trade rivals. Britain would be more vulnerable to this competition, he added, if it continued to waste money on 'needless intervention in continental wars'. He also thought the Corn Laws should be scrapped in the interests of free trade and affordable food. They were designed to sustain the high price of wheat for farmers and landowners at the record levels of the famine during the Napoleonic Wars (1803–1815). They also prevented any imports when the price fell below this high level (50 shillings a quarter). Cobden was the leading light in the formation of the Anti Corn Law League in 1838 and he threw himself wholeheartedly into the cause, addressing public meetings all over the country, until the laws were abolished in 1846. During this time, he and the league were denounced by Tory landlords as a seditious conspiracy, which should be suppressed.

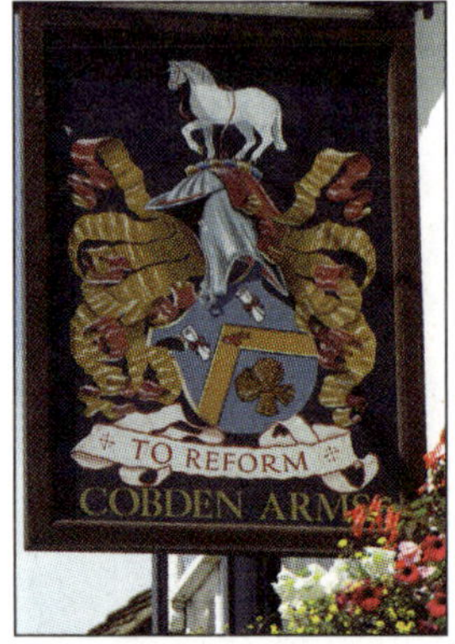

Bedhampton pub sign.

After being elected as MP for Stockport in 1841, Cobden made his voice clear on the issue in Parliament as well and he was further denounced by the Prime Minister Sir Robert Peel for using language, which 'held him up to public odium'.

When finally repealing the Corn Laws, however, Peel praised Cobden for his 'pure and disinterested motives' on the issue and his untiring and eloquent advocacy of his case. His almost complete devotion to the cause, however, had meant that his attention to his calico business had suffered. His private fortune had disappeared and the business was deeply in debt by 1845.

It was a measure of his popularity that a public subscription raised nearly £80,000, which was mostly used to pay off his debts. The remainder was used to buy the Durnford farmhouse in Heyshott, where he was born and lived out the rest of his life. A second (private) subscription raised a further £40,000 for him to live on.

His health as well as his wealth, however, had also suffered from the nearly eight-year campaign against the Corn Laws, so he travelled abroad again for two years, preaching the cause of free trade. On his return in 1847, he was elected as MP for the West Riding of Yorkshire and held the seat for the next ten years.

His views on peace, international arbitration and disarmament were not popular though, especially during the Crimea War of 1854 to 1856. So he did not even attempt to defend his West Riding seat in 1857, thinking he had a better chance in Huddersfield. But his opposition to wars with Russia and China saw him soundly beaten. Two years later, he was returned unopposed as the MP for Rochdale and was offered the post of President of the Board of Trade by the Prime Minister Lord Palmerston. Cobden

Portrait of Richard Cobden in the bedhampton pub.

declined on the grounds that he thought Palmerston was warlike. Cobden did agree though to negotiate a commercial trade treaty with France – known as the Cobden–Chevalier trade treaty – in 1859–1960, which helped preserve peace with that country.

On his death, he was buried at West Lavington Churchyard (just north of his Heyshott home) in the same grave as his only son, who had died at the age of 15. The people of Camden in North London seemed particularly grateful to him though, for 15,000 of them attended a concert in his memory, which raised enough money to erect a statue of him at the south end of Camden High Street (opposite Mornington Crescent Tube Station). Cobden's Welsh widow Catherine demonstrated her husband's favourite speaking stance to help the sculptors W. J. and T. Wills. The statue is 8 feet tall, made of Portland stone, and has sheaves on the sides of the pedestal, symbolising corn. Within a stone's throw are both a pub and a school named after him. The sign outside the Bedhampton pub carries his credo: To Reform. His portrait is displayed at the Worthing pub (about 15 miles from his birthplace), which is in the *Real Ale Pub Guide 2008.*

82. Isambard Kingdom Brunel (1806–1859)

(i)   The Brunel, 83 Fore Street (corner of Culver Road), Saltash, Cornwall, PL12 6AE (Tel: 01752 842261). Scottish & Newcastle.

(ii) Isambard Kingdom Brunel, 2 Guildhall Walk, Portsmouth, Hampshire, PO1 2DD (Tel: 023 9223 5112). Wetherspoon.

(iii) Reckless Engineer, Temple Gate, Bristol, BS1 6PL (Tel: 01179 220487).

The pub in Saltash, Cornwall.

Voted the second greatest Briton ever by BBC television viewers in 2002, Brunel was, in fact, the son of a French asylum seeker Marc Brunel (1769–1849). Isambard was born in a Portsmouth terraced house at Britain Street, Portsea. In his early childhood, the family moved to 98 Cheyne Road (4 Lindsey Row at the time), Chelsea, London, where he learned to swim in the Thames at the end of the garden. While there, his parents were imprisoned for debt.

His first engineering job was assisting his father on the construction of a tunnel under the Thames from Rotherhithe to Wapping, which started in 1825. The working conditions were appalling and several workers died from fever or drowning. Yet Isambard often deducted them a day's pay for what he considered slow work. A safety precaution, which would have saved several lives, was proposed by his father – siting a drain below the tunnel, which would be constantly pumped out – but was rejected by the penny-pinching company. In January 1828, the tunnel flooded and Isambard, after rescuing some workmen, fell into a rainwater tank and was off work for at least three months; six workmen were drowned during this incident alone.

Brunel, however, opposed any compensation for workers killed or injured on the grounds that this would interfere with market forces. For the same reason, he was against trade unions, or any laws being introduced to protect navvies from being exploited by excessive subcontracting, irregularity of payment and harsh conditions – exploitation that he nonetheless recognised. When workers demanded pay rises, as part of market forces, however, he dismissed them as blackmailers.

Another double standard of his involved his attitude towards law and order. During the civil unrest of 1831 and 1848, he signed up as a special constable to quell rioters and arrested a looter. Yet, in 1851, he led 3,000 men to violently and illegally evict a contractor on the Mickleton Tunnel in Gloucestershire (near Evesham), who had stopped work for non-payment of £34,000 owed to him. To his credit, Brunel never took out patents on his ideas as, in his view, they stifled competition and held back technical advance.

When working on the Thames Tunnel, he had lived at nearby 30 Bridge Street in Blackfriars. But after securing the lucrative job in 1833 of constructing the Great Western Railway from Bristol to London, he was able to move to Lord Devon's old house at 18 Duke Street, London, SW1, near fashionable Pall Mall, at the age of 29. He got the railway contract by just one vote, after saying he was not the cheapest but the best.

While condemning civil servants for discouraging initiative in others he, in fact, never delegated responsibility to anyone and was a strict authoritarian. So the railway took up a huge amount of his time in designing and supervising all the bridges, viaducts and tunnels, as well as the Bristol and Paddington Station contracts that he undertook. The task was finally completed in 1841, when the first train made the journey in four hours.

In the meantime, he had designed the first steamship to cross the Atlantic. This was the Great Western, which made the crossing from Bristol to New York in fifteen days in April 1838. Other projects he designed included a portable field hospital for Florence Nightingale and another ship, the Great Eastern, which was then the biggest ship in the world that laid the first cable between Britain and America.

He came close to death when swallowing a sovereign in 1843 as part of a conjuring trick, in which it appeared to go in his mouth and come out through his ear. He suffered severe coughing fits until it was finally extracted by a specialist six weeks later. His actual death though, came on 15 September 1859, just a week after an explosion on the Great Eastern had killed several crew members. One of his last achievements was

The pub, named after Brunel, opposite Bristol Temple Meads Station which he designed. He was considered reckless when he ran out of money building the Bristol suspension bridge.

the completion of the Tamar railway bridge between Saltash and Plymouth in 1859, which is still in use today.

83. William Webb Ellis (1806–1872)

(i) 24 London Road, Twickenham, Middlesex, TW1 3RR (Tel: 020 8744 4300). Wetherspoon.

(ii) 22 Warwick Road, Rugby, Warwickshire, CV21 3DH (Tel: 01788 578692). Marsdens.

Pub in Twickenham.

Pub in Rugby.

The game of rugby is said to have started in 1823, when William Webb Ellis picked up the ball and ran with it during a football match in Rugby School at the age of 16. A plaque at the school states, 'This stone commemorates the exploit of William Webb Ellis who with a fine disregard for the rules of football as played in his time first took the ball in his arms and ran with it, thus originating the distinctive feature of the Rugby game, AD 1823.' A statue illustrating this is situated on the corner of Donchurch Road and St Matthews Street, just 100 yards from the Rugby pub. It was sculpted by Graham Ibbesson and was erected in 1997.

Another one stands in the school grounds and a replica of it is situated in the cemetery, where he is buried in Mentone, near Nice, in southern France. He is also immortalised through the

A statue of the historic moment when Webb Ellis picked up the ball and ran with it, near the pub in Rugby.

Webb Ellis Trophy, which is presented to the winners of the Rugby Union World Cup, and also in Ellis Park rugby stadium in Johannesburg.

The story of his starting the game did not appear until four years after his death and there are now doubts about its authenticity, but the legend lives on. Another theory is that he was demonstrating the ancient Irish game of caid, which his father James Ellis had witnessed when serving as a soldier in Ireland, before being killed in battle in 1812.

It was after this death that William's mother Ann Webb moved to Rugby in order to get a free education for him and his brother. William attended the school there from 1816 to 1825. He then went to Oxford University for three years, where he gained a blue at cricket.

He entered the church first as chaplain of St George's in Albermarle Street, London, then as rector of St Clement Danes in The Strand, and finally rector of Laver Magdalen (now Magdalen Laver) in Essex, where there is a stained-glass window of him.

After contracting tuberculosis he went to Mentone, overlooking the Mediterranean, in the hope that the climate might cure him. He died there in January 1872, just a few months before the first ever rugby international match, which was between England and Scotland.

84. Giuseppi Garibaldi (1807–1882)

The Garibaldi, 61 Albert Street, St Albans, Herts, AL1 1RT (Tel: 01727 855046). Fullers.

Giuseppi Garibaldi was not only a successful guerrilla fighter for the liberation from kings and foreign rule of his native Italy. He was also truly an internationalist, who risked his life for the liberty of his brothers and sisters in South America and other parts of the world. This was why he was hailed as a hero on his four visits to Britain. In his own words, 'A man who defends his own country or attacks another's is no more than a soldier ... but he who, by becoming an internationalist ... offers his blood and his

sword to every people struggling against tyranny, is more than a soldier; he is a hero.'

He was born the son of a sailor in Nice, which was part of Italy for much of his life, and he became a cabin boy at the age of about 15. In 1833, he met Giuseppe Mazzini and joined his Young Italy movement. In the same year, he joined the royal navy with the task of spreading revolution and mutiny in order to seize ships on behalf of the republicans. When the revolt was crushed, he was sentenced to death for 'armed rebellion' in his absence. Although later arrested, he managed to escape and find refuge in a mountain village inn. In 1836 he made his way to Brazil and supported the revolution there, by seizing a ship and taking command of it. In sea battles in this cause, he was wounded in the head and arm, arrested, escaped, recaptured, imprisoned for two months before being released and then shipwrecked. When the republicans were finally defeated he became a commercial traveller in spaghetti and a mathematics teacher.

In 1842, he bigamously married Anita Duarte, the wife of a fisherman, and settled in the newly independent Republic of Uruguay. Argentina, with the support of the Pope, intervened to overthrow the republic and Garibaldi took command of a small fleet to defend it. But his greatest triumph was in successfully defending Montevideo, with black slaves and Italian exiles, against foreign, professional soldiers, who greatly outnumbered them and were more heavily armed. The Italian Legion seized and wore red shirts – that were waiting to be exported to Buenos Aires for workers in the slaughterhouses – and from then on they became known as the Red Shirts. Their victories inspired the Italians back home.

Garibaldi sailed back to Italy in 1848 and joined Mazzini in the revolution in Milan. The Austrians crushed it and the king surrendered to them. Garibaldi, however, battled on with 750 volunteers. The king then ordered his arrest for treason in fighting on. A republic was set up in Rome in the same year and Pope Pius IX fled. From exile, he excommunicated anyone who voted in its elections, in which Garibaldi was returned to its assembly. In 1849, the French invaded to restore the Pope to Rome and ignored notices put up, quoting the French constitution, 'France respects other nationalities. Her might will never be used against the liberty of any people.'

Garibaldi once more proved to be an inspiring leader of volunteers against superior regular troops and forced the French to retreat, despite being shot in the stomach himself. However, the King and the Italian army forbade him to pursue the French, which enabled them to gather reinforcements and to return to conquer Rome. Garibaldi was then made commander in chief of the Roman army in the mountains and raised 4,000 volunteers against 60,000 French, Austrian and Spanish troops. He was eventually arrested and exiled to Tangier and then America in 1849.

In 1854 he sailed to London, docking in the West India Dock, where he was warmly welcomed by the East Enders. He stayed for three months and met Mazzini again. The following year, he settled on the Island of Caprera, off Sardinia, as a farmer.

In 1859, there was an unholy alliance between France and Italy (royalists and republicans) against the Austrians and Garibaldi was persuaded to become a major general in the regular army in this alliance. But his fellow professional soldiers resented his success as a guerrilla leader and did everything they could to undermine him. He was given the rawest of untrained recruits and obsolete weapons and he was diverted from any fields of action.

Despite this, he managed to force the Austrians to retreat, only to be betrayed by the French and the Italian royalists, who made peace in exchange for land; the French got Nice and Savoy from Italy and northern Italy got Lombardy from the Austrians. Part of the peace settlement was that the old despotic rulers, who had been driven out of the central Italian states, would be restored to power and Italy was to become a confederation of states under the presidency of the Pope.

Garibaldi was called upon to command the forces to resist this, but resigned when he was prevented from advancing to liberate the Papal States. Instead, he went to Sicily in 1860 and with just 1,000 volunteers, he defeated 25,000 regular troops, forcing the Austrians to agree to a truce and the effective liberation of the island. He declared, 'I came here to fight for the cause of Italy, not of Sicily alone. If we do not free and unite the whole of Italy, we shall never achieve liberty in any individual province.'

The king and the Pope were among those who ordered the assassination of Garibaldi, fearing his continued successes would lead to a revolutionary system taking the place of the monarchy. Nonetheless, Garibaldi went on to liberate Naples and was seen as a communist by the British ambassador for restoring the common land, which had recently been enclosed. Garibaldi, however, believed in 'no class war ... no wanton or unjustified interference with private property ... but a steady bettering of the material conditions of the classes least favoured by fortune'. After he left Naples, all his progressive legislation was repealed en bloc, when the northern Italians took over as the new conquerors in what was effectively a civil war.

In 1862, Garibaldi was shot and wounded by the royal army as he marched towards Rome, where he was arrested and imprisoned while his followers were executed. He escaped a similar fate by a general amnesty, but was confined to bed for several months after being shot in the foot.

On his final visit to England in 1864, he was once more cheered by working men at Southampton, where he docked. When he reached London, more than half a million people packed the streets to applaud him as he went by carriage from Wandsworth to the West End. He inspected the Barclays & Perkins Brewery at Southwark, and also the railworks at Bedford, a little north of St Albans. It is rumoured Garibaldi visited St Albans on this trip – where he was a very popular figure because of the city's large Italian community – to raise funds for his campaign to unify the Italian provinces.

The Germans attacked the French Republic after it deposed the despotic Napoleon III in 1870. Garibaldi helped to defend the French, whom he had fought both with and against in Italy, from 1870 to 1871 and he was the only undefeated general of the French army.

In 1872, he supported, with reservations, the First Socialist International. He explained, 'The International wishes all men to be brothers, the abolition of priests and privileges, hence, I sympathise with it.' Forecasting that agents of the monarchy and clergy would try to undermine it by force in order to protect their state and property, he concluded, 'Only a government founded on justice for all, constitutes the safety of the State and of individual property.'

85. Dic Penderyn, real name Richard Lewis (1808–1831)

Y Dic Penderyn, 102–103 High Street (corner of Castle Street), Methyr Tydfil, CF47 8AP (Tel: 01685 385786). Wetherspoon.

Dic Penderyn was hanged for inflicting stab wounds with a bayonet on a soldier brought in to quell riots against wage cuts. Penderyn was undoubtedly one of the rioters, but almost certainly innocent of the stabbing; even the stabbed soldier Daniel Black doubted his guilt. He is described as 'a martyr of the Welsh working class' on a plaque outside the library opposite the pub, which was unveiled by TUC general secretary Len Murray in 1977. Inside the pub is a banner depicting rioters soaking white flags in calf's blood during the height of the rising, to symbolise their slogan of 'bara neu waed' (bread or blood). This is also said to be the origin of the red flag.

Dic was born into a Methodist family in 1808 at a cottage known as Penderyn in Penrhiw, Aberavon (near Port Talbot). When scrumping apples as a youngster with the blacksmith's son, he was recognised and picked out at school. But rather than inform on his companion, he submitted to a whipping. When another fellow pupil Dafi Cound fell into some water, Dic dived in and saved him from drowning.

Banner in the Dic Penderyn pub of the uprising.

In 1819, the family moved to Merthyr Tydfil, where Dic, aged 11, and his father Lewis, previously a cordwainer, or shoemaker, became ironstone miners. As a youth, Dic hauled timber at Llanelli ironworks in Brecon, but his outspokenness against the inhuman working conditions led to him being sacked in 1828. So he got another job at the neighbouring village of Penderyn, which he also had to leave to avoid prosecution for breaking a law over handling horses.

Dic was fond of his drink and, under its influence, he once thrashed the parish constable John Thomas, who was known as a bully who took bribes from beer shops to leave them alone. Dic also got involved in fisticuffs in the street with Tories, after an argument about reform. He was very much 'part of the tavern world' and known as a strong debater on behalf of rights for working people. His fight with the constable may have made him a marked man by the authorities, when they were later looking for a scapegoat for the riots.

In 1830, he married Mary Thomas (or Mari Howells), the sister of a Methodist preacher – who disapproved of Dic's 'infidel and dangerous ideas' and barred trade unionists from his chapel – and the couple moved to Ynysgau.

Wage cuts were imposed on the miners in 1830 and a mass meeting of between 2,000 and 3,000 workers took place at Pentwyn-mawr, at which Dic was one of the conveners. Apart from the wage cuts, they protested against the truck system, whereby they had to buy goods in the company shops at prices 30 per cent more than shops in the town. In May 1831, further wage cuts of 40 per cent were announced when bread prices were rising, which led to another mass meeting, where red flags were carried and a motion 'not to go to work' was carried almost unanimously. The rising began on 31 May 1831, when workers resisted bailiffs, who were seizing their property. It soon spread and starving rioters demanded bread and cheese, the price of which was still rising rapidly. Workers at the town's ironworks, the largest in the world, who resented the sacking of eighty-four puddlers as well as the pay cuts, came out on strike on 2 June and on the same day, a mass rally on the hills 'broke into insurrection under a red flag'. The flag was carried by one of the sacked puddlers William Thomas Williams, aged 32.

The following day, soldiers arrived from Brecon and took up position both inside and outside the Castle Inn (now the Castle Cinema, opposite the Dic Penderyn pub). They were surrounded by crowds protesting, 'We wanted bread, but the masters have brought the soldiers against us.' A delegation that included Penderyn went in to meet the employers and sought higher wages and immediate reforms to reduce the price of bread.

After this failed, the crowd attempted to disarm the soldiers (Dic grasped the rifle of one of them) and some were bayoneted in the process (16 were wounded but none killed). The soldiers fired on the crowd, killing at least 24 workers and wounding 70 others. The rebels, between 300 and 400 of whom were armed, responded and drove most of the military out of town and held the district for four days. Dic led a band of 200 workers to intercept army reinforcements on the Brecon Road, using boulders to block the road and forcing them to retreat. They were only defeated when an extra 800 troops were brought in. The original troops had remained cooped up in the Castle Inn for eight days, during which time they consumed 950 gallons of beer, 15 gallons of porter, 208 bottles of wine and 34 bottles of brandy.

The authorities rapidly rounded up twenty-eight of the rioters they deemed to be ring leaders, including William Williams (standard bearer of the red flag) and Dic (who was captured after a fierce struggle in a lonely pub called The Lamb Inn at Penderyn). They also included eight ironstone miners, four colliers and two women (one aged 62), who were charged with seizing arms outside the Castle Inn and other offences; four were transported for life and others were sentenced to hard labour.

At his trial at Cardiff in July, Dic was charged with 'riotously assaulting, feloniously attacking and wounding' Black. He admitted being in the deputation to the inn, but said he left by the back and was never at the front, where the stabbing took place. The main witness against him was a barber, James Abbott, who had a grudge against him, having been seen in a fight with him outside the Bush Inn on a previous occasion. Penderyn was wearing a different coloured suit to the attacker at the time and thirteen witnesses, including a chief constable, said he was not at the front, where the crime took place. There was a strong feeling that the real criminal had been shot dead by the soldiers. Even the soldier Donald Black, who had been stabbed in the right hip, could not say it was Penderyn who was responsible. After the verdict, even the judge recommended a reprieve of the death sentence, but this was overruled by Lord Melbourne, the home secretary.

Over 11,000 people, almost the entire population of the town, signed a petition for a reprieve, which led to a stay of execution. But on 13 August, he went to the scaffold in public view at the County Jail, St Mary Street, Cardiff, where a plaque now marks the spot, erroneously referring to the charge being 'murder' during the armed rebellion of the Merthyr trade unionists. His wife had walked there the night before, with their newborn child in her arms, only to find it dead when she got there.

Penderyn's dying words, amid a thunderstorm, were, 'Oh Lord, what an iniquity! I am going to suffer unjustly. God, who knows all things, knows this is so.' He pleaded mercy for those who had borne false witness against him. The Cardiff prison chaplain Daniel Jones resigned in disgust.

The body, followed by a funeral cortège of over a mile long, was taken to St Mary's Parish Church in his birthplace of Aberavon, stopping at the Bridge Inn for refreshments. At the church, a white dove settled on the coffin (Penderyn means head of a bird). He is buried next to his sister, close to the south side of the church (to the left of the path from the main entrance). The inscription on his gravestone reads: To the memory of Richard Lewis, executed at Cardiff for the part he played during the industrial riots in Merthyr Tydfil.

The grave in Aberavon of Richard Lewis aka Dic Penderyn.

A month after his death, thousands of iron workers in Merthyr refused to give up their trade union and in October 4,000 were locked out as a result. They lasted two months before being starved back to work. The pressure, however, forced the government to give the town its own MP in the following year and it soon became one of the strongest centres of Chartism in Wales.

On 14 October 1874, the Western Mail reported that on a visit to Pennsylvania, Rev Evan Evans heard the deathbed confession of Ieuan Parker that it was he who had stabbed Black.

86. Elizabeth Parker (1808–1876) and the Captain Swing Rioters

The Trouble House Inn, Cirencester Road, Tetbury, Gloucestershire, GL8 8SG. (Tel: 01666 502206). Hall & Woodhouse.

The only woman to be transported for life after taking part in the agricultural workers riots of 1830 was arrested in this pub. Mounted soldiers captured Elizabeth Parker and twenty-two of her fellow rioters on 26 November 1830, after they had destroyed several labour-saving threshing machines and after they had demanded pay rises. They were known as the Captain Swing riots. Elizabeth was transported for life to Australia, after being found guilty of smashing one of the machines to pieces with a sledgehammer.

Previously, the pub was called the Wagon and Horses and ironically, the first machine was being carried by a wagon and horses, when rioters attacked it nearby. They unhitched the horses, set fire to the wagon and destroyed the machine, which had been hidden in it underneath some hay. Afterwards, the pub was known as the Trouble House.

The rioters, enraged that each machine was costing ten farm workers their jobs, destroyed several at farms in nearby Horsley and Belverstone, as well as Tetbury. Elizabeth smashed up the one belonging to farmer Jacob Hayward in Belverstone, which had cost him £50. They also broke one of his horse rakes and a haymaking machine. They then set off to burn barns and extort beer and money from other farmers.

Between 5 and 6 p.m., they arrived at the Trouble House on Tetbury Common and ordered beer, bread and cheese. A couple of detachments of Dragoons stationed at Dursley and Wotton-under-Edge also arrived, surrounded the inn, captured the rioters and took them to Horsley Bridewell Prison four miles away. Eventually, twenty-nine were rounded up, of whom twenty-four were finally tried on 5 January 1831 for feloniously destroying the machines.

The prosecution recognised there was high unemployment and great distress in the countryside, but declared this did not excuse 'predetermined and outrageous destruction of agricultural machinery'. After just five minutes' consideration, the jury found them all guilty, but recommended mercy, as only machinery had been attacked. Those at the breaking of one machine were sentenced to seven years and seven others who had been present at the breaking of two machines were transported for fourteen years. Altogether, four hundred and eighty-one were transported for breaking machines all over the south of England and East Anglia and a further nineteen were executed.

Elizabeth Parker, who lived in Tetbury, was originally sentenced to be transported for seven years, but was pardoned after becoming paralysed down one side of her body, losing the use of her legs and becoming unable to speak. Then, after being convicted on 27 March 1832 of stealing £17 10s (£17.50), she was transported to Australia for life. She sailed on the *Frances Charlotte* and arrived at Hobart in Tasmania (which was then called Van Diemen's Land) on 10 January 1833. On 5 October 1835 she married Joseph Councel in Tasmania.

A farm labourer by trade, after being sacked as a house and dairymaid, she had also earned money as 'a common prostitute of the very worst description', according to her jail report. She admitted that she had been 'on the town' for two or three years before being transported.

Her two front teeth had been knocked out, her right cheek was scarred and she had moles on her arms and belly. Her height was 5 foot 6 inches and she had dark hazel eyes and a florid complexion. She could read and write, but was considered by the authorities to have a 'very bad character'.

In Australia, she was jailed eighteen times for being drunk, absent without leave, refusing to work, misconduct, assaulting a constable, indecent exposure and being in bed in a disorderly house after hours. She was also sentenced to three months hard labour for receiving a stolen silk handkerchief. Pardons were granted from 1836 onwards to those who had been transported, but Elizabeth had to wait until 11 August 1846, before being given a conditional pardon,

The Trouble House where the Captain Swing rioters including Elizabeth Parker were arrested.

which meant she had to stay in Australia or New Zealand. She died in Victoria in 1876.

A year before the 1830 riots, two of the last highwaymen to be hanged in the country, Matthew and Henry Pinnell, had also been arrested in the pub in April 1829, after robbing a farmer named Kearsey three miles away near Rodmarton. This was another reason for it becoming known as the Trouble House.

87. Charles Darwin (1809–1882)

Sutton Road, Shrewsbury, Shropshire, SY2 6HN (Tel: 01743 356827).

Charles Darwin, whose well-documented theories of evolution revolutionised world scientific thinking and outraged religious believers, was born and educated in Shrewsbury. In fact, he delayed publishing his findings for many years, conscious of the storm his findings would cause for challenging the theory of creation. He had studied theology with a view to having a career in the church, but over the years he became an agnostic. In 1858, he was precipitated into publishing his findings, because another naturalist Alfred Wallace sent him a paper with identical theories to his own. Their two papers were presented and published jointly in July of that year and Darwin finally published his expanded views in *On the Origin of Species by Means of Natural Selection* in November 1859.

He then braced himself for the furious public reaction, which duly came with cartoons of him looking like an ape being widely published. Darwin kept aloof from the debate over whether his findings disproved all the species had been created by God in one week. But Darwin's evidence of fossils showed how species had evolved over the centuries.

One ingenious attempt was made to reconcile the two theories by the Christian zoologist Philip Gosse, who opined God could have created both species and fossils. Christians and atheists alike scorned this theory. But the idea of God as an amiable practical joker 'scattering misleading clues' appealed to writer John Mortimer, who warmed to Gosse as 'a kindly man anxious to end a quarrel'.

Darwin, who suffered from flatulence and gout for most of his life, was born at The Mount in Shrewsbury. His mother Susannah Wedgwood died when he was 8 and the following year, he went to Shrewsbury School, staying there from 1818 until 1825. Darwin evoked the wrath of the school by constructing with his brother an amateur laboratory in a tool shed without permission. The school was then where Castle Gate Library is now sited, outside which a statue of Darwin stands, sculpted by H. Montford and erected in 1897.

After leaving school Darwin studied medicine at Edinburgh University, but was disgusted by anatomy and horrified by operations, so he abandoned the course after two years. Next, he went to study theology at Cambridge University, but spent most of his time collecting beetles, galloping across the countryside, supping and shooting.

The break that was to change his life came in December 1831, when he embarked on a five-year voyage around the southern hemisphere on *The Beagle* ship as a naturalist. His quarters were so cramped that in order to put up his hammock, he had to move one of the drawers containing his clothes. He wrote about his homesickness and dreamed of the autumn robins singing in his Shrewsbury garden. In one of the expeditions on land, he proved his endurance by being one of the few who managed to struggle on to get water, while the others collapsed from thirst and exhaustion. This voyage greatly added to his knowledge of geology and zoology ... and it also started his collection of fossils from South America, which led to his thoughts on evolution. He started sketching out the *Origin of Species* within a year of his return and his thoughts of a career in the church died a natural death.

In January 1839, he married his first cousin Emma Wedgwood (daughter of Josiah) and they moved into what was then 12 Upper Gower Street and is now 110 Gower Street, now appropriately occupied by the Biological Science Buildings of University College London. His granddaughter Gwen Darwin later studied at the Slade School of Fine Art in the same street. His first two children were born there, including his favourite daughter Annie, who died aged 11. Darwin scientifically observed their infantile behaviour and described his findings in *The Expression of Emotions*.

Darwin's statue outside the site of the school he attended in Shrewsbury.

Fondly describing the area, he wrote, 'There is a grandeur about its smoky fogs and the dull distant sounds of cabs and coaches; in fact you may perceive I am becoming a thorough-paced cockney.' But the not-so-distant sounds of troops marching past his house on the way to quell Chartist uprisings alarmed him, so he moved in 1842 to Down House near Sevenoaks in Kent. There, he kept tame pigeons and made laborious cross breeding experiments with them. He always enjoyed experiments more than writing, which might have been a contributing factor to the delay in publishing his work.

About 6 feet in height, his habitual stoop made him look less tall. Although strong, he was clumsy and unable to use his hands effectively to draw. A good listener, he was normally warm and frank in expressing his views, but cruelty was one issue that roused his indignation and made him angry.

His success as a scientist he put down to his 'love of science, unbounded patience in long reflecting over any subject, industry in observing and collecting facts, and a fair share of invention as well as common sense'.

88. William Gladstone (1809–1889)

(i) The Gladstone, 123 Lewes Road, Brighton, East Sussex, BN2 3QB
     (Tel: 01273 620888). Punch Taverns.
(ii) The Gladstone Arms, Combs Ford, Stowmarket, Suffolk
     (Tel: 01449 612339). Adnams.

William Ewart Gladstone, four times a liberal prime minister, was a regular visitor to Brighton, as shown by a plaque at the Adelphi Hotel in Pool Valley, which states he frequently stayed at the nearby Lion Mansions Hotel. After switching from Conservative to Liberal, he stated, 'Liberalism is trust of the people, tempered by prudence; conservatism, distrust of people, tempered by fear.' Chamber pots, with his portrait inside, were popular merchandise sold to Tories after his defection.

His father John had left school at 13 to work at Leith Docks, but had became a successful corn merchant and owner of sugar plantations using slave labour in the West Indies. The wealth from this enabled him to purchase a large house in Liverpool with wine cellars, where William was born. It also financed William's education from the age of 12 at Eton, where he acquired the nickname Mr Tipple, and Oxford University's Christchurch College from the age of 19.

On leaving university, he was elected as a Conservative MP for Newark at the end of 1832. In his election address he promised to press for 'labour to receive adequate remuneration, which, unhappily, among several classes of our fellow countrymen, it is not now the case'. His maiden speech in 1833, however, was against the Slavery Abolition Bill. His case was that the emancipation of slaves should be delayed until they became Christians. A slave revolt on his father's plantation had been brutally suppressed ten years earlier.

He became known as the 'people's William' after converting to the liberal cause (becoming the party's leader in 1867) and extending the vote to the working class in stages, saying he thought their representatives would serve the 'public interest' rather than class interests. He also expressed the view that the wealthy should use their surplus for the common good. This made him very unpopular with Queen Victoria, who dubbed him 'that half mad firebrand'.

Other popular measures of his included the 1844 Railways Act, limiting profits and putting legal obligations on the companies to provide cheap travel, and the lowering of duties on French wine and brandy. Gladstone himself enjoyed fine wines, champagne and strong beer. Less popular measures were the Licensing Act of 1872, which forced pubs to close at 11 p.m. in the country and midnight in London, and which brought about an increase in duty on beer.

In 1893, during his last term as prime minister, he managed to get his controversial Irish home-rule bill through the House of Commons by a majority of 34, only to see it rejected by the House of Lords by 419 votes to 41.

A family man with eight children, he raised eyebrows by picking up prostitutes late at night in order to 'save' them. He had founded the Church Penitentiary Association for the Reclamation of Fallen Women in 1848, but soon started taking them to his or their homes late at night. His diaries reveal that he made several long visits to a young prostitute called Elizabeth Collins, with whom he had oral sex, after which he whipped himself. Just before he died, he told his son he had never 'been guilty of the act which is known as that of infidelity to the marriage bed'; a very precise wording that in those days excluded sex acts short of penetration. His diaries, which were full of references to the state of his bowels, also reveal that he read pornography avidly.

Gladstone's statue in The Strand, London.

He remained fit throughout his life and climbed the highest peak in the Cairngorms at the age of 75. His sister Helen was an opium addict, who had to be restrained in a lunatic asylum in 1846.

89. Alexander Bain (1810–1877)

Market Place, Wick, Caithness, Scottish Highlands, KY1 4BS (Tel: 01955 609920). Wetherspoon.

The inventor of the electric clock and the forerunner of the fax machine, Alexander Bain started his working life as an apprentice watchmaker in Wick some sixty paces from this pub at 77 High Street (on the corner of London Close), working for John Seller from 1829 to

1830. Some of Bain's less successful inventions included unspillable inkwells, propelling pencils and apparatus enabling musicians to play their instruments from a distance.

The son of a crofter, he was born about 13 miles from Wick at Houstry in the parish of Watten, Caithness, in the far north-east of Scotland. Wick is just 17 miles from John O'Groats. In 1837, he travelled to London to become a journeyman clockmaker in Clerkenwell, where he attended lectures on electrical science. This was put to good use when he invented in 1841 the first electric clock, with an electromagnetically maintained pendulum, for which he become known as 'the father of electrical horology'.

In 1843, he patented what was, in effect, the world's first fax machine, which could send copies of drawings electronically from one place to another. This was done by the use of synchronised pendulums and scanning styluses. He discovered how fast it worked by accident, when a spring broke during an experiment. The machine stopped, but the message had already been received at the other end. Some forty years later (after his death) it was developed to transmit photographs to newspaper offices and, more recently, as standard office equipment.

The Alexander Bain at Christmas time.

After a dispute, he received £7,500 from the Electric Telegraph Company for infringements of his patents. This was a fortune he was to lose by taking further legal actions and by drinking excessively. By 1872, he had resorted to repairing clocks to scrape a living. Before that he was awarded a medal for his clocks at the Great Exhibition of 1851 in London and he set up a business manufacturing clocks at 43 Old Bond Street.

But he also kept inventing other instruments, which were to have a considerable impact on the railways and shipping, such as electrical rail signalling equipment to transmit time signals telegraphically (allowing standard time to be used throughout the country for the first time, which was vital to efficient railways), electric fire alarms on ships and electric logs to record ship speeds. His other inventions included a document copier and repeating firearms.

After he was reduced to poverty, the Royal Society came to his rescue in 1873, with a grant of £150 a year in recognition of his great contributions to science. But it was only three years later that he was admitted to the Broomhill Home for Incurables in Kirkintilloch (8 miles north-east of Glasgow), where he died a few months later. He was buried in the local Old Aisle Cemetery. A *Times* obituary stated, 'He was not a commercial man but his inventive powers were most wonderful. He has given the world some invaluable innovations.'

90. Charles Dickens (1812–1870)

(i) 5–6 Victoria Parade, Broadstairs, Kent, CT10 1QS (Tel: 01843 869865). Enterprise Inns.

(ii) 160 Union Street, London, SE1 0LH (Tel: 020 7401 3744). Free house.

The Charles Dickens in Broadstairs.

The locations of these two pubs represent the emotional depths and heights in the life of Dickens. Union Street is close to where his father John was incarcerated in Marshalsea Prison (in Borough High Street) for debt from February to May in 1824. It was also where Charles lodged at Lant Street (by Borough Station) near the prison, when it was a run-down neighbourhood.

He was just 12 years old and had to work in a much-hated blacking factory to pay the six shillings a week rent while his father was in jail. When Charles visited his father in the jail they cried together. Debt and prison life were later to feature in many of his novels, such as *A Passage in the Life of Mr Watkins Tottle*, the *Pickwick Papers*, *Little Dorrit* and *David Copperfield*. Hence, nearby streets today are named Pickwick Street, Dorrit Street, Copperfield Street and Dickens Square.

Within a few days of completing *Little Dorrit* in May 1857, Dickens returned to Borough to see if he could find any ruins of the Marshalsea. He found the room where his father had been and observed the differences, 'The spikes are gone, and the wall is lowered, and anybody can go out now who likes to go ...'

In contrast, his days in Broadstairs, where he had long holidays regularly from 1837 to 1850, were bliss. He delighted in the 'corn growing, larks singing, gardens full of flowers, and fresh air on the sea', which set him writing with 'great vigour'.

Dickens House Museum is located two doors from the pub in this seaside resort, where Mary Pearson Strong lived, on whom Dickens based David Copperfield's aunt Betsey Trotwood. Mary fought like crazy to prevent donkeys being ridden in front of her house along the cliffs, much to the amusement of Dickens, who befriended her. He completed many novels here, including *Pickwick Papers*, *Oliver Twist*, *Nicholas Nickleby*, *David Copperfield*, *The Old Curiosity Shop* and *Barnaby Rudge*, while staying at various places such as the Albion (now the Royal Albion Hotel) where he took a liking to the Hollands gin, 40 Albion Street, 12 High Street, Lawn House, and Fort House (now renamed Bleak House) overlooking Viking Bay. A book in the pub informs us that he also liked a Sherry Cobbler (made of port and sherry) and a punch (made of white wine and brandy).

He may have partaken of them when he grabbed a young woman and dragged her into the sea 'as if possessed', until she screamed as the 'wild waves overwhelmed us'. He told her not to struggle but to think of how *The Times* would report her pathetic fate: 'drowned by Dickens in a fit of dementia!' His wife intervened and so the 20-year-old Eleanor 'Emma' Picken escaped from his all too realistic play-acting. Later, she befriended Dickens's brother Frederick, who shared his love of charades and amateur dramatics.

Dickens was also an accomplished conjuror: being able to pour raw ingredients into a bowler hat and turn them into a plum pudding, as well as turn bran into a guinea pig. But he was unable to work his magic to make the pain from a fistula in his rectum disappear while he wrote *Barnaby Rudge*. Instead, he had it removed by a conventional operation, without an anaesthetic. He had a pet raven called Grip and he also liked to roam the 'more dreadful streets of London' at night, including the opium dens of Limehouse, and gaze into the black stinking waters of the Thames.

He had intimate liaisons with two of his sisters-in-law: Mary who died aged 17 and Georgina. In 1858, he left his wife and started an affair with a young actress, Ellen Lawless Ternan, who, at 18, was the same age as his eldest daughter. She wore scarlet geraniums in her hair and had 'a pretty face and a well developed figure'. Her father had died in a lunatic asylum when

Dickensian characters from Oliver Twist, The Artful Dodger and Fagin, hanging in the pub in Broadstairs.

she was 6 years old. Dickens first met her in a Manchester theatre, when he comforted her as she wept with embarrassment over the scantiness of her costume.

In June 1865, they survived a train crash that killed ten people and seriously injured forty others; one of those killed was a Frenchman, who had changed seats with Dickens a few seconds before the crash at Staplehurst Viaduct in Kent on the Dover to London train. Dickens emerged from the wreck to help the rescue work – and rescued a bottle of brandy and his manuscript *Our Mutual Friend*.

91. John Snow (1813–1858)

39 Broadwick Street, Soho, London, W1F 9QP (Tel: 020 7437 1344).
Samuel Smith.

'The most terrible outbreak of cholera which ever occurred in the kingdom' was how John Snow described the deaths of nearly 700 people in a few days in a tiny area of Soho, starting on 31 August 1854. He was convinced that it was caused by polluted water being drunk from the pump by 40 Broadwick Street (called Broad Street in those days). But despite compelling evidence presented by him to the authorities, they were sceptical and his theory that cholera was a waterborne disease was not generally accepted until nearly thirty years after his death.

He was born in York, became a surgeon in Newcastle-upon-Tyne during the 1831 cholera epidemic in that town and, after inventing a device for administrating chloroform, he became the world's first professional anaesthetist; later using his skills to assist Queen Victoria in the birth of Prince Leopold in 1853 and Princess Beatrice in 1857.

After moving to London in 1836, where he lived in Argyll Street and 54 Frith Street, Soho, he published his theories *On the Mode of Communication of Cholera* in 1849. When the epidemic struck in Broadwick Street, 127 people died in the first three days and the death toll rapidly escalated to 500. He finally persuaded the reluctant board of guardians to close the pump on the eighth day, after which the cases dropped dramatically, leaving 616 dead after a month and the final total around 700. Snow had discovered that a high proportion of those who used the street pump contracted cholera, but very few did among other locals who used alternative water supplies. The latter included 70 men working in a brewery almost next to the pump, not one of which suffered. Snow interviewed the proprietor Mr Huggins and discovered 'the men are allowed a certain quantity of malt liquor ... and do not drink water at all', although the brewery had its own well.

This inspired a poem at the time called *The Cholera's Coming*, which went:

> They say it's the water
>
> That brought on the slaughter
>
> And those that drank porter
>
> Were saved by the jar.

Those who drank in the local pubs, however, were not immune, because water from the street pump was used to mix with spirits; nine customers from one pub alone died because of this. Snow also discovered how a gentleman from Brighton died after a brief visit, during which he drank a small tumbler of brandy ... with water from the pump.

Karl Marx was living nearby at 28 Dean Street, but was spared because, despite living in squalor, he had his own water supply. Florence Nightingale joined the emergency nursing force to soothe the fear-crazed victims, mainly prostitutes, who were taken to Middlesex Hospital in nearby Mortimer Street. Rev Henry Whitehead, vicar of St Luke's Church in Berwick Street, thought all this was divine retribution. But he did discover the probable real cause: just before the epidemic, a child with cholera had its nappies steeped in water, which was then tipped into a leaking cesspool only 3 feet from the pump.

Even after deaths stopped when the pump was temporarily closed, the Board of Health dismissed Snow's claim that this was the cause of the epidemic and the pump continued to be used for another eleven years. A year after the epidemic, *The Builder* journal noted, 'Even in Broad Street it would appear that little has been done ... the open cesspools are still to be seen; in the court, as far as we could learn, no change had been made; so that here, in spite of the late numerous deaths, we have all the materials for a fresh epidemic.'

Snow himself wrote, 'Cholera may linger in the courts and alleys crowded with the poor, but I know of no instance in which it has been generally spread through a town or neighbourhood, among all classes of the community, in which the drinking water has not been the medium of its diffusion. Each epidemic of cholera in London has borne a strict relation to the nature of the water supply of its different districts, being modified only by poverty and the crowding and want of cleanliness which always attend it.'

A replica of the pump in Soho that caused the 1854 cholera outbreak in the shadow of the John Snow pub.

Yet he was a voice in the wilderness, dying four years after the epidemic, aged just 44. His theories were not accepted until further findings by Robert Koch were published in 1884. A replica pump has been erected in the street on the site of the original. A few yards away, in the John Snow Pub, the history of the epidemic is displayed in the upstairs bar.

92. Grace Darling (1815–1842)

The Bamburgh Inn, 175 Bamburgh Avenue, South Shields, Tyne & Wear, NE34 6SS. (Tel: 01914 541899). Greene King.

North Sea rescue heroine Grace Darling is graphically portrayed on this pub sign bravely battling against the waves off Bamburgh in Northumberland. The daring 22-year-old Grace was on duty in the lighthouse, where she lived on Longstone Island (one of the Farne Islands), on 7 September 1838 amid a terrible storm. At quarter to five in the morning she saw a ship had run aground on the rocks of Big Harcar Island, half a mile to the west. She awoke her father William, who considered the conditions would make it impossible to launch the lifeboat at Seahouses (2 miles south of Bamburgh).

Grace Darling's daring rescue on the Bamburgh pub sign.

At dawn, they saw through a telescope that survivors were clinging to the wreck. Grace pleaded with her father to attempt a rescue and he agreed. The pair got into the lighthouse coble, an open rowing boat 21 feet long and 6 feet wide used for fishing, which normally took at least three to row it, and struck out into the raging storm.

The tide and the wind were so strong that they could not row using the direct route, as the mountainous waves would have dashed them on the jagged rocks. Instead, they went the long way round to get shelter, which meant they had to row twice as far to reach the nine survivors of the steamship *Forfarshire*: five crew members and four passengers, including a woman, who held her two dead children. There was not enough room for them all, so two trips had to be organised. Grace held the boat steady as the woman and four men, one of whom was injured, scrambled aboard.

When they rowed back to the lighthouse, Grace and her mother tended to the injured man and fed them all, while two of the fitter men joined William to row back and pick up the remaining four. Grace's brother George and other members of the Seahouses lifeboat crew had meanwhile launched another coble and reached the rock after two and a half hours, only to find three dead bodies. The sea was too rough to row back to shore, so they went to the lighthouse instead and joined the survivors.

Grace Darling's tomb in the church.

The violent storm lasted so long that it was two days before they could be taken ashore. Over forty people on the *Forfarshire* had drowned and much of the early publicity focused on the possibility that the shipowners had deliberately put it to sea in an unfit state to get the insurance money ... the so-called 'coffin ships scandal' exposed by Samuel Plimsoll.

But soon the details of Grace's role in the rescue emerged and she was hailed as a national heroine. *The Times* newspaper asked the question, 'Is there in the field of history, or of fiction even, one instance of female heroism to compare for one moment with this?' Artists painted her, poets and minstrels wrote verses and songs about her, she was inundated with proposals of marriage and so many people asked for locks of her hair that she became almost bald. One of the most popular verses to come out was the *Grace Darling Song*, which went:

'Twas on the Longstone Lighthouse, there dwelt an English maid;
Pure as the air around her, of danger ne'er afraid;
One morning just at daybreak, a storm-tossed wreck she spied;
And tho' to try seemed madness, 'I'll save the crew!' she cried.
And she pull'd away, o'er the rolling sea,
Over the waters blue –
'Help! Help!' she could hear the cry of the shipwreck'd crew –
But Grace had an English heart,
And the raging storm she brav'd –
She pull'd away, mid the dashing spray,
And the crew she saved!

Grace and her father received gold medals from the Royal Humane Society and silver medals from the Royal National Institution for the

The Grace Darling Museum in Bamburgh.

Preservation of Life from Shipwreck. Payments of £50 from the Treasury and £750 from public subscription were also made to Grace and most of it was held in trust. But she disliked all the fuss and said she was only doing her duty. She continued living in the lighthouse and remained a hard-working, sensible woman, until her death just four years later from tuberculosis.

She was buried at St Aidan's Parish Church, Radcliffe Road, Bamburgh, where she had been baptised, opposite the cottage she was born in, which is now the Grace Darling Museum. The rowing boat used in the rescue is on display in this museum, along with other relics connected with Grace. Her tomb in the churchyard overlooks the sea. The original one carved in Portland stone had to be moved inside the church in 1885, as the weather was taking its toll on it. A replacement one made from local stone was erected in the churchyard. In 1893, its roof was destroyed in a violent storm and had to be replaced. A stained-glass window depicting Grace is sited in the Oswald chapel of the church. A lifeboat bearing her name at nearby Seahouses continues to make rescues to this day.

The Bamburgh Pub in South Shields is about 40 miles south, also overlooking the North Sea, and is quite close to Tynemouth Lifeboat Station.

93. Edwin Waugh (1817–1890)

10–12 Market Street, Heywood, Lancashire, OL10 4LY (Tel: 01706 621480). Wetherspoon.

Known as the 'Burns of Lancashire', Edwin Waugh became famous for his poem in dialect *Come Whoam to thy Childer an' Me*, published in 1856.

Born in Rochdale the son of a shoemaker, his father died when Edwin was aged 9. His mother tried to keep the business going and Edwin helped her with their stall in the market, but it was tough going and they lived in great poverty in a cellar. She taught him to read with the few books his father had collected. At the age of 12, Edwin earned his first wages as an errand boy to a local Wesleyan preacher and printer. Later in the same year he became an errand boy for Thomas

Edwin Waugh's portrait inside the pub.

Holden, a bookseller and printer, who two years later apprenticed him to become a printer. The books in his shop were read avidly by Edwin, especially histories of Lancashire, poetry and ballads.

On completion of his apprenticeship, he wandered the country as a journeyman printer for six or seven years and then returned to Rochdale, where he established a literary institute. In 1847, he was appointed assistant secretary to the recently founded Lancashire Public School Association, which campaigned for popular and unsectarian education, paid for from local rates and run by elected local boards.

When the *Manchester Examiner* accepted for publication his descriptions of rural rambles, it encouraged him to write more articles for the paper. These were collected by a local bookseller and were published as his first book *Sketches of Lancashire Life and Localities* in 1855. They featured his racy humour in Lancashire dialect. Thomas Carlyle received a copy and pronounced the author to be 'a man of decided mark'.

Offers of work poured in and from 1860 to 1875 he was able to make a living from writing alone, producing prose, songs, verse, tales and sketches. He also publicly recited his work and was a good singer. He was not spoiled by success, however, and he retained the geniality and cheerfulness he had maintained through years of poverty.

In 1862, he became deeply affected by the cotton famine and wrote in graphic detail about the districts most hit. By 1876, he was becoming infirm and so a committee of supporters took over the copyright of his works in return for a guaranteed, fixed annual income. Further security came in 1881, when Gladstone granted him a civil list pension of £90 a year.

After his death he was mourned by thousands as the 'voice of Lancashire's homely virtues' and he was praised as 'a striking specimen of the sturdy, independent, plain spoken Lancashire man'.

94. Florence Nightingale (1820–1910)

(i)   110 London Road East (corner of Litchurch Street), Derby, Derbyshire, DE1 2QZ (Tel: 01332 296885). Punch Taverns.
(ii) 132 Beckett Street, Leeds, West Yorkshire, LS9 7JX (Tel: 01332 482622).
(iii) 199 Westminster Bridge Road, Lambeth, London SE1 7UT (Tel: 020 7928 3027) (demolished 2006).

Her popular image as the 'Lady with the Lamp' was always rejected by Florence Nightingale herself, as she preferred to be seen as a thorn in the side of the military and political establishment. But it is the image that made her the world's most famous nurse and is the one depicted on the sign of this Derby pub. This pub is right next to the Derbyshire Royal Infirmary Hospital, which was redesigned, according to her plans in 1869, to reduce the mortality rate.

Florence had a pet owl called Athena and she lived in Lea just 12 miles north of Derby. She was modest about her hospital's role in reducing the death rate from 42 per cent to just 2 per cent in the Crimea during the war of 1854–1856, which was considered a huge achievement at the time.

'While devoting my life to hospital work I have come to the conclusion that hospitals are not the best place for the poor sick,' she wrote. 'The ultimate destination of all nursing is the nursing of the sick in their own homes ... I look to the abolition of all hospitals and workhouse infirmaries.'

Her wealthy landowner father at first refused to allow her into nursing, considering hospitals as little better than brothels. But he finally relented in 1853 and she worked unpaid at the Hospital for Invalid Gentlewomen in London.

The following year, during the Soho cholera epidemic, she volunteered to work at the Middlesex Hospital in nearby Mortimer

The Florence Nightingale in Derby.

Street, where many of the nurses had died or run away. She recalled a constant stream to the hospital of 'wretched shrieking creatures', many of them prostitutes, whom she described as 'poor creatures staggering off their beat'. They were, she said, filthy, drunken and crazed with terror and pain. She was up day and night undressing and bandaging them in a vain attempt to keep the mortality rate down. The hospital closed in 2007, but a pub close to it, The Champion, 13 Wells Street, London, W1, has a stained-glass window of Florence.

She was one of the few at the time who agreed with the theory put forwards by John Snow that cholera was caused from drinking polluted water. She was working at a Harley Street nursing home at this time - 1853 to 1854.

Then, in October 1854, she went to treat the wounded and diseased soldiers of the Crimean War at the Scutari Barrack Hospital in Constantinople. The hospital was built on a cesspool and poisonous gases came up from the blocked sewers, became trapped in the unventilated hospital and killed thousands of patients. From November 1854 to March 1855, the death rate trebled to three in eight.

The Florence Nightingale pub in Leeds.

Nightingale thought this was as a result of the men's treatment before they reached the hospital, having been starved and overworked in the trenches. 'The men sent down to Scutari in the winter died because they were not sent down till half dead,' she said in August 1855. 'The men sent down now live and recover because they are sent in time.'

There was some truth in this though, as over 16,000 soldiers died from scurvy and other diseases related to malnutrition (which could have been prevented by the use of supplies in army stores or food in the near vicinity), frostbite (from exposure) and exhaustion (caused by the incompetence of their officers). This was about seven times the number of those who were killed in battle.

In November 1855, a national appeal was launched for the Nightingale Fund to establish a school for nurses in a London teaching hospital. This was boosted by the publication of letters from soldiers, such as one stating, 'What a comfort it was to see her pass ... we would kiss her shadow as it fell, and lay our heads on the pillow again, content.' She also served them wine by the light of candles in beer bottles.

The war officially ended on 30 March 1856 and when she returned to London in August 1856, she was proud of eventually reducing the death rate. She dedicated herself to reforming army practices, which she thought were causing unnecessary deaths, but was strongly opposed by Queen Victoria.

The cabinet planned to use her popularity to bring the army high command under democratic control, to prevent further mistreatment of the common soldier. Nightingale on the field had been criticised by army officers for spending too much time with the common soldier and not enough on 'her equals and superiors'.

Then, in May 1857, a Royal Commission found that the real reason for the high death rate in the military hospitals was as a result of bad hygiene, overcrowding and poor sanitation. But it suppressed the specific evidence of Scutari hospital. When the statistics proved this, Nightingale had a mental breakdown and lost all interest in the Nightingale Fund and in promoting nursing schools.

A scene from the Crimean War showing Florence Nightingale tending a wounded soldier (part of the monument in Pall Mall).

When she recovered, she recognised that 14,000 soldiers had died in hospital, because she and her medical staff had neglected elementary sanitary precautions. She was determined to learn the lessons from the mistakes of Scutari hospital, where the death rate had been highest and so was good, hard evidence, in order that they were not repeated. But the government, which was conducting an internal battle with the army high command, suppressed the evidence and as a result, the same mistakes were made in the American Civil War. 'Had the conclusions that Florence Nightingale reached been heeded in the civil war in America, hundreds of thousands of lives might have been saved,' was the view of her biographer Hugh Small.

Nightingale went to enormous trouble to reveal the facts and preserve the evidence, despite the official cover-up by leading politicians and by Queen Victoria. She wrote *Notes on Nursing* in 1860, which attacked doctors, hospitals and hospital nursing, and in the same year she started up the Nightingale Training School for Nurses at St Thomas's Hospital in Lambeth Palace Road, opposite the pub that bore her name, until recently being demolished.

But her heart was not in it and so she concentrated more on social policy, such as community health-care and modifying hospital architecture. The success she had achieved, she said, was not as a result of her 'Lady of the Lamp' image, but the political power she had been given in running the hospitals free from army bureaucracy.

The Florence Nightingale Museum, 2 Lambeth Palace Road, is situated opposite where the pub once stood. There are three statues of her in Derby: one in front of the hospital, one above the Nightingale Care Unit opposite the hospital and the other in St Peter's Street.

95. Sally Purse, aka Pussey (c.1820–1885)

Sally Pussey Inn, Swindon Road, Wootton Bassett, Swindon, Wiltshire, SN4 8ET (Tel: 01793 852430). Arkells.

Faith healer Sally Purse was a formidable woman who ran the pub from 1841, until her death. Although only 5 feet 1 inch tall, she had no problem ejecting burly railway navvies if they got out of order. She possessed extraordinary healing powers over both men and beasts and became a living legend. Her name, when pronounced in the local dialect, led to her becoming known as Sarah Puss, then Sah Puss and finally, Sally Pussey. She is buried in nearby Lydiard Tregoze Churchyard.

Arkell's Brewery bought the pub, then called the Wheat Sheaf, in 1906 and renamed it after her in 1971.

96. Samuel Plimsoll (1824–1898)

Plimsoll Line, 138 High Street, Redcar, North Yorkshire, TS10 3DH (Tel: 01642 495250). Wetherspoon.

Samuel Plimsoll became known as 'the Sailors' Friend' for his dogged battle against shipowners, who callously sacrificed their seamen's lives for profit. 'I once made a voyage from London to Redcar which opened my eyes to the horror of the "coffin-ships" and led me to devote myself to the cause of the seamen,' he recalled.

Coffin-ships were unseaworthy, overloaded and heavily overinsured vessels, the owners of which were happy to see them sink in order to collect the inflated, and often fraudulent compensation ... impervious to the cost in human life. Plimsoll's proposals to improve maritime safety were naturally resisted to the end by these owners.

The voyage to Redcar to which he referred took place in 1864 and it ended in a fierce storm, which wrecked four ships. His own ship finally arrived several hours overdue, when he was met by his wife Eliza, who was sobbing with relief that he was safe.

'I mingled my tears with hers, because I was thinking of those other women who had also spent a sleepless night and who would never see their husbands again,' he stated. 'I was thinking of good and brave men who would never return home and I resolved, deep down in my heart, as I stood on the sands of Redcar, to devote myself to this work. What was the difference between me and these poor, drowned sailors? Parliament had cared for my safety by sending me to sea in a ship which had been surveyed, while the sailors went to sea in any ship any owner liked to send them in.'

After resting up at 37 High Street in Redcar (now a Marks & Spencer's store), where Bristol born Plimsol frequently stayed on holiday, he set about his campaign and in 1868, after being elected as the Liberal MP for Derby, proposed that a load-line be painted on ships to prevent overloading. The Plimsoll Line, as it became known, finally became law in 1876, when he had been nearly bankrupted by shipowners who, at one time, had thirteen writs and notices served on him simultaneously. Even then, the new law left it up to the shipowners themselves to decide where the load-line, up to which the water could reach, should be fixed. One in Cardiff showed his contempt for the law by painting it on the top of his ship's funnel. It was not until 1890 that the law made the Board of Trade responsible for determining a safe position for the line.

Plimsoll was suspended from the Commons in 1875 for his angry reaction to the announcement that the Merchant Shipping Bill, which had already been talked out several times by shipowner MPs, was being postponed yet again. He urged the Tory prime minister Benjamin Disraeli 'not to consign some thousands of living men to an undeserved and sudden death' by dropping the bill. 'Shipowners of murderous tendencies outside this house, but who are amply represented

A detail from the mural at the International Transport Workers Federation in London, showing shipowners playing poker with seamen's lives.

The labour movement pays tribute to Plimsoll in a mural at the International Transport Workers Federation in London.

inside the house, have frustrated and talked to death every effort to procure a remedy for this state of things,' he declared.

Goaded to name names, he gave notice of a question about the Plymouth MP Edward Bates, owner of three ships, which had all been lost in the previous year with the loss of eighty-seven lives. 'I am determined to unmask the villains who send these sailors to death and destruction,' he said.

As he was being led out of the chamber, his wife dropped a written statement by him from the gallery onto the press desk. It stated, 'I charge the government that they are wittingly and unwittingly playing into the hands of the maritime murderers inside the house and outside the house, to secure a further continuance of the present murderous system.'

The appalling conditions that the seamen were forced to work under were exposed in Plimsoll's book *Our Seamen*, published in December 1872. It pointed out that they had to sign articles before seeing the state of the ship and if they then refused to sail on an obviously unseaworthy vessel, they were sentenced to three months' imprisonment with hard labour.

This was the fate of seven seamen chained on the jetty at Margate in 1871 for refusing to go to sea on a ship where they had less shelter than the sheep being carried on board. Another ship fed the crew seven-year-old meat; which had been pickled in army garrisons and returned as unfit for soldiers. A dozen of them died of scurvy on passage and a further three on arrival in port.

In 1887, Plimsoll became the first president of the newly formed National Amalgamated Sailors' and Firemen's Union of Great Britain and Ireland; a position he held until 1892, when diabetes forced him to resign.

The lifeboat that rescued Samuel Plimsoll from a shipwreck in Redcar, from a picture in the Plimsoll Line.

Plimsoll had earlier been influenced by the Chartist movement after moving to Sheffield in his teens. He became a coal merchant transporting coal from Yorkshire to London and in 1860, he became known as 'the Miners'

Friend' for supporting ways to prevent colliery disasters by detecting fire damp. He also called for healthier conditions in workshops, where metal dust was causing death of three times the average rate from asthma among knife grinders.

His maiden speech in Parliament in 1868, for a repeal of the criminal laws against trade unions, helped win their legal recognition in the 1871 Trades Union Act. But it was his campaign against the coffin-shipowners that gained him growing public support. A music hall ditty of the time *A Coffin-Shipowner's Lament* went as follows:

> I bought up an old rotten ship
> And filled it with boxes of earth,
> I swore they were boxes of Indian silk
> And insured them for ten times their worth.
> At sea, of course, she went down.
> Ten thousand I got for my greed;
> But Plimsoll is putting a stop to my game,
> And hang it, I think he'll succeed.

Another song *Our Sailors on the Sea* included the verse:

> There was a time when greed and crime did cruelly prevail,
> And rotten ships were sent on trips to flounder in the gale;
> When worthless cargoes, well-insured, would to the bottom go,
> And Sailors' lives were sacrificed that men might wealthy grow.

A lifeboat was named after Plimsoll and was launched at Lowestoft in 1876, where it stayed in operation until 1905, saving 165 lives during that time. In the same year, the Liverpool Rubber Company produced a canvas rubber shoe, which was watertight as long it was not immersed above its water band ... and these shoes naturally became known as Plimsolls.

He retired to Folkestone at the age of 68 and lived there for the rest of his life. The National Union of Seamen – the successor of the Sailors and Firemen's Union, and now part of the Rail, Maritime and Transport Union – erected a memorial in Plimsoll's honour in 1929 between Charing Cross and Westminster on London's Victoria Embankment Gardens. It bears the inscription, 'in grateful recognition of his services to the men of the sea of all nations.' There is also a Plimsoll Bar in the Grand Hotel, Broad Street, Bristol, where he addressed a crowd calling for reform, when it was called the White Lion.

97. Joseph Arch (1826–1919)

7 Bridge Street (corner of Mill Lane), Barford, Warwickshire, CV35 8EH
(Tel: 01926 624365).

The rousing rhetoric of Joseph Arch on a village green in 1872 led to the formation of the first ever national agricultural labourers' union. Within two years, under his leadership, its membership rocketed to over 86,000 to make it the largest trade union in the country. Apart from winning pay increases, Arch and the union also played a significant role in winning the vote for agricultural labourers, which was denied them until 1884, seventeen years after town workers.

Back in 1872, he stood on an old pig stool under the chestnut tree on Wellesbourne Green, near Warwick, on the evening of 7 February, addressing hundreds of workers by the light of a few lanterns, because a hostile farmer had turned off the street lights. When about 300 had signed up on the spot to the union, he realised he had done his job. 'I knew now that a fire had been kindled which would catch on, and spread, and run abroad like sparks in stubble,' he wrote in his autobiography. 'And I felt certain that this night we had set light to a beacon which would prove a rallying point for the agricultural labourers throughout the country.'

On leaving school, he had started work as a crow-scarer at the age of 9. He had also become the champion hedge cutter of England and, after forming the union, he was the first farm worker to become a Member of Parliament - as a Liberal before the formation of the Labour Party. The year he left school his father John was blacklisted from work by farmers, because he refused to sign a petition in favour of Corn Laws to keep prices high by restricting imports. The family then relied on Joseph's mother Hannah taking in laundry to save them from starvation in the terrible winter of that year.

Joseph's wages as a crow-scarer were 4d (about one and a half pence) for a 12-hour day. Even on this pittance, he saved enough to buy a book or two in order to continue his self-education. At 10 years old he became a plough boy for three shillings (15 pence) a week, and then a stable boy for eight shillings (40 pence) a week.

In 1847, he married Mary Ann, who was a domestic servant. When they had children she could not afford food that was as good as that which she saw fed to the cats and dogs of her employer. This spurred Joseph to seek a rise, which was rejected out of hand by his employer, so he became a jobbing (freelance) labourer. His skills were so good, as demonstrated by his winning of ploughing and hedge-cutting competitions, that he earned enough to feed his children and ageing father.

Because he was not dependent on a single employer, and the cottage he lived in had been bought freehold by his grandfather for £30, Joseph was less vulnerable to immediate victimisation. This, combined with his skills as a Primitive Methodist preacher, made him the natural choice as leader by a group of agricultural workers who wanted to form a union. They booked the Stag's Head Inn at Wellesbourne to discuss this matter, but so many turned up that the meeting took place on the green and led to the formation of the union.

The workers were then being paid 12 shillings (60 pence) a week and asked for 16 shillings (80 pence) a week. When this was refused, 200 came out on strike on 11 March. There was such support from surrounding areas that the infant union was able to pay nine shillings (45 pence) a week in strike pay. Within a month half the workers had won the 16 shillings and within three months all of them had, or had been found work elsewhere. In the middle of all this, Arch was elected the organising secretary for 21 shillings (£1.05) a week; two and a third times the strike pay.

In December 1885, he was elected as the Liberal MP for North West Norfolk – the year after the vote was won for agricultural workers. His maiden speech contributed to the downfall of the Conservative government in January 1886 – an amendment to a Bill about allotments – in which he called for land reform. In it he made the case for cheap freeholds for rural workers, so that they could produce food for themselves and their families. He argued that with so much uncultivated land and with so many unemployed agricultural workers, Parliament should consider 'every legitimate means to bring the land that cries for labour to the labourers as soon as possible'.

At several conferences of the Trades Union Congress he had called for heavy taxation on landowners, who left their land uncultivated. And in 1879, he had written to William Gladstone a year before he became the Liberal Prime Minister again, asking 'if the land itself were made free from the

The chestnut tree on Wellesbourne Green, where the agricultural workers union was formed by Joseph Arch.

feudal fetters that bind it, that such emancipation would tend in future to prevent agricultural depression?' No reply is recorded.

Arch lost his seat by just twenty votes in 1886, after supporting home rule for Ireland, and did not return until 1892. In the interim, he succeeded in another campaign – the ending of paying agricultural wages partly in kind, with beer or cider, in lieu of wages at harvest time – through the Truck Act of 1887, which stipulated all pay should be in cash.

While staying in village pubs on recruitment tours for the union, he was said to be 'somewhat fond of a glass of brandy and a cigar'. His parliamentary career ended in 1900 and in his retirement he continued to live in his Barford cottage and renewed his home supply of whisky from visits to the Woolpack Inn in Warwick. In 1909, he offered beer and tobacco in his cottage to a visiting Norfolk agricultural worker called Tom Higdon and it was five years later in 1914 that Tom made history of his own through the Burston Strike School. Tom and his wife Annie were sacked for organising support for candidates to the parish council, who unseated the landed gentry. They then set up an independent village school, which lasted until Tom's death in 1939. This school is celebrated with an annual rally in September in Burston – as is the formation of Arch's Union in Wellesbourne every June.

Arch is remembered also in at least two songs: one in Somerset called *To See The Thousands On Ham Hill*, which goes:

> Success to gallant Joseph Arch,
> He is our leader brave
> And with him I am sure you'll march
> Your liberties to save.
> They told his poor old father
> To the workhouse he must go.
> They would have done the same with him
> But he said, 'Not for Joe!'

The other is the chorus to *We'll All Be Union Men*:

> Joe Arch he raised his voice,
> 'Twas for the working men,
> Then let us all rejoice and say,
> We'll all be Union men.

98. William Morris (1834–1896)

(i) 2 King Street, Hammersmith, London, W6 0QA (Tel: 020 8741 7175). Wetherspoon.

(ii) 20 Watermill Way, Merton Abbey Mill, London, SW19 2RD (Tel: 020 8540 0216). Faucet Inns.

The William Morris in Hammersmith.

Born into a privileged position, Morris had nothing but contempt for the system that gave this to him and he devoted his life to replacing it with something more worthwhile. From his comfortable riverside home at Kelmscott House, 26 Upper Mall, Hammersmith (near the first pub) in 1881, he saw homeless 'ruffians' outside and commented, 'It was my good luck only of being born respectable and rich that has put me on this side of the window among delightful books and lovely works of art, and not on the other side, in the empty street, the drink-steeped liquor shops, the foul and degraded lodgings.'

On a similar theme, he declared, 'If I were to work ten hours a day at work I despised and hated, I should spend my leisure I hope in political agitation, but I fear – in drinking'; his own favourite tipple was a glass of claret.

When antagonisms arose between classes, he stated that there was no other way than to renounce his privileged class and cast in his lot with the victims. This led to him being thrown into the Serpentine after one fiery speech in Hyde Park, being hit over the head with a truncheon on Bloody Sunday in 1887 at Trafalgar Square (a place which, he wrote, would be ideal for growing apricot trees) and being charged with assaulting a policeman and disorderly conduct.

The latter incident occurred in court in 1885, when Morris cried 'shame' when a tailoring worker was sentenced to two months hard labour for obstruction at an open-air meeting. Police arrested Morris and claimed he hit one of them and broke the strap of his helmet. 'There was a funny scene in the police station where they charged me,' recalled Morris. 'The inspector and the constable gravely discussed whether the damage done to the helmet was two or one and a half pennies.'

As an art pupil of Rossetti, young Morris (nicknamed Topsy) was temperamental, often flying into fits of ungovernable rage, throwing plum puddings at housemaids, throwing furniture about, tearing his hair out and chomping up spoons and forks with his teeth. His friend and fellow artist Edward Burne-Jones recalled one occasion when the hair of Morris 'was so long and he looked so wild that the servants who opened the door would not let him in, thinking he was a burglar'. In calmer moments, Morris kept an owl and amused it by imitating an eagle and jumping off chairs with a heavy flop.

He never really took to painting, however; even his most well-known picture (*Queen Guenevere*, also known as La Belle *Iseult*) he failed to complete and left it to Rossetti and Madox Brown to finish. His main artistic achievements were in writing poems and books and in designing furniture and wallpaper. Of the latter, he said, 'I have spent, I know, a vast amount of time designing furniture and wallpapers, carpets and curtains; but after all I am inclined to think that sort of thing is mostly rubbish, and I would prefer for my part to live with the plainest whitewashed walls and wooden chairs and tables.'

His main volume of verse, entitled *The Earthly Paradise*, was published in 1868 and became very popular. He responded, 'Just because I string a few rhymes together, they call me dreamy and unpractical. I can't help writing verses; I must do it, but I'm just as much a business man as any of them.'

And it was as a businessman selling furniture that he made money, which he used to help fund the Marxist Social Democratic Federation and its journal *Commonweal*, which Morris both edited and advertised as a sandwich board-man. The Federation split in 1884 and Morris and *Commonweal* went into the more anarchic and anti-parliamentary section, which called itself the Socialist League.

It was in the *Commonweal* that his greatest works *A Dream of John Ball* and *News from Nowhere* first appeared in serial form in 1886 and 1890 respectively. Varying reports exist on his views about Marxist theories, one of which quotes him as saying, 'It is enough political economy for me to know that the idle class is rich and the working class is poor, and that the rich are rich because they rob the poor. That I know because I see it

The watermill by the William Morris pub on the River Wandle.

with my eyes. I need no books to convince me of it. And it does not matter a rap, it seems to me, whether the robbery is accomplished by what is termed surplus value, or by means of serfage or open brigandage ... and what we socialists have to do is to work together for its complete overthrow, and for the establishment in its stead of a system of cooperation where there shall be no masters or slaves, but where everyone will live and work jollily together as neighbours and comrades for the equal good of all. That, in a nutshell, is my political economy and my social democracy.'

In 1892, he was considered as a successor to Tennyson as Poet Laureate, but Prime Minister Gladstone rejected the idea on being told that Morris was 'an out and out socialist' and a communist 'with unpleasant associations'. Morris mused, 'If I can't be the Laureate of reading men, I'll be the Laureate of sweating men.'

The William Morris in Merton Abbey Mill by the River Wandle.

On his last visit to Paris, he spent most of his time in the restaurant up the Eiffel Tower. A friend remarked on how impressed he must be by the tower to spend so much time there. 'Impressed!' he spluttered. 'I remain here because it is the only place in Paris where I can avoid seeing the damn thing.'

The site of the Merton Abbey Mill Pub, by the River Wandle, was originally Liberty's block shop, where their printing blocks of Morris' designs were stored, some of which are framed on the walls.

99. Harry 'Brusher' Mills (1838–1905)

The Snakecatcher, Lyndhurst Road, Brockenhurst, Hants, SO42 7RL (Tel: 01590 622348). Admiral Taverns.

Harry 'Brusher' Mills was a hermit, who believed his cleft palate was the result of a curse put on him by snakes and so he set about catching and killing 35,000 of them in his lifetime. He sold them to zoos, where they were fed to larger snakes, and laboratories, for experiments, at a shilling each. He also sold their skins to retailers and adder fat to chemists as a cure for rheumatism.

The son of a forester, he lived in a wigwam-shaped hut made out of wattle, daub, turf and branches (a bivouac) in the depths of the New Forest at Red King's hunting ground near Queen's Bower. Born at Lyndhurst, he used to give an audience to coachloads of tourists at the

Crown Hotel. There, he would display his wriggling snakes in two tins slung over his shoulder. He was such an attraction that picture postcards were sold of him showing his weather-beaten brown face and forked beard, and his clothes of several old coats, waistcoats and a battered shovel hat. Many thought he was a mystic and a snake charmer. If his crowds of admirers blocked his way to the bar, he released the snakes, which rapidly cleared a route for him. At other times he threw harmless snakes into the crowds and then rescued them for cash.

A dummy of Brusher Mills greets visitors to the Snakecatcher.

Skilled in forest crafts, he had been a gardener and an agricultural labourer before becoming a full-time snake catcher in 1855. He used a long, forked branch to pin them down behind their heads. Any venom he then extracted with scissors. He was bitten by snakes many times, but appeared immune by means of a combination of rubbing adder fat into his skin and drinking a bottle of rum a day. The rum was drunk with bread, cheese and onions at the pub now named after him, which was called the Railway Inn until 1983. His nickname of Brusher was acquired when he used a broom to sweep the cricket pitches at Balmer Lawn in Brockenhurst and Bolton Bench in Lyndhurst, where New Forest ponies roamed.

The council burned down his hut just four months before he would have acquired squatters' rights for having lived there for 21 years. Not long afterwards, he died of bronchitis and heart disease in the Railway Inn, where he was found in one of the outhouses. There was a story, however, that he actually died in a pub up the road, where the landlord put him in a wheelbarrow and dumped him at the Railway, in order to avoid his liability to pay the funeral expenses – under a law covering paupers who died on your premises. At the inquest, a juryman asked the doctor if the heart failure could have been brought on by Brusher's meal of pickled onions. The doctor solemnly replied, 'A sound heart does not fail through eating pickles.'

The gravestone of Snake-catcher Brusher Mills.

Brusher is buried in nearby St Nicholas Churchyard, Church Lane, under a tombstone decorated with snakes, close to a mass grave for ninety-three New Zealand soldiers, who died in local hospitals during the First World War.

The pub's manager Sandy Bergstorm still serves Brusher's favourite meal of bread, cheese and pickles, but only sells 'Snakebite' (a potent mixture of cider and lager) to people he knows.

100. Charlotte Despard (1844–1939)

17–19 Archway Road (corner of Despard Road), London, N19 3TX
(Tel: 08721 077077). Independent.

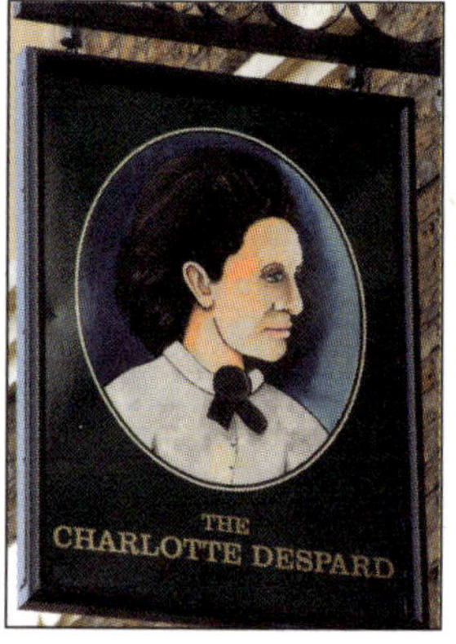

As a suffragette in the period before the First World War, Charlotte Despard was twice imprisoned in Holloway Prison close to this pub, which is on the corner of Despard Road, named after her husband who lived in the area. Charlotte was to be imprisoned again in the 1920s after she moved to Dublin and joined both Sinn Féin and helped found the Communist Party of Ireland.

She was born into a wealthy family (her father being an Irish naval officer and her brother later becoming Lord Lieutenant of Ireland) in Kent. At the age of 15, her father had died and her mother had been confined to a lunatic asylum, so she was taken to be looked after by relatives in London.

She met the wealthy Anglo-Irish banker Maximilian Despard and married him in 1870. When he died in 1890 she threw herself into social activity, being appalled at some of the poverty that existed in London. To be among the poor, she moved from Esher to Wandsworth and campaigned for the reform of the Poor Law (with its hated workhouses). George Lansbury and Keir Hardie were among those who joined her in this. She became a guardian or administrator of this law in Lambeth in 1894. At the same time she joined the Marxist Social Democratic Federation and in 1901 she joined the Independent Labour Party.

Later, in 1906, she joined the suffragettes and was soon jailed for a demonstration outside parliament. In 1907, she broke away from the more moderate Women's Social and Political Union to form the Women's Freedom Party, which was prepared to break the law with non-violent action.

In 1909, after being imprisoned again, she met Gandhi and was very impressed by his tactics of passive resistance. In the same year she visited Ireland at the invitation of the Socialist Party of Ireland. When the Dublin employers locked out all workers who refused to leave their trade unions and tried to starve them into submission, Charlotte was there to lend moral and considerable financial support.

During the First World War she was a pacifist, which made her unpopular and led to her losing as the Labour Party candidate for Battersea in the 1918 election. Now, however, there is a Charlotte Despard Avenue in her honour in Battersea.

In 1921, she moved to Ireland and joined Sinn Féin. Her house was frequently raided by the police, who suspected it was being used to shelter IRA members. The following year she founded the Women's Prisoners' Defence League, which supported the families of republican prisoners and was declared illegal in 1923.

After visiting the Soviet Union in 1931, she joined the Revolutionary Workers' Group and then the Communist Party of Ireland in 1933 when it was formed.

Her house was frequently attacked by mobs, so she moved to Belfast in 1934, after giving away her house and all her possessions. Her house in Belfast was burned down by a mob, so she moved to the nearby coastal town of Whitehead, where she was declared bankrupt in 1937.

General Secretary Harry Pollitt of the Communist Party of Great Britain said of her, 'She has done more for communism than any of us.'

She was also a prolific writer of poetry and novels.

The pub changed its name from the Settle Inn to Charlotte Despard in December 2008.

101. Charles Stewart Parnell (1846–1891)

(i) The Parnell, 19 Parnell Place, Cork, Republic of Ireland.
(ii) Charles Stewart, 98 Parnell Street, Dublin 1.

Known as 'the uncrowned king of Ireland', Charles Stewart Parnell devoted his life to attaining home rule for Ireland. He was imprisoned for his beliefs, but managed to get Gladstone in the British Parliament to support Irish home rule. In fact, it was passed by the Commons with a majority of 34 in 1893 (two years after Parnell's death), but was then rejected in the Lords by a majority of 378.

At the age of 21, he was outraged by the hanging of three Fenians in Manchester and started supporting their cause. In 1875, he was elected as member for County Neath to Parliament and before long was accused of contempt of the House for his use of obstructive tactics.

The National Land League was formed in Ireland in 1879 and Parnell was elected as its president. Its aim was to reduce rents and to promote ownership by the occupiers of the land. To achieve this, it advised tenants

The Parnell in Cork

to offer a fair rent, but pay nothing until it was agreed. The following year, sixty-eight home-rule MPs were elected to Parliament and Parnell became their chairman.

When large scale evictions of Irish tenants took place for rent arrears, he advised people to shun all those who assisted in the evictions. This was taken up vigorously and one of the first to be on the receiving end was landlord Captain Boycott. His name became the word to describe the tactic. Parnell was tried for seditious conspiracy for supporting this in 1881, but was let off by a hung jury.

In Parliament, he used filibustering to oppose the suspension of civil rights and the increase of police search powers in Ireland – and was suspended for 'disorderly' conduct in his protests. He was then arrested and jailed in Dublin for inciting tenants not to pay their rents. He made a call from Kilmainham Prison to all tenants to join the rent strike, until he and his supporters were released. But the government declared the Land League illegal and tried to suppress it. This was when Parnell's popularity reached its height and he became known as the uncrowned king of Ireland and was granted the freedom of Dublin City.

In May 1882, he and his supporters were released from jail, but five days later, two members of the government Lord Frederick Cavendish and Thomas Burke were assassinated in Dublin. Even harsher laws were brought in as a result, including trials without juries and unlimited police powers to arrest people on the merest suspicion. Gladstone tried to extend these powers when they came up for renewal in May 1885, so Parnell vowed to drive his government from office. He succeeded in the following month, by successfully voting against an increase in beer and spirits duty.

In 1886, however, Gladstone was returned to power and he supported Parnell's home rule for Ireland and introduced a bill to implement it. But ninety liberals rebelled and the bill was defeated by just thirty votes. Gladstone called another general election, which was won by a coalition of Tories and breakaway Liberals.

The National Land League, of which Parnell was still president, was declared a 'dangerous association' in 1887 by the government, which continued trying to suppress it. In the same year, *The Times* published letters, which it claimed were from Parnell, approving of the murder of Cavendish and Burke back in 1882. He was accused of inciting sedition and of conspiracy to gain independence by promoting agitation and rent strikes. During the trial in 1889, the chief witness against him admitted that he had forged the letters.

Later in the same year, however, Parnell was cited for adultery with Kitty O'Shea by her husband in a divorce case. This led to a withdrawal of political support for him and the splitting up of the Irish home rule party. The Church also disapproved of him when he married Kitty after the divorce. Undeterred, the couple had three children, living at 9 Walsingham Terrace in Brighton, on the Sussex Coast, which is where he died of inflammation of the lungs. He was buried at Glasnevin Cemetery in Dublin.

102. Dr W. G. Grace (1848–1915)

Grace's (previously Dr W. G. Grace), 1–3 Witham Road, South Norwood, London, SE20 7YA (Tel: 020 8778 4269). Spirit/Punch Taverns.

The legendary cricketer William Gilbert Grace is buried in a tomb at Beckenham Cemetery a short walk from this pub, which is shaped like a pavilion. In his 44-year career, he scored an astonishing 54,896 runs and took an incredible 2,876 wickets ... as well as being a splendid fielder. Only four batsmen have scored more runs than him and only five bowlers have taken more wickets in the succeeding

Picture of W.G.Grace in the pub.

generations, when a lot more matches are played than in Grace's day. He achieved the double of scoring over a thousand runs and taking over a hundred wickets in a season no less than ten times.

In 1876, he became the first player ever to score over 300 runs in a first class innings ... and then did it again in the same season. In that memorable season he also scored 400 runs not out in a match that was not rated first class, so did not count in his record. It was late in his career that Test matches started and even then they were much less common than nowadays, yet he still managed to appear in twenty-two of them.

Born near Bristol, he played for Gloucestershire for many years, but at the age of 51 he started playing for London County, whose ground was at Crystal Palace. He got most of his income covertly from cricket, but maintained his 'gentleman' (amateur) status, so was what later became known as a shamateur. Today, he would also be branded as a 'cheat' for some of the tactics he used to win at all costs.

One story, possibly apocryphal, tells of him being bowled out first ball but refusing to leave, telling the umpire, 'These people have come to see me bat, not to see you umpire.'

Other examples are better documented. In an 1882 Test match against Australia, when Grace was fielding, the

The pavilion-like exterior of Grace's pub.

batsman walked up to the wicket to flatten a bump. Grace had the ball and appeared to be handing it to the bowler, when he suddenly hit the wicket with it instead. The umpire had to give run out under the strict rules, but admonished Grace by adding, 'It's not cricket.'

In 1893, he was bowling to a young batsman called Charles Wright, who blocked the ball. Grace asked him to pick up the ball and toss it back to him. When he did so, Grace appealed for handling the ball. Again, the umpire had to observe the letter of the law rather than its spirit and give Wright out.

The pub, decorated with much memorabilia and pictures of him, is next to Birkbeck Station, which is on the British Rail line from London Bridge and the tram link from Croydon. The cemetery where he is buried (he died at home in nearby Mottingham) is just the other side of the rail/tram line and his tomb is in Plot U3 about 100 yards from the entrance on the right. There is a stained-glass window of him in The Champion Pub at 13 Wells Street, London, W1.

The stained glass window of W.G. Grace in the Champion pub (courtesy of artist Ann Sotheran)

103. Captain Matthew Webb (1848–1883)

Captain Webb, Bagley Drive, Wellington, Shropshire, TF1 3NP
(Tel: 01952 254150).

The first person to swim the English Channel, Matthew Webb was a daredevil character, who risked his life many times. Finally, aged 34, he took one risk too many and drowned, when swimming across the rapids of the Niagara Falls.

He was born just 4 miles south-east of Wellington in the mining village of Dawley. Here, he learned to swim in the strong currents of the River Severn and gained a reputation for being fearless. This was confirmed when, after becoming a merchant seaman at the age of 14, he dived overboard in the middle of the Atlantic in an attempt to rescue a fellow seaman. For this, he became the first person to receive the Stanhope gold medal for bravery.

In 1873, when he was captain of a steamship, Webb read of a failed attempt to swim the channel and he became determined to succeed in the feat himself. His first attempt, in August 1875, had to be abandoned in a violent storm after seven hours in the water. His historic, successful achievement started just 12 days later though, at 1 p.m. on 24 August, when he set off from Dover. After eight hours he was stung by a jellyfish but, fortified by brandy supplied by one of the boats following him, he pressed on. By dawn, he was in sight of the French coast at Cap Gris Nez, but strong tides were against him. He had to swim along the coast for another five hours, before the tide abated and he was able to step ashore at Calais at 10.40 a.m., having swum 39 miles in twenty-one hours forty minutes. An instant hero and celebrity, he was welcomed by crowds wherever he went and he made a living as a swimming showman.

Swimming the rapids of the Niagara Falls between America and Canada was considered impossible and so it became an irresistible challenge for him to tackle. He jumped in on the American side on 23 July 1883, but was dragged under by the currents of a whirlpool after just ten minutes. His body was found four days later and he was buried in the nearby cemetery.

The stained glass window of Capt. Webb in the Champion pub (courtesy of artist Ann Sotheran)

This final stunt was considered so suicidal as to be sinful back in Shropshire, so the church at Coalbrookdale (5 miles south of Wellington) barred a memorial to him from its interior. Instead, it was erected outside.

104. Lillie Langtry (1853–1929)

(i) 79 Unthank Road (corner of Park Road), Norwich, NR2 2PE (Tel: 01603 767700).
(ii) 19 Lillie Road, West Brompton, London, SW6 1UE (Tel: 020 7385 3605).
(iii) Previously in St Helier, Jersey, Channel Islands.

The Lillie Langtry in Norwich

The legendary 'Jersey Lil', as Langtry was known, became famous as the mistress of Edward VII, as an actress and as the first female member of the Jockey Club.

Born as Emile Charlotte le Breton, in St Saviour just north of St Helier in Jersey, she married Edward Langtry, owner of a 60 ton yacht, which docked in Jersey in 1874. 'I met the owner and fell in love with the yacht,' she explained. 'To become the mistress of the yacht, I married the owner.'

The couple moved to London in 1877 and lived in Eaton Place, 8 Wilton Place and at 21 Pont Street (a mile or so east of the West Brompton pub). This was when Lillie first saw Edward (then Prince of Wales) riding in Hyde Park. 'He is a very large man, but appeared to ride well for one of his bulk,' she observed, and was later to experience him more intimately.

The prince became enchanted with her reckless style, such as when she was presented to Queen Victoria at Buckingham Palace, wearing three large ostrich feathers in her hair in mockery of the prince's crest. He was less amused, however, when she spooned large dollops of strawberry ice cream down the back of his neck at a dinner and he briefly ostracised her. But he was soon lavishing gifts on her again, and once remarked, 'I've spent enough on you to buy a battleship.' Straight away, she retorted, 'And you've spent enough in me to float one!'

A journal once reported, 'There is nothing whatever between the Prince of Wales and Lillie Langtry ... not even a sheet.'

They had a special house built at Bournemouth (now called Langtry Manor, in Derby Road), with their bedrooms connected by a passage, of which her husband was kept ignorant.

When their affair ended, she formed a liaison with the prince's nephew Prince Louis Alexander of Battenberg, who fathered her only child, a daughter called Jeanne-Marie. The Prince of Wales stood by her with financial support, nonetheless, and gave her a golden statuette of herself naked, which she proudly displayed in the middle of her dining room table.

It was after the birth of the baby that her friend Oscar Wilde suggested she become an actress to support the baby. Her other friends included Whistler, who suggested she paint, and Millais, who said she should be a writer. Wilde got a retired actress friend of his to coach Lillie and her career took off. When he wrote his play *Lady Windermere's Fan* for her

about society's hypocritical attitude to her and her illegitimate daughter, however, she took offence.

After his death though, she kept an empty seat at her table 'in memory of dear Oscar'. When a guest criticised this on the grounds that he was a convicted homosexual, she turned on him and exclaimed, 'You fool, you don't understand. Oscar was a very versatile man.'

In the 1890s, after her husband had left her, she lived with a jockey, who drank himself to death. Then, in 1897, her horse Merman won the Cesarewitch running shoeless, so Lillie became the first woman to receive the prize of £39,000, which she supplemented with a bet of £10,000 at 8–1. The very same day, however, her husband died insane with drink in an asylum, after being injured on a railway line. Lillie's own tipple was a glass of champagne for elevenses and three glasses of brandy after dinner.

In her sixties, she finally took the advice of Millais (also born in Jersey) and wrote a novel called *All At Sea*. In it, she has a male character having his affair broken off by his lover and he

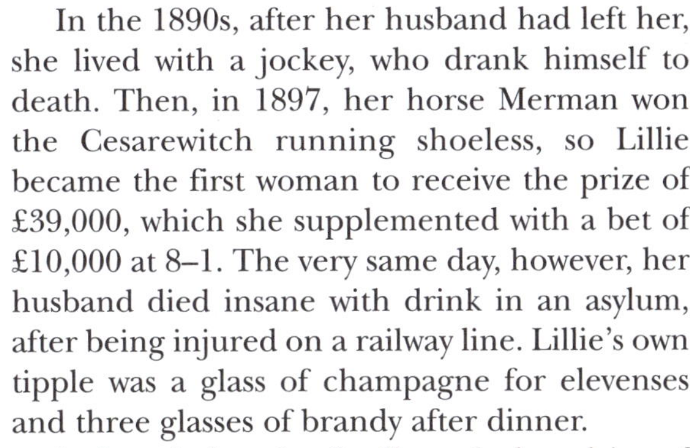

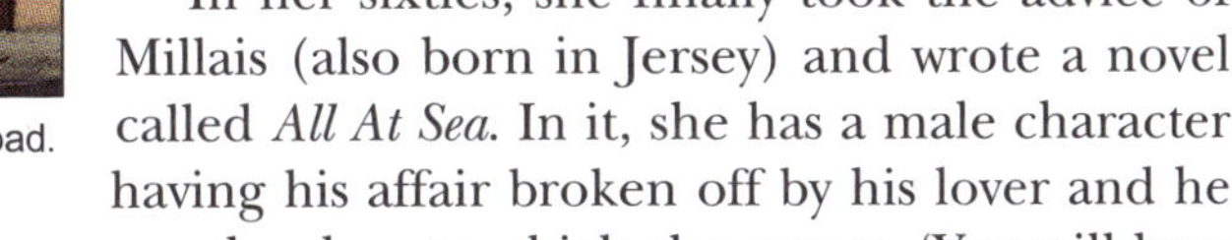

The Lillie Langtry in Lillie Road. S.W. London.

tells her he will always remember her, to which she muses, 'You will be a phenomenon if you don't ... it is the thing men find easiest to do – to forget a woman they imagined they loved.'

In her seventies she was asked how her beauty had affected her in her youth. 'Life has taught me that beauty can have its tragic side,' she replied. 'It is like great wealth in that respect. It promotes insincerity, and it breeds enemies. A really beautiful woman, like a very rich man, can be the loneliest person in the world. She is lucky if she knows her friends.'

A pub named after her in her native Jersey was sadly turned into flats in the 1990s. There is a sculpture of her over her grave in St Saviour's Church on the island.

105. Percy French (1854–1920)

Slieve Donard Hotel, Downs Road, Newcastle, Co Down, Northern Ireland,
BT33 0AH (Tel: 02843 723175. Free house.

Perhaps best known for writing the song *The Mountains of Mourne*, Percy French once performed here, in the shadows of those very mountains, in 1915. He was also a singer, painter, author, performer and engineer. A happy-go-lucky person, he was never ruffled. As a child, he saw a dog running towards him pursued by a crowd chanting 'mad dog!' Instead of running away, he went up to the dog and removed from its tail a long, thin briar, that he had spotted and which was the real reason for the dog's furious yelping and rushing.

Later, he went to Trinity College in Dublin, where he qualified in engineering after eight long years. When he explained the reason for the delay, he said, 'I think taking up the banjo, lawn tennis, and water colour painting instead of chemistry, geology and the theory of strains, must have retarded my progress a good deal. But eventually I was allowed to take out my civil engineering degree. I believe the Board were afraid I should apply for a pension, if I stayed any longer at Trinity College.'

While at Trinity, he wrote his first song *Abdulla Bulbul Ameer*, which was a great and popular success. But he got no royalties for it, as he had failed to register the copyright. This did not perturb him unduly, however, and he remained unconcerned about money throughout his life.

When still an apprentice engineer for a railway company, he used to busk at racing meetings. And while working as an engineer on a drainage scheme, he was entitled to travel and hotel expenses ... but preferred to cycle and stay with friends instead.

The money he earned from *The Mountains of Mourne* was invested in a distillery. This was lost when it went bust and when he lost his job as an engineer at the same time. As a result of this he turned to journalism, becoming editor of a comic, weekly paper called *The Jarvey*. That also went under, so he wrote a musical comedy called *The Knight of the Road*, which played to packed houses.

His first wife died on their first wedding anniversary and their baby died a few weeks later. His second wife was an actress and they had two daughters. In 1906, he and his family moved to England, where some of his paintings were bought by Edward VII.

Once, on a train journey, he overheard a passenger say, 'That can't be Percy French; he died last year in Naples of delirium tremens.' In telling a friend of this later, French added, 'As I was practically a teetotaller and had never been to Naples I did not trouble to verify the statement.'

In London during the First World War he survived one of the worst German air raids on the capital. When the 'all clear' was sounded, he remarked to his family, 'Do you know I think that was quite the pleasantest raid we ever had!'

In old age, he said, 'I was born a boy and have remained one ever since.'

A seat is dedicated to him by the Grand Canal in Dublin (at Baggot Street Bridge) which is inscribed:

> Remember me is all I ask, and yet
> If remembrance prove a task, forget.

106. Oscar Wilde (1854–1900)

112a Friedrich Strasse (next to Oranienburger Tor Station), 10117 Berlin, Germany (Tel: 0049 30 282 8166).

The Irish poet and playwright Oscar Wilde is famed for his legendary wit and for being jailed for consensual homosexual acts. Appropriately, in view of the existence of this Berlin pub, he could speak fluent German. The bisexual Wilde had an affair with Lord Alfred Douglas, who had just translated Wilde's French play *Salome* into English. The

The Oscar Wilde in Berlin.

Marquis of Queensbury, the father of Douglas, was so incensed by this that he left a misspelt message at Wilde's club in London, accusing him of being a 'somdomite' (sic). Wilde allowed himself to be persuaded by Douglas to sue for libel and lost the case in 1895. He was then charged with 'gross indecency', which had been made an offence just nine years earlier. It was the first law passed specifically against homosexual acts; sodomy had been unlawful for both homosexuals and heterosexuals, and was until quite recently.

The Marquis of Queensbury had also accused the Prime Minister Lord Rosebery of having a homosexual affair with his other son Francis. Lord

Alfred Douglas was of the view that those in high places insisted on Wilde's prosecution to distract attention from this other accusation. Wilde, who was already the bane of the establishment for his foppish dress and appearance, as well as his support for socialism, faced a hostile judiciary. As working-class young men gave evidence of having had sex with Wilde, the judge and prosecution seemed equally shocked that he was mixing with the lower orders. Despite the hostile atmosphere, Wilde was applauded in court for his reference to the 'love that dare not speak its name'. After the jury failed to agree in the first trial, he was found guilty in the second and was sentenced to the maximum of two years jail with hard labour.

During this time, he lost 22 pounds in weight, working six hours a day on the treadmill, picking oakum until his fingers were numb, sleeping on bare boards and existing on a subsistence diet. The only visitors he was allowed were the vengeful Marquis of Queensbury, to serve a bankruptcy petition on him, and Wilde's wife Constance, to tell him she was divorcing him and that his mother had died. He described his and his fellow inmates' suffering in *The Ballad of Reading Gaol*, which was published in 1898.

After his release, he described the case in a treatise called *De Profundis*. He admitted homosexual acts short of sodomy with the young men, but felt no shame about it. They were, he said, 'delightfully suggestive and stimulating' and it was 'like feasting with panthers, the danger was half the excitement'. He found more shame in having to lie to lawyers, he added. 'Sins of the flesh are nothing,' he concluded. 'Sins of the soul are shameful.'

On his release, he was refused a place in a Catholic Retreat, so went to live in France. While in Dieppe his friend the poet Ernest Dawson took him to a female brothel in order to acquire 'a more wholesome taste'. On hearing of his presence, a large crowd had gathered outside, to whom he announced on leaving, 'The first in ten years – and it will be the last. It was like cold mutton. But tell it in England, for it will entirely restore my character.'

He died in Paris from an ear disease caused by an injury in prison. On his deathbed, he said, 'I am dying beyond my means,' and finally, 'It's the wallpaper or me – one of us has to go.'

The Irish pub is in the Mitte area of Berlin, right next to the Oranienburger Tor Underground Station on the U6 Line. Strangely, there is no pub or bar named after him in Dublin, but there is a plaque there marking his birthplace at 21 Westland Row.

107. Ned Kelly (1855–1880)

1 Sir Thomas Street (corner of Victoria Street), Liverpool, L1 6BW
(Tel: 0151 236 1561). Punch Taverns.

The son of an Irish convict transported to Australia, Ned Kelly ended up being hanged for murdering three policemen, but became a folk hero. His vendetta with the police started at the age of 14, when he was jailed for three months for hitting a constable for accusing him of stealing a horse. Ned got an additional three months for sending the officer's wife a parcel of calves' testicles with an obscene note. He was also bound over to keep the peace for a year.

Within that year, however, he was accused of horse stealing on what he claimed was perjured police evidence. He was found guilty of receiving and was sentenced to three years' imprisonment. In 1873, he was transferred from Beechworth Jail to Pentridge Jail in Melbourne, then to prison hulks, where he was made to work in chain gangs in quarries and road building.

On his release, he managed to go twenty rounds of bare-knuckle boxing against Isiah 'Wild' Wright, who was the finest fighter in the region. He also spent three years as a timber cutter and mill foreman in Victoria.

Then, in September 1877, he was arrested for drunkenness and was put in the cells overnight. When a number of police tried to handcuff him to take him to court the next morning, he resisted and was involved in a brawl. He was then fined a total of £4 for hitting the policemen, who he claimed had 'caught me by the privates'. One of these was Constable Thomas Lonigan, whom Ned was reported to have threatened with shooting. And it was for his murder that he ultimately hanged. Another of those involved in the handcuffing brawl was Constable Whelan Fitzpatrick, who later became Sergeant at Greta (a village near Glenrowan), where the Kelly homestead was.

Fitzpatrick went there to arrest Ned's young brother Dan for horse stealing without a warrant in April 1878. He came out with a gunshot wound in his wrist, which he accused Ned of causing, although he claimed not to be there, and a sore head from being hit with a shovel by Ned's mother Ellen, for which she was jailed for three years. She claimed Fitzpatrick was drunk and had made advances on her daughter. A reward of £100 was offered for the capture of Ned for the attempted murder of Fitzpatrick, so he and Dan took to the hills with two friends. They built a cabin in the wild and trackless region of Wombat Ranges, an area they knew from cattle-thieving days, and they lived there for six months.

Then on 25 October 1878, they came across a camp of four policemen, who were hunting them at Stringybark Creek, Victoria. The next day, Kelly told them to put their hands up, but they went for their guns, so he shot three of them, including Lonigan, but the fourth escaped. He later stated, 'I was compelled to shoot them in my own defence or lie down like a cur and die.'

On 10 December 1878, they rode into Euroa in Victoria and robbed the national bank of £2,000. Ned showed the locals the gold watch belonging to one of the policemen he had shot and delivered a statement of justification to the press, which suppressed it. A couple of months later, the gang stopped at the Woolpack Inn near Jerilderie and the next day they went into town and captured the local police station, locking the officers in the cells with the local drunk, who was most amused by the development.

They then put on police uniforms and told the locals they were reinforcements brought in to hunt for the Kelly gang. They slept overnight in the police station, making the sergeant's wife cook them supper, then took her to church in the morning, before robbing the Bank of New South Wales of another £2,000. Again, Ned tried to get his statement published in the press without success. They rode out of town to a wave of public sympathy and songs were being sung lauding him as a hero and loathing the authorities as oppressors.

On 27 June 1880, they had a drinking spree in the Glenrowan Inn, near the Kelly homestead, where Ned displayed his poetic qualities.

Hearing that a train full of police in pursuit of them was on its way, they tore up the railway track with the aim of making it plunge down a ravine. But someone flagged down the driver.

The next day saw the Siege of Glenrowan, which took most of the day, during which Ned took on the entire police battery clad in armour made out of stolen ploughshares. But after being shot twenty-eight times in his unprotected legs he was captured. The police set fire to the inn and later dragged out the burned bodies of the other members of the gang.

Ned, who was much admired for his boldness and chivalry towards women, was nursed back to health and was brought to trial in Melbourne on 28 October 1880. It was the same judge, Sir Redmond Barry, who had sentenced his mother to three years in prison and Ned treated him with utter defiance. He was found guilty of the murder of Lonigan and was hanged on 11 November. His last words on the scaffold were, 'Such is life.' His skull was acquired by a minor civil servant who used it as a paperweight.

108. Arthur Conan Doyle (1859–1930)

Conan Doyle, 71–73 York Place (corner of Broughton Street and Cathedral Lane), Edinburgh, EH1 3JD (Tel: 0131 524 0031). Mitchell & Butler.

The author of the famous *Sherlock Holmes* detective stories Arthur Conan Doyle was born almost opposite this pub at 11 Picardy Place, where a statue of Sherlock Holmes now stands outside. Conan Doyle qualified as a doctor in the city and lived at 23 George Square when a medical student. In fact, he based *Sherlock Holmes* on the eminent Edinburgh surgeon Dr Joseph Bell, who had taught him.

After qualifying, Doyle set up as a general practitioner in Portsmouth on the south coast of England, where he played as goalkeeper for the Football League club's first team. He also became a regular at Portsmouth Eye Hospital, ordering glasses for his patients. He decided to specialise in this field of medicine and studied it for some months in Vienna. Then, in 1891, he set up as an oculist at 2 Devonshire Place in London near Harley Street ... and not far from Baker Street, the address he gave to Sherlock Holmes.

Statue of Sherlock Holmes outside Conan Doyle's birthplace opposite the pub.

Doyle was not getting much work in his surgery and started writing the *Sherlock Holmes* stories for *Strand* magazine to fill in the time. During a virulent attack of influenza in the days when it was often fatal, he decided 'with a wild rush of joy' to sell the practice and to concentrate on writing full-time. This enabled him to move to 12 Tennison Road in South Norwood.

The stories became more and more popular, but he felt he had become 'entirely identified with what I regarded as a lower stratum of literary achievement'. So he killed Holmes off in 1893 in a fight with arch villain Moriarty over the

Reichenbach Falls in Switzerland. 'The general protest against my summary execution of Holmes taught me how many and how numerous were his friends,' wrote Doyle, who received a certain amount of hate mail for this heinous crime. Holmes was brought back from the dead ten years later and

A portrait of Conan Doyle in the pub.

continued until his final case in 1926. His name lives on through the Sherlock Holmes Pub at 10 Northumberland Street, London, WC2.

Doyle was also a spiritualist, writing a history of it in 1926. He believed, for example, that the great escapes performed by Harry Houdini were achieved by dematerialising himself and reassembling his molecules beyond the reach of danger.

109. Archibald Knox (1864–1933)

Avondale Road, Onchan, Isle of Man, IM3 4EZ (Tel: 01624 620457).

Now hailed as the inspiration of the British art nouveau movement, Archibald Knox always shunned publicity in his lifetime and much of his work is unsigned. He was born in the village of Cronkbourne, near Douglas in the Isle of Man, in a terrace of small houses for workers at the nearby Tromode Timber Mill, where his father Robert worked. It was at this mill that Archibald lost the tip of the index finger of his right hand in an accident with a mechanical saw, when he was aged 8 or 9. In another accident, his young brother Carmichael drowned in Douglas Harbour.

Archibald's three elder brothers all went into the marine engineering business, which their father set up in Lake Road, Douglas. But Archibald refused to join it, preferring to roam the area painting and drawing, much to the annoyance of his father, who once exclaimed in exasperation, 'Why, he doesn't even know how to hold a hammer!' He thus became something of an outsider at home, which may have explained some of his rather eccentric behaviour later in life.

At the age of 16, he enrolled at the newly formed Douglas School of Art and was taught by the avant-garde artist John Miller Nicholson (a student of the French revolutionary sculptor Aime-Jules Dalou, who had fled from Paris to save his life after supporting the commune). Nicholson encouraged Knox and his other students to be 'venturesome modernists'.

Archibald excelled, winning medals for ornamentation and design, as well as winning a national art competition for his studies of ancient Manx crosses. He then became an art master at the school from the age of 20 for four years.

In 1892, he visited Dublin to study Celtic art and was drenched by the rough sea on the quay, but warmed himself up by sampling 'the innumerable best ales that were to be had'. He never seemed to mind getting soaked when on sketching missions.

In Douglas, the architect M. H. Baillie Scott employed him in Athol Street as a designer from 1892 to 1896; earlier, Scott had worked as a designer of wallpapers and furniture coverings for Liberty & Co in London's Regent Street, where Knox later became chief designer.

In 1897, Archibald moved to Fulham in London and taught at the Redhill School of Art, where the principal was Alfred James Collister, who had been at the Douglas School of Art with him. Knox also did some design work for the Silver Studio of Decorative Design at Brook Street, Hammersmith, which supplied Liberty & Co.

Before long, he became Liberty's greatly acclaimed chief designer of art nouveau silver, pewter and jewellery (plus carpets, fabrics and metalwork), and his work was immensely popular. It was not the policy of the company, however, to identify the designers. After he had worked for Liberty for four years it wrote to him as 'Mr A Know'.

Portrait of Archibald Knox in the pub.

He moved back to the Isle of Man in 1900 and lived in a small cottage in the remote village of Sulby, where he spent four years at his most creative, producing metalwork designs, hundreds of drawings ... and a claret jug.

During this period, he took on an untrained, private art student called Phyllis D. Wood and told her to 'see with her own eye', without previous indoctrination by copying, which was completely against the guidelines of the Board of Education. She became a respected Manx artist, but Knox's snub to established teaching methods was soon to land him in trouble.

It came at Kingston-on-Thames School of Art, where Knox started teaching upon his return to London in 1904. The school had no problem with his teaching, but the Board of Education inspectors disliked his new ideas, because they threatened the established order. They claimed that, far from encouraging students' individualism, he was standing in their way. Enraged by this and by the lack of support he got from the school, he resigned in 1912. His students were equally enraged and they left the school in protest and set up their own one called the Knox Guild of Craft and Design in the same town, which lasted until 1937. Knox then moved back to the Isle of Man again to live at 70 Athol Street, Douglas, overlooking the harbour.

In August 1912, he set off from Liverpool to Philadelphia, where he got work teaching at the School of Industrial Arts for a term and he also had a sideline in designing carpets. But his attempts at getting work as a proper designer came to nothing. He supplied Liberty catalogues as examples of his work, but the Americans were unimpressed. 'One firm called it the art of the drug store,' he wrote. So he returned to Douglas again in March 1913.

When the First World War broke out, he got a job as censor at the Aliens Internment Camp at a farm known as Knockaloe Moar, near Patrick, on the south-west coast. Originally, the internees had been housed in Douglas,

The Archibald Knox in the Isle of Man.

where their food was infested with weevils, which led to a riot and five internees being shot. By 1916, over 20,000 of them were held at Knockaloe and Knox's job was to make sure no news of the war in Europe reached them from letters or parcels from their home countries. Not being terribly creative or inspiring work for Knox, he found solace by studying the cloud formations over the Irish Sea.

In his later years, he was a part-time teacher of art at his old art school, Douglas High School for Girls, and Ramsey Grammar School. His other activities included drinking beer with his friends, designing theatre programmes, collecting old axe hammers and other fossils, attending the Conister Lodge of Freemasons, organising culture festivals, interior designing, architecture and designing gravestones.

His own gravestone was one that he had, in fact, designed for the brother of Thomas Quayle, the stonemason who sculpted it. His own name was added to it with the epitaph: A humble servant of God in the ministry of the beautiful.

A wreath made entirely of snowdrops came from his loyal students at Kingston, with the message: It is the skies' benediction I look for (one of his favourite sayings).

He was buried at Braddan Cemetery, near his birthplace, and many of his original works are displayed in the pub, named in his honour, which opened in 1988.

110. Grigorii Rasputin (c. 1864–1916)

Rasputin's, Walker Street (junction with Duke Street), Wellington, Shropshire (Tel: 01952 255234). Admiral Taverns.

Grigorii Rasputin was a drunken, lecherous peasant, whose apparent healing powers earned him the friendship of the Russian royal family and a certain amount of political influence. This was resented by the nobility, who assassinated him with great difficulty.

A wagoner by trade, he was born in western Siberia in a village called Pokrovoskoe near the Ural Mountains. By the age of 15, he was a heavy vodka drinker and sometimes thieved to pay for it. At 16, he was seduced by the wife of a general and her six maids. Around the age of 20, he married Praskovia Dubrovina, who bore him three children and was tolerant of his sexual excesses with other women. 'Grigorii has enough to go round for everybody,' she said philosophically. The name Rasputsvo means debauched. His daughter Maria stated that his over-abundance of natural lust seemed to radiate from his 13 inch penis.

While on the run following horse-stealing charges, he visited a monastery for three months, after which he became a pilgrim and walked 10,000 miles in two years around Syria and Jordan. He continued having sex with many women, justifying this on the grounds that you had to sin in order to repent and God was pleased by repentance. He also said that salvation could only be achieved by annihilating pride and rejecting his sexual advances amounted to pride. Alternatively, he said sex was not degrading but purifying and grace ... and purification could be achieved through orgasm. He was able to assist in this more than most, as he had a large wart strategically situated on his penis, which vastly enhanced its capacity to stimulate.

In 1903, he moved to St Petersburg, where public notices urged people to drink beer rather than water in order to avoid contracting cholera. He was doing just that, drunkenly dancing and singing in a gypsy camp by the river, when he was sent for by a royal messenger on 19 July 1907. Tsar Nicholas' 3-year-old haemophiliac son Aleksey was bleeding seriously and one of the court had heard of Rasputin's healing powers. At first, he refused to go and shouted 'more dancing', but he was finally persuaded and the boy recovered when he visited him.

When people went to him as a healer and heard he was visiting the Tsar, they asked him to use his influence to get positions for their relatives, which is how he was sucked into politics. This included receiving bribes to keep people out of armed service. But, invariably, he gave any cash away to the next poor person that he met.

In 1912 or 1913, he moved to Flat 20 on the third floor at 63–64 Gorokhavaya Street (since renamed Dzerzhinsky Street) in St Petersburg, where he lived for the rest of his life. There, he loved to eat fish and vegetable soup – never using cutlery but getting women to lick his fingers clean – washed down with red Russian Madeira fortified wine that could 'fell an elephant', for which he had a gargantuan capacity.

In 1914, he was stabbed by a syphilitic woman, who claimed he had raped a nun. As a result, he was in hospital for months, during which time Russia entered the First World War. Rasputin believed he would have been able to keep the country out of the war, and prevent its waste of peasant lives, if he had been well enough to advise the Tsar. His outspoken opposition to the war led to the popular belief that he was a German spy. His intake of vodka increased to relieve the pain from the stabbing and he was often intoxicated in the middle of the day.

Prince Felix Yusupov, a transvestite who believed Rasputin was a German spy, had first met Rasputin in 1909 and been hypnotised by him. Yusupov lured Rasputin to his palace on the night of 16 December 1916 and fed him some cakes laced with potassium cyanide and some Crimean wine, which was also poisoned. But because he had alcoholic gastritis, which thickened the lining of his stomach, the cyanide did not have any effect.

Rasputin suggested they visit the gypsies, adding, with a wink, 'with God in thought, but with mankind in the flesh.' A couple of hours after the poison had been administered without effect, Yusupov shot Rasputin in the chest with a revolver. After slumping to the ground, however, Rasputin suddenly leapt to his feet, foaming and bleeding at the mouth, and attacked his assassin with a roar. The extreme right-wing politician V. M. Purishkevich then came to Yusupov's aid and shot Rasputin twice in the back, kicked him in the head and battered him with a steel press.

A third assassin finished the job off with a shot to Rasputin's forehead. He was identified as Oswald Rayner of the British Secret Service, according to a BBC2 *Timewatch* programme on 1 October 2004. He was involved because the British government feared Rasputin's advice to pull out of the war would be heeded by the Tsar.

Yusupov was then said to have cut off Rasputin's penis, whereupon he flung it across the room, where it was retrieved by the maid. She preserved it in a velvet-lined, polished wooden box 'like a blackened, overripe banana, about a foot long' in Paris, where she was last heard of in 1968. Paris is also where Rasputin's daughter Maria became a dancer. The assassins then threw the body into the frozen river, where Rasputin still managed to break free from the bonds tied around his hands, but was trapped by the ice above him. In March 1917, his body was disinterred and burned.

In the last month of his life, he had written to the Tsarina Alexandra stating he did not think he would live more than another month and if he was killed by nobles, there would be civil wàr for twenty-five years and no nobles would survive in the country. But if he was killed by royalty, then the entire royal family would be killed by the Russian people within two years. This proved to be the case just over eighteen months later.

Years later, Yusupov sued the makers of a film about Rasputin for *not* identifying him as the murderer, and he won substantial libel damages.

111. Edith Cavell (1865–1915)

7 Tombland, Norwich, Norfolk, NR3 1HF (Tel: 01603 627719).

This British nurse was executed by a German firing squad in Brussels for helping British and Allied soldiers to escape to neutral Holland. After the war, her body was exhumed and reburied in 1919 at Norwich Cathedral.– a stone's throw from this pub – just 4 miles from her birthplace, the village of Swardeston.

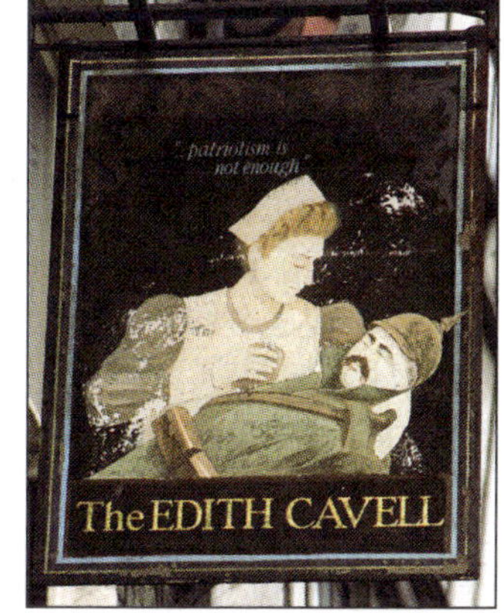

She was educated for a short while at Norwich High School in Theatre Street and first went to Brussels as a governess to the children of a lawyer at 154 Avenue Louise in 1890 for five years. She then returned to Norfolk to nurse her sick father, the Vicar of Swardeston, and decided this was to be her vocation. So she became an assistant nurse at Tooting in London at the end of 1895 and the following year she was accepted for training at the London Hospital at 99 Bow Road. During the typhoid epidemic of 1897–1898 in Maidstone, Kent, she was drafted in to help, for which she was awarded a medal.

She worked in two Poor Law institutions, as night superintendent at St Pancras Infirmary in 1901 and assistant matron at Shoreditch Infirmary in 1903. Then, in 1907, it was back to Belgium as matron of its first training school for nurses: the Ecole Belge d'Infirmieres Diplomees at 149 Rue de la Culture, Ixelles, Brussels. It started with four trainees and ended with about sixty under her leadership and was eventually renamed the Institute Edith Cavell.

She took the maxim of the patient always coming first to the limit. For instance, one evening a male patient, intoxicated by her beauty and a surfeit of alcohol, got out of bed and made advances towards a female nurse. After beating off his third attempt, she escaped through the ground-floor window. The next morning, she indignantly reported this to Cavell, who merely asked, 'Did the patient suffer?'

In July 1914, she was holidaying between her mother's house at 24 College Road, Norwich and Cumberland Cottage in the nearby coastal village of West Runton (between Sheringham and Cromer), when news reached her of the imminence of war. So she returned to Brussels on 2 August, just two days before war was officially declared.

The Germans occupied Brussels on 20 August, but allowed her to continue working in the training hospital. A few days later, there was the Battle of Mons, 30 miles south-west of Brussels, which resulted in a huge defeat for the British and hundreds of soldiers were stranded.

A couple of the wounded were hidden by the resistance movement, who had difficulty in finding a haven for them in Brussels. Almost as an afterthought, somebody suggested Edith at the hospital. Instinctively, she took them in, treated their wounds, gave them bottled beer from the hospital kitchen, dressed them in civilian clothes and took them towards the border; one of whom reached it, but not the other. This success encouraged the resistance to bring more and more soldiers – over 600 in the eight months that the escape route lasted. She found herself treating wounded German soldiers in the main ward and hiding British ones in cellars at the back of the clinic. Even when some of them got drunk and started singing raucously, and indeed incautiously, *It's A Long Way To Tipperary*, she did not chastise them, merely remarking that they were not prisoners.

A local youngster wanted to enlist in the exiled Belgian army in England and went to her for help. When she gave him a form to sign for an operation, he exclaimed, 'But, Madame, there must be some mistake. I am perfectly well. I do not need an operation. I thought you were going to help me cross the frontier!' She smiled and explained, 'That, Monsieur, is the operation!'

Another she helped was Private Robert Mapes of the 1st Norfolk Regiment, who told her he lived in Hethersett. She told him that was near where she was born and kissed him. When he finally got home, he discovered his own name on the Roll of Honour in the local church; he had been reported missing, believed dead.

After several German police raids, she and others were arrested on 5 August 1915. They were treated with civility, being given a glass of Faro (a local beer of light gravity) twice a day. The first question put to her was whether she had received 5,000 francs from a resistance member to cover expenses in helping escapers. Her reply was, 'No, not 5,000, it was only 500.'

The trial of her and thirty-four others took place on 7 and 8 October. She was asked only twelve questions, one of which related to the charge of conducting soldiers to the enemy; the one for which she was shot. Her reply was, 'My preoccupation has not been to aid the enemy but to help the men who applied to me to reach the frontier; once across the frontier, they were free.'

The sentences were delivered three days later, in which five were sentenced to death, nine were acquitted, including one who had hanged himself in a cell awaiting the verdict, and the rest got sentences of up to fifteen years' hard labour.

Edith Cavell's statue in Norwich.

Edith was shot by a firing squad at dawn the next day on 12 October. While waiting, she was visited by an English chaplain and she told him the ten weeks she had spent in prison had been a relief from the tension which had been building up. Then she came up with the immortal words, 'This I would say, standing as I do in view of God and Eternity. I realise that patriotism is not enough. I must have no hatred or bitterness towards anyone.' This was originally omitted from the engraving on her statue in St Martin's Place, London, WC2, but was soon added. The chaplain then said that she would always be remembered as a heroine and martyr, to whom she responded, 'Don't think of me like that, think of me only as a nurse who tried to do her duty.' The engraving on her monument opposite the pub refers to her as 'Nurse, Patriot and Martyr'.

The War Office reacted to news of her death by telling an official to telephone her mother. Having got through and confirmed he was speaking to Mrs Cavell, he got straight to the point, 'I rang up to tell you that your daughter in Brussels has been shot by the Germans.' There was a pause and then came the reply, 'When you get in touch with the right Mrs Cavell you won't put it quite like that, will you? She's a very old lady and she isn't very well.' It was the cousin of her late husband.

The British press bayed for revenge and suggested the formation of an Edith Cavell (Machine Gun) Regiment to kill Germans; not quite in keeping with her message of not hating anyone.

When her statue in London was unveiled, the artist Whistler did not think it looked much like her, so he quipped, 'My God, they've shot the wrong woman.'

When a film of her life *Nurse Edith Cavell* was made, the title role was played by Anna Neagle, who was the niece of a nurse who had served with Edith.

112. Ma Egerton, real name Matilda Powles (c. 1866–c. 1962)

Ma Egerton's, 9 Pudsey Street, Liverpool, L1 1JA (Tel: 0151 708 1570).

This pub is situated opposite the stage door of the Empire Theatre, where Ma Egerton herself performed. Later, she became licensee of the pub

(when it was called the Eagle) and it became a meeting point for music hall artists. Among these was Dr Crippen's wife, who sang under the name Belle Elmore ... until he murdered her in 1910. He was said to have called in at the pub, before fleeing to America, and Ma Egerton informed on him to the police to help secure his capture and execution.

Vesta Tilley (1864–1952) was one of Ma's contemporaries and frequent visitors. She was a male impersonator, whose painting is displayed in the pub.

In 1889, Ma appeared as principal boy at a panto in Liverpool's Gaiety Theatre, where she met local music hall manager Walter de Freece, whom she married in the following year. The marriage certificate gives her name as Matilda Powles, her age as 23 (which would mean she was born between 17 August 1866 and 16 August 1867) and her father as Henry Powles, a comedian who had died.

Walter took over several theatres and turned them into music halls. In 1906, he set up the New Tivoli Theatre of Varieties in Liverpool's Lime

Street, where Vesta topped the bill and laid the foundation stone. But because it was so close to the Empire, it never prospered.

Ma Egerton lived until the1960s. Chris Haddley remembers when he was just 16 in 1962 and asked to be served by her. 'She was a very beautiful lady but frail by then,' he recalled. 'She admired my cheek and let me have a mutton and potato pie with gravy and a drink as long as I sat in the corner at the back.'

A later Liverpool entertainer to drink in the pub and to have his oil painting displayed in it is comedian Ken Dodd (born 1927). With his buck teeth and toilet-brush hairstyle, Ken would be the first to admit he is no oil painting in reality. But he is certainly a masterpiece of comedy. A couple of his gags give a flavour of his genius. After explaining cat's eyes (light reflectors in the road) were invented by a Yorkshireman, who got the idea from shining his car lights in the eyes of a real cat, Ken mused, 'If the cat had been facing the other way he may have invented the pencil sharpener instead.' The other was his remark, 'What a great day it is for pushing a cucumber into your neighbour's letter box and shouting out The Martians are Coming!'

113. Marie Lloyd (1870–1922)

24 Chart Street (corner of Bache Street), Hoxton, London, N1 6DF.

The "Queen of the Music Halls" Marie Lloyd was born, went to school and made her stage debut at the age of 15, all within a few hundred yards of this pub, which now bears her name. She was born Mathilda Wood at Hoxton's 36 Provost Street (called Plumber Street at the time), went to school at Bath Street and trod the boards for the first time at the Grecian Theatre/Eagle Tavern on the corner of Shepherdess Walk and City Road.

Her father John Wood was an artificial flower maker, who supplemented his meagre income by working as a waiter in the music halls and pubs of Shoreditch. Marie had nine younger brothers and sisters – two of whom died in infancy, one being smothered in an overcrowded bed – and they became her first audience.

She was still only 15 years old when she made her first West End appearance at The Oxford Music Hall on the corner of Tottenham Court Road and Oxford Street. She had been warned that its audiences – who were well plied with pots of beer by waiters during the performances – had a raucous reputation and were 'distinctly crude' in their reactions both for and against an act.

But the young Marie took them by storm with her mischievous rendering of *The Boy I Love Sits Up In The Gallery* and also with another song, full of innuendo, about a young woman in a garden 'surrounded by various vegetables' with a line about how she 'sits among the cauliflowers and peas'. When told this was too suggestive for a later royal performance, she changed it to 'sits among the cauliflowers and leeks'.

The Oxford nearly lost its licence when Marie, dressed as a schoolgirl and accompanied by various phallic objects, sang *What's That For, Eh?* (also known as *Johnny Jones*), with lines such as 'I want to know the in and out'.

But it was often her nods, winks and gestures rather than the actual words which had the audiences in tears. The poet T. S. Eliot observed, 'There was nothing about her of the grotesque, none of her comic appeal was due to exaggeration; it was all a matter of selection and concentration.' The novelist Arnold Bennett added that it was her silences, for the audiences to fill with their own imagination, which were so deadly.

She toured the world to become an international star, but always had a strong feeling of solidarity with less known and poorly paid entertainers.

In 1906, she was elected the first president of the Music Hall Ladies Guild and the following year, she called a meeting (in the Bedford Head Pub, Tottenham Court Road) of the Variety Artists' Federation in support of it joining a national alliance with the National Association of Theatrical Employees, and the Amalgamated Musicians' Union. This alliance called the music hall strike of 1907, which was about resisting management attempts to make smaller turns do extra performances for no extra money and which restricted the number of rival theatres they could work at. As a star, Marie was not directly affected by these issues, but she joined the strike over the principle and declared, 'I will never go back upon the music hall stage until the wants of every musician and stagehand are satisfied.'

She was also on the picket line at The Euston Palace, when one of the strike-breakers was the singer Belle Elmore (later to be murdered by her husband Dr Crippen) and some performing animals. It was said that one of the pickets told Belle not to be a blackleg, but Marie shouted, 'Go on, let her work. She'll do the strike a lot more good by going on and singing than by stopping out! You go and work Belle!' When Belle started singing, the word was put around that Marie was singing for free on the picket line outside and the entire audience streamed out of the theatre. Marie disliked the meanness of Crippen and said, 'When Crippen asks you to have a drink, pay for your own. It's a damn sight cheaper.' She also supported alternative performances on behalf of the union when it hired the Scala Theatre in Charlotte Street, by Tottenham Court Road.

The quality of Marie's evidence to the Board of Trade arbitration body impressed it so much that it ruled in favour of the strikers that extra payments should be paid for matinees and that the ban on performing at rival theatres be greatly restricted.

Marie was also active in the cause of votes for women and had a small part in a suffragist play at The Oxford in 1909. At one performance of this, she smuggled the militant suffragette Annie Kenney in her theatrical hamper through the police cordon, so she could make a speech on stage.

When the first ever royal command performance was organised in 1912, Marie, still at the height of popularity, was excluded and it was widely assumed this was because of her involvement in the strike five years earlier. Unperturbed, she hired another theatre nearby on the same night to put on a rival performance, with placards proclaiming: Every performance by Marie Lloyd is a command performance, by command of the British public.

Always true to her roots, she was generous with her money, buying a pair of boots for each pupil in her old school, for example. She died after collapsing on stage singing *A Bit of a Ruin that Cromwell Knocked About a Bit.* Thousands attended her funeral and T. S. Eliot wrote that it was 'her capacity for expressing the soul of the people that made Marie Lloyd unique'.

An empty champagne bottle is preserved over the fireplace in the saloon bar of the Warrington pub in Maida Vale (93 Warrington Crescent, London, W9 1EH); one of many she emptied on her way home from the Metropolitan Theatre in Edgware Road.

The Marie Lloyd Pub took that name in around 1949 (it was previously The Globe) after the area was bombed and rebuilt. Nearby in Murray Grove is the Marie Lloyd House block of flats.

114. Harry Lauder (1870–1950)

Lauder's, 76 Sauchiehall Street (corner of Renfield Street), Glasgow, G2 3DE (Tel: 0141 331 5181). Mitchell & Butler.

The great Scottish singer comedian Harry Lauder composed the classic songs that made him famous ... from *Stop Your Ticklin', Jock* to *Keep Right on to the End of the Road.* He projected an image of meanness, as he said it was good for business. For example, he gave a particularly miserly tip to the porter at Queen Street Station in Glasgow and then explained to a friend, 'He will be so outraged that he will tell all his friends ... and everyone will know I am back appearing in Glasgow.' It was much cheaper than advertising, he added.

He also slipped something into the hand of a caddy, saying it was 'for a glass of hot whiskey'. It turned out to be a lump of sugar. English comedian Tommy Cooper did a similar trick to a cabbie, giving him something 'for a drink', which turned out to be a tea bag.

In reality, however, Lauder was quite generous (strictly on the QT). On a tour of America, for instance, a young soprano went ill and was absent for several weeks. Lauder not only paid her wages in full, but also her hospital bills.

He was born in Portobello near Edinburgh and then moved to Arbroath, where he worked in a flax mill while still a child. He then worked for ten years as a miner down Eddlewood Colliery in Hamilton. While there, he befriended a pit pony and later gave substantial sums of money to campaign for a reform of working conditions for both men and beasts.

A signed picture of Harry Lauder in the pub.

It was through his participation in mining community sing-songs that his talent as an entertainer emerged. His first professional engagement was in Belfast. He also tried his luck in London in 1900 and his money was just about running out and he was preparing to return to Glasgow, when a performer went ill and he was hired as a last-minute replacement at Gatti's Theatre, Westminster Bridge Road.

His rendition of *Stop Your Ticklin', Jock* went down a bomb and he rapidly became the rage of London. From there, he conquered the world, touring the continents of America, Africa and Australia. These were built on the international success of his records, such as *I Love a Lassie*, first performed at the Theatre Royal, Glasgow, in Christmas 1905.

When he first arrived in New York, his agent's junior clerk, who had been sent to meet him, failed to see an international star in the making. 'Say, chiefs, we've booked a complete bum!' he exclaimed. 'This guy Lauder is only four feet nothing, he has crooked legs, his nose is all over his puss and if he gets three hands on Broadway I'll undertake to eat him, legs, nose and foreign accent!'

A hit song eluded him, however. Young Will Fyffe was appearing on the same bill as him at the Alhambra Theatre in Glasgow and offered him a song he had just written called *I Belong to Glasgow*. He turned it down on the grounds he never sang songs in praise of drink. 'But what about your song *A Wee Deoch an' Doris*,' replied Will 'Isn't that praising drink?' Harry explained he always emphasised the word 'wee' so 'it's really warning people against taking too much drink.'

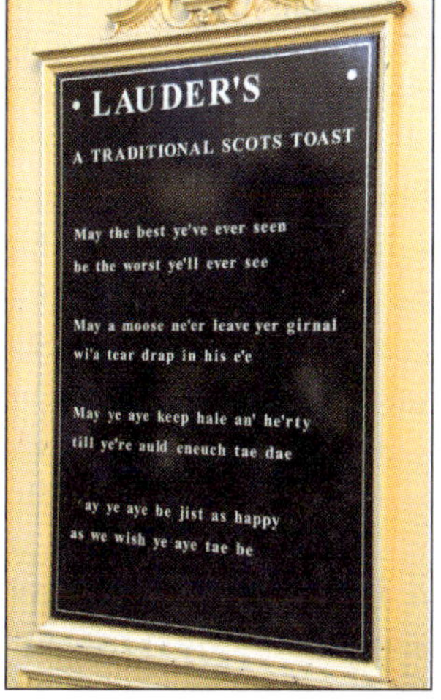

A Scottish toast outside Lauder's.

In his early days he was occasionally booed by the audience, as at the Palace Theatre in Dundee. Another singer on the same stage asked the crowd to stop booing, as he was trying to earn his bread and butter. Sure enough, he was rewarded with a stale loaf of bread hurled at his head.

Even when a wealthy star, Harry preferred to live simply and stay at the old guest houses, where landladies had been kind to him in the past, rather than luxury hotels. Plenty of photographs of him in his heyday adorn this traditional, old pub.

115. Edgar Wallace (1875–1932)

40 Essex Street (corner of Devereux Court), Strand, London, WC2R 3JF (Tel: 020 7353 3120). Enterprise Inns.

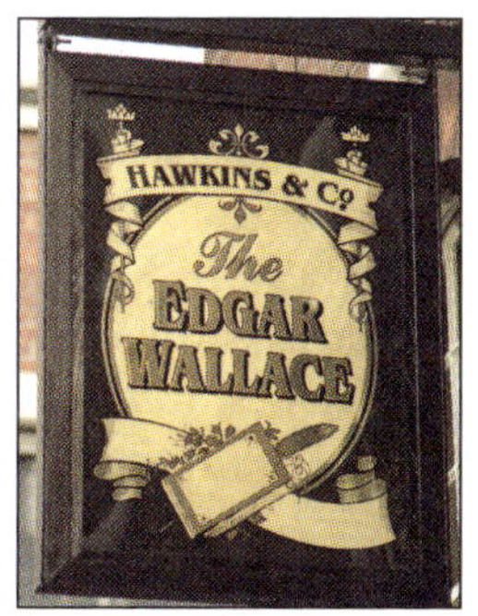

Abandoned at birth by his actress mother, Edgar Wallace was raised by a Billingsgate fish market porter in Greenwich and Camberwell. After various jobs – newspaper seller, trawler cook, building labourer and soldier – he eventually became a reporter and author. The 150 books he had published made a fortune, but he died owing £140,000.

His mother Marie 'Polly' Richards had been widowed in her early twenties and was practically starving when she gave birth to Edgar in Greenwich. His real father was Marie's employer's son-in-law, but the name of comedian Walter Wallace was put on the certificate. Before continuing her theatrical tour around the country, she agreed to pay five shillings a week to fish porter George Freeman to foster Edgar, who was just nine days old. A couple of years later she returned and said she could no longer afford the five shillings a week and would have him put in a home. George and his wife would not hear of this and adopted him instead.

At the age of 11, Edgar was playing truant in order to sell newspapers at Ludgate Circus (on the north-west corner of Fleet Street, where a bronze plaque now commemorates this). He mixed this preoccupation with petty theft from type founders.

He left school at 12 and got another job in the print trade as a reader's boy in Farringdon Street. Then, at the age of 15, he met a seaman in a music hall, who got him a job on a Grimsby trawler as a cook. After signing on for a year, he soon discovered that he suffered from seasickness and could not cook. So at the end of his first trip in gales and freezing weather in the North Sea, he ran away (a criminal offence of desertion) and walked all the way from Grimsby to London. It took him three weeks, stealing food and clothes en route.

A brief period as a milk roundsman was followed by a stint as a road maker, which was heavy work. One day, Keir Hardie was passing by and asked how much he was being paid. When he heard it was only 15 shillings (75 pence) a week, he suggested he ask for more. Instead, Edgar, on an impulse, joined the army, signing on for the 3rd Battalion of the West Kent Militia at Woolwich for six years. It was a bit like the Territorials in those days, which meant he was on call most of the time and that he could also work as a building labourer. Eventually, he signed on for seven years full time and got into the medical staff corps.

He wrote songs for army concerts and got one accepted by the music hall comedian Arthur Roberts, who sang it on stage. Edgar went absent without leave to witness the performance and was punished with ninety-six hours' imprisonment with hard labour. This included a torturous routine of lifting up heavy iron cannonballs and picking oakum.

In 1896, he sailed to South Africa to serve in Simonstown Hospital. A poem he had published in the *Cape Times* was seen and admired by Rudyard Kipling and was reprinted in a number of newspapers, including some in London. A follow-up poem led to him being paid a guinea and to an invitation to dine with Kipling himself. Kipling's advice to him was, 'For God's sake, don't take to literature as a profession. Literature is a splendid mistress, but a bad wife!'

Just before the Boer War was officially declared, Edgar bought himself out of the army for £10; he was getting £4 a week for columns and poems in local papers at the time. Some five months later he became Reuter's war correspondent and was given £100 advance for expenses – equivalent to half a year's pay in the army.

Later, he became the London *Daily Mail's* correspondent and proved highly inventive in getting around the strict censorship imposed by Lord

Kitchener. On one occasion, Kitchener ordered that he be removed from the front at Johannesburg under military escort to Cape Town.

When peace talks were taking place at Pretoria in 1902, Kitchener tried to block any reports on them, until agreement had been reached, by banning the press from the venue. Edgar was, however, able to report daily progress on the talks to *Daily Mail* readers. He knew one of the sentries on duty, who signalled to him the progress of the talks with three different coloured handkerchiefs. Red was no progress, blue was making progress and white was treaty definitely signed. So the final deal was reported in the *Mail* twenty-four hours before the official announcement.

Kitchener had Edgar's war correspondent credentials withdrawn for evading the rules of censorship. Edgar immediately reported this to the press and commented, 'One scarcely knows whether to be amused or saddened by the puerility of the War Office.'

He then became the editor of the *Rand Daily Mail* for £2,000 a year; six times what he was getting on the London *Daily Mail*. But he fell out with the owner after just nine months and returned to London with just £80, which he lost at poker on the voyage.

From previously selling newspapers in Fleet Street, he progressed to writing for them as a £15 a week *Daily Mail* reporter and he then became acting editor of the *Evening News*.

When he started writing crime thrillers, such as *Four Just Men*, he had an office at 21 Temple Chambers, off Fleet Street, just the other side of Temple Gardens from Essex Street, where the pub is situated.

In 1907, he was sent by the *Daily Mail* to disprove stories of Belgian atrocities in the Congo, which he found to be true. His stories were suppressed and when he refused to write lies he was sacked. His Congo experiences proved useful, however, when he used them to write the *Sanders of the River* stories, which proved best sellers and were later turned into a film.

When writing fiction or reporting real events he was equally inventive ... writing his report of King George's coronation for the *Evening Times* the day before the event, for example. Another story for this paper involving Edgar was the publication of a disputed confession by the murderer Crippen, which led to it going bust.

Edgar boasted in one of his plays that reporters never carried notebooks - why let the facts get in the way of a good story? Another unethical practice he indulged in was to plug commercial products in his stories for payment by the manufacturers.

Neither was he above 'recycling' material. In 1913, for example, he was made editor in chief of a journal called *Ideas*, which had offices in Temple Chambers. He was ghosting the life story of a chorus girl in this and when the deadline came for the next instalment, he 'lifted' large chunks from a previous life story he had ghosted for an artist.

When the First World War broke out, he was still barred as a war correspondent, but was appointed miliary correspondent of the *Birmingham Daily Post*, based in London. This, he combined with guarding Buckingham Palace at night as a member of Lincoln's Inn branch of the Special Constabulary.

Many of his early books he sold for one-off payments, but he finally got a royalty deal with Hodder & Stoughton, who published forty-six of his books in ten years, the sales of which ran into millions.

In 1926, Edgar's first successful play was staged. In the next six years he had seventeen produced, including three in the West End at the same time, which earned him £100,000.

Memorial to Edgar Wallace in his beloved Fleet Street.

But he was spending it faster than he was earning it ... on such luxuries as a string of twenty-one racehorses and a luxury flat with a large staff of servants in Portland Place. At this flat, he dictated a gangster play *On the Spot* in just four days and a novel about the murderer Charles Peace *The Devil Man* over a weekend. He was so prolific that he would be planning six or seven novels simultaneously.

In 1927, he became chairman of the newly formed British Lion Film Corporation and he sold his rights to all his writing to it, which earned him £26,000 in five years.

In 1931, he was heavily defeated as a Liberal candidate in Blackpool. His only previous Liberal connections were as a youngster being paid a shilling a night by Rotherhithe Liberals to break up Tory public meetings. Asked why he was standing for Parliament, he replied, 'A writer of crook stories ought never to stop seeking new material.'

Later that year, he sailed to Holywood to work as a screenwriter for RKO Pictures on the film *King Kong*. When he collapsed, diabetes was diagnosed, aggravated by hourly drinks of sweet tea when he was writing. Double pneumonia developed and he died in February 1932.

His liquid assets amounted to practically nil and claims on his estate totalled £140,000; the main claim being from his own limited private company set up to avoid income tax, from which he had overdrawn £58,000. A couple of years later, however, royalties had reduced this debt to just £64,000 and future royalties cleared it altogether.

116. Oliver St John Gogarty (1878–1957)

58–59 Fleet Street (corner of Anglesea Street), Temple Bar, Dublin 2
(Tel: 00353 1 671 1822).

A flamboyant figure, Oliver St John Gogarty excelled in many fields: cycle racing, writing poetry and plays, flying early aeroplanes and performing surgery being among them. His bravery was proved by risking his own life in hiding Irish Republican Army members on the run, operating on injured ones and rescuing more than one person from drowning in the River Liffey.

His life was even more at risk after he became an Irish Free State Senator, and was kidnapped by rebels, who were about to shoot him, when he managed to escape into the icy waters of the Liffey. As a Senator, he was dedicated to the clearance of the slums in Dublin, having seen how they spawned disease.

He was a top footballer and cricketer at a Jesuit school in Kildare, where he saved his first life – that of a fellow pupil who was choking on a fish bone, which Gogarty pulled out of his gullet. Progressing to Trinity College in Dublin, he acquired a reputation as a prankster. On one occasion, he sold the slumped body of a drunken medical student inside a sack to the Royal College of Surgeons as if it was a corpse for medical research. Luckily, it sobered up in time to evade the knife.

During the Boer War, Gogarty wrote articles for Sinn Fein urging Irishmen not to join the British army to fight in South Africa. When the Irish regiments returned from there in 1909, he wrote an *Ode of Welcome* to them, which was published in the snobbish social magazine *Irish Society*. Only afterwards was it realised that the first letter of each line spelled out 'the whores will be busy'.

He became the Irish cycling champion in 1899, completing 20 miles in fifty-three minutes thirty-five seconds (a record that stood for many years) and he then beat the English champion over 10 miles in London. But he gave up the sport for good in 1901 after being suspended for swearing at three rivals, who were trying to ram him out of a race.

From 1901 to 1903, he won the Trinity College gold medal prize for verse three times in succession, which was another record. To collect the third one he borrowed a gown from a rag-and-bone man for the ceremony and then pawned the medal and sent the ticket to the university. He also got bronze medals from the Royal Humane Society for rescuing three people on separate occasions from drowning in the Liffey, one of which, in 1901, was trying to commit suicide and Gogarty had to knock him out to stop him resisting the rescue.

During 1904, he spent two terms at Oxford University and passed the initiation test of drinking five pints of beer from a silver cup in one go, without letting the cup down from his lips.

In 1905, he spoke at the first annual conference of Sinn Fein – Irish for Our Selves – in support of national self-determination and declared, 'The British government is a tyranny because it forces on Ireland legislation which the people of Ireland repudiate ... from Leonidas to Emmet the best blood in the world has been shed for the principle we are in danger of foregoing.'

After failing anatomy exams for three years, he finally qualified as a doctor in 1907 and became an ear, nose and throat specialist at Meath Hospital. His great skill was to work quickly with just a local anaesthetic, while simultaneously joking with the patient. On one of the rare occasions he used a general anaesthetic, his patient the actor Michael Scott became conscious during the operation and tried to alert Gogarty, only to hear him say, 'Nurse, kindly put your hand over that man's mouth – we are not interested in an actor's subconscious.'

At the age of 33, he became only the second surgeon ever to remove a patient's larynx and was watched by a crowd of medical students in the gallery. The theatre was over a river and when a knocking was heard under the operating table, he made a joke about the local fish thinking

they were salmon and trying to leap out, which had the audience in stitches. At the end, he flipped the extracted larynx from behind his back into the gallery, saying, 'There you are boys have a look at it.' He never charged poor people for operations and he had a reduced rate for nuns and actors.

The conditions in the slums and the effect they had on children's health so enraged him that he wrote a play about tenement life called *Blight,* which was performed in 1917 and caused a sensation. It used Dublin proletarian dialect for the first time and indicted the social system, one line being, 'We shall shake capitalism off our backs as a terrier shakes canal water out of its hide.'

In 1918, Sinn Fein achieved an overwhelming victory in the general election with a mandate for refusing to take up seats in Westminster, but for setting up a home Parliament known as the Dail. This was suppressed and the leaders were arrested, resulting in a campaign of armed resistance. Gogarty's second play in 1919, called *A Serious Thing* satirised British rule in Ireland.

Michael Collins became the most wanted man in the country in 1920 after organising the execution of fourteen British spies. Gogarty hid him in his house at 15 Ely Place in Dublin and also operated on wounded IRA men there.

Gogarty had a passion for fast cars and used one of these to pick up some IRA prison escapers and to get them to safety at this time.

After the Treaty with the British was negotiated by Michael Collins and others, it was approved in the election of 1922, but only very narrowly, and civil war followed. Collins was killed in an ambush on 22 August 1922 and on his bloodstained body, which Gogarty embalmed, was found the key to Gogarty's house in Ely Place.

Gogarty became a Senator of the pro-Treaty Irish Free State, even though the rebels had a policy of shooting senators on sight. On 20 January 1923 he was kidnapped at gunpoint by six men and was driven to a house on the bank of the Liffey. As they got out, he asked, 'Are you not going to tip the driver?' His captors later remarked on his confident and courageous manner.

Claiming that his bowels were loosening with fright, he persuaded them to let him out, which enabled him to jump into the swirling river, which was in flood on an extremely cold night. After being almost overcome by the foam in his nostrils he managed to grab an overhanging branch and haul himself out after fifteen minutes in the icy waters. He had no feeling in his legs below the knees, but managed to stumble to a house, where he was refused entry. Even when he reached the police barracks in Phoenix Park he was incapable of speech, so it was some time before he was admitted and given brandy to restore his circulation.

A month later, his house in Conamara was burned down by the rebels. He was instructed by the security forces to carry a revolver, but he rarely did so, because it put his suits out of shape.

While struggling in the Liffey during his escape he had vowed that if he managed to survive, he would release two swans into the river. When keeping this promise, the swans were reluctant to leave the safety of their box and had to be kicked out to freedom.

As a sequel to this he published a book of poems in May 1924 entitled *An Offer of Swans*, which won him yet another gold medal. A couple of these poems were included in the *Oxford Book of English Verse*. Yeats described him as being one of the finest lyrical poets of the age.

After gaining a pilot's licence, he often flew over to London to perform operations there. Once, his parachute opened while he was still in the cockpit and almost blew him out into the sea, so he had to make an emergency landing at Chester. In 1928, he founded the Irish Aero Club, which lay the foundations for the formation in 1936 of Aer Lingus.

During his years in the Senate, up to its abolition in 1936, he ceaselessly campaigned for better housing for working-class families and was largely responsible for the housing estates that were built on the outskirts of Dublin in the late 1930s. In his later years he published more poems and novels.

117. Augustus John (1878–1961)

Peach Street (off Brownlow Hill), Liverpool, L3 5TX (Tel: 0151 794 5507). Free house.

'I become more rebellious in Liverpool,' wrote the bohemian artist Augustus John, who taught at the university art school on Brownlow Hill from February 1901 to July 1902. Some of the other staff were flustered by his long hair and beard, earrings and singing of bawdy songs.

After falling off a ladder in his studio he broke his nose, which needed two stitches, and dislocated a finger. This meant he had to wear a nose patch, which drew more students to his class; as did his behaviour, which grew wilder after the fall.

He refused to stand when the King's health was toasted at the university and his application for membership of the Liverpool Academy was rejected. But he found the cosmopolitan atmosphere inspiring and explored the Chinese quarter (off Pitt Street and Upper Frederick Street) with the whiff of opium, and mixed with the tinkers around Scotland Road and the gypsies at Cabbage Hall wasteland, whom he painted and learned Romany from.

When his first child was born he named him temporarily after the anarchist bomber Ravachol, but finally settled on David.

He drank in a local pub called The Duke and lived at various Liverpool lodgings, including 9 St James's Street, 4 St James's Road, 146 Chatham Street, 66 Canning Street and 138 Chatham Street.

Shortly after leaving Liverpool when travelling the world, he claimed to have met Abdul Hamid II, Sultan of Turkey, before he was deposed in 1909. The sultan asked him to paint the beheading of John the Baptist and the pair argued over what a severed head would look like. So the sultan sent for one of his wives and had her beheaded on the spot. 'See how right I was,' he said calmly to the artist.

Augustus had been trained at Slade School of Fine Art in Gower Street, London, from 1894 to 1898, when he was often thrown out of local music halls for sketching the performers. When attending anarchist meetings in Tottenham Court Road, those present were more tolerant of his sketching. At these meetings he saw Peter Kropotkin (the exiled Russian prince) and Louise Michel (known as the Red Virgin), who had fought on the barricades of the Paris Commune.

A fellow Slade art student was Iris Tree, who had a studio in Fitzroy Street, where she served him sardines, wine and hashish. 'I had already tried smoking this celebrated drug, without the slightest result,' he wrote. 'It was Princess Murat who converted me. She contributed several pots of the substance in the form of a compote of jam. A teaspoonful was taken at intervals. Having helped myself to the first dose I had almost forgotten it when, catching the eye of Iris across the dinner table, we were both simultaneously seized with uncontrollable laughter about nothing at all. This curious effect repeated itself from time to time throughout the evening.

'During the intervals we were completely lucid and even grave but, as it were, in another world ... in the silence we seemed to hear the tick-tock of the clockwork of the Universe, and voices reached one as if from across the frozen wastes between the stars. Ping! A shifting of the slats of time and space!

'The crises of laughter continued with some of us till dawn, with further repercussions as I made my way home with Violette Murat, who had only been slightly amused by the night's proceedings.'

He found Tottenham Court Road a fruitful place for finding models, including one particularly stunning redhead, who dozed off while posing, when her wig slipped off to reveal her baldness. Augustus withdrew, so that she could replace it on awaking.

His paintings were said to improve after he received a bang on the head when diving into a rock pool on the Welsh coast; he was already partially deaf from being hit by a cricket ball at school.

When his wife Ida Nettleship died in 1932, he got so drunk he was unable to attend the cremation. Indeed, being drunk in 1939 led to him missing an appointment to paint Queen Elizabeth (later the Queen Mother) at Buckingham Palace and he sent a rather impertinent telegram explaining this. Unperturbed, she supplied him with a bottle of brandy by his easel when the sitting was rearranged.

John considered himself an anarchist and was fond of quoting Charles Fourier: 'When the state ceaseth look my brothers, do you not see the rainbows and the bridges of beyond?'

His favourite pub was the Fitzroy Tavern in Charlotte Street, where he learned Yiddish from the governor Papa Kleinfeld. When in this tavern he used to pat any children on the head, in case any of them were his as he had sired countless children. His second wife was a gypsy, Dorelia 'Dodo' McNeil, and he often took to the road in a caravan himself.

Another of Augustus' drinking holes was The Wheatsheaf in Rathbone Place, where he took one of his lovers Caitlin Macnamara in 1936 and introduced her to the poet Dylan Thomas, whom she married the next year. Caitlin had not appreciated John's foreplay technique though, saying he had 'leaped on her, ripped off her clothes and penetrated her like some mindless hairy goat.'

Among Augustus' legitimate children were Edwin, who became a middleweight boxing champion of Wales, and Casper, who could beat his father in fights and who became an admiral, losing both of his legs in battle.

118. Alexander Fleming (1881–1955)

16 Bouverie Place, Paddington, London, W2 1RB (Tel: 020 7723 6061).
Free house.

Penicillin was discovered by Alexander Fleming when he was Professor of Bacteriology at St Mary's Hospital, Paddington, where he had first studied medicine, near this pub. This great breakthrough in antibiotic medicine may never have happened but for two random decisions made on the basis of Fleming's love of sport.

The first was his choice of St Mary's between the three medical schools he was offered. He chose it because he had played water polo against its team. Then came his great decision in 1905 to switch from specialising in surgery to bacteriology. This was made on the basis that it enabled him to stay at St Mary's and join its rifle club. While there, he was one of the first to use a compound called Salvarsan in the treatment of syphilis with the new technique of intravenous injection.

Born on a farm in Lochfield, a remote area in Ayrshire, Scotland, he moved to London aged 14 to study at Regent Street Polytechnic. On leaving, he worked for a shipping firm, which he did not like, before joining a Scottish regiment to fight in the Boer War in South Africa. After that, one of his uncles died and left him £250, which enabled him to study medicine at St Mary's.

During the First World War, he set up a bacteriology lab on the French battlefield and felt a similar chemical could be used to fight microbe infection in wounds caused by exploding shells. He continued this search after the war back at St Mary's, where he discovered that lysozyme (contained in human mucus, saliva and tears) had a natural antibacterial effect, but not against the strongest infections.

The breakthrough came in 1928, when he was testing dishes in which he had been growing bacteria, one of which had mould on it, which he had grown accidentally, and he noticed that the bacteria all around it had been killed, unlike in the other samples.

This was not what he had been looking for at all, but it led him to take a sample of the mould, which was penicillium notaturm. After developing it he called it penicillin. The full potential of its usage was finally realised during the Second World War.

Fleming received the Nobel Prize for this finding in 1945 and said, 'One sometimes finds what one is not looking for.' Another honour bestowed upon him was to be made the honorary Chief Doy-gei-tau of the Kiowa Tribe.

119. James Joyce (1882–1941)

(i) 89 Kenton Road, Harrow, Middlesex, HA3 0AN (Tel: 020 8907 9237)
(ii) (Renamed Spice Lounge), 125 Cleveland Street, London, W1T 6QB
     Tel: 020 7168 8469).

The Dublin born novelist and poet James Joyce had to educate himself for two years from the age of 9, when his alcoholic father lost his job and could not afford to send him to school. He wrote one story during this time called *Et Tu Healy* that so impressed his father that he had it printed up and distributed to friends.

James lost his virginity at the age of 14 in Dublin's brothel area of Nighttown, which in his later student days he revisited with his friend Oliver St John Gogarty. This led to Joyce contracting syphilis, which he treated himself by cauterising the chancre. The presumably painful treatment only eliminated the symptoms, however, and not the disease itself. His eye problems may have been caused by this disease. He had

twenty-five operations on them from 1917 to 1930, during which time he was completely blind for short periods.

He gave up using prostitutes, saying he wished to 'copulate with a soul'. This came in the form of the red-headed chambermaid Nora Barnacle of Galway, whom he met in 1904 in Dublin's Nassau Street and was struck by her wonder and beauty. Joyce told Barnacle he would love to be whipped by her and the thought of her soiled underwear made him horny. He asked her if his remarks about her drawers offended her and she replied, after commenting he was weak and did not fully understand women, 'I know they are as spotless as your heart.' He was an underwear fetishist who, when drunk, slipped underpants over his fingers and cakewalked them across cafe tables. Joyce, according to Nora, also asked her to go to bed with other men 'so he'll have something to write about'.

Certainly, his experiences in Dublin's brothels appear in his novel *Ulysses*, which was published in Paris in 1922 and was banned from America and Britain (but not Ireland) for obscenity. These experiences are also depicted in the very first scene in this book, which is set in Martello Tower in Sandycove, Dublin, where Joyce lived for six days with Gogarty – until Gogarty shot his revolver at pans over Joyce's bed and he left hurriedly.

Joyce then travelled abroad with Nora, where they had two children, but did not get married until 1931 (in London), and only then under pressure from their daughter Lucia.

While in Zurich during the First World War, he wrote *Portrait of the Artist as a Young Man*, which was published in America in 1916. In it, he wrote, 'I go to forge in the smithy of my soul the uncreated conscience of my race.' Yet, when he was sitting for a portrait and the painter Patrick Tuohy told him how important it was for an artist to capture his subject's soul, he replied, 'Never mind my soul. Just be sure you have my tie right.'

The success of *Portrait of the Artist as a Young Man* encouraged him to write *Ulysses* when in Paris. This was also where he wrote *Finnegans Wake*, which was published in 1939, starting with the finish of a sentence which, on the last page, is started and left unfinished.

During a bout of blindness, he dictated part of *Finnegans Wake* to Samuel Beckett. Somebody knocked on the door, which Beckett did not hear, and Joyce said 'come in', which Beckett took down as part of the story. When Beckett read it back, Joyce queried the line, then, after a pause, he said 'let it stand', so it was published with the line intact.

When back in Zurich, a young man approached him and said, 'May I kiss the hand that wrote *Ulysses*?' Joyce replied, 'No, it does lots of other things too.'

After he died in Zurich, his widow Nora admitted she had never read *Ulysses* and opined, 'Jim should have stuck to music instead of bothering with writing.'

As a young man he had trained as a singer and he had also composed music to his own poems and those by his friend W. B. Yeats, whom he visited in London in 1902.

Another pub at 125 Cleveland Street, London, W1 (previously the Cunarder and the Cleveland) was named the James

The sign at the former pub in Cleveland Street

Joyce from 1997 to 2000 and is now the Spice Lounge. It is near the Euston Hotel in Gower Street where Joyce stayed in 1926, the manager of which, E. H. Knight, is mentioned in *Finnegans Wake*.

Finnegans Wake, in turn, was the name from 1996 until 2003 of another nearby pub, now called The Fitzrovia, at 18 Goodge Street.

120. Clem Attlee (1883–1967)

1–2 St Thomas's Way (corner of Rylston Rd), Clem Attlee Estate, Fulham, London, SW6.

The original sign of the Clem Attlee (Inn Sign Society picture).

The first prime minister to have an overall Labour majority in government, Clem Attlee was reputably described by Winston Churchill as 'a modest little man with much to be modest about'. But there was nothing modest about the Attlee government's founding of the welfare state, including the national health service, improved pensions and proper unemployment pay.

He was born and raised just south of the river from Fulham at Portinscale Road in Putney. But it was in the East End that he developed a social conscience and concluded socialism rather than charity was the best means of tackling the poverty that he witnessed there.

In 1906, he volunteered to help a school friend to run a boys' club in Durham Road, Stepney. It took up more and more of his time and he eventually became the club manager and lived over its premises.

His road to socialism was a gradual, almost reluctant one, as it involved a complete break from his upbringing. But after eliminating all the alternatives, he came to the inescapable conclusion it was the only way to channel, as he said, 'the burning anger which I felt at the wrongs which I could see around me.' Charity, by contrast, 'tends to make the charitable think that he has done his duty by giving away some trifling sum, his conscience is put to sleep and he takes no trouble to consider the social problem any further.'

In 1907, he joined the Independent Labour Party and wrote a poem called *Socialism* that included the lines:

Surely some day we'll make an ending

Of all this wretched state of want and greed.

Children shall reap, glad cries forth sending,

In fields where we have sown the seed.

More poetry was to come from his pen in 1910, with a piece about *Boozers*, which went:

We have no solace to delight

Our poor and hapless folk

Only the boozer shining bright

Where men can sit and soak.

Whereby the worried housewife knows

The way the money flies

When half the scanty earning goes

To purchase paradise.'

During the First World War, he temporarily lost the use of both legs after being hit by shrapnel. In hospital, he joked in a letter to his ILP friends, 'It may interest the comrades to know I was hit while carrying the red flag to victory. I had a large artillery flag of that hue and was just planting it on the parapet when strafed. I pointed out to the commanding officer that I thought the colour was a delicate compliment to my political persuasions.'

After becoming Mayor of Stepney in 1919, he increased the rateable value of pubs in the area to raise £200,000 to provide work for unemployed ex-soldiers.

In 1922 he was elected on an anti-profiteering platform as the MP for Limehouse and a couple of years later he became Minister of War in Ramsay MacDonald's Labour–Liberal coalition government and was

Snooker champion Jimmy White at the re-opening of the Clem Attlee in 2006.

made Postmaster General the following year. But he refused to join MacDonald's national coalition government in 1931 and replaced George Lansbury as leader of the Labour Party in 1935.

During the Second World War, Attlee was deputy to Churchill as prime minister and replaced him when victorious in the 1945 general election. Churchill regained power in 1951, even though Labour received more votes than the Conservatives. Attlee said his proudest achievement in that historic Labour government was the granting of independence to India. As for his tipple? He liked a sherry before dinner and a claret during it.

121. Rupert Brooke (1887–1915)

(i) 2 The Broadway, Grantchester, Cambridgeshire, CB3 9NQ (Tel: 01223 840295). Free house.

(ii) 8–10 Castle Street, Rugby, Warwickshire, CB21 2TP (Tel: 01788 576759). Wetherspoon.

Popularly seen as the epitome of patriotism, the poet Rupert Brooke was in fact an atheist socialist, who once spoke of never returning to England. At the age of 12, during the Boer War, he spoke on a public platform in Rugby on behalf of the Boers against England. And two years before his death he wrote from America 'I have come to the conclusion that if I'm always so happy out of England, it is absurd ever to return'. So his patriotism was far from blind and jingoistic.

He became regaled as the nation's war poet with the publication of *The Soldier* in 1915, just before he died of blood poisoning on the way to fight in the Dardanelles. It includes his most famous lines:

> If I should die think only this of me,
>
> That there's some corner of a foreign field
>
> That is for ever England. There shall be
>
> In that rich earth a richer dust concealed.'

He was, in fact, buried in the Greek island of Skyros, even though he had written a song in praise of cremation, expressing horror at being buried and being 'changed by the worm's unnatural cold lust, to slime and dust!'

Rupert was born at 5 Hillmorton Road, Rugby and there is a statue of him barefooted in the town's Regent Place.

Because his mother Ruth wanted a daughter, she treated him as a girl. He was sent to a Rugby prep school and then, in 1901, he was accepted into Rugby School itself without a scholarship, because his father William worked there as a teacher. At this famous, traditional public school, he described himself as a rabid socialist and spoke against a motion deploring the rise of the Labour Party at the school's debating society in 1906. In the same year, he won a prize for prose, got into the cricket first team and took 'unheard of liberties in his hair and dress styles'.

At the end of the year, he went to King's College, Cambridge University (living first at Room 14 in Fellows' Building and then Room 1 of Gibbs Building), where he expressed his radical and rational atheism.

The Grantchester church clock stands at ten to three..."And is there honey still for tea?"

He also described himself as 'a William Morris sort of socialist' and joined the Cambridge Fabian Society, eventually becoming its president. He was a particularly enthusiastic supporter of its campaign to abolish the outdated poor laws and workhouses and he took part in a national caravan tour supporting it.

A couple of gypsy caravans soon visited him at Grantchester (2 miles south-west of Cambridge on the River Cam), where he had moved to in 1908. They were occupied by the painter Augustus John with his six horses, seven children and one of his two wives. Brooke had moved to Grantchester because he was 'passionately enamoured of solitude' and he later immortalised the village in his poem *The Old Vicarage, Grantchester.*

He first lived next door to the vicarage in the Orchard tea room, where he had two rooms for 30 shillings a week, which he paid to Mr and Mrs J. W. Stevenson, who disapproved of his bohemian ways. 'This is a divine spot,' wrote Brooke. 'I eat only strawberries and honey.' He also wandered about barefoot and almost naked, or sat in the rose garden writing all day.

He frequently bathed naked in a nearby river pool known as Byron's Pool with his fellow 'Neo Pagans', including Virginia Woolf, who was impressed by his trick of jumping in and emerging almost immediately with a full erection. He would then hang upside down on a poplar tree to dry, with his long locks brushing the grass. He got to recognise the sound of this poplar tree rustling in the wind, so knew where to stop when canoeing back from Cambridge in the dark.

At the end of 1910, he moved into the Old Vicarage itself, renting three rooms for 30 shillings (£1.50) a week from Henry and Florence Neve, whose beehives supplied the honey to the Orchard tea room. They were much more tolerant than others of his bohemian ways and he often slept on the lawn; partly to get away from the fleas and woodlice in his rooms.

He was convinced the vicarage was haunted by 'the ghosts of generations of mouldering clergymen' and he felt the tug of the vicar's children as he climbed the stairs to his bedroom where they had slept. It was here he lived for the rest of his life. Its appeal was summed up in the aforementioned poem:

> Ah God! to see the branches stir
>
> Across the moon at Grantchester!
>
> To smell the thrilling-sweet and rotten
>
> Unforgettable, unforgotten
>
> River-smell, and hear the breeze
>
> Sobbing in the little trees.'
>
> And of course,
>
> 'The lies, and truths, and pain? ... oh! yet
>
> Stands the Church clock at ten to three?
>
> And is there honey still for tea?'

Another of Brooke's skills was to be able to draw pictures or to pick up tennis balls with his toes, which were long and prehensile.

A more unpleasant task he had to perform was to poison the family cat Tibby, when moving his mother to new premises at 24 Bilton Road, Rugby (where pets were not allowed) after his father died and she had to move out of the quarters provided by Rugby School.

As for Brooke's sexual ambivalence, he 'estimated his own nature was one-quarter homosexual and half heterosexual'; maths was not his strong point, or perhaps the other quarter reflected his inactivity.

He described his first homosexual penetration with a friend, Denham Russell-Smith, which took place in 1909, 'My right hand got hold of the left half of his bottom, clutched it, and pressed his body into me. The smell of sweat began to be noticeable ... the boasted jump from virginity to Knowledge seemed a very tiny affair after all.'

Rupert Brooke's statue in Rugby.

His first heterosexual penetration took place in Stanberg, Germany in February 1912 with Katharine (Ka) Cox, who had been treasurer of the Fabians at Cambridge. This was when he was in the middle of a severe mental breakdown, for which he was prescribed stout and bullocks' blood to fatten him up, on the grounds that depressed people got thin and neglected to eat. When Ka told him she was pregnant, Brooke went to the New Forest, searching in vain in the shops of Lyndhurst and Brockenhurst for a gun to shoot himself. Ka later had a miscarriage.

He was to have a daughter, however, by a young woman called Taatamata, whom he met in Tahiti, where he stayed from January to April 1914. He described with joy his time there with scarlet flowers in his hair, singing songs to the concertina, drinking French red wine, dancing and bathing in a soft lagoon by moonlight and eating squelchy tropical fruits. Taatamata nursed him when he ripped his leg on a jagged coral reef.

After he left, she wrote a letter to him in England with news of her pregnancy, saying she wished he were with her as she got fat, drinking beer and eating sardines on the beach through the night. The ship carrying the letter, however, was sunk at the bottom of the Atlantic ... but the letter was rescued from the wreck by divers and was eventually delivered to Brooke in the following January. 'I think life is far more romantic than any books,' he commented. His daughter from this union Arlice Raputo lived until about 1990.

While in Tahiti, he sent two guineas to the Dublin transport strike fund, run by James Larkin, with the message, 'I suppose there'll be no peace anywhere till the rich are curbed altogether'. On this world tour Rupert dropped off in Fiji and wrote a poem about cannibalism there to the then prime minister's daughter Violet Asquith, in particular the practice of cutting off limbs and eating them in front of the victim while still alive:

> Broiled are the arms in which you clung
>
> And devilled is the angelic tongue ...
>
> Of the two eyes that were your ruin,
>
> One now observes the other stewing.

In February 1915, Brooke joined the Royal Naval Division and set sail for the Dardanelles. En route, he was bitten by a mosquito in Cairo, which left a sore swelling on the left side of his upper lip. Later, when anchored in Trebuki Bay in the Aegean Sea, he complained that the hock that they were drinking was making his lips swell again. This was followed by pains in the back and chest and he became semi-conscious, before dying of rapid septicaemia.

He was taken to Skyros and was buried by lamplight in an olive grove, where he had rested a few days before, remarking on its peace and beauty. The local Greeks added the following inscription: Here lies the servant of God, sub-lieutenant of the English navy, who died for the deliverance of Constantinople from the Turks.

122. Barnes Wallis (1887–1979)

Station Road, (North) Howden, East Yorkshire, DN14 7LF (Tel: 01430 430639).

Inventor Barnes Wallis is best known for designing the bouncing bombs used to destroy German dams during the Second World War. The 1954 hit film The Dam Busters, with its equally popular theme tune by Eric Coates, graphically tells this tale, including the scorn and official opposition that Wallis (played by Michael Redgrave) was subjected to. Wallis was never deterred, however, and he summed up his philosophy as 'half the joy in life consists in the fight, not in the subsequent success'. 'Bomber' Harris, chief of bomber command, said of his bouncing bomb idea in February 1943, 'This is tripe of the wildest description.' Others described it as 'mad', 'crackpot', 'freak', 'crazy' and 'far fetched.'

Some nine days later, Wallis was ordered to stop work on the project by the chairman of Vickers and he offered to resign as a result. Another three days later, however, the order was reversed and Wallis continued experimenting with his design until the bombs finally worked. They were designed to bounce in order to avoid torpedo nets and to provide greater accuracy.

In March, a squadron under Wing Commander Guy Gibson (played by Richard Todd in the film) was formed to practise dropping the bombs. On 16 May they finally targeted the dams of Germany. The vast floods that resulted killed 1,294 workers and destroyed 125 factories, 3,000 homes, 25 bridges, and 6,500 acres of arable land. The loss of the electricity generated by the dams also hit the production of steel in the manufacture of arms.

Pub landlord with the sign he painted himself.

Wallis also designed very large bombs, such as Grand Slam and Tallboy, which were used in the war. His inventive skills were also used for peaceful means, however, such as lighter calipers for polio victims, improved rigging to prevent trawlers capsizing in icy conditions and radio telescopes. Another of his ideas, producing cargo-carrying nuclear submarines, was not developed.

He lived in Howden from 1923 to 1929, when he was chief designer for the Airship R100 that was being built in the town a mile from this pub. Initially, he actually lodged in the pub (when it was the Station Hotel) while finding a place to live. He then moved in opposite the pub and finally into a bungalow near the site of the Airship Guarantee Company.

He was born in Ripley, Derbyshire, but moved to London at the age of 4. At school, he failed his matriculation exams and became an engineering apprentice, aged 17, for four shillings (20 pence) a week at Thames Engineers, Blackheath. From there, he moved to Samuel White's Shipyard in Cowes, Isle of Wight, and by the age of 26 he was earning 25 shillings (£1.25) a week and was sending one shilling (5 pence) of this back home to his mother.

He resat and passed his matriculation exams and was an airship designer when the First World War broke out. Winston Churchill was First Lord of the Admiralty at the time and he ordered White's to stop building the airships because he thought the war would be over in three months. Wallis therefore enlisted in the Artists' Rifles and served for nine months, before going back to designing airships.

In 1925, he married Molly Bloxham and they had four children. When Molly's sister and her husband were killed in an air raid in 1941, Barnes and Molly adopted their children.

After the war, he developed tailless high-speed aircraft. His work on the dam-

The Dam Busters' bouncing bomb invented by Barnes Wallis in the Yorkshire Air Museum.

busting bombs was rewarded in 1951, with an award of £10,000 from the Tribunal on Invention, which he used to endow a foundation for the education of RAF personnel.

He did not retire from Vickers company until he was 84 years old, and then only on condition that his office was moved to his home, where he spent much time on his woodcarving hobby.

An entire room is devoted to his work at the Yorkshire Air Museum in Halifax Way, Elvington, York, about 12 miles north of this pub. A life-sized bronze statue of him by sculptor David Norris stands at the RAF Museum in Hendon, North London.

123. Jack Phillips (1887–1912)

48–56 High Street, Godalming, Surrey, GU7 1AU (Tel: 01483 521750). Wetherspoon.

Portrait of Titanic hero Jack Phillips.

The chief wireless telegraphist on the ill-fated *Titanic*, Jack Phillips stuck bravely to his post sending out distress signals in Morse code as it sank. He went down with the ship two hours and forty minutes after it had struck an iceberg on 15 April 1912, the day after his 25th birthday, resulting in the loss of 1,490 lives. But Jack's heroic actions in alerting other ships to come to the rescue, instead of abandoning his post, saved 700 lives.

He was born in Farncombe, near Godalming, and lived above a drapers shop in the high street there. He sang in the choir at St John's in Farncombe and went to Godalming Grammar School (which is now the Red Lion Pub). His first job was as a telegraphist in the local post office (now the Midland Bank).

In 1906, he started working for the Marconi Company and after completing his training, he worked for the company on various ships, including the *Lusitania*. In 1908, he was transferred to a Marconi Station on the Irish coast, transmitting messages to and from Nova Scotia in the world's first transatlantic wireless operation.

In March 1912, he was sent to Belfast shipyard to take up his post on the *Titanic*. After the disaster, his body was never recovered, but there is a memorial headstone in his family's grave in Godalming Old Cemetery and a memorial to him on the River Wey in the shadow of St Peter and St Paul's Parish Church.

124. John Logie Baird (1888–1946)

(i) 29–31 Havelock Road, Hastings, East Sussex, TN34 1BE
     (Tel: 01424 448110). Wetherspoon.
(ii) John Baird, 122 Fortis Green Road (corner of Princes Avenue), London,
     N10 3HN (Tel: 020 8444 8830). Punch Taverns.

The John Baird near Alexandra Palace, London.

The inventor of television John Logie Baird was seen as 'a bit of a crank' when experimenting in Hastings and he was finally thrown out by his landlord for causing an explosion. This was the second explosion to get him into trouble, the first being in the First World War at a Clyde Valley factory, where he was trying to make diamonds out of carbon rods during a slack period. He connected electricity to each end of them in a pot of concrete and the resulting explosion blew all the main fuses in the plant, cutting off most of Glasgow's power supply in the process.

His personal safety was also endangered by other experiments, such as a glass razor blade that would not need sharpening – with which he cut himself and was taken to hospital – and a pair of pneumatic shoes containing balloons that burst and caused him to fall over.

But even when he demonstrated the success of television he received opposition from the British Broadcasting Corporation in the form of its Director General Sir John Reith; whom Baird had first met at college in Glasgow, where they formed a dislike of each other. Reith saw it as a threat to radio and tried to prevent Baird from developing television with sound, saying the BBC had a monopoly on sound! It was only after Baird went to Germany to transmit pictures with sound from Berlin to his studio in London that the BBC grudgingly agreed to cooperate with developing television. Even then, however, it charged him for the use of its transmitters when he broadcast events, such as the Derby horse race in 1931 ... whereas the Germans had paid him for the use of his apparatus.

Baird was born in the seaside town of Helensburgh, near Glasgow and at the age of 2 he developed a serious chest illness, which plagued him for the rest of his life. At the age of 10, he became president of the photographic society in the local school. As a youngster, one of his first experiments was to build a glider and to push it off the roof with him on board, resulting in some bad bruises as it plunged to the ground. More successful projects were to make a generator to supply electricity to the family home – which unfortunately caused his father to fall down the stairs when the lights failed on one occasion – and also to set up a telephone service between other houses in the same street.

His three-year course at the Royal Technical College in Glasgow took five years because of his illness. This was followed by a science course at the University of Glasgow, which he left without taking his final exams in 1915 in order to join the army during the First World War. He then failed the medical and became a mains engineer instead at the Clyde Valley Factory, where he had caused the explosion.

This hastened his branching out on his own and he successfully produced 'damp proof socks', until failing health caused him to close the

John Logie Baird's invention of television featured in Hastings Museum.

business. In order to improve his health he went to Trinidad in 1919, where he promptly contracted dysentery and malaria. He tried exporting marmalade from there to Britain, but it became infested with maggots.

Back in Britain he tried manufacturing jam, which was a failure and he then moved practically penniless to London, where he marketed 'a revolutionary soap', which was a success. Once more, his health failed, so he sold the business and moved to Hastings in 1923.

His lodgings were at 21 Linton Crescent, which proved too small for his television experiments and so he also rented a small room in the attic at 8 Queens Avenue (which was called Queens Arcade in those days) for five shillings (25 pence) a week. It was there that in 1924 he produced his first crude transmitter from a tea chest, a hat box, a darning needle, a biscuit tin, a bicycle lamp and a coffin lid from the local undertaker. He managed to give himself two electric shocks with this and then cause the small explosion, after which his landlord Mr Twigg evicted him.

So, in November 1924, Baird moved to 22 Frith Street in the Soho area of London for £2 a week, where he continued his experiments. The breakthrough came on 2 October 1925 when he managed to transmit an image of Stooky Bill (a ventriloquist's dummy) onto a screen in the next room. Excitedly, Baird rushed downstairs and dragged up a bemused office boy called William Taynton to become the first human to appear on television. He set the lad up before the camera and went next door to look at the screen, only to see a blank. The lights had been so hot that William had moved away from them and was out of shot. The sum of half a crown (12.5 pence) persuaded him to stay in position and he at last appeared on the screen.

Baird improved on the equipment and demonstrated it publicly to forty members of the Royal Institution on 26 January 1926 and he celebrated afterwards with a large brandy or two. He transmitted pictures from London to Glasgow in May 1927 and to New York in February 1928. And he demonstrated colour television as early as July 1928.

Often, the events that he televised he had to provide himself, such as boxing matches between members of his own staff. It was not until August 1932 that the BBC took responsibility for making programmes and he introduced its first official broadcast. The first high-definition service started in Alexandra Palace, North London (close to where the John Baird Pub is) in 1936.

A double disaster then hit Baird. First his studios in Crystal Palace were destroyed by fire in November 1936. And then the BBC decided to use Marconi EMI equipment in preference to that manufactured by Baird's company in February 1937. Baird persevered, however, and from his new studio at 3 Crescent Wood Road in Sydenham, South London, he transmitted colour television pictures to a 12 foot screen in Tottenham Court Road's Dominion Theatre in 1938. In August 1944, he demonstrated the first fully electronic colour television. He was still developing colour television when he died at home at 1 Station Road, Bexhill, Sussex, where he spent the last five years of his life, a few days after transmitting a victory parade at the end of the war. He was buried in a small graveyard in his birthplace of Helensburgh, Scotland.

125. Charlie Chaplin (1889–1977)

26 New Kent Road, Elephant & Castle, London, SE1 6TJ (Tel: 020 7703 6117). Unique Pub Company.

The world's greatest comic genius was born in squalor in East Lane, Walworth (near this pub) and was to spend much of his childhood being flogged in the poorhouse or sleeping rough. 'Victorian England was a cruel, damnably cruel place. It was a pitiless time,' he wrote of those years.

Both his parents were vaudeville artistes. His father of the same name, from a French Huguenot/Jewish family, spent most of his money on drink, eating only raw eggs in port wine, and he died of alcoholism when young Charlie was about 10. His mother, who sang under the stage name of Lily

Charlie Chaplin and the Kid looking out from the pub wall.

Harley, was half-Spanish/Jewish and half-Irish/Gypsy on the side of her father Charles Hill, a revolutionary cobbler.

Charlie was only 5 when he was pushed on stage to sing an old coster song *Jack Jones*, because his mother was too ill to perform. He was showered with coins as a result. When she was declared insane and taken to an asylum, he made a living doing chores in Covent Garden Market, dancing in the streets, selling paper boats and as a lather boy in a barber shop. At nights he slept in the market or in the park. By the age of 10, he was appearing at the London Hippodrome and got enough money together to transfer his mother to a convalescent home, but she never regained her sanity.

Stage work was going through a lean time in 1905 and Charlie got a job in a glass factory, but it only lasted one day before he burned his hand. His act was transformed by chance though, when he was performing in the Channel Islands. The audience knew little English, speaking a French patois, so his jokes were not being understood. He resorted to miming and this became a major element in his art; he continued to make silent films years after talkies were introduced.

But his big break came at the age of 17, when his brother Sidney got him into the Fred Karno Company. This company toured America from 1910 to 1913, at the end of which Charlie signed up for the New York Motion Picture Company, makers of the *Keystone Cops* films, who trebled his salary to $150 a week.

In 1915, the year of his huge success with the film *The Tramp*, he was being paid $1,250 a week. Explaining the success of this character, he said, 'That costume helps me to express my conception of the average man, of almost any man, of myself. The derby (bowler hat), too small, is a striving for dignity. The moustache is vanity. The tightly buttoned coat and the stick and his whole manner are a gesture towards gallantry and dash and front. He is trying to meet the world bravely, to put up a bluff, and he knows that, too. He knows it so well that he can laugh at himself and pity himself a little.'

The following year, he signed a deal with the Mutual Company for $6.7 million a year. After that, he said, 'Well, I've got this much if they never give me another cent. Guess I'll go and buy a whole dozen neckties.' He continued to live in a small room in downtown Los Angeles and wandered at night through the poorer quarters of town.

He said that much of the humour in his films hinged on attempts to maintain dignity. 'Perhaps the best example is the intoxicated man who, though his tongue and walk give him away, attempts in a dignified manner to convince you that he is quite sober. He is much funnier than the man who, wildly hilarious, is frankly drunk and doesn't care a whoop who knows it.

'For that reason, all my pictures are built around the idea of getting me into trouble and so giving me the chance to be desperately serious in my attempt to appear as a normal little gentleman.

'That is why, no matter how desperate the predicament is, I am always very much in earnest about clutching my cane, straightening my bowler hat, and fixing my tie, even though I have just landed on my head.'

In his autobiography in 1964, he stated, 'Because of humour we are less overwhelmed by the vicissitudes of life. It activates our sense of proportion and reveals to us that in an overstatement of seriousness lurks the absurd.'

In the 1920s, he brought his confused mother over to America. When she saw him in make-up, she said, 'Why do you want to make yourself look hideous, you who are so beautiful?'

In 1923, he joined United Artists for the rest of his career and by 1931, with *City Lights*, he was writing, directing, acting, composing music and conducting the orchestra for the soundtrack; his interest in music dated back to hearing *The Honeysuckle and the Bee* being played on clarinet and harmonica in the streets of Kennington as a boy.

In 1940, he made the film *The Great Dictator* satirising Hitler, which eventually got him into trouble with the American authorities for being a communist.

Back in 1921, he had been asked if he was a Bolshevik and had replied, 'I am an artist. I am interested in life. Bolshevism is a new phase of life. I must be interested in it.'

Shortly after *The Great Dictator* had been released (it was later banned by cinema chains), he said, 'I'm no communist ... just a human being who wants to see this country a real democracy, and freedom from this infernal regimentation which is crawling over the rest of the world.'

In 1943, on being warned his failure to take US citizenship might see him discredited, he said, 'I am an internationalist, not a nationalist, and that is why I do not take out citizenship.'

Told he might be called before the House of Un-American Activities Committee, he asserted, 'I am not a Communist, I am a peacemonger.'

After the war he was asked if he was a Communist sympathiser and he replied, 'During the war I was sympathetic with the Russians who were holding the front. I believe we owe her thanks and in that sense I was sympathetic.'

His ideology, he explained, was a defence of 'the little man – his right to have a roof over his head and to work and raise a family'. If anything, he was a 'social anarchist'.

Statue of Charlie Chaplin in Leicester Square.

In 1952, when touring Europe, he was barred from returning to America for being a Communist and for 'making statements that would indicate a leering, sneering attitude towards a country whose hospitality has enriched him'.

His film *Limelight* was banned and he spent the rest of his life in Switzerland, declaring himself a 'citizen of the world'. There, he fathered the last of his children in his early seventies. He disliked condoms – describing them as 'aesthetically hideous' – and so had eleven children in all, through four wives; three of whom were 18 or under when he married them.

While in Monte Carlo, he entered a Charlie Chaplin lookalike competition – and came third.

126. Stan Laurel (1890–1965)

Stan Laurel Inn, 31 The Ellers (corner of Chapel Street and Ellerside), Ulverston, Cumbria, LA12 0AB (Tel: 01229 582814). Free house.

Laurel and Hardy became the world's best known comedy double act. But although Stan was half the weight of Ollie, he was paid nearly twice as much, because he also wrote and directed most of their films.

He was born Arthur Stanley Jefferson, near the pub at what is now 3 Argyle Street (it was called Foundry Cottages) on 16 June 1890, when

Ulverston was part of Lancashire. His father Arthur Jefferson was a comic actor, which meant the family was always on the move.

In 1897 they moved to 8 Dockwray Square, North Shields and Stan was banished to a nearby boarding school in Tynemouth, because of his 'incorrigible naughtiness'. This included setting fire to the house and falling into a barrel of fish guts in his best suit.

When aged 12 he was at King James I Grammar School in Bishop Auckland and his comic skills (jokes and impressions) caught the eye of a teacher, Master Bates, who persuaded him to entertain other teachers after hours over a tipple.

By 1905, the family was living at 185 Stonelaw Road, Glasgow and Stan was playing truant from Stonelaw High School and Queens Park Secondary School.

His first stage appearance was at Glasgow's Britannia Theatre on an amateur night in 1906. Spotting his father in the audience and fearing punishment, he tried to escape. When catching him, however, his father rewarded him with a whisky and soda. Still aged 16, Stan had a short career as a solo comedian, but the following year he joined a theatrical juvenile company for £1 5s (£1.25) a week. The company's rules forbade him to be intoxicated or to ad lib on stage.

Then, in 1909, he met the showman Fred Karno, who took him on tour for £2 a week. The following year, the tour extended to America, during which Stan shared rooms with Charlie Chaplin. Because they were not paid for the long periods of travelling between shows, Stan demanded a rise. When this was rejected, he returned to England in 1911 and stayed with his brother Gordon in High Holborn, London. On one particular day in Leicester Square he bumped into one of Karno's managers Alf Reeves, who asked Stan if he was starring in the West End. 'Starving in the West End,' replied Stan, who was taken on again and sailed back to America at the end of 1912.

In April 1917, he teamed up with an Australian female comedian Charlotte Mae Dahlberg under the stage name of Stan and Mae Laurel, after opening a history book on the page of a Roman general wearing a laurel of leaves. They also lived with each other until 1925 without getting formally married. From then on, his stage name was Stan Laurel, but he did not change it to that officially until 1931.

He made his first film for Hal Roach in 1918 and the following year he appeared in a supporting role in a film starring Oliver Hardy; but it was not until 1927 that they appeared as Laurel and Hardy in *Putting Pants on Philip*.

Stan wrote roles for himself as a lumberjack, a street cleaner, a miner, a door-to-door salesman, a laundry worker, a petrol station attendant, a fruit picker, a cook and a waiter ... with plots being recognisable to the ordinary man in the street. He also wrote and directed at least twenty films starring Oliver Hardy.

Then, in 1926, when Stan was directing *Get 'Em Young*, Ollie became injured. So Stan stepped in to replace him and used his famous crying on screen. Such was Stan's standing that he was allowed to shoot his film scenes in the chronological order that they appeared, which was much more expensive. It was also in 1926 that Stan married actress Lois Neilson, when he was living at 6075 Franklin Avenue, Hollywood.

In 1929 – the year of the first Laurel and Hardie talkie *Unaccustomed As We Are* – Stan moved with his wife and baby daughter to 718 North Bedford Drive, Beverly Hills. But he still cycled to the studio and kept his telephone number (Oxford 0614) in the public directory, and even used it in the film *Blotto*. But in 1932, Stan and Lois separated because, as Stan explained, 'we got on each other's nerves.'

On a tour of the UK in 1932, Laurel and Hardy were mobbed everywhere they went, but the people of North Shields and Glasgow were impressed at how success had failed to spoil Stan. They also made an appearance at

Another fine mess ... picture in the pub.

the cinema run by his father at 49 Colebrooke Avenue, West Ealing, London, W13. On this tour, Stan analysed his comedy as an exaggeration of the daydreams of children. 'The comedian who knocks down the policeman is the small child rebelling against authority,' he stated. 'The custard pie is the symbol of revolt – revolt against an ignorant world of grown-ups which cannot appreciate that the dirty puddle at the end of the garden path is really the most romantic of lakes, on which there are boats to be sailed and bridges to be built.'

In 1934, he met vivacious Virginia Ruth Rogers and they got married on 3 April and again on 26 September, after it was pointed out his divorce from Lois had not been finalised in April. His new wife separated from him in 1936 and she filed for maintenance. A month later, his earlier common-law wife Mae also filed for maintenance. Both women wanted half his property each and $1,000 a month. Mae claimed they had actually been married, but was unable to prove it. In court, Stan admitted he introduced her to landladies as his wife, but only because 'it was the gentlemanly thing to do'. Eventually, they settled out of court.

In January 1938, his third (or fourth) marriage took place, this time to Russian singer Vera Illiana Shuvalova, when the ceremony was heckled by his previous wife (vivacious Virginia). Vera turned out to be a drunk, who was found guilty of reckless driving. Also, while wearing just her socks, she threw sand in Stan's eyes when he was at the wheel, making him swerve and end up being arrested for drunken driving. They were divorced within a year.

In 1941, when living at 20213 Strathern Road, Reseda, in the San Fernando Valley, he remarried Virginia, but separated again after a few

months, formally being divorced in 1946. A month later, he married his fourth (or fifth) wife, another Russian singer Ida Kitaeva Raphael and they remained together for the rest of his life.

Back on tour in Britain in 1947, he and Ollie once more impressed whoever they met, such as stagehands they mixed with, at how unassuming they were for top of the bill stars. Stan's classless approach was said to be inherited from his egalitarian father and, even when he was a star, he welcomed ordinary people in his apartment and always wrote back to fans who sent him letters.

In 1957, he moved from 1111 Franklin Street to a one-bedroomed flat at 25406 Malibur Road by the sea in Santa Monica and then the following year to 849 Ocean Avenue, where he remained.

He developed cancer of the palate and, on 23 February 1965, as the nurse prepared his injection, he remarked, 'I'd much rather be ski-ing than doing this.' When she asked 'Do you ski?' he replied, 'No, but I'd much rather be ski-ing than what I'm doing now,' and then he died.

Laurel and Hardy fans from all over the world converge on the Stan Laurel Inn (which changed its name from The Britannia in 1977) on the first Saturday of July during the town's annual parade.

127. Richmal Crompton (1890–1969)

23 Westmoreland Road (corner of Masons Hill, opposite Bromley South Station), Bromley, Kent, BR1 1DS (Tel: 020 8464 1586). Wetherspoon.

The creator of the hugely popular anti-authoritarian *William* books, Richmal Crompton was a teacher in a girls' public school in Bromley from 1917 until polio forced her to resign in 1923. This was a blessing in disguise, as she herself conceded, giving her a far more interesting and rewarding life as a full-time author, which enabled her to live in the area for the rest of her life.

For the first decade of her life she was treated as an invalid, forced to lie on a backboard to prevent curvature of the spine, so she sought escape to the attic, which is where she scribbled stories. She developed this by writing comic stories for her school magazine. Even when she became a classics mistress at Bromley High School (which was then just north of this pub at Elmfield Road off the high street), she was writing stories for magazines under her pen name; which was an abbreviation of her full name of Richmal Crompton Lamburn.

William first appeared in *Home Magazine* in 1919 and was transferred to *Happy Mag* in 1922. The character was modelled on her young brother Jack, named after their grandfather, who killed himself with prussic acid the year before young Jack's birth. Jack detested homework, just like William, and he preferred an adventurous life. He joined the mounted police in Rhodesia (as Zimbabwe then was) for a few years and then travelled the world, being captured by bandits in China. During the war, he served as a pilot in Iceland with Air Commodore Cecil George Wigglesworth, on whom the *Biggles* stories were based. Jack eventually became quite a successful novelist, basing his plots on his own escapades.

When Richmal contracted polio she lost the use of her right leg, which remained stiff for the rest of her life. For a while, she persevered with teaching, cycling the three and a half miles to school (from her home in Cherry Orchard Road) with her stiff leg sticking out at a dangerous angle. But after some months she was advised to give it up.

Her books became so successful that after just three years, she was able to move to a much larger house, The Glebe, in Oakley Road, Bromley Common. In her forties she developed breast cancer and had a mastectomy performed in her own home.

During the Second World War she joined the Bromley auxiliary fire service at the station set up in Bromley County Grammar School for Boys. She also worked in the Toc H canteen for service personnel on Bromley Common and then nearby Keston.

Early in the 1950s, she moved to the village of Chislehurst, near Bromley, about the time she performed the opening ceremony of Bromley Junior Library. In her speech she deplored the library's policy of grading books by age groups and urged the children to experiment by reading all kinds of books.

In the 1960s, she had a heart attack and broke her legs twice. The second time it was her stiff leg, which she used as a prop by sticking it out at an unusual angle. When the doctor tried to set it at the usual angle, she insisted he do it at the odd one instead.

She died of a second heart attack in 1969. The funeral was held at St Nicholas's Church in Chislehurst and the cremation at Eltham. Among her prized possessions were newspaper cuttings of *William* being banned from various libraries.

In one episode *Great Aunt Jane's Treat* (*William the Fourth*, 1924), his puritannical relative lets her hair down with William at a funfair and goes wild with excitement on a roundabout, where she 'mounts a giant cock'. She seemed 'to find the circular motion anything but monotonous. It seemed to give her a joy that all her blameless life had so far failed to produce'.

The last *William* book was published posthumously in 1970. Summing up the appeal of *William,* the child rebel against adult authority, Richmal stated, 'The boy of eleven is at the stage of the savage – loyal to his tribe, ruthless to his foes, governed by mysterious taboos, an enemy of civilisation and all its meaningless conventions.

'He dislikes little girls, not only because he considers them to belong to an inferior order of being, but also because he suspects them of being allies of the civilisation that threatens his liberty.'

She also described him as well meaning, sensitive, generous and affectionate beneath his tough exterior, which his pride made him conceal. His favourite tipple was liquorice water and lemonade, whereas Richmal's was sherry. The pub was named after her in January 2003.

128. Ellen Wilkinson (1891–1947) and the Jarrow Crusaders

Jarrow Crusaders, 76 Walter Street (behind the town hall), Jarrow, Durham, NE32 3PQ (Tel: 01423 862598). Punch Taverns/Pubmaster.

When long-term unemployment in Jarrow reached 80 per cent in 1936, after the closure of the shipyards, the town council decided something dramatic had to be done. It approached local Labour MP Ellen Wilkinson to help organise a march to London calling for the reopening of the shipyards.

'Red' Ellen, as she was known because of her politics and the colour of her hair, in turn, approached Wal Hannington (leader of the National Unemployed Workers' Movement) for advice. He advised her to make it part of a national hunger march of the NUWM, which was to take place in October. The NUWM was considered too militant by the official leadership of the Labour Party and the TUC at the time, so this suggestion was rejected by the Labour town council. So the 200 Jarrow Crusaders set off on the 280 mile march to London a week before the Tyneside and Durham contingent of the NUWM march, led by communist councillor Tom Richardson.

Ellen, who had been a member of the Communist Party from 1920 to 1924, joined the Jarrow Crusaders for as much of the march as she could. She had to take time off, however, for the annual conference of the Labour Party, where she was amazed to find her marchers denounced from the platform. 'I thought that we were so guaranteed 100 per cent respectable,' she wrote. 'With the blessing of bishops, priests and clergy, subscriptions from business men, the paternal interest of the Rotary Club, and the unanimous vote of the town council, could anything have been more constitutional?' However, the Labour Party, as she added, 'drew out, and the TUC circulated the trades councils advising them against giving help.

Landlord proud of the pub's heritage.

'So in places like Chesterfield, where the trades and Labour council obeyed the circular, the Conservative Party weighed in with hot meals and a place to sleep.'

When they reached London, some of them were allowed into the public gallery of the House of Commons to witness their petition being formally handed over on 4 November. They were amazed when there was no debate about it. As their MP Ellen recalled, 'The men, who were entertained to tea in the House, were rather disappointed. They had imagined an imposing ceremony and a long discussion.' As Wal Hannington remarked in his book *Never on our Knees,* the government never showed any inclination to reward the Jarrow men for their good conduct and they left, unheralded, on Saturday 7 November.

A sculptured plaque commemorating the Jarrow Crusade.

The very next day, the officially disapproved of NUWM marchers were greeted by a crowd of 250,000 people as they arrived in Hyde Park, demanding a withdrawal of dole cuts and the means test. The leader of the Parliamentary Labour Party Clem Attlee joined the communist Wal Hannington on the platform in denouncing the means test. The national government had said it would not receive a deputation of the marchers. But four days after their arrival they were forced to do so and the Minister of Labour Ernest Brown announced a suspension of the dole cuts.

Ellen Wilkinson described the Jarrow experience in her book *The Town That Was Murdered,* published in 1939, as 'a picture of capitalism at work' and an indictment of the politics that made the town 'a workhouse without walls'.

A sculpture of the Jarrow Marchers was unveiled in the town's Morrisons car park in 2001. In the year 2002, a local heavy rock band Crashed Out recorded on their CD *Back for More* the *Jarrow Song* by Alan Price. The lyrics go:

> My name is Geordie McIntyre, and the bairns don't even have a fire,
>
> and the wife said Geordie go to London town
>
> and if they don't give us half a chance,
>
> don't even give us a second glance,
>
> then Geordie with my blessings burn them down.

129. Wilfred Owen (1893–1918)

17 Willow Street, Oswestry, Shropshire, SY11 1AJ (Tel: 01691 653435).
Wetherspoon.

Killed in action a week before the end of the First World War, Wilfred Owen lives on through his poetry, which condemns both the horror and the purpose of the war. A plaque marks where he was born at Plas Wilmot in Weston Lane, Oswestry on 18 March 1893. He was baptised in St Oswald's Church, in Church Street, where his parents had got married, alongside which is a memorial to him in Broad

Owen's birthplace in Oswestry.

Walk (there is also a Wilfred Owen Road, Avenue and Close in the town).

The family moved in 1897 to Birkenhead, where a stained-glass window commemorates him in the central library. In 1906, they moved to Shrewsbury, where there is a memorial to him in the abbey grounds.

In 1915, he joined the Artists' Rifles Brigade of the 28th London Regiment as Private Number 4756, at Dukes Road, Bloomsbury (near Euston Road). Immediately after being sworn in, he was injected against typhoid. The after-effects were so painful that he felt a horse had got its teeth in his arm, so he was given three days' sick leave. That night, he went to poetry readings at the Poetry Bookshop at nearby 35 Boswell Street. He went through the shop's yard and up a steep wooden staircase to 'what seemed to be an old stable loft, the only light coming from a pair of candles on the reader's desk. The effect was intentionally church-like. For half an hour the new soldier could rededicate himself to his true creed, forgetting the war and his aching arm.' He was to revisit the bookshop many times when on leave and actually lodged there in 1916, 'drafting poems and looking for inspiration across the narrow street'.

A photograph of Wilfred Owen in the pub in Oswestry.

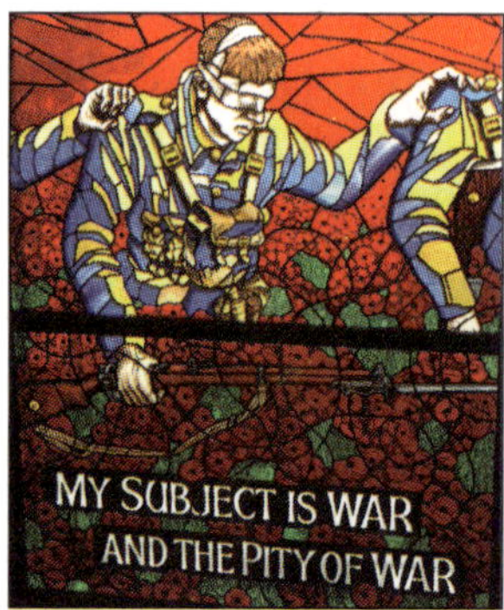

A detail from the stained glass window dedicated to Wilfred Owen in the Birkenhead Library.

The main inspiration, however, was to come from his service on the Somme in the first five months of 1917 ... the worst French winter for forty years. He witnessed 'unnameable tortures' and was to be almost buried alive, half-frozen to death and nearly blown to pieces.

In April 1917, a big shell exploded a few yards from his head and blew him into the air. When he landed, he was buried under corrugated iron for several days before being rescued. Suffering from shell shock, he was taken to Craiglockhart Hospital near Edinburgh, where he was pronounced unfit for service for six months – the longest period which could be recommended. It was here that he met fellow soldier poet Siegfried Sassoon and he discussed with him not only the horrific reality of the war, but also its aims, which they considered had become those of aggression and conquest. Sassoon had, in fact, been sent to the hospital to try and silence him after he had published a letter in *The Times* (as the holder of a Military Cross for bravery) accusing the British and French governments of keeping the war going in the hope of grabbing colonies. Owen, who had a 'wicked sense of humour and an ironic eye for social pretensions', wrote a poem about a shell shock victim called *The Dead Beat* while in hospital.

Throughout September and October of 1917, the two poets discussed the war intensely and decided the people of England must be told what was happening, so they would agitate against it. They decided poetry was the best form of protest for this, as it was easier to get past censors than prose. The aim was to strike at the civilian conscience to bring pressure on politicians. With this in mind, Owen produced *Anthem for Doomed Youth*, with the lines:

> What passing-bells for those who die as cattle?
>
> Only the monstrous anger of the guns.
>
> Only the stuttering rifles rapid rattle
>
> Can patter out their hasty orisons.

He also collected photographs of wounds and mutilations to show people who glorified war. The same people were the target of a gas poem he wrote; to the effect that those who experienced the reality of war would not tell their children it was 'sweet and meet to die for one's country'.

In 1918, he returned to the front and received the Military Cross for his bravery in action. He was shot while attempting to cross the Sambre Canal near Ors on a floating bridge. Some ten minutes later, the attempt was called off. A week later, the war ended. Shortly afterwards, his mother received his last letter to her, written while he was sheltering from shells in the cellar of a destroyed house. It read: There is no danger down here – or if any, it will be over before you read these lines ...

130. Burn Bullock (1896–1954)

315 London Road (corner of Cricket Green), Mitcham, Surrey, CR4 4BE
(Tel: 020 8640 2093). Punch Taverns.

If you expect to see scalding genitals on this pub's sign you will be fortunately disappointed, because it is named after the cricketer Burn Bullock. The pub is situated right next to the ground of the oldest cricket club in the world, Mitcham, being formed over 300 years ago, which Burn first played for at the age of 15.

Born Burnett Wedlake Bullok locally, he signed up for Surrey County Cricket Club and played for them, mostly in the second team, from 1921 to 1925. His highest innings was 153 runs, which he hit in 1923. Before that, he had joined Mitcham Junior Cricket Club at the age of 11. At the age of 15, he made his first century for the adult second eleven (against Carshalton) and was rapidly promoted to the first team.

During the First World War he fought for the Royal Flying Corps in France for three years. On being demobbed, he resumed playing for Mitcham and in 1919 he headed its batting averages, which prompted Surrey to sign him up. He captained their second team and played in many Minor Counties Championship games with the likes of Jack Hobbs in his side. In his first season he scored over 1,500 runs and took over 50 wickets.

He turned professional in 1921, but by 1926 he became the coach and cricket organiser of a millionaire Bradford wool manufacturer called Jimmy White. Later, he returned to Mitcham and became an all-rounder for the team in the Surrey Championship League.

When his playing days were over, he became a licensee in 1929 at Croydon, and then Borough and Vauxhall, before taking over the King's Head (as it then was) at Mitcham in 1941 - the pub that he ran for the rest of his life and now bears his name. He also became President of Mitcham

A dismissed batsman has to cross the main road to get back to the pavilion.

Mitcham Cricket team in action in front of the Burn Bullock.

Cricket Club and played regularly for the North and South of the Thames Licensed Victuallers' Cricket Club, which he captained for 14 years.

For many years he used his contacts to bring first-class sides (Burn Bullock's XI) to Mitcham for annual charity matches on the green. 'He was a great big bloke and a very well known character,' recalled Herbert Rattle, who has been a regular in the pub since 1956. 'He had these huge Alsatians which he walked around the ground every day.

'When he died, Taylor Walker, who owned the pub then, changed its name in his memory. His widow Lil took it over and she was a real diamond. She stayed until the mid 1960s.'

The cricket green was common grazing land in medieval times and it escaped the enclosures of the eighteenth and nineteenth centuries. Horatio Nelson often watched cricket being played there. A peculiarity of the ground is that the batsmen have to cross a main road to get from the pavilion to the pitch. One of the club's best batsman, apart from Burn, was the South African Dave Morley, who worked in the pub as a barman and who met his wife there. One day, he hit a six over the scoreboard and it hit an old lady, who was out shopping, while she was walking along the road. An ambulance came to take her away and the game recommenced. Dave hit the very next ball for six – and hit the ambulance!

Chelsea footballers using Tooting and Mitcham's ground for training were regulars in the pub, including Peter Osgood, who owned a local boutique, and goalkeeper John Phillips, who still has a local radio spare-parts shop.

131. Percy Hobbs (1898–1983)

Alfresford Road (corner of Chapel Lane), Alfresford, near Winchester, Hants, SO21 1HL (Tel: 01962 849631). Mitchell & Butler.

Local farm worker Percy Hobbs drank in this pub for sixty-three years. It was called the New Inn when he started drinking here in 1920 ... and a shilling (5 pence) could buy 6 pints of beer. Mind you, the statutory minimum wage for farmworkers under the Corn Production Act was only 25 shillings (£1.25) a week, although the Agricultural Wages Board recommended 42 shillings (£2.10) for those aged over 21. Even that was well below the poverty line of 48 shillings (£2.40) required to feed a couple with one child.

After sixty-two years of solid drinking and eleven changes of landlord, Percy's loyalty was rewarded by owners Whitbread, when they renamed it after him in 1982 and had his portrait painted on the signs outside. Percy, who lived in nearby Firmstone Road, Winnall, said at the time it was the happiest moment in his life.

But even more happiness was to come when the publicity about the event reached his long-lost sister Alice, whom he had not seen for sixty years. As a result, they were reunited. Sadly, this was short-lived, because Percy died a year later, just before Christmas 1983 in Winchester's Royal Hampshire County Hospital, after developing a chest infection.

By then, the minimum wage for an agricultural worker was £79.20 a week. His tankard remains behind the bar, although it is considered unlucky to touch it. Barmaid Louise Sims, however, made an exception and drank a toast to Percy's memory with his tankard.

Barmaid Louise Sims hold up Percy's tankard.

132. Charlie Butler (1899–1980)

40 Mortlake High Street (corner of Vineyard Path), London, SW14 8HR
(Tel: 020 8878 2310). Youngs.

The head horse keeper of Young's brewery for forty-three years, Charlie Butler won over 3,000 first prizes and championships with his dray horses over that time. Born in Lincolnshire, he left school at 15 to work for Forshaw's Stud in Carlton-on-Trent, Nottinghamshire.

In 1923, Henry Young, the young chairman of the Wandsworth brewery, decided to keep show horses as well as working ones. So he went to Forshaw's to buy a shire horse called Wandle Bob. Charlie, the groom and studman, was initially lent to the brewery for 'a short period' to get the horse ready for competing at the Islington Agricultural Show. He never returned and stayed with the brewery until retiring in 1966.

He bought and trained black-and-white shires and became skilled at picking the best young horses for looks and gentleness. He looked, he said, for 'muscle and manners'. It took at least six weeks to teach them the manners needed for the show ring and up to a year to develop the muscle.

The secret of his success he put down to treating the horses individually. 'There is not two horses alike,' he explained. 'They are exactly the same as humans. They don't look like each other and they are not alike in any way. Train them as individuals and prepare them as a team.'

It certainly worked for, apart from winning more prizes than any other brewery before or since, his horses were completely unbeaten in the show ring from 1945 to 1954. He respected them so much that he said they should 'replace the lion and the bulldog as the symbol of Britain.' Lions, he added, did not originate in Britain and 'they have never pulled a plough and they have never produced any food.'

The horse that really made his reputation was Bower King John, whose enormous harness was the largest ever made. But because he tended to be temperamental, he was considered unsuitable for stud in retirement so, instead, was castrated.

In 1942, Charlie took over control of the working horses (from John Cornish, who died in the harness at the age of 84) as well as the show ones. The horses worked for twelve hours a day delivering beer as far as Croydon, Hampstead, Stepney and Surbiton.

Just before Charlie retired he added one more record to his impressive list of achievements: to produce the first ever eight-horse team to be driven at the Royal Show, in which four working horses were groomed and prepared to match four show horses. This was considered extraordinarily ambitious, because they all had to start at exactly the same time. But the feat was accomplished and history was made.

In August 1968, two years after his retirement, the brewery honoured him by naming a new pub after him. It replaced the Old George, which had been demolished for road widening. As the brewery's official history states, 'It is most unusual for a pub to be named after a living person, particularly a commoner.' It was, it added, 'a unique memorial to a unique man.'

One of its present customers Idris Richards remembers Charlie as a 'charming man', who got 'drunk out of his brain' at brewery functions.

In 1997, the brewery decided to stop deliveries by horse-drawn drays, but the public outcry was so great that it had to retract its decision and the pubs around Wandsworth

continued to be visited daily by a pair of horse-drawn drays. This practice finally ceased in 2006, when the brewery moved production to Bedford.

The sign on the new pub was painted by artist Michael Francis and the horse depicted on it with Charlie was a 23-year-old called Steve. The pub is decorated by horse brasses, bridles and harnesses.

133. Charlie Hall (1899–1959)

49 Barnabas Road, Erdington, Birmingham, B23 6SH (Tel: 0121 384 2716). Wetherspoon.

After starting off as a film set carpenter, Charlie Hall progressed to acting and starred as Laurel and Hardy's foil in forty-eight of their films. Born at 23 Washwood Heath Road, Ward End, Birmingham (where the fire station now stands), he left school at 14 and became a carpenter like his father had been. To earn some extra money he worked in local clubs and theatres.

At the age of 16 he went to America to visit his sister and stayed there for the rest of his life. He settled in New York and readily found work as a

carpenter, often in the film studios. When the studios moved to California, he followed them and continued to find work there as a carpenter. In 1921, he was working at the Hal Roach Studio as a part-time carpenter and as a film extra. By 1923, he had become a bit player and befriended Stan Laurel.

His first billing was in that year in *The Soilers*, a Hal Roach film starring Stan Laurel and Jimmy Finlayson, the Scottish actor, who appeared in many Laurel and Hardy films. The first Laurel and Hardy movie that Charlie appeared in was *Love 'Em and Weep* in 1927, after which he became a regular. The best known ones he appeared in were *Them Thar Hills* in 1934 and *Tit for Tat* in 1935.

After that he found less work, as the short films, which were his forte, were replaced by feature-length movies, for which his skills were less suited. Indeed, between 1950 and 1956, he only featured in five films.

He died in Hollywood three years later and his ashes were buried at Forest Lawn Memorial Park Cemetery in Glendale, California.

134. Louis Armstrong (1901–1971)

59 Maison Dieu Road, Dover, Kent, CT16 1RA (Tel: 01304 204759). Free house.

The world's most famous jazz trumpeter Louis 'Satchmo' Armstrong was born to Mayann, the 15-year-old daughter of an ex-slave, in New Orleans at 723 Jane Alley (sometimes called Jane's or James Alley). Mayann soon became a prostitute ('selling fish' as Louis described it) and she left Louis and his sister with their grandmother Josephine, who told them of her personal experiences of slavery. When his mother became sick, 5-year-old Louis was sent to look after her. On his way to her he had his first experience of segregation: being dragged from the front (Whites only) end of the bus to the back (Coloureds only).

To support his mother, he did various jobs as a youngster including, at the age of 7, working on a rag-and-bone cart. To attract attention to the cart, he played a tin horn, which cost him a dime, and this proved very popular, especially when he learned different tunes. One day, he saw an old cornet in a pawn shop, costing $5, which he borrowed off his boss (a White Lithuanian).

At the age of 11, he dropped out of school and joined a quartet of street musicians called the Uptown Boys. Then, aged 12, he was arrested for firing a pistol into the air during New Year's Eve celebrations. After a fifteen-minute trial, he was sentenced for an indefinite period to a reform school called the Coloured Waifs' Home, which had been an asylum.

After going on hunger strike for three days, he knuckled under and was rewarded by being allowed into the brass band (playing tambourine) and then becoming the home's bugler. The music teacher gave him a cornet and he became the leader of the band, where he first started doing comedy dances. When marching with the band through his old neighbourhood of Storyville, he was recognised by all the gamblers, prostitutes, and thieves, who gave so much money to the collection that it paid for new uniforms and instruments for the whole band.

Louis (he always pronounced it Lewis) was released on 17 June 1914 and he got a job playing blues on his cornet in Storyville bordellos. But these brothels were outlawed and closed in 1917, so Louis made a living by delivering coal in a hand cart and by playing in funeral bands.

He then got a permanent job playing cornet in a Mafia-run club called Matranga's, after the owner bought his cornet from the pawn shop for $15 and deducted it from his wages. While there, he witnessed a shoot-out in which a disgruntled gambler was killed by the bouncer ... and then the band played on.

At the age of 15 he was taken home drunk. His mother reacted by saying she would teach him how to hold his liquor. She did this by taking him on a drinking spree to sample raw whiskey and two bottles each of extracts of Jamaican ginger until daybreak, during which they fell over each other dancing.

The day after he registered (under age) for the draft in 1918, he was arrested by police looking for a Black man who had committed a robbery, but any Black would do. He was only released after the Mafia at his club exercised its influence.

After joining Kid Ory's band, Louis wrote a song called *Take Your Finger Outta Katie's Ass* and he performed it on stage while shimmying (a dance described as lewd in the White press). A man in the audience, Clarence Williams, scribbled down the lyrics and offered Louis $25 for the rights, which he accepted. The money was never paid, but Williams made a fortune cleaning it up as *I Wish I Could Shimmy Like My Sister Kate*.

At the age of 18, Louis joined the Fate Marable Orchestra playing on the Mississippi riverboats; to Whites for six days and Blacks on Mondays.

In 1922, he played with Joe Oliver in Chicago while living at 421 East 44th Street, then in 1924 to Harlem in New York with the Fletcher 'Smack' Henderson dance orchestra. Henderson gave him arrangements with notes such as 'pp', meaning play soft. Louis played at full volume and said, when challenged, he thought it stood for 'pound plenty'. This was when he switched from the cornet to the trumpet.

It was also at this time that he won a singing prize at a club and he took on this role as well, which included a preacher act, satirising avarice and lechery of the clergy. He called himself Reverend Satchelmouth for this part, which an English journalist later shortened to Satchmo.

While in Chicago he had his first stick of 'gage', his favourite name for marijuana. 'It's a thousand times better than whiskey,' he commented and, from then on, always smoked it before a recording session, as he considered it enhanced his performance. His recording career had started in 1923 and critics say the records got better after he started smoking. He explained to one record producer who disapproved of the drug, 'It relaxes you, makes you forget all the bad things that happen to a Negro. It makes you feel wanted, and when you're with another tea smoker it makes you feel a special kinship.' It was certainly safer than the bootleg booze that was available in those days of prohibition, he reckoned.

At one session in 1927, he playfully recorded a piece he had written called SOL Blues, based on a traditional one known as *Shit Out of Luck Blues* or *If You Don't Like This Song, You Can Kiss My Fucking Ass.*

His show at the Cotton Club in Harlem was regularly broadcast on the radio and after one-such performance he was arrested for smoking a joint, which then carried a six-month jail sentence. A rival bandleader had tipped off the police and Louis was held without bail for nine days in the Downtown Los Angeles City Jail. He shared a cell with two others, already sentenced to forty years, one of whom bit the other's finger off in front of him. Louis got off with a suspended sentence and the publicity seemed to increase his popularity. The two policemen who had arrested him came every night to listen to him.

After being threatened with a pistol by a gangster called Frankie Foster, who ordered him to play for a different Mafia club, Louis went on the road instead. This eventually took him to New Orleans, where he received a huge welcome from Black and White alike. But while there, performing a concert broadcast on the radio, the White announcer refused to introduce 'that nigger man' as he called him. So Louis seized the microphone and introduced himself and became the first Black man to speak on radio in that area.

When the tour reached Memphis, the bus was stopped by police, who saw Louis sitting next to the White wife of his manager, which prompted them to take all the Blacks to the jailhouse amid racist threats. The management of the theatre, where they were due to play, bailed them out with a condition that they make a radio broadcast with all proceeds to go to the police. At the event, Louis announced he was dedicating the next song to the Memphis Police Force and then launched into *I'll be Glad When You're Dead, You Rascal, You*, at the end of which the police rushed over and the band feared for their lives. But the police just thanked them, as it was the first time they'd had a tune dedicated to them.

In 1932, Louis came to London and was initially barred from all the hotels around Paddington because of his colour. Finally, he was accepted by the Howard Hotel in Norfolk Street, off the Strand. It was here that he was met by journalist Percy Brooks, who greeted him as 'Satchmo' for the first time.

The publicity posters for his appearance at the London Palladium depicted him as a monkey wearing a tuxedo, blowing a trumpet, which

Louis duly put in his scrapbook. On the opening night he was attacked by a former girlfriend in his dressing room and had to knock her out in order to go on stage.

The audience had only ever heard his records before, so they were unprepared for his 'vaudeville jinks' and improvisations – and most walked out. The *Daily Herald* reviewer Hannen Swaffer wrote, 'He looks, and behaves, like an untrained gorilla. He might have come straight from some African jungle'. That, too, went into the scrapbook. After this tour Louis went, in 1934, from London to Paris, probably passing through Dover.

Another savage review came when he appeared in the 1937 film *Artists and Models*, which showed a White actress dancing seductively as he blew his horn. The *Shreveport Journal* proclaimed, 'For negroes and whites to be shown in social equality is offensive in this part of the country'. In his films from then until the 1960s he was not allowed to be seen interacting socially with Whites, but could only be a musician playing a number unconnected with the rest of the plot.

In 1942, he married his fourth and final wife Lucille Wilson, to whom he gave away his collection of pornographic films. He took laxatives three times a day to cleanse his bowels and mischievously referred to this on a publicity handout picture of him on the toilet, captioned: Satchmo says 'Leave It All Behind Ya!'

In 1956, he went on his first tour of West Africa and drew 100,000 to an open-air concert in Ghana. He noticed how the locals looked like him and was convinced that this was where his roots were.

In the following year there were scenes in Little Rock, Arkansas, where the state government was resisting desegregation of schools. Louis saw on television a White mob spitting at a small Black girl, terrified, on her way to school. He was so infuriated that he called off his next international goodwill tour and told the press, 'The way they are treating my people in the South, the government can go to hell. It's getting so bad, a coloured man hasn't got any country.' He criticised President Eisenhower for being two-faced and gutless, was slated in the press and had a file opened on him by the FBI. Louis responded by refusing to play anywhere in Louisiana, including his hometown of New Orleans, because of a law that prohibited integrated bands like his. It had been ruled as being unconstitutional in 1956, but was still enforced illegally. While touring Connecticut in the supposedly more tolerant North, he was barred from using a toilet in a restaurant because he was Black.

He had two hits in 1964: *Hello Dolly*, which sold millions all over the world, and *What A Wonderful World*, which sold less than a thousand in America but 600,000 in England.

After all this success, his wife wanted them to move from their house at 34–56 107th Street, Corona, Queens, New York to fashionable Long Island. But he refused, saying, 'We're right out here with the rest of the coloured folk and the Puerto Ricans and Italians and the Hebrew cats. We don't need to move out in the suburbs to some big mansion with lots of servants and yardmen and things.' He liked to do his own shopping, visit the local barber and buy ice creams for the local kids. He also refused an honorary doctorate from Harvard University and an invitation from the newly elected President Richard Nixon in 1969 to play at the White House.'The only reason he would want me to play there now is to make some niggers happy,' he explained.

He died on 6 July 1971 and 25,000 attended his funeral procession – but there was no music at the service in Corona Congregational Church – before he was buried at Flushing Cemetery. Shortly afterwards, The Grapes Pub in Dover had its name changed to the Louis Armstrong in his honour by landlady Jackie Bowles, who celebrated 47 years running the pub in September 2009. The sign was unveiled by British jazz star Chris Barber, who has since played there at the traditional jazz nights.

135. George Orwell (1903–1950)

(i) The Orwell at Wigan Pier, Wallgate, Wigan, Lancashire, WN3 4EU (Tel: 01942 323034). Free house.

(ii) The Orwell, 382 Essex Road, Islington, London, N1 3PF (Tel: 020 7359 4651).

Author George Orwell visited Wigan in 1936 to research his book *The Road to Wigan Pier*, a study of working-class poverty in the North, which was published by the Left Book Club in 1937. 'Look at the filthy chemical by-products people will pour down their throats in the name of beer,' was one of his observations in the book. He backed up his evidence of poverty in the town with statistical data collected in Wigan Library. The 'pier' in the title is on the opposite bank of the Leeds and Liverpool Canal from this pub, which in Orwell's day was at the end of a railway line used for transporting coal from the pits to canal boats. The book received a mixed reception. The Independent Labour Party, for example, derided it for its author's lack of socialist principle. This did not prevent it accepting Orwell as a member two years later.

Orwell was born as Eric Blair in Bengal, but was taken a year later to England to live first at Henley-on-Thames and then at a boarding school in Eastbourne, where he was beaten by the sadistic headmaster for bed-wetting; Orwell's memoirs of this school were considered too libellous to publish until 1968. At the age of 14 he won a scholarship to Eton, which later convinced him of the need for educational reform; while there he plotted to kill one of the school bullies.

From 1922 to 1927, he worked for the British colonial police in Burma, which instilled in him a hatred of imperialism. He later described public executions there, which sickened him, and the joy of sex with Burmese women in public parks. He was also struck by a fever.

After returning to Europe he went to Paris, where he contracted pneumonia. He was forced to wash dishes for fourteen hours a day to survive after a woman, whom he had picked up, stole all his money from his pocket.

On reaching London, by now describing himself as a Tory anarchist, his book *Down and Out in Paris and London* was rejected by T. S. Eliot at Faber. Frustrated, he gave it to a woman to throw away 'but keep the paper clips'. Instead, she took it to Victor Gollancz, who accepted it. Because Blair was not proud of it, he insisted it be published under a pseudonym and chose Orwell from the name of a river near Southwold in Suffolk where his parents lived.

His conversion to socialism came in 1936, when he visited the flat of Sir Richard Rees to borrow some money. Sir Richard was at a socialist meeting, which is where Orwell went in pursuit of him. 'I spent three hours with seven or eight socialists harrying me, including a South Wales miner who told me – quite good naturedly, however – that if he were a dictator he would have me shot immediately,' recalled Orwell.

Within days of completing *The Road to Wigan Pier* at the end of 1936, he pawned the family silver to go to Spain to fight for the Republicans in the civil war. He tried, but failed, to sign up for a communist regiment, so joined the militia of the Workers' Party of Marxist Unification (POUM), which had the support of the Independent Labour Party, but was accused by the communists of being Trotskyist.

Orwell was on the battle front against Franco troops from January to April 1937. When he was shot in the neck, however, it was from the Republican side. This was in Barcelona after POUM and the anarchists had been outlawed by the Republicans. Material unearthed decades later from the Soviet archives showed just how close he had come to being liquidated by the Stalinists at this time. In this climate, Orwell fled to France with his wife Eileen O'Shaughnessy, a psychology student whom he had married in June 1936 after meeting her at a London party in 1935.

From 1937 to 1939 he proclaimed himself a pacifist, during which time he joined the Independent Labour Party on the grounds that it was the only one 'likely to take the right line either against imperialist war or against Fascism'.

When the Second World War was declared in 1939, however, he supported it, justifying his change of stance by stating, 'We are in a strange

The actual pier at Wigan, where coal was unloaded onto barges.

period of history in which a revolutionary has to be a patriot and a patriot has to be a revolutionary.' He also explained (in *The Lion and the Unicorn* published in 1941) that the only way the people could pull together enough to win the war was if the country was transformed on socialist lines. He thought this would be possible as 'the working class, the middle class and even a section of the business community could see the utter rottenness of private capitalism'.

This transformation should be brought about, he suggested, by nationalising key industries, land and the banks, limiting top incomes and reforming the education system. 'Our talk of defending democracy is nonsense while it is a mere accident of birth that decides whether a gifted child shall or shall not get the education it deserves.'

Weak lungs kept him out of the army, so he joined the Home Guard. And from 1941 to 1943 he

'wasted' two years at the BBC, which he described as 'a mixture of a whoreshop and a lunatic asylum', producing programmes to be broadcast to India and South East Asia. From there, he went to *Tribune* (the Labour left newspaper), where he became their literary editor for fifteen months.

During the 1940s, Orwell lived near the Islington Pub that now bears his name in a third-floor flat at 27b Canonbury Square, as is confirmed by a plaque. He described it as a slum at the time and used the bombed out surrounding area to describe the Proles area in his novel *Nineteen Eighty-Four*. He wrote this and his other classic novel *Animal Farm* in this flat.

The draft of *Animal Farm* was completed in early 1944 and it was initially accepted by the publisher Jonathan Cape. But he was then warned off by the government, which thought its publication would upset its Russian allies in the war. The government official who did this, Peter Smollett of the Ministry of Information, later turned out to be a Soviet agent. The book was then rejected by T. S. Eliot at Faber on the opposite grounds – that it was too pro-communist. An American publisher, missing the point that the book was an allegory, turned it down because animal stories were not popular in the USA. A small publisher called Frederic Warburg finally accepted it and published it in August 1945.

The book was widely seized upon by right wingers as an attack on socialism rather than totalitarianism. Orwell felt compelled to put the record straight, 'I meant the moral to be that revolutions only effect a radical improvement when the masses are alert and know how to chuck out their leaders as soon as the latter have done their job ... What I was trying to say was, you can't have a revolution unless you make it for yourself; there is no such thing as a benevolent dictatorship.' He later added, 'Every line of serious work that I have written since 1936 has been written, directly or indirectly, against totalitarianism and for democratic socialism.'

Just before *Animal Farm's* publication, Orwell's wife died while having a hysterectomy, leaving him with their 11-year-old adopted son Richard, whom he took to raise at a farmhouse in the Hebrides off the west coast of Scotland.

Nineteen Eighty-Four was published in June 1949 and it features one of Orwell's favourite drinking haunts called the Newman Arms (situated at 23 Rathbone Street in London's Fitzrovia), which was known as 'the Proles' Pub'. This is where the book's hero Winston seeks information about life before the revolution, only to learn that a litre of beer was too much and

half a litre was not enough. Orwell predicted the book would not sell more than 10,000. But in the first year it sold 170,000 in America, 50,000 in Britain and 190,000 through the Book of the Month Club.

Once more, it was commandeered by the right as an attack on socialism alone. Orwell again had to dissociate himself from this by stating it was, 'not intended as an attack on socialism or on the British Labour Party (of which I am a supporter) but as a show-up of the perversions to which a centralised economy is liable and which have already been partly realised in communism and fascism. I do not believe that the kind of society I describe necessarily will arrive, but I believe ... that something resembling it could arrive.'

In the very year that he was warning of the dangers of Big Brother and the thought police it has since been discovered that Orwell was feeding information about 'subversives' to the British Secret Intelligence Services. A list of Nazi sympathisers he had compiled had evolved into one also taking in those he considered too close to the Soviet Union and communism, eventually numbering one hundred and five. This included Charlie Chaplin, whom, in 1941, Orwell had praised for, 'his power to stand for a sort of concentrated essence of the common man, for the ineradicable belief in decency that exists in the hearts of ordinary people.' From this, Orwell selected thirty-six to be blacklisted by the government, which he gave to his friend Celia Kirwan, of the Information Research Department; it had been created by the government in 1948 to disseminate anti-communist propaganda. Perhaps she did not know Orwell's dog was called Marx.

By then, however, Orwell was dying from tuberculosis. He was taken into the University College Hospital of London, in April 1949, where he married his second wife Sonia Brownell in October and died there of a lung haemorrhage in the following January.

136. Harold Larwood (1904–1995) and Bill Voce (1909–1984).

Larwood & Voce, Fox Road (next to Trent Bridge Cricket Ground), Nottingham, Notts, NG2 6AJ (Tel: 0115 981 9960). Punch Taverns.

Ex-miner Harold Larwood is best known for his controversially aggressive bowling for England during their cricket tour of Australia in the winter of 1932–1933. This was known as the Bodyline test series. It was all a little too rough for the genteel nobs at the MCC, who selected the side. They demanded that Larwood apologise for the way he had bowled at the Australians or they would never pick him for England again. He refused to do so on principle and never did play for his country again. 'I'm glad to this day that I never apologised,' he said in later life.

Born in the mining village of Nuncargate (about 10 miles north of Nottingham), he was just 2 years old when he drank some paraffin he found in the scullery and had to have his stomach pumped by a doctor to save his life. To keep the lad out of further trouble, his father made him a tiny cricket bat out of an old fence paling. He practised with it so much that the balls had to be replaced every week, at a cost of nine pence (about 4 pence) to his father. Young Larwood carved his own bats out of any old pieces of wood he could find.

He went down the local pit at the age of 14 for 32 shillings (£1.60) a week. At the age of 15, he played for Nuncargate's second eleven as a fast bowler against players ten years older than him. In his first season he took seventy-six wickets at an average of less than five runs each.

'Two years later I was promoted to the village's first team, bowling in sandshoes because I did not own a pair of boots,' he recalled. 'I sent down

20 overs during the first match, even though I had worked down the mine all the previous night.

'After a few overs my nose began to bleed. Team mates urged me to leave the field. I refused and kept on bowling. Down the mine I dreamed of cricket. I bowled imaginary balls in the dark and sent the stumps spinning in the tunnels. No mishap was going to stop me from bowling in the real game, especially this one.

'My nose bleed got worse than ever, splattering my shirt. I was again advised to go off but I continued to bowl. Then a ball caught the middle stump. My next delivery scattered the incoming batsman's wicket. Although feeling a bit weak by now I got ready for one more, and hit the off stump. It was my first hat-trick.'

A year later, at the age of 18, he got a trial for Nottingham County Cricket Club and was signed on for a year's probation. At the end of the year he was taken on permanently. In just his second game for the first team he took the wicket of the Yorkshire legend Herbert Sutcliffe for a duck with his second ball, at Sheffield's Brammall Lane.

Larwood went on to play 361 matches for Nottingham's first team, and 21 times for England. When retiring from cricket in 1938 he had taken 1,427 first-class wickets for an average of 17.15 runs.

In the 1950s he emigrated with his family to Australia where, despite the hostility shown to him in that country during the Bodyline series, he became very popular. Larwood's great friend and fellow Nottinghamshire and England bowler Bill Voce was also an ex-miner, who had gone down the pits at the age of 14.

While playing village cricket he was spotted by Nottinghamshire's fast bowler Fred Barratt and was taken on by the club in 1926. In his first match in the county side against Gloucestershire at Trent Bridge the following year he took five wickets for thirty-six runs and followed it up with six wickets for thirty-nine runs against Essex a few weeks later. Voce, a left-arm bowler, topped the team's bowling averages in 1929 when they won the championship. He also fell out with the England selectors during the Bodyline series and was dropped from the side. When he was recalled by England in 1934, he took eight Australian wickets for sixty-six runs, but was again criticised for bowling bouncers.

In 1939 he was given a benefit, which produced just £980 for him. His playing career ended in 1947, when he became Nottinghamshire's coach, playing in a few emergencies until 1952. In all first-class matches he took 1,558 wickets (for 23.08 runs each) and in 27 England matches 98 wickets (for 27.88 each). On the pub sign Larwood is on the right and Voce on the left.

137. John Jacques (1905–1995)

72–82 Fratton Road (corner of Cornwall Road), Portsmouth, Hants, PO1 5BZ (Tel: 023 9277 9742). Wetherspoon.

John Jacques became chief executive of the Portsea Island Mutual Co-operative Society (which had a store where the pub now stands) in 1945. But his commitment to the cooperative movement started thirty years earlier at the age of 10, when he attended co-op evening classes. When he left school to become a miner in Ashington, Northumberland, at the age of 13, he continued going to the co-op classes two nights a week to further his education.

At the age of 15 he took a cut in wages to leave the mines and become a grocery apprentice at the Ashington Co-op. A couple of years later he won a scholarship of ten shillings (50 pence) a week to attend the Co-operative College in Manchester, where he gained an honours diploma in management and secretaryship.

Aged just 21, he became managing secretary of Moorsley Co-operative Society (Durham). Then, in 1929, he became a tutor at the Co-operative College and stayed there until 1942; during which time he had three volumes on *Book-Keeping* published.

After that he travelled south to Plymouth, where he became an accountant for the local co-op for three years, having gained a commerce degree at Manchester University in 1939. His ground breaking time with the Portsea society then followed. Building on the historic past of Portsmouth – the country's earliest cooperative society was founded there

by dockyard workers in 1796 – he opened the country's first ever completely self-service store in Albert Road in 1947.

During his 20 years with the society its sales multiplied sixfold and its membership doubled. In 1961, he was president of the Co-operative Congress and impressed many, including future Prime Minister Harold Wilson, before he became leader of the party, by memorising his half hour speech instead of reading it, even though it had been printed for delegates. He was also a magistrate in the town from 1951 to 1975.

He had two more books published: one on *Management Accounting* in 1966 and the other a *Manual on Co-operative Management* in 1969. For relaxation, he liked walking his West Highland terriers, gardening and playing snooker – in the Portsmouth Co-operative Club, naturally.

He died three weeks before his ninety-first birthday, leaving three children and numerous grand and great-grandchildren; his first wife had died in 1987, after which he married his brother's widow in 1989.

138. Eva Hart (1905–1996)

1128 High Street (corner of Station Road, near Chadwell Heath Station), Chadwell Heath, Romford, Essex, RM6 4AH (Tel: 020 8597 1069). Wetherspoon.

The last survivor of the *Titanic* disaster, Eva Hart was just 7 years old when she embarked on the voyage with her parents for Canada. She and her mother Esther were rescued by a lifeboat as the so-called 'unsinkable' ship headed for the bottom of the Atlantic Ocean on 15 April 1912. Her father Benjamin went down with it and drowned.

The family were migrating from Seven Kings (near Chadwell Heath) to Winnipeg in Canada, where Benjamin, a master builder, was to enter a partnership with his friend. 'My mother had a premonition from the very word go,' recalled Eva. 'She knew there was something to be afraid of and the only thing that she felt strongly about was to say a ship to be unsinkable was flying in the face of God. Those were her words.

'She never went to bed in that ship at night at all. She sat up for three nights so she slept during the day and I was with my father. My memories are of being with him and playing in a nursery and meeting a lot of other children and generally enjoying myself. But inside I was thinking how odd it was that my mother was never up during the day.'

Her mother's strange actions were commented on by other passengers, but saved the lives of her and her daughter, because when the ship hit the iceberg she felt a 'minor jolt'. Her premonition spurred her to wake her husband and insist he went on deck to check what had happened. Reluctantly, he did do, but soon returned pale and shaken. They knew about the danger before most of the other second-class passengers and were able to get to the lifeboats early. Benjamin gave his sheepskin coat to his wife, wrapped a blanket around Eva, waved them goodbye as their lifeboat left with fifty-eight on board and helped other women and children into the other lifeboats.

'The sounds of people drowning are something that I cannot describe to you, and neither can anyone else,' said Eva. 'It is the most dreadful sound and there is a terrible silence that follows it. It was not until we were in the lifeboat and rowing away that I realised the ship was going to sink. I remember thinking that everything in the world was standing still.'

From the Titanic Disaster Fund, Eva was paid 3s 6d (17 and a half pence) and her mother £1 1s (£1.05) a week. Eva, who lived in Chadwell Heath, first at Rose Hatch Lane and then at Japan Road, had a very good soprano voice and she played piano well. At the age of just 16, she opened a small music school to teach local children.

During the Second World War she sang to entertain the troops, distributed emergency food to bombing raid victims and volunteered for the Women's Junior Air Corps. In 1956, she became a magistrate and later was on the local prison parole board. She worked at the local Stirling's Steelworks. Her community work was rewarded with an MBE in 1974. In her later life she was a frequent guest on radio and television

Portrait of teetotaller Eva Hart in the pub.

programmes and she also featured in documentaries about the *Titanic*.

The year after her death a biography of her called *Shadow of the Titanic* by Ronald C Denney was published. A teetotaller all her life, she would have been amused that a pub was to be named after her, on the site of where the village stocks and the police station had been. A portrait of her in later life by local artist Edward Simmons has been hung in the pub.

139. John Hewitt (1907–1987)

51 Donegall Street, Belfast, BT1 2FH (Tel: 028 9023 3768). Free house.

A portrait of John Hewitt outside the pub named after him is held up by his great friend and fellow poet John Campbell

A socialist poet, John Hewitt opened the Belfast Unemployed Resource Centre next door to this pub on May Day 1983. In return, the centre opened the pub in his honour in December 1999. In keeping with Hewitt's humanist, non-sectarian attitudes, the pub won the 2001 Aisling Award for Inter-Community Endeavours in recognition of the fact that it hosts both sides of the community, enabling them to mingle and muse with each other.

All profits from the pub go to the unemployed resource centre and it has proved to be very popular (winning the Dining Pub of the Year award in both 2001 and 2002), with live music every night of the week, except Monday, when art exhibitions are frequently launched.

Hewitt was born in Belfast and he was educated at the Methodist College and Queen's University. From 1930 to 1957, he was the art keeper at the Ulster Museum, then, after being rejected for the top job there, he moved to Coventry. Here, he became the director of the Herbert Art Gallery and Museum until 1972, when he retired and returned to Belfast.

In 1968, his *Collected Poems* were published, followed by *Out of My Time* in 1974 and *Time Enough* in 1976, which won the Poetry Book Society Award. He described himself as 'an Irishman of planter stock, by profession an art gallery man, politically a man of the left'. His poetry and other writings were described as 'anti-sectarian in feeling and radical in direction'.

His memory lives on through the John Hewitt International Summer School in the last week of July each year at St MacNissi's College, Garron Tower, Carnlough, Co Antrim. It is a week long festival of literature and arts, including poetry readings, commemorating Hewitt, and is attended by hundreds of people from all over the world.

A great friend of his was John Campbell, a poet and retired docker, who said of Hewitt, 'He was an enigma – a rich man who stood up for the socialist cause.

'He could pass in any company, a wee man with a wee goaty beard, and a chain on his cane walking stick. Once he asked me to take him to the dockside bars. We squeezed into one of the packed bars on the North Queen Street peace line in the protestant district before making our way to a tough dockers' pub in Pilot Street. Blending into each company I introduced him to, he sipped stoically at his half pint of ale. He was so pleased that he wanted to visit the area again. So we went in July during the marching season.

'While drinking in the Rotterdam pub in Pilot Street (a catholic area) I noticed a group of young men at another table eyeing us up with considerable interest. My built-in hassle detector went into top gear when one of them rose and moved quickly out of the door and into the street. Naturally I assumed the worst. Most of the catholics in that community were broad minded but generally they did not get an influx of prods during the marching season. So we rose to leave and were in the car ready to depart when the lad who had left the bar came running towards us. As he approached the car he dug his right hand into the inside pocket of his jacket. Our worst fears were unfounded when the hand came out clutching a book, which turned out to be a copy of John's latest publication. He pushed it through the open window and asked him to sign it.

'Our next stop was the Grove Tavern, a bustling bar on the predominantly protestant York Road. One of my friends called Bouncer, slightly under the weather, approached our table. For a moment he gazed with what I took to be awe at the imposing figure of the poet. Then he leaned over and playfully tugged at John's grey beard, grinning 'What about ye, oul han'. I was rather angry but John later said it was the best part of the outing. I think he was tickled by the irreverence. He had a unique way of blending into whatever environment he found himself in. He seemed to be as equally at home with the punters in the American Bar as he was with the academics of Queen's University.'

Hewitt was also a director of the Lyric Theatre in Belfast and a play about him was written and performed by the actor Ian MacElhihey. A portrait of Hewitt by local artist Joe O'Kane is displayed in the Laganbank Social Club in the Markets area, where he often attended the annual Poets and Pints night.

140. Richard Llewellyn (1907–1983)

20–24a High Street, Gilfach Goch, near Llantrisant, Rhondda Valley, Mid Glamorgan, South Wales, CF39 8SP.

The unostenatatious sign of the Richard Llewellyn.

The author of *How Green Was My Valley* Richard Llewellyn based his classic book on this village, where he lived and even worked briefly in the pits. So it was no surprise that this was the location for its filming by the BBC as a drama serial in 1976, starring Stanley Baker and Sian Phillips. Previously, Twentieth Century Fox had filmed it in 1941, starring Walter Pidgeon and Maureen O'Hara.

The book, originally published in 1939, was republished as a Penguin Classic in 2001. It tells the story of how harsh life was for the mining communities of South Wales during the reign of Queen Victoria. Llewellyn wrote it during spells of unemployment in Wales and London, having drafted the original version while serving in the army in India.

Born Richard Doyle Vivian Llewellyn Lloyd in St David's, Pembrokeshire, on the far west coast of Wales, he went to Venice at the age of 16 to work in a hotel kitchen. While there, he used his spare time to study printing and sculpture. Later, he worked with an Italian film unit.

Having had what he described as a 'turbulent' life, he felt he needed some discipline, so joined the British army at the age of 19, serving around the world. Some five years later he returned to Britain and worked for a film unit, first as assistant director, then as production manager and finally as film director.

After *How Green Was My Valley* became a best seller, he joined the Welsh Guards as a captain in 1940. His second novel *None But the Lonely Heart* was published in 1943 and was also filmed. He had several more novels and two highly successful plays, *Poison Pen* and *Noose*, published right up to the year before his death, shortly before which he revisited Gilfach Goch.

The pub depicted in *How Green Was My Valley* was the Three Bells at the bottom of the hill of the mining village ... which is where the pub now named after him, with his initials R. L. on the green door, is situated between Jack Brown the bookies and Lol's fish and chip shop. It was at the Three Bells that the men discussed forming a union after wage cuts had been imposed by the mine owners.

Some of them quoted Keir Hardie, Hyndman and Marx, to the effect that the mines and land should belong to the people. But the father of Huw Morgan (the narrator) threw in his view, 'I am not in favour of anything put up by a lot of old foreigners. Owain Glyndwr said all there is to be said for this country hundreds of years ago. Wales for the Welsh. More of him and less of Mr Marx, please.'

How Green was my valley ... Gilfach Goch in the Rhondda Valley, where Richard Llewellyn lived and worked.

The novel also gives the recipe for part of the village's staple diet, which was Brandy Broth, 'A good chicken and a noble piece of ham, with a little shoulder of lamb, small to have the least of grease, and then a paste of the roes of trout with cream, a bit of butter, and the yolk of egg, whipped tight and poured in when the chicken, proud with a stuffing of sage and thyme, has been elbowing the lamb and the ham in the earthenware pot until all three are tender as the heart of a mother. In with the carrots and turnips and the goodness of marrow bones, and in with a mixing of milk and potatoes. Now watch the clock and every fifteen minutes pour in a noggin of brandy, and with the first a pint of home brewed ale. Two noggins in, and with the third, throw in the chopped bottoms of leeks, but save the green leaves until ten minutes from the time you sit to eat, for then you shall find them still a lovely green. Drink down the liquor and raise your eyes to give praise for a mouth and a belly, and then start upon the chicken.'

Richard Llewellyn landlord Gerry McLoughlin (with coal shovel) in the archway, made of the supporting rings from the old Tower Colliery.

The Three Bells, in the novel, was bought by Dai Bando with the money he won in a prize boxing match on the mountain against Big Shoni Mawr, who was much taller and broader than him. Dai had challenged Big Shone because of his bullying behaviour; he had a loud voice and a habit of punching little men and drinking their beer in the Three

Bells. 'Many times he had been hit across the head with pick handles to teach him, but he was not the kind to learn.'

Dai was nearly blinded in the fight, but was able to buy the pub with his purse. He was there when everybody in the village got drunk in it after one of the mine workers scored a try against Scotland at Cardiff Arms Park.

The present landlord of the Richard Llewellyn is another rugby international, Gerry McLoughlin, who played for the British Lions and nineteen times for Ireland. The support rings from the closed Tower Colliery are used as an archway between the two bars of the pub.

141. Dixie Dean (1907–1980)

Dixie Dean's, London Street (on junction with Hotham Street), Liverpool 1.

The greatest goalscorer ever in English football, Everton's Dixie Dean amassed an incredible sixty league goals in a single season. That was in the 1927–1928 season, when Everton won the league championship. It is also a record, which will surely never be beaten.

Born in Birkenhead as William Dean, he first played for Tranmere Rovers before signing for Everton in 1925. The following year he was involved in a motorcycle accident in which his skull and jaw were broken. Doctors feared he would not live for more than a few hours and when, to their astonishment, he recovered, they pronounced he would never play football again. Once more he defied them and went on to score 383 goals in 433 games for Everton. A high proportion of these were scored with his head, prompting a rumour that surgeons had inserted a steel plate in his skull during the operation to save his life.

One reporter noted, 'Ordinary players butt the ball with the crown of their heads. Dean artistically glides it downwards with the side of his head.'

His sixty goals in 1927–1928 included five scored in a match against Manchester United, a satisfying away hat-trick against Mersey rivals Liverpool, and another hat-trick against mighty Arsenal in the last match of the season. He captained Everton to a further league championship in 1932, scoring forty-five goals in thirty-eight games, and the winning of the FA Cup at Wembley in 1933. Strangely, he played for England only sixteen times.

Despite much provocation, including one kick, which led to him losing a testicle, he refused to retaliate and was never even cautioned in a match. Symbolically, he died at Everton's ground Goodison Park just after the final whistle in a match against Liverpool.

142. Douglas Bader (1910–1982)

Bader Arms, Malcolm Road, Tangmere, West Sussex, PO20 6HS (Tel: 01243 779422). Hall & Woodhouse.

Douglas Bader was the extraordinary pilot who, after having both legs amputated, shot down twenty-two German planes in the Battle of Britain, before becoming a prisoner of war and escaping four times. At school in Eastbourne he was captain of the rugby, soccer and cricket teams. In one year, he scored seven tries in a rugby match and topped both batting and bowling averages at cricket.

When he was 18 he won a scholarship to the RAF Cadet School at Cranwell in Lincolnshire, where he earned his colours at rugby, cricket, boxing and hockey. At boxing he knocked out nineteen of his twenty opponents and then got knocked out himself by the last one. At rugby he played for the Harlequins, the RAF and the Combined Services (as fly-half against the Springboks). At cricket he played for the RAF at The Oval and scored sixty-five runs in thirty minutes.

Then, in 1931, he performed an aerobatic display before a quarter of a million spectators at the Hendon Air Show. In December of the same year he crashed his plane at Reading, resulting in the amputation of both legs. He was fitted with artificial ones and through sheer will and determination he learned to walk on them.

With two other friends, missing various limbs, they managed to drive a car between them on an outing one day and stopped at a tea shop, where they were served by Thelma Addison. Bader married her in secret, because of her parents' disapproval, in 1932 and then publicly five years later.

He was pronounced fit to fly, but was pensioned off by the RAF, because his legless state was 'not covered by King's Regulations'. But when the Second World War broke out this technicality was waived and he became the leader of the only Canadian squadron in the RAF, which had one of the best records in the Battle of Britain.

In March 1941 he was posted to Tangmere as the RAF's very first Wing Leader, where he commanded three squadrons, taking on the Luftwaffe over France. In August of the same year he collided with a German plane and as he prepared to parachute out, his artificial leg got stuck. He simply detached it and mused how lucky it was that it was not a real one. He also mulled over the fact that if he had not removed the tin one then it would have split his groin on landing.

The Germans captured him and put him in a French hospital. They managed to recover the leg he had left behind in the plane and repaired it for him – and also obligingly contacted the RAF to send over his two spare legs, which were dropped by parachute. They were soon confiscated at night, however, after a series of escapes, which all ended in recapture. Finally, he was transferred in 1942 to the famous Colditz escape-proof castle in Germany, where the most troublesome prisoners of war were confined. During this time he became only the third ever pilot to be awarded a bar for both the Distinguished Flying Cross and the Distinguished Service Order.

In June 1945, after the war had ended, he was posted back to Tangmere as a group captain running the fighter leader school. But he soon got bored with that and got a job as a rep selling aeroplane fuel for Shell with his own private plane.

In 1946, he became the first ever legless player to compete in the national amateur golf championships. He had first taken up this sport at Goodwood (near Tangmere), accompanied by his golden retriever Shaun, who had a habit of distracting his opponents. In one match, his tin legs were creaking and his opponent joked that he should put some Shell oil on them. On another occasion, a club member admired Bader's new golf shoes and asked if they kept the water out. He retorted, 'How the hell would I know?'

His famous biography *Reach for the Sky* was written by Paul Brickhill (author of *The Dam Busters*) and was made into a film starring Kenneth More, which was released in 1965. The success of this film made him world famous and he was honoured by the Canadian Black Foot tribe, who made him Chief Morningbird. He also served as a member of the Civil Aviation Authority from 1972 to 1978.

In the International Year of the Disabled on 20 November 1981 he opened the Bader Arms in Tangmere. In the same village is a military aviation museum, where spitfires as flown by him can be seen.

143. Dylan Thomas (1914–1953)

Samlet Road, Llansanlet, Swansea, SA7 9AQ (Tel: 01792 701670). Spirit.

The first published work of Swansea born writer Dylan Thomas was a piece of blatant plagiarism. Aged just 12, he recycled a piece from *Boy's Own Paper* into the *Western Mail* and got paid ten shillings (50 pence) for it.

The Lewisham, London, pub showing Dylan Thomas.

He was born at 5 Cwmdonkin Drive, Uplands, Swansea and he went to school at 22 Mirador Crescent in the same district. It was by winning the school cross-country race that he made his second appearance in print, with his picture in the local paper. His interest in poetry was inspired by local Marxist poet Bert Trick, who ran a grocery shop at 69 Glanbrydan Avenue, where Dylan discussed politics and literature with him twice a week.

At the age of 18 he became a junior reporter on the local paper, but got sacked for being drunk, late and for fabricating stories. He moved to London at the age of 20 and within three years he was 'drinking in earnest, and pissed and shat himself on many occasions'. At the age of 21 he was barred from the Cafe Royal in Regent Street for 'scraping his tongue with the menu and presenting the detritus to another diner'. Obsessed with jokes about contraceptives, bestiality and the sexual habits of deformed people, he earned the name of 'The Ugly Suckling' for sponging off friends, even when earning good money.

When he was 22 he met his future wife Caitlin Macnamara, a showgirl and dancer, in the Wheatsheaf Pub in Rathbone Street in the Fitzrovia quarter of London's West End. They spent the next five nights together in the Eiffel Tower Hotel nearby in Percy Street; charging it to the account of artist Augustus John without his knowledge.

The Swansea pub.

Caitlin found Dylan's clothes were stinking and his knowledge of foreplay non-existent. They just clung to each other as she showed him, as best she could, what to do. They had no food throughout the whole five days and just drank with artists and writers in local pubs, including the Fitzroy Tavern in Charlotte Street, which now has a Dylan Thomas Bar in the basement. They arranged to get married twice, but spent the licence fee on drink instead, and then finally made it third time lucky in 1937.

Augustus John, an anarchist, recalled Dylan left the Communist Party 'when asked to become a poetic mouthpiece for Moscow and confined his political activity to sponging off the rich by writing magnificent begging letters'.

Dlyan Thomas statue in Swansea Quay.

Theatre producer Thomas Taig recalled meeting Dylan in the Fitzroy Tavern and being fascinated by his 'chameleon act' when circulating between different groups of drinkers. 'My guess is that what we call life was for him a hectic dream in which he took an active part.'

Author Anthony Burgess recounted how, during this period, Dylan 'technically committed adultery' with his wife, but 'he was usually too soused to perform and, when not soused, he foresaw his morning guilt and was inhibited. All he really wanted was female warmth and a protective cuddle.'

During the war he got a job writing scripts for the Ministry of Information and he befriended the Soviet spies Guy Burgess and Donald Maclean. After the war he often got work from George Orwell and then John Arlott on BBC radio, reciting poetry. On one famous occasion he turned up drunk and read *Ode on St Cecilia's Day* as Shaint Sheshiliash.

His masterpiece was *Under Milk Wood*, set in the Welsh village of Llareggub ('bugger all' spelled backwards). When writing it he would recite parts of it in The Wheatsheaf, including parts which were censored from the final version; such as town hall messages about fish declaring war on the area and the Anti-Christ reaching the district. Eli Jenkins Ale House at 24 Oxford Street, Swansea is named after a character from this play.

Despite his liking for its pubs, he described living in London as 'the capital punishment'. Caitlin summed it up neatly, 'He needed London for talk and pubbing – for stimulation – but he could only write away from it.'

He died in America on a tour reading Under Milk Wood, having consumed a large amount of whiskey. At the funeral in Laugharne, Carmarthen Bay, the poet Louis MacNeice, having imbibed, became confused and 'threw his sandwiches on the coffin in the belief that they were a bunch of daffodils'. It is not recorded if he ate the daffodils though, as Dylan once did for a bet with another poet Roy Campbell.

A statue of Dylan sculpted by John Doubleday stands on the quay at Swansea Marina (between the Dylan Thomas Theatre and The Pump House Pub), a few hundred yards from the Dylan Thomas Centre, which is at Somerset Place, Swansea, SA1 1RR (Tel: 01792 463980). The poet also appears on one side of the sign of Dylans in Lewisham. A Dylan Thomas Festival takes place in Swansea each year in October.

144. Joe Fagan (1920–1985)

Fagan's, 69 Broad Lane, Sheffield, South Yorkshire, S1 4BS (Tel: 0114 2728430). Punch Taverns.

Fagan's pub sign.

Joe Fagan was a member of Bomber Command, who had beer in his blood. He was born in a nearby pub, the Royal Oak, and ran The Barrel for thirty-eight years before it was renamed after him. Just two weeks after, he died from a stroke and cirrhosis of the liver; his wife and two children had all died before him. The pub was already nicknamed Fagan's before the official name change and Joe was known as one of the city's great character landlords.

'He was curmudgeonly and had a heart like a bucket,' commented landlady Barbara Boulding, who took over from Joe and still runs the pub. 'He had a pump labelled Fagan's Fun House and there was always laughter when he was around.

'Somebody stole the sign (bearing his portrait), which was very heavy, some years ago but we managed to get it replaced.'

In 1940, Joe became a rear gunner in Bomber Command and pictures of him at that time remain on the walls of the pub; surviving members of Bomber Command in the area still meet in the pub once a month. Joe spent three years as a prisoner of war in Stalag 4B, near Colditz, after being shot down during a bombing raid on Hamburg in 1942. On being freed by the Russians in 1945, he returned to Sheffield and collected £1,000 back pay from the RAF.

In 1947, the money ran out and he borrowed more to buy the Barrel. He was always proud that the pub could attract a wide mix of regulars – from barristers to steelworkers and millionaires to people on the dole – without there ever being any trouble.

A keen boxer when in the RAF, he used his skills to help local youngsters as a trainer for Croft House Club in Garden Street, which he co-founded, and St Vincent's Club in Solly Street.

During his thirty-eight years at the pub, the price of a pint rose from 11 old pennies (just under 5 pence) to 74p.

145. John Brunt (1922–1944)

John Brunt VC, 24 Church Road (corner of Old Kent Road), Paddock Wood, Kent, TN12 6HB (Tel: 01892 838414). Punch Taverns.

The daredevil antics of John Brunt in the Second World War read like a comic-book adventure. Perched on top of a tank amid heavy fire, he led his men to a victory over the Germans, who outnumbered them by at least three to one. This happened on 9 December 1944 in Faenza, Italy, and resulted in him being awarded the Victoria Cross. Sadly, the VC had to be awarded posthumously, because he was killed the very next day by a stray mortar shell, the only one that was fired on that day. *The Daily Mirror* front page of 9 February 1945 proclaimed the award and described how his platoon of thirty infantry smashed a counter-attack from the crack German 90th Panzer Grenadier Division. He jumped on the turret of a Sherman tank and shouted orders to his men, under heavy machine gun fire, and then killed thirty Germans with bazookas one by one, until they retreated, it continued. This brought the total number of notches on his Tommy gun to one hundred and seventeen enemy soldiers he had killed during the war, reported *The Mirror*. The official citation for his VC gives more details of his heroism in battle.

As the Germans advanced in strength, they destroyed the house where Brunt's platoon was dug in and they also destroyed the British anti-tank defences. Brunt rallied his men and took them to an alternative position, where they were outnumbered by at least three to one, and he personally killed fourteen of the enemy with a Bren gun.

His wireless set was then destroyed by shellfire and he withdrew by 200 yards. When his ammunition ran out, he picked up a mortar gun from a casualty and dashed over ground to a new position. This aggressive action caused the enemy to pause, so he took a party of soldiers back to his previous position under fire.

When the Germans mounted another attack, he seized a spare Bren gun and advanced to a forward position and rallied his men. Then he leaped on to a Sherman tank and ordered the tank commander to drive from one position to another, while he sat on the turret directing fire at the enemy regardless of the hail of small-arms fire.

Then, on seeing small parties of the enemy armed with Bazookas trying to round the left flank, he jumped from the tank and, taking a Bren gun, he stalked these parties, killing more of them and causing the rest to withdraw in haste. His coolness, bravery and personal example were the major factor in the successful repulse of the fierce enemy attacks.

His teenage years were spent in Paddock Wood, where his father, a senior marketing officer for the Ministry of Food, lived at Woodlands. At school, Brunt was outstanding at sport, excelling in rugby, swimming, hockey, shot-putting, hurdling and steeplechasing. On leaving school in July 1941, he immediately enlisted and won several army boxing medals when serving with the Queens Own Royal West Kent Regiment.

In January 1943, he was commissioned to the Sherwood Foresters. In Italy, he was awarded the Military Cross in December 1943 and he was promoted to captain in May 1944.

A poem about him is framed in the pub containing the following lines:

> He sought no glory of a wide renown;
>
> Looked for no fame, aimed at no laurelled crown;
>
> Lived with his men as brothers in the fray;
>
> He would not claim a greater name than they.

146. Tom Finney (born 1922)

Central Drive, Penwortham, Preston, Lancashire, PR1 0LN (Tel: 01772 752299). Enterprise Inns.

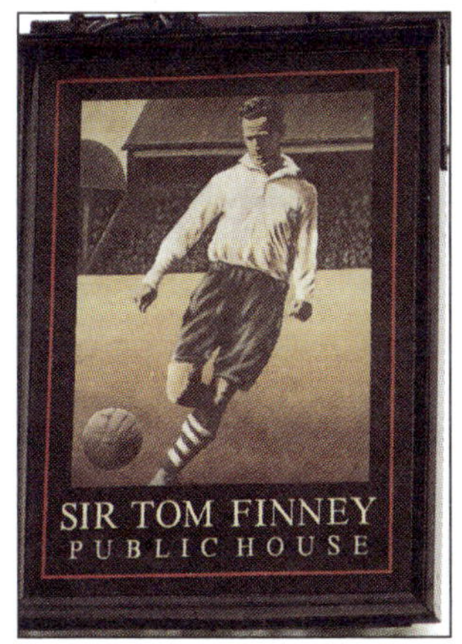

Tom Finney would, according to the legendary Liverpool football manager Bill Shankly, have been great in any team in any age 'even if he had been wearing an overcoat'. Shankly maintained until his dying day that Finney was 'the greatest footballer ever'. Asked in 1968 if the footballing genius George Best, then aged 22, was beginning to at least come close to Finney, he said grudgingly, after much thought, 'Possibly.' This seemed an astonishing concession. Then he added, 'But you must remember Tom is 46 years old now.'

Finney spent his entire career at Preston North End, making his first team debut in 1940 at Liverpool, with Bill Shankly playing alongside him for Preston. Finney's last game for the club was in 1960, when he retired without ever having been sent off or even cautioned.

In 433 league games, he scored 187 goals. He was the club's most capped player, appearing for England 76 times (on both wings and as centre-forward) scoring 30 goals and only losing 12 games. He was also Footballer of the Year twice: once in 1954 and once in 1957, becoming the first player to achieve that honour.

He was born into a poor family in St Michael's Road, just 200 yards from Preston's ground at Deepdale. When his mother Margaret died when Tom was 4 years old, his father Alf, an electricity board clerk, had to work nights in pubs to support his six children. As a toddler, Tom kicked a rubber ball around in the back fields of Holme Slack, near Daisy Lane where the family had moved, still within earshot of the football ground. He recalls the spirit of camaraderie when playing as a youngster for Holme Slack even when they had no changing room.

When he went to Deepdale School, he played inside-left for the under 12 team and scored the winning goal to take the Dawson Cup (the major local school tournament) in the final at Preston North End's ground in 1934. He left school at the age of 14 and became an apprentice plumber. In the same year, when he was just 5 stone in weight and 4 foot 9 inches tall, Preston did not even bother replying to his request for a trial.

But his father, who was a waiter in The Sumners Pub, was serving the Preston trainer and persuaded him to give Tom a trial, after which the club offered him a professional contract for £2 10s (£2.50) a week. His father did not think this was secure enough, however, and got him to sign as an amateur instead.

Some three years later, aged 17, he signed as a wartime professional for ten shillings (50 pence) a game, and was in the team that became the Northern Section champions and won the Wartime Cup (drawing against Arsenal at Wembley and then winning the replay), both in 1941.

The following year he was called up into the Eighth Army as a tank driver in Egypt. He played football for the army against Egyptian sides, one of which included the film star Omar Sharif ... often having to sweep the pitches for mines before the kick-off. Towards the end of the war he played for England in a friendly against Switzerland in Berne ... before having played in the Football League proper. That debut came against Leeds in August 1946 and his first full international was a month later, when he scored in a 7–2 victory over Northern Ireland in Belfast. The highlight of his international career was scoring four goals in a 5–3 win over Portugal in Lisbon in 1947.

Preston was often described as a one-man team, hence the joke that 'Tom Finney should claim income tax relief ... for his ten dependants'. When he asked for a rise, however, he was told he was getting too big for his boots.

At the age of 30, when still on the £20 a week maximum at Preston, he was offered a £10,000 signing on fee plus £130 a month basic, with bonuses up to £100 a game, as well as a Mediterranean villa and a car, by the Italian club Palermo. But he stayed with Preston.

The following year, in 1953, Preston were only pipped on goal average by Arsenal for the league championship and in 1954, they reached the FA Cup Final, but lost 3–2 to West Brom.

In 1956, Cliff Britton was made Preston's manager and he switched Finney to centre-forward with great success, as he scored twenty-three goals to take the team to third place. But Finney found Britton too much of an authoritarian and it came to a head when the manager told the players they could not have any alcoholic drink on the train home after a match.

'Out of devilment, and in view of the manager's on-going miserable attitude,' he recalled, 'I ordered a glass of beer. That was unheard of because I didn't drink and when the lads saw what the skipper was doing they followed suit.' He was carpeted but stood his ground. In fact, he likes a drink and a meal in the Dog and Partridge pub in the village of Chipping, 10 miles north of Preston.

After retiring from Preston he was signed up for one game by the Irish team Distillery to play against Benfica (including Eusebio) in the European Cup and he headed the opening goal in a 3–3 draw at the age of 41.

He continued playing in testimonial matches to raise money for retiring players right up to the age of 50. One stood out at Grimsby, when he was playing alongside England striker Nat Lofthouse. As a token reward, Tom got a box of plaice and Nat one of cod. 'Hang on a minute,' said Nat, tongue in cheek. 'We have both made the effort to come here tonight but while I get cod as a thank you that fellow Finney ends up with plaice. How come?' The organiser replied, 'Oh, that's quite easy to explain. Mr Finney is a better player than you are.'

There was another joke at the time about Lofthouse playing for England and heading in goals from crosses by Finney on the left wing and Stanley Matthews on the right. Lofthouse kept thanking Matthews but frowning at Finney. Asked to explain, he said that Matthews crossed the ball with the stitching away from his forehead!

Throughout his football career, Finney continued working six to eight hours a day as a plumber until 1984, when he became chairman of the Preston Health Authority for four years. Preston had been top of the infant mortality league with a rate of 25 per cent at the end of the nineteenth century because, as he stated, the cotton mill 'tyrants' had demanded too much of the workforce, with no regard for proper housing or public health. So he was very proud to be responsible for the opening of a new maternity unit in the town. He also made a point of consulting the public before making decisions in this role. 'I believe in the voice of the people, always have and always will,' he stated.

It was, however, another Sunday newspaper, *The News of the World*, for which he reported football matches for many years.

147. Nat Lofthouse (born 1925)

(i) Lion of Vienna, 158 Chorley New Road, Bolton, Lancashire, BL1 4PE
     (Tel: 01204 843172). Samuel Smith.
(ii) The Pineapple, 562 Blackburn Road, Bolton, Lancashire, BL1 7AL
     (Tel: 01204 303303).

England footballer Nat Lofthouse became known as the Lion of Vienna for the courage he showed in an international match away to Austria in 1952. The match was 2–2 with just eight minutes to go, when Nat, who had already scored, picked up the ball in his own half. He then raced all the way to the goal area with defenders closing in on him all the way. As the

goalkeeper came out, they clashed and Nat was knocked out cold ... a price he was prepared to pay for knocking in the winning goal. Such bravery resulted in the press dubbing him the Lion of Vienna. This was probably the best known of an incredible thirty goals he scored for England in just thirty-three games.

Probably his best remembered goal for Bolton Wanderers also involved a clash with a goalkeeper. It was in the 1958 FA Cup Final against Manchester United, which had just lost some of their star players, such as Duncan Edwards, in the Munich air crash. Nat scored both goals in Bolton's victory, the second by barging the United goalkeeper Harry Gregg over the goal line as he held the ball, at a time when shoulder barging was allowed.

Nat was just as much a one-club man as his friend Tom Finney of Preston. Born and bred in Bolton, Nat was just 14 years old when he signed for Wanderers and he was 15 when he made his debut against Bury (scoring twice in a 5–1 win). He was also to score two goals in each of two other debut matches: against Chelsea in his first league match and against Yugoslavia in his first match for England in 1950.

After scoring a record six goals in a match for the Football League against the Irish League in September 1952, he was elected Footballer of the Year at the end of that season.

He finally retired as a player after an injury in 1960, having scored a club record of 256 goals for Bolton in 452 league games. A few months later, he became the club's assistant trainer, then chief coach and then manager in 1968 for a short while. This was followed by becoming administrative manager, chief scout, executive manager and caretaker manager in 1985 at the age of 60. The following year he was appointed club president.

His final accolade came in 1997, when the east stand in the club's new ground was named The Nat Lofthouse Stand. In 1998, he was named among football's top 100 legends and he was described by the Football League as 'a working class hero who stayed true to his northern roots and his beloved Bolton Wanderers'.

Strangely, Nat does not appear on the sign of this pub, which is named after him, but he does feature on the sign of another Bolton pub: The Pineapple.

148. Marilyn Monroe (1926–1962)

Monroe's, 2 Elmton Road (junction of Sheffield Road and Mansfield Road), Creswell, Derbyshire, S80 4HE (Tel: 01909 890724).

Marilyn Monroe, one of the most enduring pop icons of the twentieth century, was born as Norma Jeane Baker in the charity ward of Los Angeles General Hospital. Her father, a baker called Edward Mortenson, was listed on her birth certificate as address unknown. He had left her mother, a Mexican called Gladys (maiden name Monroe, whose first husband was Jap Baker), when she became pregnant.

One of Marilyn's earliest memories was as a baby – she slept in a drawer for lack of a crib – being smothered by her mother, who was later diagnosed and detained as a paranoid schizophrenic when Marilyn was 9.

When Gladys returned to her job as a negative cutter in a film laboratory, she paid $25 a month to a deeply religious couple Wayne and Ida Bolender to bring up Marilyn in their house at 459 East Rhode Island Street, Hawthorne, Los Angeles, California. This was opposite the bungalow of Marilyn's grandmother, Della Monroe, who went mad and died in a straitjacket when Marilyn was fourteen months old.

At the age of 7, she was reunited with her mother at a bungalow she acquired at 6812 Arbol Drive, near the Hollywood Bowl. To pay the rent they took in lodgers and one of these, according to Marilyn, molested her. But when she informed her mother, she was scolded for making it up. About this time a neighbour attacked Marilyn's pet dog Tippy with a garden hoe and sliced the animal in two in front of her; just as her mother had seen her own pet kitten killed by being thrown against a brick wall by her drunken stepfather.

Before long, Gladys lost her job and so had to foster Marilyn out again, this time to her friend and workmate Grace McKee, who encouraged her to dream of being a film star. She then went to more foster homes and, at the age of 9, was dragged screaming into the Los Angeles Orphans' Home. From her dormitory, she could see the tower of the RKO film studios nearby.

Just before her eleventh birthday, she went to live with Grace McKee again, who was now with her fourth husband, who drank heavily and made sexual advances towards Marilyn, so Grace farmed her out to another foster home. By the time she was 12, she had been assaulted in at least two other homes. Each time, she was the victim and each time, she was the one that was expelled.

When Marilyn was 15, Grace (her legal guardian) announced she was moving to West Virginia, but that she could not take her with her. Marilyn was given the choice of marrying a 21-year-old neighbour or returning to the orphans' home. So three weeks after her sixteenth birthday she married James Dougherty and dropped out of high school.

In 1944, James joined the Merchant Marines and went into service overseas. Marilyn, aged 17, went to work as a chute-packer and glue-sprayer in a factory making planes. An army photographer covering women in the war effort took pictures of her there in 1945. Following their publication, she got into modelling and within a year she had an acting contract with Twentieth Century Fox and was divorced.

In 1952, when she was becoming well known, a calendar was published with nude photographs taken of her in 1949. She was advised by the studio to deny they were of her for fear it would damage her career. Instead, she announced that they were of her and she was not ashamed of them – and her popularity increased as a result. When one reporter had asked her if she had been photographed with nothing on, she replied, 'Well, I had the radio on!'

She married the baseball star Joe DiMaggio in 1954, but they were divorced in the same year after he witnessed the filming in a New York street of the scene in *The Seven Year Itch* of her skirt being blown over her shoulders while standing over some grating. It was shot countless times

and gathered an audience of 1,500 fans, one of whom quipped he could see she was a natural blonde; her pubic hairs were visible through sheer nylon panties, but were, in fact, also bleached.

After this, she demanded more artistic control over her parts, which was resisted by the studio. She held out for a year and a half though, until her demands, including choice of directors, were conceded at the end of 1955.

The following year, she married the playwright Arthur Miller at a time he was being threatened by the House Un-American Activities Committee with contempt proceedings, unless he named others at communist writers' meetings he had attended in 1947. He refused to do so and was fined $500 and given a suspended jail sentence, both of which were turned over on appeal.

In the middle of all this they came to London, where one of his plays was being performed and where Marilyn was filming *The Prince and The Showgirl* with Laurence Olivier. The Lord Chamberlain, who in those days could censor theatre plays, objected to a man kissing another man in Miller's play, but instead of cutting this out, the producer Binkie Beaumont put it on at a private club set up for the purpose – and 13,000 people joined when Marilyn was photographed signing up.

The couple were staying at Parkside House in Englefield Green, near Windsor Great Park, Surrey, which is where Marilyn found notes for future play ideas that Arthur had made, including how she had failed to live up to his ideal of her. This sowed the seeds of the end of their marriage. He tried to make amends by writing a film *The Misfits* to prove his love for her. But because it idealised her rather than accepted her for what she was, it had the opposite effect on her.

Her heavy intake of alcohol – she often drank vermouth, vodka, sherry and gin from teacups on the set, and champagne at the end of psychiatric sessions – was one of the reasons she had her second miscarriage at the end of 1958.

Just three weeks after her divorce from Miller, and after trying to jump out of a window, in 1961, she unwittingly signed herself into a psychiatric clinic and had to be sedated and restrained when trying to escape. She was eventually released and her lover Frank Sinatra gave her a fluffy poodle, which she named Maff, because of his Mafia connections. Sadly, it never became house-trained and stained her carpets frequently.

Another of her pet dogs Hugo, a basset hound, was fed brandy by her when it was depressed.

In 1962, she could scarcely stagger to the podium to accept, with slurred speech, the Golden Globes Award as the World's Favourite Female Star. A couple of months later, she seductively sang happy birthday to another of her lovers President Jack Kennedy on his forty-fifth birthday in a flesh-coloured gown (Marilyn, not the President) before 15,000 people at Madison Square Gardens and 40 million television viewers.

She returned to making the film *Something's Got to Give* with Dean Martin, when photographers were invited to a skinny-dipping scene in which she wore a flesh-coloured bikini. But she took it off in the water and posed nude for them. Shortly afterwards, she was sacked by the film company and Dean Martin quit in solidarity.

Then, on 4 August, she was found dead from an overdose. Numerous theories have been put forwards over whether it was an accident, suicide, or murder to prevent a scandal involving the White House.

Regular Monroe lookalike competitions are run in the pub now named in her honour (called the Portland until 2001) in what used to be a pit village, as can be seen from the winding gear in the forecourt. It is run by Chelsea Rosewell, who has bedecked it with numerous pictures of Marilyn.

149. Che Guevara (1928–1967)

El Comandante, 10 Annette Road, Islington, London, N7 6ET
(Tel: 07958 296031). Independent.

The most famous photograph in the world, according to a Maryland Institute of Art survey in 2001, is the iconic one of Che Guevara, hero of the Cuban Revolution. This was taken of Che (a qualified doctor) after he had given first aid to victims of an explosion on a ship in Havana in 1960. He was attending the memorial service of the 100 victims which took place the next day. The photographer, Alberto Korda, never got paid anything from the picture's ubiquitous use worldwide.

Che's father, Ernesto Guevara Lynch, was partly Irish and later stated, 'In my son's veins flowed the blood of the Irish rebels.'

Che himself acknowledged that he had picked up some of his guerilla warfare tactics from the Welsh rebel Owain Glyndwr.

Che was born in Argentina and at the age of 20 he studied medicine at the University of Buenos Aires. After three years he took a year off to do voluntary work at a leper colony in Peru, travelling there with a friend on a motorcycle. It was on this trip through South America, well chronicled in his book *The Motorcycle Diaries* and the 2004 film of the same name, that he witnessed the poverty and hunger of those employed on American owned plantations.

This led him to conclude that this suffering could only be overcome by a revolution throughout Latin America and that his role was in that rather than medicine. Nevertheless, he qualified as a doctor in 1953, before heading off to Guatemala, to support the land reforms being introduced by the democratically elected President Jacobo Arbenz Guzmán. When this government was forcibly overthrown by an American CIA sponsored coup, it convinced Che that armed struggle was the only way to defeat American imperialism's opposition to any egalitarian reforms.

He moved to Mexico where, in June 1955, he met Fidel and Raúl Castro, who had just set up a movement to overthrow the Cuban dictator Batista. Che was one of the eighty-two on the leaky ship *Granma,* which sailed from Mexico to Cuba in November 1956, and he was one of just twenty-two to survive after being attacked by the army on landing. It was during this bloody battle that he dropped his medical supplies and picked up a box of ammunition. The survivors reassembled in the mountains and started the movement which grew and finally succeeded in overthrowing Batista in December 1958. By then, Che had been promoted by Castro to Comandante (commander).

In the year following the revolution, Che was made a director at the National Institute of Agrarian Reform and became President of the National Bank of Cuba. He famously led by example, including cutting sugar cane in the fields.

A couple of attempts to assassinate him were made in New York when he was there to address the United Nations in December 1964. One was by a woman who broke through the barricades with a hunting knife but was restrained and the other was by a man who fired a bazooka from a boat but missed the target.

'It is better to be killed by a woman with a knife than by a man with a gun,' mused Che drily. Sadly, he was eventually killed by a man with a gun.

Shortly after making his speech to the United Nations, denouncing the brutal repression practised by the USA and South Africa, he set off on a world diplomatic tour that took in Ireland, China, Eastern Europe and Africa – ending up in the Congo in April 1965, where he supported the Marxist guerilla movement. However, a CIA spy ship in the Indian Ocean was monitoring all his communications, so the South African mercenaries were able to anticipate all his attacks and ambush his forces.

Following this failure, he went to help the guerillas in Bolivia. Again, the CIA sent in a large force of commandos. Che's radios proved to be faulty, which meant his forces were unable to communicate with each other and they became isolated. His camp was located by the Bolivian Special Forces, who surrounded it on 7 October 1967, wounding and capturing Che.

He was executed two days later, having said he thought nothing about his own immortality, only 'the immortality of the revolution'. He was shot nine times, after which his hands were amputated, to prove his identity through his fingerprints, and he was then buried in an unmarked grave with the rest of his captured comrades. Their remains were discovered twenty years later – Che was identified by his teeth – and were taken to be buried at Santa Clara in Cuba, where he had led the decisive battle of the revolution.

A 'Che Guevara' brand of Cuban rum can be bought in the pub, which assumed its present name in 2009.

Rum do: The bar has its own Che Guevara brand of liquor which packs a punch.

150. Rohan Kanhai (born 1935)

1–4 Woodham Road, Ashington, Northumberland, NE63 9UX
(Tel: 01670 857692). Wetherspoon.

The West Indian international batsman and wicketkeeper Rohan Babulal Kanhai won the Northumberland League title and the Wilson Cup for Ashington Cricket Club in 1964. His contribution was a record 1,217 runs (an average of 93.62).

In his autobiography, he explained why he preferred league to county cricket at that stage, 'Everyone gets on with the job of providing entertainment for the locals even if it means losing the match.'

Later, he moved to Warwickshire and scored at least 1,000 runs in each of the ten seasons he was with them; including 213 in a record undefeated stand of 465 with John Jameson against Gloucestershire at Edgbaston in 1974.

He was born on a little sugar plantation called Port Mourant in Guyana, where his father worked in the sugar factory, and he learned his cricket, entirely uncoached, as a child in the narrow backstreets and open wasteland with his friends. They used a bat made of fronds (dried leaves of coconut palms), a ball made of a piece of cork covered with rags and bound with twine and stumps made from twigs snapped from trees. None of them could afford pads or gloves and he would keep wicket with bare hands and legs.

His uncle John Trim lived next door and became opening bowler for the West Indians in the 1940s. Other near neighbours of Rohan's, who played with him in the streets, included three other Test players: Basil Butcher (who lived 200 yards down the same road), Ivan Madray (a further 100 yards along) and Joe Solomon (half a mile away).

When making his international debut in Australia as a 19-year-old, Rohan scored fifty-one against Keith Miller, who afterwards advised him to change his style of batting. This style was to hit across the ball, which was against all the rules. Rohan ignored the advice and went from success to success.

Another bowler called him a rabbit when he was out for a duck in India in 1959. He responded by scoring his highest Test score of 256 in the next match at Calcutta, including a partnership of 217 with Basil Butcher; for which Kanhai was presented with a stuffed tiger's head.

A small but powerful player, he had a habit of falling on his back as he cracked the ball to the boundary, which became his hallmark. He was also an excellent and athletic fielder, who took 315 catches and made seven stumpings in first-class cricket. But he was deprived of one in the last over of the legendary tied Test during the 1960–1961 tour of Australia. With four balls to go, the Australians needed four runs to win, when Wally Grout spooned the ball in Kanhai's direction. He was about to catch it, when the bowler Wes Hal, also went for it and bumped into Kanhai, elbowing him in the head and sending him spinning. The ball went into Wes' hand, but he dropped it as the batsmen completed a run. The next ball saw Grout run out with an amazing 90-yard throw from just inside the boundary as he was going for the third and winning run. As the batsmen were going for the winning run off the final ball, Kanhai's childhood friend Joe Solomon threw the ball from 12 yards to hit the stumps direct and save the day at 737 each.

Later in the same series, at Adelaide, Kanhai became the first ever West Indian to hit Test centuries in both innings of a match (117 and 115). This helped him towards a record aggregate of 1,093 runs, which won him the Karl Nunes Trophy for the outstanding West Indian of the tour.

He was made the West Indian Captain in 1973 and held the position for thirteen Tests. Of his seventy-nine Test appearances, sixty-one were in consecutive matches, a run which was only broken when he had to have a cartilage operation. In 1975, his half-century (in a stand of 149 with Clive Lloyd) won the World Cup Final for the West Indians.

Other clubs he played for included Aberdeen, Blackpool (he married a Lancashire lass called Brenda Hague in 1963), Western Australia and Tasmania. His first-class career lasted from 1955 to 1977, during which time he scored 28,639 runs (an average of 49.29). His Test total was 6,227 (an average of 47.53).

Despite this, he preferred to watch football rather than cricket and he recalled seeing Gary Sobers playing as goalkeeper for the police cadets in Barbados. He explained this by stating that people did not expect an usherette to go to the cinema on her night off.

Rohan Kanhai, early and late in his career, pictured inside the pub.

151. Julian Cayo Evans (1937–1995)

The Cayo Arms, 36 Cathedral Road, Pontcanna, Cardiff, CF11 9LL
(Tel: 029 2039 1910). Tomos Watkin/Masterson.

Julian Cayo Evans was a founder member of the Free Wales Army, who was jailed for fifteen months for causing explosions in protest at the investiture of the Prince of Wales in 1969. He formed the FWA and became its commandant in the early 1960s. Members wore paramilitary uniforms, trained with firearms, learned how to make bombs in remote areas of the mountains and marched at nationalist rallies calling for Welsh independence, often burning the Union Jack in the process.

Evans denied rumours that their guns were supplied by the Official Irish Republican Army. 'We bought, begged, and borrowed what we could,' he stated. 'To be honest I think any folk museum would have been pleased to acquire some of our arms.'

He did, however, lead a contingent to Dublin in 1966, at the invitation of Sinn Fein, to take part in a parade celebrating the 50th anniversary of the Easter Rising.

Nobody was ever injured by FWA action, it was claimed, as their protests were achieved by damaging property. They also got publicity in other ways, such as when Cayo disrupted the *David Frost* television programme live on air.

Evans had been trained by the South Wales Borderers in the army, fighting communist guerrillas in Malaya, during his national service after leaving school. He then became a horse breeder at Lampeter (30 miles north of Swansea), where he was born and died. Often he would be seen riding a white horse in the area and a Welsh flag would always be flying over his stud farm when he was 'in residence'. He was half Spanish, played the accordion, but surprisingly never learned the Welsh language.

In 1981, on the wedding day of the Prince of Wales, the FWA had a reunion at Cayo's farm and unveiled a memorial of its insignia, a Snowdon Eagle, in memory of old comrades. In the local pub afterwards, he roared with laughter when a policeman told them, 'Don't worry, the terrorists aren't here.'

Some four hundred people attended his funeral at St Sulien's Church in Carmarthenshire, many in paramilitary uniforms, with dark glasses and black berets. The FWAs clenched-fist salute was given and wreaths were carried in the shape of the Snowdon Eagle. The coffin was draped in a Welsh red dragon flag. Police were also in attendance.

The FWA anthem was also sung:

> Tramp, tramp, tramp, the boys are marching
>
> To join up to the Free Wales Army.
>
> Beneath the Union Jack, Wales will never be free
>
> So let's strike a blow for Wales and Liberty.

This pub is recommended in Camra's *Beer, Bed & Breakfast* guide, edited by Jill Adam and Susan Nowak.

152. John Lennon (1940–1980)

Lennon's Bar, 23 Mathew Street, Liverpool, L2 6RE (Tel: 0151 236 5225). Glassline.

John Lennon was unique as a rock 'n' roll superstar, who was able to write meaningful anti-establishment songs that were entertaining and immensely popular. *Give Peace a Chance* and *Imagine* have become international anthems, while *Revolution, Power to the People*, and *Working Class Hero* were all breakthroughs in their time.

He also expressed raw, personal feelings in some heart-rending songs, which departed starkly from the saccharine lyrics of the day. If these drew criticism, he was willing to debate the issue, but never allowed it to inhibit him.

It all started at the Cavern Club in the same street as this pub at 10 Mathew Street, where John's first band The Quarry Men appeared in July 1957, shortly after he had bought his first guitar at Hessy's, 60 Stanley Street, nearby for £17. The name came from Quarry Bank School, which he attended in Harthill Road, Liverpool 18. The headmaster there described John as 'the worst Teddy boy among the pupils in my charge'. His name was often in the punishment book and one report said he was 'on the road to failure ... rather a clown in class'. He failed each of his 'O' level exams by a single grade, moving the headmaster to comment that he 'could clearly have passed if he had wanted to'.

By May 1960, the group had changed its name to the Silver Beatles and they had turned professional. Until then, John had been at Liverpool Art School, but spent most of his time drinking 'black velvets' (Guinness and champagne) at Ye Cracke pub in nearby Rice Street. The group soon dropped the 'Silver' from its title and appeared at the Cavern as the Beatles 275 times in the period from 9 February 1961 to 3 August 1963. Their first single *Love Me Do* was released in 1962 and the extraordinary phenomenon of 'Beatle mania' spread around the world.

In 1963, they appeared before the Queen at a Royal Command Performance in London and John famously told the upper-class audience to join in by 'rattling your jewelry'.

The Beatles were awarded MBE's in 1965 for their contribution to the country's exports and four years later, John returned his to the Buckingham Palace tradesmen's entrance with a letter to the Queen, saying it was in protest against the government's support of the American War on Vietnam, for involvement in the Nigeria/Biafra Civil War 'and against *Cold Turkey* [his latest record] slipping down the charts'. He explained to the press that he was basically a socialist and the MBE represented the 'hypocritical snobbery' of the class system. 'I only took it to help the Beatles make the big time,' he

John Lennon statue on the site of the old Cavern Club.

added. 'I know I sold my soul when I received it, but now I have helped to redeem it in the cause of peace. Of course my action was a publicity gimmick for peace.'

He appeared in the film *How I Won the War* in 1967 and announced at its premiere, 'I hate war. If there is another war I won't fight and I'll tell all the youngsters not to fight either. I hate all the sham.'

In 1968, he wrote and released *Revolution*, which denounced radicals 'carrying pictures of Chairman Mao' and ended with 'you can count me out'. Later, he changed it in performance to 'you can count me in' and in 1971 he was wearing a Mao badge on stage with Black power speakers in New York. Even later, he expressed an interest in going to China, but was told that country's government might disapprove of the lyrics of *Revolution*. He reacted with a laugh, 'I'll just tell them that Paul wrote it' - his fellow Beatle and song writing partner Paul McCartney.

Later, in 1968, John and Yoko Ono, who was carrying his child, were arrested in the London flat of Beatles' drummer Ringo Starr and they were charged with possession of cannabis. Lennon always maintained it was planted by Detective Sergeant Norman Pilcher, who four years later was charged with 'conspiracy to pervert the course of justice'. John agreed to plead guilty in return for the dropping of charges against Yoko, who later had a miscarriage. John said he was attracted to her because she was 'like me in drag'.

In 1971, he was interviewed in the Marxist journal *Red Mole* and was quoted as stating, 'I've always been politically minded and against the status quo. It's pretty basic when you're brought up, like I was, to hate and fear the police as a natural enemy and to despise the army as something that takes everybody away and leaves them dead somewhere ... I'd like to incite people to break the framework, to be disobedient in school, to insult authority.'

He concluded, 'You can't take power without a struggle, because when it comes to the nitty gritty they won't let the people have power. They'll give us all the rights to perform and dance for them, but no real power.'

A few days later, he wrote *Power to the People* and sang it at a peace march in Washington, where Vietnamese veterans hurled their medals onto the steps of the Capitol. It sold a million records worldwide, but was criticised by some, to whom he responded, 'I think that everyone should own everything equally and that the people should own part of the factories and they should have some say in who is boss and who does what.'

Near Lennon's Bar.

A couple of months later, he was back in London, marching against British policy in Northern Ireland (with a placard reading: For the IRA, Against British Imperialism) and supporting the Upper Clydeside Shipbuilders workers' occupation, which was resisting closure, with £1,000 a week to its fighting fund.

He then returned to New York, where his campaigning against the Vietnam War needled the authorities into starting proceedings to deport him, using his drug conviction as an excuse. His FBI file was upgraded from 'New Left' to 'Revolutionary Activities' in May 1972. He described himself as 'an instinctive socialist' to *Playboy* magazine and as a 'Zen Marxist' to *Newsweek*.

In his last interview he summed up his views, 'Maybe in the sixties we were naive and like children and later everyone went back to their rooms and said "We didn't get a wonderful world of flowers and peace ... The world is a nasty horrible place because it didn't give us everything we cried for". Crying for it wasn't enough.

'The thing the sixties did was show us the possibility and the responsibility that we all had. It wasn't the answer. It just gave us a glimpse of the possibility.'

In December 1980 he was shot dead in New York by paranoid schizophrenic fan Mark Chapman, for whom he had earlier signed his autograph. When Lennon had controversially said the Beatles were more popular than Jesus, the teenage Chapman had reacted by singing 'Imagine John Lennon dead' at his high-school prayer group.

A statue of Lennon, sculpted by Arthur Dooley, now stands near the pub that bears his name. And Liverpool's Speke Airport has been renamed John Lennon Airport, where another statue of him, sculpted by Tom Murphy, was unveiled by Yoko on 15 March 2002.

Larger than life...John Lennon at the airport in Liverpool named after him.

153. Bob Dylan (born 1941)

Dylans, 66 Lewisham High Street, London, SE13 5JH.

Legendary folk singer and composer Bob Dylan is on the hanging sign of this pub in London, a city he is very familiar with. It was in a London pub that he met singer Martin Carthy, who was to have a huge influence on him, which he acknowledged. Dylan was also involved in a public slanging match with another singer Nigel Denver in the same pub.

The pub was the King & Queen at 1 Foley Street (on the corner of Cleveland Street), London W1, where he went in December 1962 to sing and play to an extremely good reception in the folk club upstairs, which was run by Carthy, who later became a member of Steeleye Span. Carthy introduced Dylan to traditional English songs. 'His time in England was actually crucial to his development,' said Carthy, as could be seen by comparing his album *Freewheelin,* before the visit with the one after *Times They Are a-Changin.*

Dylan confirmed, 'Martin Carthy's incredible. I learned a lot of stuff from Martin. *Girl from the North Country* is based on a song I heard him singing (*Scarborough Fair*).'

Another of Dylan's songs *With God on Our Side* was adapted from a Dominic Behan song *The Patriot Game*, which he heard sung by Nigel Denver. But Dylan took offence when Denver told him he 'couldn't sing his way out of a paper bag' or play the guitar. The showdown came in the King & Queen on New Year's Day 1963.

Folk singer Ron Gould was there and recalled, 'Dylan came in and stood at the back of the audience. Straight away he began to create a disturbance, talking very, very loudly, saying What's all this fuckin' shit or

something of that nature, really nasty. What's going on? Where's the drink? How do you get a drink here? And this went on all through the song, with people in the audience telling him to be quiet. Nobody knew who he was. Then Nigel said I don't know if you realise it but we allow the performers to perform, during which time the audience keeps quiet. And Dylan looked up and said I don't fuckin' have to keep quiet, I'm Bob Dylan, which really enamoured him with the audience!'

Guitarist Dave Stewart of the Eurythmics once played on tour with Dylan in America and the two became friends. At the end of the tour, Stewart told Dylan, 'If ever you're in London look me up where I have my own recording studio in Crouch End Hill, Hornsey, London N8,' and he told him the street number of the studio.

Years later, Dylan turned up unannounced. But instead of going to Crouch End Hill, he went to the similarly named Crouch Hill nearby, where at the appropriate number lived a plumber, whose first name (like Stewart's) was Dave. The plumber's wife could not believe it when she answered the door to see her hero Bob Dylan standing there and was even more amazed when he asked, 'Is Dave in?'

She replied, 'He's out on a job just now but will be back soon. Would you like a cup of tea while you wait?' It was only when plumber Dave returned that the error emerged and they redirected him to Dave Stewart's studio.

A Lewisham link is that in 1968, The Hollies performed a live tribute show to Dylan at the Lewisham Odeon, covering all his tracks on *The Times They Are a-Changin* and releasing it as an album.

154. Freddie Mercury (1946–1991)

Queen's Head, 3/10 Steine Street, Brighton, East Sussex, BN2 1TE
(Tel: 01273 602939).

Freddie Mercury, head of Queen the pop group, is portrayed on the sign of this gay community pub. Voted the seventh greatest pop icon of all time, Freddie met his first long-term gay lover in this seaside city in 1979 after performing there. This was Tony Bastin, 5 foot 11 inches tall, with fair hair and 'a very winning smile', which was what attracted Freddie in a local club. He took him back to his suite at The Grand Hotel, where the partying continued.

Tony moved into Freddie's flat in Stafford Terrace (off Kensington High Street), London W8, with his ginger tom cat Oscar, whom Freddie was wild about. When Freddie heard that Tony was seeing another younger man, however, he summoned him to America, where he was touring in August 1980, to break off the relationship. He told him to take the next plane back to London and to clear his belongings from their flat, but to leave Oscar (Freddie's favourite pussy) behind.

Freddie's after-show parties were riotous affairs. Naked women in body paint attended the toilets, dwarves circulated with bowls of cocaine and fires started by guests were extinguished with champagne. His favourite tipples were Stolichnaya Russian vodka, spearmint schnapps and St Saphorin wine from Switzerland. His favourite pub was a sleazy dive called The Coleherne in Brompton Road, Earls Court, not far from his flat.

An Iranian Parsee, Freddie was born Farookh Bulsara in Zanzibar, Tanzania. After attending boarding school in India, he came to London and took a degree in graphic design at Ealing Tech; a skill he was to later use in designing Queen's album covers, making much use of his favourite colour oxblood.

In 1975, the band's seven-minute record *Bohemian Rhapsody* was plugged on Capital Radio by disc jockey Kenny Everett, who befriended Freddie. They broke up in 1980, however, both accusing the other of cadging their drugs. Both were destined to die of AIDS.

Freddie spent much of his time in America, where he had an apartment at The Sovereign (fit for a Queen) Building, 425 East 58th Street, New York. This is where he entertained lovers, such as the aptly named barman Dick Dick and a lorry driver from the Queens district. 'What's the queen from Queen doing with a queen from Queens?' quipped Freddie.

But the band's popularity in America waned when they dressed up in women's clothing for the video to promote *I Want to Break Free* in 1983. When he was super rich, he offered £500,000 to buy a Goya painting in Spain. When told it could not be exported from the country he nearly bought a house there to keep it in.

On his death, he was cremated in West London after a Zoroastrian funeral service, which was the religion of his parents.

The Queen's Head is where camp comedian Julian Clary made one of his earliest appearances, at the age of 21, in 1980 as part of a double act called *Housewives Extraordinaire*. They were introduced by local gay comic Simon Fanshawe, who correctly predicted Julian would be a huge star.

155. John H. Stracey (born 1951)

West End, Briston, Melton Constable, Norfolk, NR24 2JA (Tel: 01263 860891).

Former world welterweight boxing champion John H Stracey took over this pub from a sparring partner after retiring in 1978. As a youngster, he lived behind the Blind Beggar Pub (infamous as the scene of a murder by the Kray gang) in London's East End. He often fought as an amateur at the York Hall, which was three bus stops away, but John always ran there instead. At the age of 18 he won the light-welterweight amateur title at Wembley Arena.

After turning professional, he became the undefeated British and European welterweight champion. Then 1975 saw the highlight of his career, when he became the undisputed world champion by beating Jose Napoles in Mexico City. Out of fifty professional fights, he won forty-five of them (a 90 per cent success rate).

John Newman was his sparring partner, whose father Tom bought the pub (which had been called the Horseshoe since 1615) in 1974. It was renamed after Stracey, who attended the renaming ceremony on 5 November 1976. Since retiring from the game he has carved out a new career as a part-time actor and club entertainer.

156. Matthew Le Tissier (born 1968)

Le Tissier Arms, 40 Albert Road North (corner of Anglesea Terrace), Southampton, Hampshire, SO14 5GB. Punch Taverns.

Matthew Le Tissier became the first Channel Islander to play football for England and was then dropped by his club Southampton! That was in the 1993–1994 season and the enraged fans kicked up such a stink that the manager Ian Branfoot was forced to reinstate him after five games. Le Tissier proved the wisdom of this decision, and the folly of dropping him, by scoring twenty-five goals, which saved the club from relegation from the Premier League.

He was born in St Peter Port, Guernsey, and went to Southampton as a 16-year-old schoolboy footballer in 1984. The following year he became an apprentice and scored fifty-six goals in the youth team in his first season. In August 1986, he made his league debut as a substitute and two months later he turned professional. In the same season he became the club's youngest ever player to score a hat-trick against Leicester.

He was regularly the club's leading scorer, with over twenty goals a season. In 1992, he scored in his Wembley debut (in the Zenith Data Systems Cup Final, which Southampton lost to Nottingham Forest). He was offered the chance to play for France, but turned it down in the hope of playing for England, which he eventually did eight times. Many managers thought he should have played in more internationals. Graham Souness, for example, thought he was the best player he ever managed. One reason given was that, to get the best out of Tissier, the team had to be built around him. And that was difficult at England, because 'too many other egos had to be massaged'.

In the 1994–1995 season he scored thirty goals, including all four in a League Cup tie against Huddersfield.

He retired in 2002, having scored a total of 209 goals for the first team out of 462 starts and 78 substitute appearances. And out of 48 penalties he only missed one. During that time, all at the old ground at The Dell, he played under ten different managers.

In his testimonial game between England and Southampton he played number seven for both sides, one in each half. In the programme he was asked if he was 17 again whether or not there be anything he would change. 'My haircut' was his reply.

He opened the pub named after him, which is close to Southampton's new ground at St Mary's, on 16 August 2002. Previously called The Anglesea Tavern, it was bought by Peter Young, a long-term fan of the club, who asked the star if he could name it after him. It is crammed full of football memorabilia, much of which is for sale, including a replica FA Cup. And, in honour of the Le Tissier feet that have scored so many goals, the pub title on the exterior has 'Arms' crossed out and it has been replaced with 'Legs'.

Matthew Le Tissier picture in the pub.

Le Tissier Arms landlord Peter Young holds a replica FA Cup.

Gone But Not Forgotten

The following are pubs that were named after commoners, but have either had their names changed or ceased to be pubs:

157. Jack Straw (executed 1381)

Jack Straw's Castle (now Jack & Lulu's restaurant), North End Way, Hampstead Heath, London, NW3.

Jack Straw was the comrade and chief lieutenant of Wat Tyler in the Peasants' Revolt of 1381. He addressed the peasants on Hampstead Heath from a hay wagon, which became known as Jack Straw's Castle. Straw and his men, about 20,000 of them, burned down the Manor of Highbury on 14 June early in the revolt. They continued into the centre of London and reached The Savoy, which they robbed and pillaged. Straw was also with Tyler when they entered The Tower of London and executed the Archbishop of Canterbury, who was also the Treasurer of England, responsible for the hated poll tax, which had sparked off the revolt.

In fact, the revolt started in Straw's birthplace of Fobbing in Essex, as commemorated in a plaque outside The White Lion in that village. It reads: To commemorate the villagers of Fobbing who, in the year 1381, stood for the freedom of the English people against oppression. Oh what avail the plough and sail, or life, or land, if freedom fail.

Inside The White Lion a notice describes how Straw was born and bred in the village and how he took part in driving out poll tax investigators and demanding a freedom charter. Other Fobbing villagers executed for their part were John Gildborne (Gildborne Close in the village is named after him), and Thomas Baker; the first identifiable rebel, who was hanged in Chelmsford. A monument commemorating the revolting peasants was erected behind The White Lion in 1990, but was soon moved to the recreation ground, as it offended the more establishment-minded residents.

The peasants met King Richard II at Blackheath, where he agreed to concede to many of their demands. When Straw and his colleague John Ball were later found hidden in an old house after the rebels had been betrayed, they were both decapitated and their heads were placed on London Bridge. Straw was said to have confessed that they had planned to kill all the king's knights, but take the king himself 'around with us so the common people would willingly join us'. Then, when they had got 'an enormous crowd of common people throughout the country', they would have murdered all the lords who opposed or resisted them, killed the king, driven out all 'possessioners' and clergy from the land and made their own laws.

Jack Straw's Castle, originally a coaching inn from about 1721, was rebuilt in the nineteenth century, when it was frequented by novelists Charles Dickens and William Thackeray, and communist author Karl Marx.

The second husband of music hall star Marie Lloyd, the ex-docker and singer of coster songs Alec Hurley, lodged in the pub with his dog Mike after Marie left him. He died there on 6 December 1913 of pleurisy and pneumonia at the age of 42. He, like Marie, had joined the music hall strike of 1907.

During the Second World War, the pub was severely damaged after being bombed by a land mine and was rebuilt again from 1962 to 1964.

In 2007 it became 'Jack and Lulu's' restaurant, despite a condition of the planning permission (to allow the rest of the building to be turned into flats) being that a replacement pub be retained on the ground floor.

158. Jack Cade (executed 1450)

(Recently renamed the Half Moon), Cade Street, about a mile south-east of Heathfield, East Sussex (on the B2096), TN21 9BS.

A notice in the bar proclaimed that 'Jack Cade was a wild Irishman who led an insurrection in 1450, defeating the king's forces at Sevenoaks, and marching on London with 30,000 men. His blaze of riot did not last and he was mortally wounded by an arrow from the bow of Alexander Iden, Sheriff of Kent, just outside Heathfield.'

The Kentish revolt, led by Cade, was in protest at the excessive war taxation imposed by King Henry VIs corrupt government.

Apart from peasants and labourers, Cade's army included many from the middle classes, who were against the misgovernment by the nobles and the mismanagement of the French war.

On 2 May 1450, the Earl of Suffolk was beheaded by sailors and thrown on the beach at Dover. Suffolk's group had controlled the king, but it had been banished by the supporters of the Duke of York, who was leading opposition to the king. This led to reprisals against the people of Kent, who were known to support the Duke of York.

This provoked the revolt and on 1 June an army of 50,000 men from all parts of Kent marched on Blackheath to place their demands before the king's council. In a coherently written programme, they listed complaints of the corruption of royal ministers, extortionate taxation and bribery in the choice of the king's collectors in Kent. They were refused a hearing, but beat off attacks from the royal army, after which the king retreated to Kenilworth in Warwickshire. Cade and his men entered London on 2 June and received much support from the people.

There they captured and executed the unpopular Sheriff of Kent William Cromer, and Lord Saye, an unpopular minister and the Treasurer of England, seen as responsible for the taxes. Cade resisted the temptation to loot in order to feed his men and instead introduced a levy of rich London merchants. They reacted by withdrawing their support for the rebels and by seizing London Bridge to shut them off from the city on 5 July.

The next day, the government falsely promised to consider the rebels' demands and to offer a free pardon to all if they dispersed. Most did, but Cade and a few of his followers, naturally suspicious, retained arms, but were eventually hunted down and executed.

Cade met his end near where the pub, which bore his name until recently, stood. A stone pillar marks the precise spot where he was shot with an arrow and it carries an inscription stating that his body was carried to London and that his head was fixed on Tower Bridge.

Shakespeare, in *Henry VI, Part II*, portrays Cade as a vicious character. But he was seen to be part of a wider movement when Henry was defeated in the War of the Roses in 1461 and his successor Edward IV, the Duke of York's son, reduced the power of the great nobles.

159. John Horne Tooke (1736–1812), John Glynn (1722–1779), and John Thelwall (1764–1834)

The Three Johns (now J3), 73 White Lion Street, Islington, London, N1.

This pub was named after John Wilkes (who also has his own pub the Wilkes' Head), John Horne Tooke and either John Glynn or John Thelwall, all four of whom were social reformers.

John Horne Tooke befriended Wilkes when in France in 1765. Tooke had lost an eye as a child, while fighting at school in Soho Square, London, with a pupil who had the advantage of a knife.

At the age of 24, he was ordained as a priest in Brentford, Middlesex, but gave it up after being 'too fond of cards and society'. When Wilkes stood as MP for Middlesex, Tooke promised to secure him the support of 'the two best inns at Brentford'. And it was Tooke who suggested the formation of the Society for Supporting the Bill of Rights at a meeting in the London Tavern.

Tooke was jailed for a year in 1777 for supporting the Americans against the English. While in prison he was allowed claret, which he blamed for his gout, and to have a weekly dinner in the Dog and Duck.

In 1794, he was tried for high treason, but was found not guilty. He then chaired a debate at the Crown and Anchor denouncing aristocracy.

At his dinner parties he had ample supplies of port and Madeira and at one of these dinners he settled an argument with James Boswell through a drinking match, at which he drunk Boswell under the table.

When someone suggested he take a wife, he replied, 'With all my heart. Whose wife should it be?'

John Glynn was another friend of Wilkes and he defended him in court. He was also a leading member of the Society for Supporting the Bill of Rights. He, too, suffered from gout.

Wilkes said of him, 'He was a Wilkite, which I never was.'

A portrait of him with Wilkes and Horne Tooke by Richard Houston was published in 1769, leading to the Three Johns title.

John Thelwall in 1789 'became intoxicated with the French doctrines of the day'. After likening 'a crowned despot to a bantam cock on a dunghill', he was tried at the Old Bailey for seditious libel, but was found not guilty. Later, a government spy claimed he saw him cut the froth (head) from a pot of porter and invoke 'a similar fate on all kings.'

In 1794, he was arrested for sedition and was taken to the Tower with Horne Tooke and Thomas Hardy. At the Old Bailey trial, Thelwall told his counsel Erskine he would defend himself, to which Erskine commented, 'If you do you will be hanged.' In reply, Thelwall coined the phrase, 'Then I'll be hanged if I do.' They were then acquitted.

After this he published *Poems written in Close Confinement in the Tower and Newgate* in 1795. He also taught oratory and how to cure stammering, which he had originally suffered from. The pub was renamed J3 in the 1990s.

160. Charles James Fox (1749–1806)

(i) The Intrepid Fox (now boarded up), 99 Wardour Street (corner of Peter Street), Soho, London, W1.

(ii) Now reopened at 15 St Giles High Street, London, WC2.

As a radical Whig MP in a period of repression, Charles James Fox had to be intrepid to keep up his fight for freedom and votes for the people. After he had drunk a toast in 1798 to 'the majesty of the people' (instead of to the king), the government considered incarcerating him in the Tower for treason, but settled for striking his name from the Privy Council list instead. This meant he could no longer be addressed as the Right Honourable.

The freeholders of Kent burned a live fox to show their contempt for him. But others admired his stand and struck a commemorative medal to 'The Intrepid Fox'. The Soho pub acquired the name after the landlord gave free beer to those who voted for Fox in the election of 1784.

He had a tremendous appetite for alcohol and gambling as well as for politics. Once, a friend found him surrounded by seven empty bottles of port and asked if he had drunk them all unassisted. Fox replied, 'No, I was assisted by a bottle of Madeira.'

When just 17 years old, he stopped at an alehouse in Nettlebed, Oxfordshire and pawned his watch for the price of a beer. On returning to London, he told his father he must send half a guinea to the alehouse keeper 'to redeem the gold watch you gave me years ago'.

Even earlier, at the age of 14, he had been introduced to gaming tables when his father gave him five guineas a night to play with while on holiday; a decision he was later to regret, when paying off £140,000 of his son's gambling debts before dying in 1774.

Young Fox became an MP for Midhurst in his teens and was the youngest Junior Lord of the Admiralty at the age of 21. Even so, he was seldom in bed before 5 o'clock in the morning, or up again until 2 o'clock in the afternoon.

At one important debate in the House in 1772 he had been playing cards until 5 a.m. the night before and after it had finished, he drank until 7 a.m. the next day. In the same year, he introduced a bill and got it through against the government by just one vote, after racing at Newmarket the day before and drinking through the whole night on the journey back to London.

All this drinking resulted in him having a rather rotund figure, which caused some amusement when he fought a duel in Hyde Park in 1779. His second, Richard Fitzpatrick, advised him to stand sideways to reduce the target area for his opponent William Adam. Fox laughed, 'Why, I am as thick one way as another.'

Adam invited Fox to fire first, but he politely replied, 'After you.' Both fired in turn without hitting each other. Adam then took another shot, which hit Fox in the groin. Fox fired in the air and they became friends.

Fox campaigned hard for the extension of the franchise – at the time only 214,000 out of a population of six million had the vote. In the 1790s, he unsuccessfully opposed the suspension of Habeas Corpus Act, the use of torture to extract confessions in Ireland and the introduction of Bills to ban public meetings.

Often, he would be joined by only thirty or forty other MPs in voting against these repressive measures. But he remained widely admired as a man even among his political opponents. So when he got heavily into debt, a fund was set up, which raised £61,000 in six months to settle his debts and to provide him with an annuity of £2,000 a year. Nervous in case he would feel patronised by this gesture, one subscriber asked a friend, 'How do you think Fox will take it?' He replied, 'Why, quarterly.' And, indeed, he did, also writing a letter of thanks.

Fox had a political revival in the last year of his life after the death of William Pitt, when he was made Foreign Secretary and Leader of the Commons. He rose for the last time in the House on 10 June 1806, to successfully propose the abolition of the slave trade. He died three months later.

Sadly, the 200th anniversary of his death was marked by the owners of the pub boarding it up and offering it for sale. But, more recently, another pub has taken up the name at 15 St Giles High Street, WC2 - on the junction with the music industry's 'Tin Pan Alley', officially called Denmark Street.

161. Charles Kemble (1775–1854)

Kemble's Head (now a Greek bar), 61 Long Acre (corner of Bow Street), Covent Garden, London, WC2.

The Shakespearean actor Charles Kemble was said to have been able to portray a greater range of roles than any other actor, except David Garrick. But it was in comedy that he excelled.

Like his older sister Sarah Siddons, he was born in Brecon, Wales, while his parents were on tour. At first, Charles worked in the post office, but after four years he got bored with this and became an actor in 1792.

His brother John Philip Kemble (1757–1823), already an established actor and theatre manager, advised him against a career on the stage. When this advice was ignored, however, he helped him to get work at the theatres he managed: the Drury Lane Theatre and the Covent Garden Theatre.

In 1806, Charles married the ballet dancer-turned-actress Maria Theresa de Camp (1774–1838), who had been accused of plagiarising a plot for one of her plays from another writer in a well-publicised case a few years earlier.

Catastrophe hit the Kemble family when both the theatres managed by John, and where they performed so much, were burned down within six months of each other. The Covent Garden Theatre was destroyed on the night of 30 September 1808, tragically killing thirty people. A piece of wadding fired from a musket during the play had lodged in the scenery without being noticed and started smouldering. Also destroyed in the blaze was the entire costume collection of Sarah Siddons (built up over thirty years) and an extensive library of plays and music scores.

In the following spring, the Drury Lane Theatre was also levelled to the ground by fire. The co-manager Richard Brinsley Sheridan watched it from the nearby Piazza Coffee House while drinking wine. When someone remarked upon how calmly he appeared to be taking the calamity, he replied, 'May not a man take a glass of wine by his own fireside?' The theatre, already on the verge of bankruptcy, had been greatly under-insured and it was four years before it reopened.

The Covent Garden Theatre, however, was rebuilt and it reopened in September 1809, a year after its fire. But because the rebuilding costs had been much greater than estimated, it was decided to increase admission prices and to install private boxes. This provoked an unprecedented reaction by the punters, who disrupted performances every night, demanding the restoration of the old prices and the abolition of the hated private boxes, which were seen to symbolise class privilege.

On the first night, magistrates were called to read the Riot Act from the stage, which only served to further incite the audience, who smashed up the seats. The Bow Street Runners were then called, but it was not until 2 a.m. that they managed to disperse the crowd. After sixty-seven successive nights of these 'old price riots' as they were called, the Kembles gave in and restored the old prices in the pit, reducing the number of private boxes in the process.

In 1822, Charles took over the management of the Covent Garden Theatre from his brother and was accused by purists of putting on too much melodrama for commercial reasons. Even this failed, however, and by 1829, its finances were in such a shambles that it was possessed by bailiffs and warrants were issued for unpaid rates and taxes of around £2,000.

Famous performers came to the rescue, giving free performances at benefit concerts for ten nights, which paid off £13,000 worth of debts. When Charles paid some of this to the Inland Revenue, he accompanied it with a note protesting, 'I now pay you this exorbitant charge, but I must ask you to explain to Her Majesty that she must not in future look upon me as a source of income.'

The following year, he was involved in another altercation, when a magazine called *The Age* commented unfavourably on his actress daughter Fanny Kemble (1809–1893). The fuming father went to its office and assaulted the editor, one Westmacott.

Fanny and Charles sailed to America in 1832 for two years of highly successful touring. He was particularly acclaimed for his portrayal of *Hamlet* in New York. Fanny married an American actor Pierce Butler in

Philadelphia. Another famous actor who married into the Kemble family had a less pleasant experience in America. This was Charles Macready (1793–1873), who was expelled from that country in 1848, for causing a riot after quarrelling with a rival American actor.

Charles Kemble, on returning to England, was given the post of 'examiner of plays', which he gave up after four years in 1840, when he also retired from acting. The pub became a Greek bar and restaurant in 2006, while retaining the name and sign.

162. Robert Emmet (1778–1803)

(Renamed G. F. Handel in 2000), 28 Thomas Street (corner of Thomas Court), Dublin 8.

Robert Emmet at his trial as pictured in the Village Inn, Dublin.

The Irish nationalist Robert Emmet was hanged and beheaded in the street outside this pub in front of St Catherine's Church, after leading an unsuccessful rising. There are two plaques that commemorate the fact that he died there 'in the cause of Irish freedom': one was erected in 1953 by the Thomas Moore Society and the other, including a picture of him in relief, in 1978 by the Corporation of Dublin and the American Irish Foundation. The date of the public execution was 20 September 1803.

Emmet, the Protestant son of a doctor, went to Trinity College, Dublin in 1793 to study science and he shone as an eloquent orator, particularly at Historical Society debates. He also became a leading light among the United Irishmen students at the university. The United Irishmen had been formed in 1791 by Wolfe Tone, Thomas Russell and others, who had their first meeting in the Eagle Tavern, Eustace Street, Dublin, on 9 November of that year.

His brother Thomas Addis Emmet, who was secretary of the Supreme Council of the United Irishmen, was arrested after the failed uprising of 1798.

Robert was also named as a ringleader at Trinity, where he was expelled, and a warrant for his arrest was issued in 1799, but this was not enforced.

Thomas was placed in Kilmainham Prison in Dublin and he was visited there by Robert, who later ended up there himself just before his execution. Robert, by then a member of the United Irishmen's executive, took messages from Thomas to his comrades. In 1799, Thomas was moved to Fort St George in Scotland, where he again was visited by Robert.

In 1801, Robert went to France, which was then at war with England, as a representative of the United Irishmen, in an attempt to persuade Napoleon to invade and liberate Ireland. While there, he studied military textbooks and met American armament specialist Robert Fulton, who taught him about rockets and explosives.

In 1802, France and England made peace and the United Irishmen prisoners, including Thomas, were released, but exiled to France. At the end of that year, the United Irishmen were planning another uprising and the police were hunting for Robert again.

In May 1803, France and England were at war again, boosting hopes that the French would support the Irish against the English. Thomas, in Paris, tried to get Napoleon to supply arms and money, but failed. Robert resolved to press ahead anyway, 'without the hope of foreign assistance'.

The planned uprising had to be brought forwards, however, when an accidental explosion at one of their arms dumps in Patrick Street drew the attention of the security forces. Saturday 23 July was fixed as the date to take over Dublin Castle and the city, with the help of men from Wicklow and Kildare, which would be a signal to the rest of Ireland. Thomas Russell, one of the United Irishmen exiled to France, came over to organise this response in the north.

At 9 p.m., Emmet issued the proclamation, 'You are now called upon to show the world that you are competent to take your place among the nations, that you have a right to claim their recognisance of you as an independent country ... We therefore solemnly declare that our object is to establish a free and independent republic of Ireland.' It was followed by 30 decrees, which

The statue in Dublin of Anne Devlin who helped Robert Emmett when he was hiding in the mountains.

abolished tithes, made church lands the property of the nation and called for a new sovereign assembly elected by universal suffrage and proportional representation.

Some of his men came across the Lord Chief Justice, Lord Kilwarden – one of the few humane judges of the time – and, mistaking him for the notorious hanging judge Lord Norbury, they piked him and his son-in-law to death. News of this and the disappointing number of men who had joined him led Emmet to call off the revolt.

He could have fled to France and safety, as did Miles Byrne, leader of the Wicklow men, but he wished to keep in touch with his lover Sarah Curran, so he hid in the Wicklow Mountains. He then went to see her at Harold's Cross, which is where he was betrayed by an informer. He was captured on 25 August and was locked up in Kilmainham Prison. Sarah's father, the lawyer John Philpot Curran, who had defended other United Irishmen, including Wolfe Tone, was so infuriated by Emmet's affair with his daughter that he refused to represent him. Instead, his counsel was Leonard MacNally who,

Commemorative relief opposite the pub that used to bear his name.

it emerged later, was the informer who had betrayed him.

Tried for high treason in Green Street Courthouse on 19 September, Emmet moved even the notoriously callous judge with his speech from the dock. He declared, 'I have but one request to ask at my departure from this world. It is the charity of its silence. Let no man write my epitaph; for as no man knows my motives and character dares now to vindicate them, let not prejudice or ignorance asperse them. Let them rest in obscurity and peace, my memory be left in oblivion and my tomb remain uninscribed, until other times and other men can do justice to my character. When my country takes her place among the nations of the earth, then and not till then, let my epitaph be written.'

The verdict was a foregone conclusion and he was sentenced to be hanged, drawn and quartered the following day. In the event, he was hanged, cut down after half an hour and beheaded with a butcher's knife. Dogs licked up the blood and some of the crowd dipped their handkerchiefs in it to preserve a part of him.

At first, his body was interred in Bully's Acre, near Kilmainham Hospital, but it was later moved to an unmarked tombstone in either St Michan's Churchyard or Glasnevin Cemetery. A month later, on 21 October, his co-conspirator Thomas Russell, friend of Wolfe Tone, was also hanged.

Emmet's friend the poet and songwriter Thomas Moore wrote two songs about him: *She is Far From the Land, Where her young hero sleeps* (about Sarah Curran) and *Oh Breathe Not His Name.* Another song entitled *Bold Robert Emmet* concludes with the chorus:

> Bold Robert Emmet, the darling of Ireland,
>
> Bold Robert Emmet will die with a smile,
>
> Farewell companions both loyal and daring,
>
> I'll lay down my life for the Emerald Isle.

At Wolfe Tone's funeral in 1915, Padraic Pearse – later commander of the Easter rising of 1916, who was shot by firing squad in Kilmainham prison – stated, 'No failure, judged as the world judges these things, was ever more complete, more pathetic than Emmet's. And yet he has left a prouder memory than the men of Brian, victorious at Clontarf, or of Owen Roe, victorious at Benburb. It is the memory of a sacrifice Christlike in its perfection.'

A pub in the south of the city was called Sarah Curran at 19 Main Street, Rathfarnham, Dublin 14, until 2003, when it was renamed The Village Inn. It still has a picture on the wall of Emmet at his trial. Sarah lived at the Priory, Grange Road, Rathfarnham.

A few yards away is a statue to Anne Devlin (c. 1778–1851), who worked for Emmet and who acted as a messenger between him and his friends in Dublin, when he was hiding in the mountains. When arrested, she refused to give any information about him or his whereabouts, despite being tortured and imprisoned for two years. The rest of her life was spent in poverty in the slums of Dublin.

Her uncle Michael Dwyer (1771–1826) was transported to New South Wales for his part in the uprising, after arriving from his hideout in Wicklow Mountains too late to be of assistance.

163. Thomas de Quincey (1785–1859)

De Quincey's (now Boozie Rouge), 7 Renfield Street, Glasgow, G2 1LP.

The author of *Confessions of an Opium Eater*, Thomas de Quincey lived in Glasgow for much of the 1840s. Born in Manchester, he was a brilliant scholar, but had a rebellious nature, so ran away at the age of 17 to London, where he slept rough in Soho. There, he befriended a 15-year-old prostitute called Ann. When he collapsed in the street, she revived him with a glass of port wine and spices, which she bought with her last sixpence. Sadly, he lost contact with her but dreamed about her for the rest of his life.

His first purchase of opium took place when he was 19 at 173 Oxford Street (near his lodgings at 82 Great Titchfield Street) in London. By the age of 27, he was addicted to the drug. Its effects made him incapable of serious work and it also gave him nightmares about monstrous crocodiles and other creatures.

In 1821, however, his *Confessions of an Opium Eater* was published as a serial in the *London Magazine* and the following year as a book. It was a great success and went into six editions over the following thirty-four years.

He moved to Edinburgh, where his wife Margaret Simpson and seven children had followed him by 1830. Because they were so noisy, he took separate lodgings at 42 Lothian Street ... until his wife and two children all died between 1835 and 1837. He relapsed into opium excesses after the shock of this.

During this period he would often let beggars move into his lodgings after they borrowed babies to get his sympathy. Rather than throw them out, he moved elsewhere. But others followed him there, until he was paying rent on six different places. This soon used up all his earnings from writing. To earn more cash he did public readings, during which he set fire to his hair to alarm the audience. His writings about dreams were to influence many later writers, including Edgar Allan Poe.

In 1841, Quincey moved to Glasgow and stayed there until 1847. He loved solitary, nocturnal rambles and would often sleep under hedges. After dying in poverty he was buried in Edinburgh's West Churchyard. The pub named after him changed its name in 2004.

164. Thomas Willingale (1798–1870)

(Renamed Station House), 134 Station Road, Chingford, London, E4 6AN (Tel: 020 8529 8576).

Willingale's action celebrated at Lopping Hall, Loughton.

A stout defender of commoners' forestry rights, Thomas Willingale saved Epping Forest from being completely enclosed by the lord of the manor. In about 1840, Willingale, a labouring man, built himself a cottage on the edge of the forest at Baldwin's Hill in Loughton, Essex. He planted a bramble hedge around it, which gradually grew further away from the cottage, because he cut it back from the inside each year and encouraged it to root outwards. The land, however, belonged to the local lord of the manor Rev. John Whitaker Maitland, who wanted to build on it, encouraged by legislation passed in 1851, which allowed 2,000 acres of woodland to be destroyed. Maitland agreed to build Willingale another cottage nearby.

Further legislation was proposed to allow the lords of the manors in Epping Forest to enclose most of their lands and to leave just 600 acres for public use. This was withdrawn as a result of huge public opposition organised by the newly formed Commons Preservation Society. But

Maitland and the other lords of the manors were determined to undermine the ancient rights of the commoners to graze their animals and to collect firewood in winter (known as 'lopping' rights).

To maintain the lopping rights, the commoners had to lop at least one branch at midnight on 11 November each year. On that night in 1860,

Thomas Willingale's descendant Gwendoline Gathercloe outside her forest cottage.

Maitland tried to prevent this happening, by inviting all the loppers to a supper at the Kings Head Pub in the High Road at Loughton – in order to get them so drunk they would be incapable of exercising their right. He even locked them in as well.

But Willingale kept his wits about him. Using his axe to break down the door, he left at 11.30 p.m., walked to Staples Hill and on the stroke of midnight, he lopped off a branch ... and returned triumphantly to present it to Maitland and so to preserve the ancient right.

In December 1865, Maitland took Willingale to Epping Court, accusing him of injury to the forest trees. The charges were dismissed. In March 1866, however, Willingale's son Samuel and two nephews Alfred Willingale and William Higgins were summoned at Waltham Abbey petty sessions on similar charges and they spent seven days in Ilford Prison rather than pay the fines.

Maitland's actions in enclosing more land – leaving just 50 acres for the commoners to cut firewood and to graze animals – spurred Willingale to take action. With the support of the Commons Preservation Society, he took legal action in 1866 against Maitland to restrain him from enclosing the forest. Willingale refused to accept a considerable sum of money to drop the case and he went on to win in court.

Willingale's staunch campaigning paved the way for the Epping Forest Act, which was passed in 1878, eight years after his death. This guaranteed that it be kept unenclosed as an open space for the public and its natural aspects be protected. Because the trees were protected, this meant an end to the cutting of wood. But compensation for the loss of lopping rights was used to construct Lopping Hall (between High Road and Station Road, Loughton), which was opened in 1883. A sculpture depicting lopping can be seen over the entrance in Station Road.

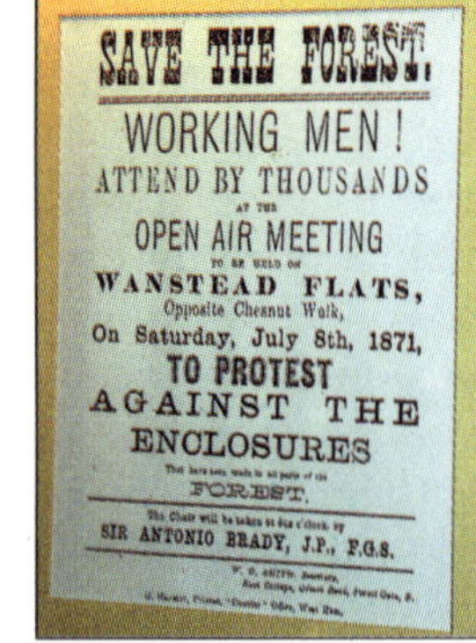

Poster in the pub calling for a big meeting to save the forest.

Willingale was buried in an unmarked grave at St John's Church in Loughton. Apart from the Chingford pub, which was renamed Station House in 2007, his name lives on in Loughton through Thomas Willingale School (in The Broadway) and Willingale Road.

His great-great-granddaughter Gwendoline Gathercloe lives in Ye Olde Loppers Cottage in Forest Road, Loughton and she is very proud of him. 'He must have been quite a guy to stand up to the lord of the manor like he did,' she said. 'But if he had not taken up the fight there would be no forest left today.'

165. William Abendigo Thompson (1811–1880)

Bendigo's (now The Hermitage), Thurgarton Street (corner of Sneinton Hollows), Nottingham, NG2 4AG (Tel: 0115 9584133).

The first southpaw to become heavyweight boxing champion of Britain in the days of bare-knuckle fighting, William Abendigo Thompson was jailed twenty-eight times for being drunk and disorderly. He fought under the title of 'Bold Bendigo', when fights were much longer than today ... one of his memorable contests lasting ninety-nine rounds.

A statue of the boxer Bendigo on top of the Hermitage pub, formerly named after him.

Born into poverty in Nottingham – one of triplets named Shadrach, Meshaach and Abendigo – he went into the workhouse at the age of 15 after his father died. He then scraped a living selling oysters in the streets, until becoming a prize fighter at the age of 21. He was 5 feet 9.75 inches tall and weighed 11 stone 12 pounds.

His reputation grew when he beat the formidable Ben Caunt in 1835 in the twenty-third round. Caunt was goaded by Bendigo's taunting laughter into landing a foul blow, which led to his disqualification.

Victories followed over fifty-two rounds, ninety-two rounds and ninety-nine rounds. The heavyweight title became his in 1839, when he beat Deaf Burke. In the tenth round, Burke butted Bendigo twice and the referee ruled the blows as being foul. Bendigo's championship belt was presented to him at Liverpool shortly afterwards 'amid the acclamations of a large assembly of people'.

He was out of the sport for two years from 1840, having injured his knee in Nottingham while throwing a somersault. Apart from somersaulting, he also excelled at stone throwing, cricket, cock fighting, badger baiting and fishing.

On his return to the ring he was arrested by the police in 1842 and was bound over to keep the peace to prevent him fighting. He finally retired from fighting in 1850, aged 39, whereupon he became a boxing coach at Oxford University for a while. This way of life did not suit him, however, and he returned to Nottingham and fell in with some local drunks, being jailed frequently for being drunk and disorderly. His tarnished reputation was repaired at the age of 59 though, when he rescued three people from being drowned in the River Trent.

Bendigo's grave in a memorial garden near the pub.

In 1872, he took the pledge and became a dissenting minister and preacher. If his old cronies barracked him, he would set about them with his fists.

Although the pub changed its name from Bendigo's in 1999, his statue in pugilistic pose remains over the front entrance. His grave is a short distance away in Bath Street Memorial Garden (formerly St Ann's cemetery), where it is guarded by the statue of a lion. It is inscribed:

In life always brave fighting like a lion
In death like a lamb, tranquil in Zion.

166. Bram Stoker (1847–1912)

Bram Stoker Tavern (now the Duke of Clarence), 148 Old Brompton Road, South Kensington, London, SW5 0BE (Tel: 020 7373 1285).

Dracula, the fictional vampire, was created by Bram Stoker, whose novel was published in 1897. Although set in Transylvania, where Vlad the Impaler had lived in the fifteenth century, the story was probably first planted in Stoker's mind as a child by his mother, Charlotte in his native Dublin. She came from Sligo, where she had witnessed the cholera epidemic of 1832, and she told him how sufferers had been buried alive by others fearful of catching the disease.

Traditional Irish stories were also told of 'undead' ghouls, who lived off the blood of others and were said to have bad blood, which in Irish was *droch fhola* (pronounced druc ula).

Stoker was born at 15 Marino Crescent, Clontarf, Dublin, overlooking the sea. When a builder bought land in this road and started constructing houses, one of the residents tried to prevent him by erecting a toll gate and charging him an exorbitant rate to go through it. The builder got his revenge by transporting his materials by barge across the bay instead and then by building his houses purposely to block the other residents' view of the sea.

In 1864, Stoker went to Trinity College, where he excelled at athletics, football and road walking. Uniquely, he also became president of both the Philosophical Society and the Historical Society. A fellow student at Trinity was Oscar Wilde, who courted Florence Balcombe, who became Stoker's wife.

A great theatregoer, Stoker was enraptured by a performance in Dublin by Henry Irving in 1876. He looked for a review in the *Dublin Evening Mail* the next day, only to find there wasn't one. After complaining to the paper about it, he was given the job of drama critic.

His main job, however, was as a civil servant in Dublin Castle, which he found tedious. Yet it led to his first published book called *Duties of Clerks of Petty Sessions in Ireland*; a far cry from *Dracula*!

When Henry Irving returned to perform in Dublin, he was impressed by Stoker's review of the play and asked to meet him. They became friends and in 1878, Stoker accepted Irving's offer to become his manager. He and his wife moved to London where, apart from managing Irving for thirty years, he also managed the Lyceum Theatre.

Stoker died at the age of 64 and was cremated in Golders Green after being described in a Times obituary as 'the master of a particularly lurid and creepy kind of fiction'. His widow lived on to see *Dracula* made into a play and a series of popular films.

The Bram Stoker Tavern opened in 1998 as one of the 'eerie' chain of pubs, but by 2005 it had taken on the more sober name of the Duke of Clarence.

167. John Burns (1858–1943)

Burns, Isle of Dogs, London, E14.

John Burns made his name leading the great dock strike of 1889, which was sparked off at the West India Docks near this pub. The half-starved dockers, sick of scrambling among themselves for a day's poorly paid employment at a time, went on strike on 14 August for a rise in the hourly rate to 'a tanner', which was six old pence (2 and a half pence).

Burns swiftly threw himself wholeheartedly behind their cause, making thirty-six public speeches on their behalf in the first three days of the dispute. It was his

Dockers strike leader John Burns addressing a mass meeting. (Picture courtesy Workers' Beer Company).

brainchild – possibly hatched in the strike headquarters at the Wade's Arms Pub in Jeremiah Street, Poplar, where the landlady Mrs Hickey provided free meals – to organise marches through the City and to demonstrate to the magnates what appalling food the dockers were forced to eat because of their poverty.

This was done by holding stinking onions, old fish-heads, rotten meat and other scraps on poles. Others demonstrated their inability to afford proper clothes, by holding up poles with red rags on them; which inspired Jim Connell to write the labour anthem *The Red Flag.*

Burns led the processions each day 'conspicuous with his black beard and white straw hat'. There were 20,000 people on the first procession and, as the strike spread throughout London, it grew every day, building up to a Sunday rally in Hyde Park on 27 August, at which 200,000 heard Burns speak.

The strike funds were just running out, when the Australian trade unions came to the rescue in September with donations totalling £25,000, which enabled the strike to continue, until the 'dockers' tanner' was won later that month. Burns was made a trustee of the Dock, Wharf, Riverside and General Trade Union.

He was born at South Lambeth, when it was a swampy area, in a narrow road called Simpson Street that then existed off Wilcox Road, between Wandsworth Road and South Lambeth Road. At the age of 9, he moved to Battersea – where he was to be elected MP twenty-five years later – and at 10 years old he became a pot boy at the Winstanley Arms in Winstanley Road (near Clapham Junction).

Later he worked locally at a bakehouse, a candle factory and, like his father Alexander, an engineering works (as a riveter). But he was sacked for making a political speech on a lemonade box in Battersea Park and was arrested for speaking on Clapham Common at the age of 19.

He got married on 1 July 1882 at St Philip's Church, Queenstown Road, Battersea and he immediately pawned the wedding ring to pay for the feast and a one-day honeymoon in Hampton Court.

In 1884, he joined the Social Democratic Federation, a Marxist party, which had just been formed by H. M. Hyndman. He and Hyndman were speakers at a Trafalgar Square rally on 8 February 1886, which culminated in the West End riots, as the unemployed looted shops in the area, and Burns became notorious as the 'man with the red flag'.

Burns, Hyndman and two others were tried for sedition at the Old Bailey, but were acquitted, although the jury condemned Burns for being highly inflammatory. From the dock, he proclaimed, 'Against this system of society I frankly confess I am a rebel, because society has outlawed me. I have protested against this state of society by which at present one and a half million of our fellow countrymen, adult males, are starving – starving because they have no work to do.'

He was agitating, he explained, 'to change the existing system of society to one in which men should receive the full value of their labour, in which society will be regarded as something more than a few titled nonproducers who take the whole of the wealth which the useful workers alone produce.'

It was better, he concluded, 'to die in prison, or better to die fighting than to die starving.'

The following year, he was at Trafalgar Square again for the banned 13 November demonstration protesting against the arrest of the Irish nationalist William O'Brien, which became known as Bloody Sunday. Burns and others were charged with riotous assembly, being armed, and with assaulting the police. From the Old Bailey dock at the three-day trial in the following January, he declared, 'I expected when I was the age of 16 or 17 that at some time in my life I should be brought face to face with the authorities for vindicating the class to which I belonged.' Although acquitted of the more serious charges, he was found guilty of assault and served six weeks in prison.

Some twenty years later, when the king praised him on the Court uniform he was wearing as they dined at Windsor Castle, Burns said he had worn his majesty's uniform before. When the king asked him where, he replied, 'In Pentonville prison.'

In 1889, just before the dock strike, he was elected as a socialist to the newly formed London County Council. In 1892, he was chosen as the chairman of the Trades Union Congress and was voted in as the Independent Labour Party MP for Battersea.

By then, he had moved to 108 Lavender Hill, playing for the local cricket and football teams, which was three doors from The Crown public house. Although partial to ginger beer, it was brandy that he was imbibing in this pub when he got into an altercation that led to him being charged with assault. The case was dismissed and he was at liberty to celebrate Christmas Eve 'with roystering boozers from the Crown' singing until one o'clock in the morning.

In 1906, he was the first working man to become a government minister; as president of the local government board in the Liberal government. He was promoted to President of the Board of Trade in 1914, but resigned later that year in protest against entering the First World War. His last speech in Parliament in 1918 was in support of the police strike.

In later years, he enjoyed taking the number 37 bus to The Plough in Clapham for a few pints and he also enjoyed playing billiards in the National Liberal Club with the Australian cricketer Don Bradman among others.

Burns died a few months after being thrown to the ground by flying debris during the Blitz and he was buried alongside his wife and son, a casualty of the First World War, at St Mary's Cemetery in Battersea Rise. The pub named after him survived the Blitz, but sadly not the building of yuppy flats in the docklands during the years of the Thatcher government.

He does, however, live on through another pub. The Bread and Roses pub, owned by the Workers' Beer Company, at 68 Clapham Manor Street, London, SW4, has on display a magnificent painting of him addressing the striking dockers at Hyde Park in 1889.

The pub takes its name from the verse:
Our lives shall not be sweated from birth until life closes;
Hearts starve as well as bodies, give us bread but give us roses.

168. Bob Fitzsimmons (1862–1917)

Fitzsimmons Arms (renamed Seven Stars in 2007), Coinagehall Street, Helston, Cornwall, TR13 8EQ (Tel: 01326 574897).

The 'fighting blacksmith' Bob Fitzsimmons was the first Englishman to become heavyweight boxing champion of the world in 1897. He was also the lightest boxer ever to take the title. A few hours before the fight he weighed 156 pounds, within the middleweight limit, so he added weights to his pockets to bring him up to 167 pounds at the official weigh in. This was still 16 pounds less than his opponent Jim Corbett, whom he knocked out in the fourteenth round.

In the sixth round, however, Fitzsimmons took a count of nine and then took further punishment. His wife Rose, a famous acrobat, shouted, 'Hit him in the slats, Bob!' He took the advice and attacked Corbett's ribs before knocking him out with a punch to the solar plexus.

'Heavyweight champion of the world, and I'm only a bleeding middleweight,' he told the press afterwards.

This was the first heavyweight title fight to be filmed and so was seen all over the world, billed as the fight of the century. Viewers seeing the footage must have been surprised by his slight build and physical characteristics, which earned him nicknames such as the 'knock kneed crane' and the 'bald headed kangaroo'. But by concentrating on punches to the body rather than the head, he beat much heavier opponents and coined the phrase 'the bigger they come the harder they fall'.

His strength had been built up as a blacksmith from the age of 10, when he left school in Helston, where he was born at 61 Wendron Street, a thatched, terraced house, which now bears a blue plaque in his honour. He was always proud of his skills making horseshoes and made this part of his training for a fight; one of his horseshoes is in Helston Folk Museum in Market Place.

At the age of 11, he and his family emigrated to Timaru in New Zealand, where there is a statue of him, and seven years later he became that country's amateur middleweight champion, by knocking out four opponents in one night! He later turned pro and moved to Australia. After winning his first purse of $500, he generously gave it to the loser, whose mother was sick and in need of

The cottage in Helston where Bob Fitzsimmons was born.

medical care. In 1890 he moved to America, where he became world middleweight champion the following year by knocking out the famous Jack Dempsey. He never lost this title.

After becoming world heavyweight champion, a play was written about him called *The Honest Blacksmith*, which he appeared in with his wife on tour, sometimes making horseshoes on stage and giving them to the audience. Hitting a punchbag made of tough calfskin was also part of the show; until once he hit it so hard that it shot off the stage and hit a female spectator in the face and knocked her out of her seat. Bob had to pay her damages. On another occasion, he hit the punchbag with such force that it exploded, when he was training in front of reporters. He finally surrendered the heavyweight crown in 1899 to James Jeffries, who outweighed him by 39 pounds.

At the age of 41, Fitzsimmons won the world light-heavyweight championship in 1903. This made him the first ever boxer to have won three world titles in different weight divisions.

After retiring from the ring at the age of 51, he toured with a vaudeville troupe. He came out of retirement at 53 to box exhibition matches with his son Robert. A year later, he died of pneumonia and was buried in Chicago, Illinois.

169. Ras Prince Monolulu (1881–1965)

(Now the Potion Bar), 28 Maple Street (corner of Fitzroy Street), Fitzrovia, London, W1.

Ras Prince Monolulu brightened up British racetracks from the 1920s to the 1960s, dressed in tribal robes, with plumes in his hair, selling tips to punters. 'I've got an 'orse' was his catchphrase as he offered envelopes containing the name of a 'winner' for the next race; each one, of course, recommending a different horse.

Born in Ethiopia, he was the son of a chieftain but not a real prince and his history was as colourful as his garb and gift of the gab. Press-ganged onto a ship at an early age, he landed in America, where he carried the Salvation Army flag for General Booth and then sailed to Russia.

On the outbreak of the First World War, he was taken prisoner in Germany, but managed to escape. Eventually, he made his way to London, where he settled at 55 Howland Street, near the site of this pub.

In the early 1930s, he was a guest on the popular radio programme *In Town Tonight* on several occasions, because of his great gift of narrative. He would sing 'I'm Ras Prince Monolulu from sunny Honolulu' and would give tips saying all the other runners would be arrested for loitering. He also used his entertaining eloquence to attract crowds at Speakers' Corner in Hyde Park on Sundays, denouncing the rise of Adolf Hitler.

During the Second World War, Monolulu changed his official name to Peter McKay and then moved round the corner to 83–85 Cleveland Street, where he lived for the rest of his life. Here, he was visited by his friend Paul Robeson, the Black American radical singer.

Just before his death in the nearby Middlesex Hospital (on the corner of Cleveland Street and Mortimer Street), he was visited by the famous alcoholic columnist Jeffrey Bernard, who was then working for the *Sporting Life*. Bernard offered him some chocolates, but Monolulu made a joke about them being poisoned, because Bernard was jealous of his reputation as being a better tipster than him. He did, however, eat some of them and died shortly afterwards.

The pub, previously called the Yorkshire Grey, was renamed the Prince Monolulu in 1991 in a ceremony attended by his three sons: Peter born in 1924 (who became the jitterbug champion of the British Empire), Ronald born in 1932 and Raymond born in 1935. In 2002, it was renamed Liquid Blue and the following year, The Potion Bar.

170. Jean Harlow (1911–1937)

(Now Quattroz), Bird Cage Walk, Stonecross, Harlow, Essex, CM20 1BX (Tel: 01279 425875).

With her platinum-dyed pubic hair and ice-rubbed nipples, Jean Harlow was the screen sex goddess of the 1930s. She never wore any underwear and enjoyed sex unashamedly in her films. This met with the wholehearted approval of moviegoers, who flocked to see her. It also led to the puritanical disapproval of many in the industry, who responded by delivering a stern edict against adultery going unpunished on the screen.

Born in Kansas City, she was discovered at the age of 19 by Howard Hughes, who put her in the

1930 film *Hell's Angels.* She was given the flimsiest of dresses to show off her breasts 'and the oceanic roll of her hips'. Despite this, she was given the immortal line, 'Excuse me sir while I slip into something more comfortable.'

Another film *Platinum Blonde* in 1931 supplied her with her nickname, one which she could share with the many Essex girls that frequent this pub named after her. In another film *Dinner at Eight,* Jean speculated that machinery would eventually replace every profession. 'That is something you need never worry about,' replied a fellow actress in the scene.

Her 'oldest profession' status was referred to in a conversation she was said to have had with Dame Margot Asquith: 'Your name is spelled with a T at the end but is pronounced with an O,' said Jean to Margot. 'That's right,' replied Margot. 'The T is silent as in Harlo.'

At the age of 16, Jean had eloped with the 21-year-old Charles McGrew, the son of a wealthy banker. When they had sex, she recalled, it was 'messy' and not very satisfying. They split up almost straight away and divorced in 1929. Her second marriage was in 1932 to Paul Bern, who was twice her age and who worked for MGM. He used to like reading poetry to naked women, and then drink tea and leave. On his wedding night, he upset Jean by biting her thighs and beating her with a cane. A few nights later, he went into her bedroom wearing a large dildo, with huge testicles and a bulb, which shot water out of the artificial penis. Jean burst into hysterical laughter as he pranced around the room with it.

The following night, he shot himself and left a suicide note, which stated, 'This is the only way to make good the frightful wrong I have done you, and to wipe out my abject humiliation. You understand that last night was only a comedy.'

Desperate to have a baby, Jean picked up a series of random men, including one outside a cinema, where one of her films was showing. He told her she looked like Jean Harlow and should try to get work as her double.

A short marriage with cameraman Hal Rosson and an affair with actor William Powell followed, before her early death from uraemic poisoning, which bloated her body and made her breath smell. Because her mother was a Christian Scientist, proper medical treatment was refused her until it was too late.

The pub was originally named, like many in the town after a butterfly, the Painted Lady. But this apparently gave the wrong impression about the customers, so it was renamed the Jean Harlow. Then, in 2005, it was renamed yet again as Quattroz.

171. Henry Cooper (born 1934)

508 Old Kent Road (corner of Bowles Road near the junction with Rotherhithe New Road), London, SE1 5BA.

The British Commonwealth and European heavyweight boxing champion Henry Cooper was best known for flooring future world champion Muhammad Ali with his left hook in 1963. Ali, fighting under his original name of Cassius Clay, took a count of four, before he was saved by the bell at the end of the fourth round. His trainer then broke the rules by bringing him round with smelling salts, which could have led to his disqualification, and by ripping his glove to delay the start of the fifth round.

This gave him time to recover from the full effects of ''Enery's 'ammer' as his left hook was known. Ali admitted, 'He hit me so hard, he jarred my kinfolk in Africa.' Sadly, Henry's eye then got cut and he had to retire from the fight.

Henry had turned professional in 1954 and he trained at 320 Old Kent Road in the gymnasium over the Thomas-a-Becket Pub, where his manager Jim Wicks had his office. A research team from the RAF visited the pub to measure the speed of the fighter's famous left hook. Its acceleration was thirty times the force of gravity and had an impact of 4 tons per square inch. Henry's diet when training switched from eggs and sherry to double port and Guinness, washed down with half a bottle of Fleurie wine (or Krug).

Born in Camberwell Green, he was raised in a council house at 120 Farmstead Road, Catford, sharing a bedroom with his twin brother George. They both qualified as plasterers and kept it up after becoming boxers. Henry became British light heavyweight amateur champion in 1952 and won seventy-three of his eighty-four amateur bouts before turning pro.

He became British and Empire heavyweight champion in 1959, after beating Brian London in one of the bloodiest battles ever in the ring. In 1968 he became European champion. In defending it in Rome, he knocked out Italian Piero Tomasoni in the fifth round. But Henry was so enraged by a punch in the testicles that he had received from Tomasoni that he showed his battered protective box to the television cameras and declared, 'I don't care what anybody says, that was bloody low.'

A few years later, he was involved in a television debate about boxing. Dr Edith Summerskill, who thought the sport should be banned, said, 'Mr Cooper, have you looked in the mirror and seen the state of your nose?' He rapidly responded, 'Well, have you? Boxing is my excuse, what's yours?'

After retiring, he starred in several television commercials, most famously for Brut aftershave lotion, with his catchphrase 'splash it on'.

The Henry Cooper Pub was named in his honour in 1980 and he was there to perform the opening ceremony; it had previously been called the Lord Wellington. Sadly, the pub closed in 1987. Even sadder for Henry was when he had to sell his three Lonsdale belts – he was the only boxer ever to have that many – having lost heavily through his investment in Lloyd's Insurance Company in 1993.

172. Duncan Edwards (1936–1958)

Priory Road, Dudley, Worcestershire, DY1 4EH.

Rarely has a footballer been canonised as much as Duncan Edwards, who was killed in a plane crash at the age of 21. A stained-glass window in Dudley's St Francis Church Assisi Chapel in Laurel Road and a statue in the town's Market Square both commemorate him.

He was born and raised 100 yards from the pub in a two-bedroomed council house at 32 Elm Road and he went to school in Wolverhampton Street. By the age of 11, he was starring in the town's boys' team, when most of the others were at least four years older than him. One of his teachers predicted he would play for England and noted Duncan 'told the other 21 players what to do, where to go – and that included the referee and linesmen!'

A couple of years later, Duncan wrote a school essay musing about playing at Wembley for England. This dream came true in the same year, when he played there in a schoolboy international against Wales in April 1951. Manchester United signed him as an amateur when he was 15 years old. Aware that other clubs were interested in him, the United coach turned up on his doorstep before sunrise on his sixteenth birthday on 1 October 1952 and signed him up as a professional; the earliest date he could legally do so. Some six months later, Duncan made his debut in the first division, before the premiership existed, for United at left-half.

Just two years later, aged 18 years and 183 days, he became the youngest player to be capped for England in the twentieth century; a record that lasted until Michael Owen beat it in 1998. Duncan played like a veteran at Wembley as England beat Scotland 7–2. Although mainly a left-half, he could play anywhere, including centre-forward, and he scored five goals in his eighteen games for England.

In the 1955–1956 season, Matt Busby's young Manchester United side – known as the Busby Babes – won the league championship, with Duncan playing a prominent role, for £15 a week. This enabled them to play in the European Cup in the following season, when they reached the semi-final, before losing 5–3 on aggregate to the eventual winners Real Madrid, who had monopolised the competition up until then. In the same season, United won the league again by eleven clear points; when there were only two rather than three points for a win. They could have won the FA Cup as well, but goalkeeper Ray Wood broke his neck

Stained glass window of Duncan Edwards in St Francis Church, Dudley.

early in the final and substitutes were not allowed. The ten men of United narrowly lost 2–1 to Aston Villa.

The following season they were again going well in the European Cup, when tragedy struck. On 5 February 1958, the team drew 3–3 in Belgrade against Red Star and so won 5–4 on aggregate to reach the semi-final again. The next day, their plane back to Manchester stopped to refuel at Munich on a snowbound afternoon, but hit the perimeter fence when taking off again. A total of twenty-one people, including seven of the Busby Babes, died. Duncan fought on for fifteen days, before he finally died from the terrible injuries he had sustained.

Over 50,000 stood outside Dudley Cemetery in Aston Road when he was buried there and three years later, crowds also gathered at St Francis Church, when Matt Busby unveiled the two stained-glass window pictures of him: one in Manchester United kit and the other in England kit. He said, 'There will only be one Duncan Edwards and any boy who strives to emulate Duncan or take him as his model won't go far wrong.'

A book entitled *Tackle Soccer This Way*, which Duncan had completed just before the crash, was published unchanged after his death. It is on display, along with all his caps and medals, at Dudley Leisure Centre in Wellington Road.

Football fans in the Duncan Edwards rejoice as England qualify for Euro 2004 by drawing in Turkey.

The pub, previously called the Wren's Nest, was renamed in his honour in 2001, under licensee Colin Ward, an ex-Aston Villa player who, at the age of 11, was one of a number of local children to attend a training session run by Duncan in 1957. He left to open up a Duncan Edwards Bar in Spain. The pub had an under 11 youth team, which maintained links with Manchester United, until it was demolished in 2007.

173. Ricky Tomlinson (born 1939), Des Warren (1937–2004) and Vic Turner (born 1927)

Flying Picket Bar (now closed), 24 Hardman Street, Liverpool, L1 9AX.

Liverpool's Ricky Tomlinson is one of the most famous flying pickets for his part in the national building official strike of 1972, before he became a television star. He and fellow picket Des Warren were jailed for two and three years respectively, after what they insisted was a political trial. They had been on strike against the increasing use of casual labour and blacklisting of trade unionists.

Based in Des' hometown of Chester, where the strike headquarters met in the Bull & Stirrup Pub, they picketed Shrewsbury, where they lodged in the Warwick Arms Pub. At the time, they were congratulated by Chief Inspector Meredith of the police force on how peaceful the picket had been; so much so that Ricky had taken his toddler son along.

When the dispute was settled and the unions were seen to have made some pay gains, the Tory government, under pressure from the employers, decided to prosecute strike activists, accusing them of intimidating strike breakers. It was several months after the Shrewsbury picketing of September 1972 that the police, who had earlier praised Ricky and Des, first interviewed them. And it was over a year before the highly publicised trial started in Shrewsbury.

Instead of charging them with intimidation, which carried a maximum sentence of three months' jail, they were charged under an obscure and previously unused 1875 conspiracy law, which had no maximum sentence and had a lower burden of proof.

At the trial, Chief Inspector Meredith admitted shaking Des by the hand and congratulating him on the peaceful picket on the day of the alleged crimes. When asked why, he replied, 'I didn't know he was a criminal then.'

Liverpool striking docker in his "Calvin Klein" T-shirt.

After being found guilty, Des stated from the dock, 'The conspiracy was between the government, the employers and the police.'

When severe sentences were announced by the judge, two members of the jury, including the foreman, walked out in disgust. Apparently, the 10–2 vote for guilty had only been achieved when some had switched sides, on the understanding that there would be no jail sentences. Des served all but four months of his three years, but after tranquillizing drugs were forcibly administered to him, he developed Parkinson's disease.

On his release, he proclaimed, 'My sentence was to have been a deterrent to trade unionists. It appears that trade unionists are not deterred, and neither am I.'

He took action against the prison authorities and won £3,000 compensation. His book *The Key to My Cell* was published in 1982. Ricky went on to become a famous television and film actor, using his earnings to set up an acting school for unemployed kids in Liverpool.

His most famous role is probably as Jim Royle in the television comedy *The Royle Family*, with his popular catchphrase 'my arse!' In one episode, he disputed the use of the word 'finger', by blurting out, 'Finger, my arse!' Then he burst out chuckling at the innuendo that he was inviting the family to insert a digit up his rectum.

Another famous flying picket, still active in employment rights, is retired London docker Vic Turner. He hit the headlines in 1972, when he and four others were locked up in Pentonville Prison for picketing a container depot, where work was being transferred away from the docks. The new Industrial Relations Act, brought in by the Conservative government earlier in the year, was used to jail them. This sparked a huge response, as thousands of workers in all industries went on strike in solidarity, until

The ceiling of the Flying Picket Bar..

the men were released a few days later. The freed men then jokingly complained they had been kept awake at night by pickets outside chanting round the clock for their release.

A large mural of a picket in the 1995–1998 Liverpool Dock Dispute adorned the front entrance of this pub until its closure in 2005. He was sporting the T-shirt that proclaimed: Support the sacked Liverpool Dockers. It also cheekily incorporated the CK logo initials of fashion stylists Calvin Klein in the word 'doCKers'. Calvin Klein put an injunction on them to stop using the logo, but by then thousands had been sold. They were even displayed by Liverpool football 'strikers' Steve McManaman and Robbie Fowler to the television cameras, after they scored goals at Anfield in the 1997 European Cup match against Bran Bergen; for which they were disciplined. McManaman's uncle was one of the striking dockers.

Dockers Vic Turner (foreground) and Bernie Steer released from Pentonville prison in 1972

The pub predates this dispute, however, and it came out of the People's March for Jobs in 1983, which led to the establishment of The People's Centre; incorporating Merseyside Trade Union, Community & Unemployed Resource Centre. The People's Centre moved from Hardman Street to nearby 52–54 Mount Pleasant in 2005 but, unfortunately, The Flying Picket did not follow and was closed.

Recommended Renamings

The following are pubs that we recommend should be named after commoners who have associations with them:

174. Gerrard Winstanley (1609–1663) & The Diggers

(Currently The Running Mare), 45 Tilt Road, Cobham, Surrey, KT11 3EZ (Tel: 01932 862007).

Gerrard Winstanley (1609–1663) and 'the Diggers' started cultivating common wasteland on St George's Hill near Cobham on 1 April 1649. Originally called the 'True Levellers', they grew beans, carrots, parsnips and barley. Their number increased from ten to fifty in four months. But then attacks on their crops and huts, organised by the Lord of the Manor Rev John Platt, forced them to move about a mile from St George's Hill, near to where Weybridge Station now is, to Littleheath Common in Cobham; near where the Running Mare Pub is now. At least seventy-three of them grew corn on 11 acres and had eight homes on the new site, until Easter Day in April 1650, when Rev Platt's flock demolished and burned their homes and threatened to kill them if they stayed.

Mosaic of Winstanely and the diggers in Cobham by local school children.

Winstanley had been an apprentice tailor, until moving to Cobham to become a herdsman in 1643. It was in 1648 though, that he started writing tracts in support of digging and cultivating the land for the common good. This followed a vision he had that 'the earth should be made a common treasury of livelihood to whole mankind without respect of person' and that everyone should 'work together, eat together, and declare this to all'.

He was expecting tough opposition from the landowners, reasoning that they had got the land by murder, violence and theft, so would be willing to keep it by the same means. But he was hoping for support from Cromwell in revising the land laws. Cromwell, however, refused to do so and denounced the True Levellers.

When they moved to Cobham Heath, the local gentry met in the local inn The White Lion to plan their attack. A pub called The Little White Inn still exists at 17 Portsmouth Road, Cobham, near the original. Once more,

Memorial stone to the diggers in Weybridge.

the diggers and their homes were attacked, but once more, they offered no resistance, because of their non-violent principles. Needless to say, it was Winstanley and fourteen other diggers who were charged with disorderly and unlawful assembly, rather than those who assaulted them.

Winstanley became a corn chandler and moved to London, where he attended Quaker meetings in The Bull and Mouth Tavern in Aldersgate. On his death, he had a Quaker funeral and was buried in Long Acre. A memorial stone to him now stands close to the original diggers' settlement on the corner of Cobbetts Hill and Brooklands Road (200 yards from Weybridge Railway Station). Sculpted

by Andrew Whittle, it has a spade engraved on the back and an inscription on the front proclaiming: Worke together, eat bread together – Gerard Winstanley, a true Leveller, 1649. Ironically, it could not be placed on the actual site, because that is now a gated community surrounded by walls and barriers. In Cobham, however, is a mosaic of the Diggers in Holyhedge Road by the corner of the High Street, constructed by local pupils. A campaign to rename the Running Mare after the Diggers has been backed by Labour veteran Tony Benn and singer Billy Bragg.

175. John Frost (1784–1877)

(Currently the Westgate Inn, boarded up), 6 Westgate Buildings, Commercial Street, Newport, Monmouthshire, South Wales, NP20 1JL.

John Frost was one of three Chartists to be sentenced to death on charges of sedition and high treason for rioting outside this pub. He had led a crowd of 5,000 workers from surrounding areas through the rainy night of 3–4 November 1839 to Newport.

In July of the same year, the People's Charter, signed by 1,280,000, had been submitted to Parliament, where MPs had rejected it by 237 votes to just 48. Peaceful and constitutional means were seen to have failed. Demand for more direct action increased when Chartist leaders were rounded up and imprisoned on dubious charges of sedition. One of these was Henry Vincent, who had been jailed in Monmouth Prison for a year for using seditious language to 'set one class against another'. The mass convergence on Newport was to demand the release of Vincent. The authorities had reacted by arresting many of the prominent Newport

Chartists and detaining them in the Westgate Inn guarded by twenty-one soldiers.

When the protesters heard about this, they decided to rescue their comrades. The troops responded by firing into the crowd and killing twenty-four people. Frost, a local tailor, was arrested with Zephaniah Williams (1784–1874), who ran the Royal Oak Inn at Coalbrookvale near Ebbw Vale, and William Jones (1809–1873), a watchmaker, who ran the Bristol House Beer House in Pontypool. They were sentenced to death by being hanged and quartered, but after a huge public clamour, the sentences were reduced to transportation for life to Tasmania. There then followed a new workers' campaign demanding their release. In 1854, they were granted pardons on the condition that they did not return to Britain. More agitation followed and they finally got an unconditional pardon in 1856.

Frost, who had become a teacher in Tasmania, returned and settled in Stapleton, near Bristol. His mother ran a pub in Newport, where he was an extremely popular folk hero. In 1835, he had been elected mayor of the town and shortly afterwards he became a magistrate. The Home Secretary Lord John Russell threatened to sack him from the bench for a speech attacking the government. Frost remained defiant and said the job was not worth having if it depended on government goodwill. He was, however, removed from the bench after chairing a meeting, where threats of violence were made in 1839.

The town has honoured him by naming John Frost Square after him. The pub was renamed The Toad in about 2001 and was later turned into a nightclub called Baltica. By 2007, it had been boarded up, but was purchased by brewers Marston's, who were considering reopening it as a pub.

Bullet holes remain where troops fired on the Chartists.

176. Mary Seacole (1805–1881)

(Currently the Pillars of Hercules), 7 Greek Street (corner of Manette Street), Soho, London, W1 (Tel: 020 7437 1179).

Plaque at Mary Seacole's home in Marylebone, London.

Gunfire and cannonballs did not deter Black nurse Mary Seacole from tending the wounded on the battlefields of Crimea in 1855. Eyewitness reports of her bravery under fire by reporter William Russell were published in *The Times*, making her just as famous at the time as her contemporary Florence Nightingale. The difference between the two women was that Mary was told by the military authorities that she was not wanted as a nurse; despite written accounts of her competence from army doctors. This was not the first time she had suffered from racial prejudice, for as a 12-year-old child visiting London, she had been upset by unkind treatment from people because of her colour.

Born Mary Grant in Kingston, Jamaica, her mother was a Black African slave, who had managed to save enough from selling vegetables to buy her freedom and to run an inn (The Blundell Hall, East Street, Kingdom). She used herbs to treat British officers who stayed at the inn, one of whom, a Scotsman, she married.

Mary keenly watched her mother treating officers and by the age of 12 she was assisting her, becoming known as a 'doctress'. She also picked up hints on the treatment of cholera from army doctors staying at the inn. At the age of 31, Mary married an English officer, Horatio Seacole, who died shortly afterwards.

When the Crimean War started in 1854, she went to London to offer her services as a nurse and was rejected. Undeterred, she set off under her own steam in January 1855. For a short while, she helped Florence Nightingale in her hospital there, but was offered no accommodation. So she slept on ships in harbour, until able to set up 'Mrs Seacole's Hut' (also known as the British Hotel), which sold food and drink to soldiers ... even being marked on military maps.

After the war ended in March 1856, she sailed back to London penniless. Because of her popularity, she was given two medals and a grand military festival, attended by 40,000 people, was organised to raise money for her.

In 1857, while living at 14 Soho Square (a few yards from the Pillars of Hercules), she wrote her best-selling autobiography called *The Wonderful Adventures of Mrs Seacole.*

Later, she lived at 157 George Street, Marylebone, London, W1 and was buried at St Mary's Catholic Cemetery, Kensal Rise, Harrow Road, West London.

177. Peter Kropotkin (1842–1921)

(Currently The Farwig), corner of Farwig Lane and College Road, Bromley, Kent (near Bromley North Railway Station).

The great anarchist writer Peter Kropotkin, who was jailed in Russia and France for his beliefs, lived at 6 Crescent Road (a stone's throw from this pub) from 1894 to 1907. The house, called Viola, was like a cave covered in vines, according to writer Ford Madox Ford. Kropotkin held Sunday dinner parties here, where he played the piano and sang revolutionary songs. As each guest arrived, he added water to the soup to provide an extra helping. The guests included Bernard Shaw the socialist playwright, Tom Mann and Ben Tillett (trade union leaders, who had led the great dockers' strike of 1889) and international anarchists such as Rudolf Rocker (German), Errico Malatesta (Italian) and Louise Michele (French).

The plaque at Kropotkin's home.

Kropotkin wrote two books while living at Bromley: *Mutual Aid* in 1902, a study based on years of observation of animals in which he concluded animals that cooperated with each other survived the evolutionary process better than those that competed with each other; and *Fields, Factories and Workshops* in 1905, on how to start an agricultural recovery in Russia - which was greatly admired by Tolstoy, Gandhi (who used it to develop ideas on village communes in India), and Mussolini before he became a fascist.

Kropotkin was born in Moscow, the son of a prince from Smolensk in western Russia. Very conscious of the evils of serfdom, he renounced his own title of prince as a child. In 1860 he was sent to military school, where he was locked up for ten days for his part in a revolt against discipline. He left the army in disgust, after witnessing the shooting of Polish exiles for insurrection.

After exploring and charting the mountains and rivers of Siberia and publishing theories about its glacial history, he was offered the prestigious job of Secretary to the Geographical Society. But he turned it down in order to become an anarchist agitator, posing as a peasant named Borodin.

In 1872 he spent two years in a fortress prison in St Petersburg, before escaping. He took refuge in London, where he made a living contributing to the *Encyclopedia Britannica* and other journals. When in France in January 1883 as striking miners caused dynamite explosions, he was sentenced to five years' imprisonment and fined 1,000 francs for being a member of

the banned International Working Men's Association. In prison, he contracted scurvy and malaria, so was released after three years.

After the revolution in 1917, Kropotkin returned to Russia, to be greeted by a crowd of 60,000. He settled in a smallholding near Moscow, where he kept a cow, a few chickens and a vegetable garden to feed himself.

Kropotkin's daughter Sasha attended Bromley High School for Girls in Elmfield Road, until 1904 when she was 17. A crowd of 100,000 attended his funeral, at which he requested the *Internationale* not be played, as it reminded him of 'the howling of hungry dogs'.

178. Kitty (1864–1946) and Tom (1869–1939) Higdon

(Currently Burston Crown), Crown Green, Mill Road, Burston, Norfolk, IP22 5TW (Tel: 01379 741257).

The 25-year school 'strike' of teachers Kitty and Tom Higdon still inspires trade unionists and others to this day, with a rally being held on the green every September on the first Sunday of the month. This rally commemorates the stand that they, and the whole village, took when they were sacked and evicted after beating the local school governors in parish council elections. They responded by teaching the children on the green and eventually, through donations from across the country, they were able to build their own school, which lasted from 1914 until Tom's death twenty-five years later.

The Burston Crown, close to the school run by the Higdons.

The Higdons were Christian Socialists, he the son of a Somerset farm labourer, she the daughter of a Cheshire shipwright. They moved to Norfolk in 1902, teaching first at Wood Dalling School, 14 miles north of Norwich. They then moved to the council school in Burston in 1911 to avoid the sack, after annoying school board members by defeating them in parish council elections; a crime they were to repeat in Burston.

The Higdons were appalled by the dilapidated cottages the local farmworkers had to live in under extremely overcrowded conditions, sleeping several to a room. But when they asked the chairman of the parish council Rev Charles Tucker Eland to build new cottages, he refused to do so; while living in a house with twenty rooms himself. So, in 1913, Tom and others contested the elections and swept the board. Tom topped the poll and the vicar Rev Eland – who was paid £581 a year, compared to the farmworkers £35 a year – was humiliated by coming bottom.

As chairman of the school managing body, the vicar was ideally placed to gain revenge. He dismissed them on a charge of caning two pupils, which was

The graves in Burston of school teachers Kitty and Tom Higdon.

later disproved. On the first day after they had left on 1 April 1914, a 13-year-old pupil Violet Potter went to the front of the class and chalked on the blackboard: We will go on strike. Then she led them all out and they marched around with placards proclaiming: 'We want our teachers back,' and singing: 'We'll all cling together like the ivy on the old garden wall.'

The parents clubbed together to provide the Higdons with food, so they could teach the children on Crown Green, and the National Union of Teachers supported them with victimisation pay. Support grew around the country and by 1917, collections had raised £1,250, which was enough to buy land and to build a new school for the Higdons.

179. Robert Tressell (1870–1911)

(i) (Currently John's Cross Inn), Battle Road (A21), Mountfield, near Robertsbridge, East Sussex, TN32 5JH (Tel: 01580 882154)
(ii) Baraka Cocktail Bar (previously The Cricketers), South Terrace (corner of Waldegrave Street), Hastings, East Sussex.

The classic socialist novel *The Ragged Trousered Philanthropist* was written by Robert Tressell between 1906 and 1910, when living and working in Hastings. For most of this time from 1907, he was living in an attic flat at 241

London Road, which is now marked with a plaque. But he actually started writing it when living at Flat 5 (also in the attic), Grosvenor Mansions, 115 Milward Road, to where he had moved in 1903.

His real name was Robert Noonan and he was a decorative artist and signwriter. Born in Dublin, he worked his passage to South Africa at the age of 18. After joining a brigade of United Irishmen and fighting against the

British in the Boer War, he sailed with his daughter Kathleen in 1902 to Britain and settled in St Leonards, near Hastings.

His first job in Hastings was with Bruce & Co in York Buildings, for 7d (just under 3 pence) an hour, where he had to work from 6 a.m. until late at night. The 'Misery' character in the book is based on the foreman there, with whom Noonan had a row and left as a result.

The pub in Mountfield where Tressell attended a works beano, later described in his book.

He then worked for Adams & Jarrett in its workshop at 20 Alfred Street, St Leonards. It was the works beano of this firm in August 1905 to John's Cross Inn, 7 miles north of Hastings, that was recorded so splendidly in the *Ragged Trousered Philanthropists*. The Cricketers Arms (now the Baraka Bar), near where Noonan lived, featured in this novel as the place where workers would try to get jobs by buying foremen drinks. Noonan drank there himself, but kept sober by eating raisins at the same time.

The *Ragged Trousered Philanthropists* graphically depicted, and analysed in simple terms, how the cut-throat, competitive nature of capitalism could not avoid causing poverty and misery. It was not published until three years after his burial in an unmarked pauper's grave, and then only in an extremely abridged form. It was later published in full and has sold millions of copies since.

He believed in a cooperative commonwealth, in which the means of production were owned by the community and in which goods were produced for use by all. A mural that he painted in St Andrews Church was rescued when the building was demolished in 1970 and it is now on display in Hastings Museum and Art Gallery.

Plaque in London Road, Hastings.

Acknowledgements

Brian Curtis of the Inn Sign Society supplied several invaluable pictures of pub signs that have become obsolete, and others.

Ann Sotheran kindly supplied pictures of her stained-glass portraits of Captain Webb, W. G. Grace, Florence Nightingale and Bob Fitzsimmons; which are hung in The Champion Pub, London.

Photographers who supplied pictures (in addition to those of Peter Arkell) were Carlos Guarita, Martin Jenkinson, Pat Mantle, Roy Peters, Peter Everard Smith and Mark Thomas.

Clifford Harper allowed us to use his illustration of Peter Kropotkin, Camden Library the drawing of Jinney Bingham (Mother Red Cap) and Marx Memorial Library the drawing of Chartists attacking Westgate Inn.

John-Michael Fisher and David Wilson researched the brewery details of the pubs.

Others who helped with suggestions, information or photographs were Lionel Addis, David Arkell, Eddie Barrett, Gordon Bentley, Chris Birch, Bob Blackman, Jack Boddie, Angela Bolam, Sid Brown, Sarah Browne, David Bull, Ken Cameron, John Campbell, Martha Campbell, Matt Campbell, Rab Campbell, Colin Carr, Pal Carter, Chadwell Heath Robert Jeyes Library, Tony Child, Jim Clayson, Barrie Clement, Tom Condon, Colin Coughlin, Tony Cox, Mark Croucher, Alan Dalton, Frank Deacon, Carolyn Dixon-Marshall, Andrew Dodgshon, Siobhan Endean, Essex County Council Libraries, Roger Foster, Alan Green, Mrs M. Griffiths, Robbie Griffiths, Derek Hanlin, Jo Harfleet, Arthur Harper, Pete Harvey, Keith Hatch, Pat Hatch, David Jobbins, Jack Jones, O. Jones, Maureen Jopson, Jim Jump, John Juniper, Chris Kaufman, Rose Keeping, Hugh Kirkbride, Derek Kotz, Danny Maher, Arthur Malinowski, Billy McColl, Viv Miller, Richard Milner, Jack Mitchell, John Morgan, Robbie Morris, Dick Muskett, Geoffrey Newman, Andrew O'Neill, Mick O'Reilley, Ivor Pearce, Jan Pickering, Bernard Plymsell, Don Pollard, Lisa Povey, Linda Quinn, Herbert Rattle, Richard Rawles, Paul Redgate, Sean Redmond (Irish Labour History Society), John Richards, Roy Rogers, Felix Rooney, Keith and Dina Singleton, Wilf Sleight, Ken Smith, Martin Smith, South Shields Local History Library, Ted Thake, Wendy Thirkettle (Manx National Heritage), S. W. J. Thompsett, Ron Todd, Ken Tuckwell, Kathleen Vick, A. J. Wade, Lynda Walker, Keith Wallbridge, Fred Wilson, Winchester Local Studies Library and Pete Wyatt

Index of People and Pubs

Places Entries Index

Numbers refer to entries not pages:

Real Ale Guides

The following pub entries are listed in *The Good Beer Guide 2009*, edited by Roger Protz, published by CAMRA Books (the Campaign for Real Ale):

5,	Wat Tyler, Dartford, Kent
6(ii),	Owain Glyndwr, Llanddona, Isle of Anglesey
14,	Oliver Cromwell, St Ives, Cambs
24,	Nell of Old Dury, London WC2
26,	Daniel Defoe, London N16
32,	Tom Cobley Tavern, Spreyton, Devon
41,	Wilkes Head, Leek, Staffs
42,	Captain Cook Inn, Staithes, North Yorkshire
45,	James Watt, Greenock, Scotland
66,	George Stephenson, West Moor, Tyneside
67,	Dolly Peel, South Shields
71,	Richard Oastler, Brighouse, West Yorkshire
75,	Land of Liberty, Heronsgate, Herts
88(ii),	Gladstone Arms, Coombs Ford, Suffolk
90(ii),	Charles Dickens, London SE1
92,	Bamburgh Inn, South Shields
93,	Edwin Waugh, Heywood, Lancashire
115,	Edgar Wallace, London WC2
117,	Augustus John, Liverpool
122,	Barnes Wallis, Howden, East Yorkshire
123,	Jack Phillips, Godalming, Surrey
126,	Stan Laurel, Ulverston, Cumbria
127,	Richmal Crompton, Bromley, Kent
134,	Louis Armstrong, Dover, Kent
138,	Eva Hart, Chadwell Heath, Essex
139,	John Hewitt, Belfast
144,	Fagans, Sheffield, South Yorkshire
153,	Cayo Arms, Cardiff, Glamorgan

The following pub entries are listed in *The Real Ale Pub Guide 2009*, edited by Nicolas Andrews, published by Foulsham:

5,	Wat Tyler, Dartford, Kent
6(i),	Owain Glyndwr, Cardiff, Glamorgan
11,	Old Dr Butler's Head, London EC2
14(i),	Oliver Cromwell, St Ives, Cambs
15(iii),	Mother Red Cap, Luton Beds
26,	Daniel Defoe, London N16
32,	Tom Cobley Tavern, Spreyton, Devon
41,	Wilkes Head, Leek, Staffs
42,	Captain Cook Inn, Staithes, North Yorkshire
62,	Dairyman's Daughter, Arreton, Isle of Wight
66,	George Stephenson, West Moor, Tyneside
67,	Dolly Peel, South Shields
75,	Land of Liberty, Heronsgate, Herts
81(iii),	Richard Cobden, Worthing, West Sussex
82(ii),	Isambard Kingdom Brunel, Portsmouth, Hants
84,	Garibaldi, St Albans, Herts
90(ii),	Charles Dickens, London SE1
95,	Sally Pussey's Inn, Wootton Bassett, Wiltshire
98(i),	William Morris, Hammersmith, London W6
115,	Edgar Wallace, London WC2
117,	Augustus John, Liverpool
122,	Barnes Wallis, Howden, East Yorkshire
132,	Charlie Butler, London SW14
135(i),	Orwell at Wigan Pier, Wigan, Lancs
151,	Cayo Arms, Cardiff, Glamorgan
155,	John H Stracey, Briston, Norfolk

J. D. Wetherspoon Pubs:

22,	Pennsylvanian, Rickmansworth, Herts
25,	William Dampier, Yeovil, Somerset
45,	James Watt, Greenock, Scotland
55(i),	William Wilberforce, Hull, East Yorkshire
71,	Richard Oastler, Brighouse, West Yorkshire
82(ii),	Isambard Kingdom Brunel, Portsmouth, Hants
83(i),	William Webb Ellis, Twickenham, Middx
85,	Dic Penderyn, Merthyr Tydfil, South Wales
89,	Alexander Bain, Caithness, Scottish Highlands

93,	Edwin Waugh, Heywood, Lancs
96,	Plimsoll Line, Redcar, North Yorkshire
98(i),	William Morris, Hammersmith, London W6
121 (ii),	Rupert Brooke, Rugby, Warwickshire
123,	Jack Phillips, Godalming, Surrey
124(i),	John Logie Baird, Hastings, East Sussex
127,	Richmal Crompton, Bromley, Kent
129,	Wilfred Owen, Oswestry, Shropshire
133,	Charlie Hall, Erdington, Birmingham
137,	John Jacques, Portsmouth, Hants
138,	Eva Hart, Chadwell Heath, Essex
150,	Rohan Kanhai, Ashington, Northumberland